WITHDRAWN

Modern French Drama 1940–1990

Modern French Drama 1940–1990

DAVID BRADBY

Professor of Drama and Theatre Studies, University of London

SECOND EDITION

*The right of the
University of Cambridge
to print and sell
all manner of books
was granted by
Henry VIII in 1534.
The University has printed
and published continuously
since 1584.*

CAMBRIDGE UNIVERSITY PRESS

Cambridge
New York   Port Chester
Melbourne   Sydney

Published by the Press Syndicate of the University of Cambridge
The Pitt Building, Trumpington Street, Cambridge CB2 1RP
40 West 20th Street, New York, NY 10011–4211, USA
10 Stamford Road, Oakleigh, Melbourne 3166, Australia

First published 1984
Second edition published 1991

Printed in Great Britain at the University Press, Cambridge

British Library cataloguing in publication data
Bradby, David
   Modern French drama 1940–1990 2nd ed
   1. Drama in French, 1945. Critical studies
   1. Title   11. Bradby, David. Modern French drama 1940–1980
   842.91409

Library of Congress cataloguing in publication data applied for

ISBN 0 521 40271 9 hardback
ISBN 0 521 40843 1 paperback

FP

Contents

Jacques Copeau at the Vieux-Colombier and afterwards. The Cartel:
Louis Jouvet, Charles Dullin, Georges and Ludmila Pitoëff, Gaston
Baty. Surrealist theatre and Antonin Artaud; Jean Cocteau; Jean
Anouilh. Firmin Gémier and the Théâtre National Populaire; the
Front Populaire and political theatre. Léon Chancerel and Catholic
theatre. Dullin's report on decentralisation. The state of French
theatre at the outbreak of war.

Conditions for theatres. Cocteau's plays and films. Giraudoux's
Sodome et Gomorrhe; his death and last works. Henry de
Montherlant; the collapse of the hero. Joan of Arc plays. Jean-Louis
Barrault and his production of *Le Soulier de satin* by Paul Claudel;
Barrault's production style and Claudel's dramatic technique;
contrast between Montherlant and Claudel; Barrault: an observer
and a visionary. Copeau's *Le Théâtre populaire*; touring groups and
companies performing outside Paris; popular culture and educational
movements of the Resistance.

Anouilh's *Antigone* and differing interpretations; his later plays: a
theatre of masks. *Les Mouches* by Jean-Paul Sartre: the tragedy of
free choice; bad faith dramatised: *Huis Clos*; the struggle for
authenticity: *Le Diable et le bon Dieu*; history as dialectical process:
Les Séquestrés d'Altona; Sartre's theatre: a world of dramatic conflict
set within traditional conventions. Albert Camus: *Caligula*, the
Absurd and the response to it; later plays; Camus's failure to find an
original dramatic form. Armand Salacrou and social melodrama. The
limitations of naturalistic or melodramatic form.

Contents

Contents

Illustrations

Illustrations

Preface

The transformation of the French theatre between 1940 and 1990 has been colossal: there have been changes in styles of acting, directing, writing, stage design, and a massive redistribution of resources away from Paris towards the provinces. Before the last war, almost every significant event in the life of the theatre took place in Paris. By 1990 there were over one hundred well-established theatre companies working permanently outside Paris. Before the war, a new play normally received its premiere in an unsubsidised, privately-owned theatre in Paris. By 1990 a new author was just as likely to have his work performed in a publicly-owned, state-subsidised theatre in Caen or Strasbourg, Marseilles or Villeurbanne. Before the war, with the notable exception of Artaud, the theatrical avant-garde displayed austere literary or poetic tastes and was content to be an elite. Since the war, it has welcomed the most diverse influences: Brecht and the *théâtre populaire* movement, Strehler and Dario Fo, Grotowski, the Living Theatre, Bread and Puppet, Bob Wilson and many more.

Some of the changes that were to come had been foreshadowed in the inter-war years. The work of the art theatres between the wars had shown a tendency to move away from the naturalist theatre style towards less realistic forms, and a few companies had shown an interest in community theatre. But the influence of Marxist theory, the importance of Brecht and the development of Epic theatre in France were as unexpected as the rapid expansion of the decentralisation movement. Equally unanticipated was the emergence of the New Theatre of the fifties and its world-wide influence, followed by the division of the theatre world into 'absurdist' and 'political' camps. This symbolic division, an expression of the real gulf still dividing Paris from the provinces, was bridged in the best work of the sixties and seventies. New forms of theatre were created in which the social concerns of the Brechtians combined with the atavism of the Artaudians to achieve entirely new dramatic effects.

Developments in theatre practice over this fifty-year period have been accompanied by startling developments in theatre criticism, partly in response to new methods of dramatic construction, partly following the advance in sociology, anthropology and structural linguistics. Sociological criticism has shown that the meaning of a drama is not simply generated by the play text, but also by the place of performance, the type of building, the relationship between the stage and auditorium, the class composition of the audience. An increased awareness of the controlling socio-cultural factors influencing any production, and of the essentially political nature of theatrical activity, has in turn helped to influence dramatic experiment, especially experiments with unusual playing spaces not confined to theatre buildings.

Criticism of the Structural Linguistic School has complemented sociological insights by showing how plays communicate by means of non-verbal signs. Roland Barthes and his followers have analysed the codes of signification at work in the rituals of theatre-going and have promoted the techniques of demystification, which were adopted by many dramatists of the sixties (though decried by others). This school of criticism has provided a new way of theorising the relationship of signs to reality in the theatre, showing that its specificity lies not in imitating reality, but in developing conventions that may *signify* reality. This has led to a rich and subtle exploration, by both critics and creators, of the familiar modes of representation previously taken for granted. It has produced a lively awareness in French theatre circles of the close relationship between ideology and dramatic form.

This book deals only with published plays, concentrating on those whose performances have been documented in secondary literature. Before the war, a playwright expected that his play would be judged by readers as much as by theatre-goers. But more recently, playwrights have tended to write specifically for performance, taking the view that the complete realisation of their work is to be found, not on the page, but on the stage. Several have benefited from a close relationship with directors or theatre companies and some have worked as resident playwright to the company that has performed their plays. In extreme cases, such as the plays of the Théâtre du Soleil, the text of the play has not been written down at all in the conventional sense. For this reason the accounts of particular productions given in this book are combined with interpretations of the plays that allow for the construction of different performance possibilities, showing where there has been a fruitful interplay between critical methodology, playwriting and theatrical practice.

Much of the most original work in the French theatre since the war has been apparent, not in new plays, but in new approaches to the classic repertoire. Shakespeare, especially, has taken on a new lease of life in France as a result of productions stressing material and historical conditions and employing a physical and gestural acting style. The outstanding pioneer of this new approach has been Planchon and, since he is also an important playwright, his career is traced in some detail in this book. As well as its intrinsic interest, Planchon's work provides a unique opportunity for studying the point at which the arts of acting, directing and writing intersect.

For references, the author–date system has been used. This means that there are no footnotes and the reader should consult the bibliography at the end of the book for the source of a quotation. The bibliography is divided into two sections: Section 1: authors and practitioners; Section 2: critics and theatre historians. Under each author or practitioner is a list of cross references to critics that may be found particularly helpful. Where direct quotation is made from a French source, the translation into English is my own.

Acknowledgements

Among the many people who have helped in the formulation and elaboration of this book, I should like to express my special gratitude to the following: Robert Abirached, Rachel Anderson, Michel Bataillon, Edward Bradby, John Burgess, Richard Coe, Bernard Dort, Edward Freeman, René Gaudy, Austin Gill, Denis Gontard, Bill Howarth, Bridget Jones, Dorothy Knowles, Jim Knowlson, Joseph Long, John McCormick, Bernard Sharratt, Sarah Stanton, Clive Wake.

I am also grateful to André Veinstein for allowing me access to the 'fichier permanent de la production théâtrale' at the Bibliothèque de L'Arsenal, Paris.

Introduction: the inter-war years

When the second war broke out in Europe, the French theatre had come to the end of an era. The inter-war period had witnessed the triumph of literary drama and poetic production style; Jouvet, Dullin and other outstanding directors had achieved world-wide fame with glittering productions of plays by a new school of playwrights led by Giraudoux, Cocteau, Salacrou. By the end of the thirties, this literary and poetic theatre was firmly established in the public eye as the distinctive French contribution to modern drama. It received the official seal of approval when Jacques Copeau, the man who was considered to be its chief architect, was appointed director of the Comédie Française in 1940.

Four decades earlier, at the time of *la belle époque*, Copeau had set himself the task of purifying the decadent elements of the French stage. His career in the theatre started, not as a director, but as an author and critic. In the early years of the century he published a series of theatre reviews in which he developed a searing criticism of the state of Parisian theatre. The terms of his attack were more moral than artistic: he claimed that the modern theatre was guilty of cunningly corrupting the public's tastes in order that they might more easily be satisfied. He accused the actors of vanity, the theatre managers of rapacity, and claimed that 'fine craftsmanship' and 'aesthetic dignity' were dead (see Borgal, 1960: 29–42). He was offended by superficial bedroom farces, and by lavish productions in which sensational stage effects were sought as ends in themselves.

In place of this corruption, he wanted to see a theatre that was simple but inventive, one in which the play and its performance became an integrated whole, and in which the audience's attention would be directed towards the playwright's ideas rather than towards the effects displayed by actor or designer. He could see no evidence of good playwriting among his contemporaries, and claimed that the only way to make a new beginning was to return to Molière and Shakespeare. He valued these playwrights, not only for the quality of their ideas, but also for their ability to write plays that found natural expression in performance, plays that did not call for extraneous spectacular effects: 'with them there is no intermediary between poetic creation and its true theatrical realisation. Dramatic invention and stage production are merely the two phases of a single action' (Borgal, 1963: 18).

In 1913 Copeau founded the Théâtre du Vieux-Colombier in the student quarter of Paris, far from the fashionable boulevard theatres, where he hoped to produce a repertoire of plays combining revivals of the classics and good plays of the previous decades as well as occasional new plays of quality. For a theatre that is now considered to have been so influential, the Vieux-Colombier company had a remarkably short and troubled existence. It played for only one season before war broke out, then spent two seasons (1917–19) in America before returning to Paris, where it performed for only four and a half seasons before its final dissolution. Moreover it did little to reveal vigorous new playwrights: the only new play of lasting merit 'discovered' by Copeau was *Le Paquebot Tenacity* by Charles Vildrac (1920). But for Copeau the founding of his theatre school was more important than the success or failure of these professional seasons, since he believed that the profound transformation of the French stage would take a generation. This theatre school flourished alongside the theatre in the early twenties and it followed Copeau to his home in Burgundy when he withdrew from the Vieux-Colombier in 1924.

The training given at the school was based on a quasi-religious search for truth through a mystical trinity of qualities: *le Beau, le Bien* and *le Vrai*. Emphasis was laid on cultivating the complete man, not just the technical faculties, and on training actors to work for the group rather than for themselves. Discipline was harsh, control of the body a major priority. The early stages of training relied solely on physical exercise and cultivation of expressive faculties of the body, with an absolute ban on using words. After he had left Paris, he continued to work along similar lines with a shifting group of followers known for a while as Les Copiaus, later branching out on their own as La Compagnie des Quinze.

One of Copeau's central preoccupations was with the need for the skills of playwright, actor and director to be so closely integrated that they became indistinguishable. Another was the need to develop a new performance vocabulary of modern types similar to the old masks of the Commedia dell'arte. In both these respects, though he himself failed, he anticipated later developments. The Compagnie des Quinze helped to realise the first by taking on André Obey as resident dramatist and working closely with him on a number of plays, the most successful of which was *Noé* (1931). The practice of employing a resident dramatist has become much more common since the war, especially in some of the decentralised companies. The second aim was to be fulfilled, quite literally, by the Théâtre du Soleil in 1975 with their play *L'Age d'or* (see chapter 9). In order to achieve these aims, Copeau believed that the Italianate theatre with boxes, footlights, and trompe-l'oeil scenery must be abandoned in favour of something more like the Elizabethan stage. His architectural restructuring of the stage of the Vieux-Colombier became a model for later directors, actors and designers with similar aims.

During the 1930s Copeau occupied a more marginal position in the French theatre, acknowledged as the originator of a great movement of renewal, but doing relatively little in the way of production work. There were some notable exceptions however, especially two open-air festival productions in Florence of large-scale plays on religious themes. In their attempt to do more than just entertain, and in their use of multiple acting areas, these productions also anticipated the work of the Théâtre du Soleil. Copeau's name was often mentioned during this period, as a likely director of the Comédie Française. When his appointment finally came, it was in 1940 as the replacement for Edouard Bourdet, knocked down by a car in the black-out. Bourdet had been appointed under the Front Populaire to reform the old institution. He had initiated a system of inviting in guest directors (of whom Copeau was one) and survived the fall of the Government that appointed him. But 1940 was the worst possible time for someone with Copeau's reforming zeal to take over that post. He was not prepared to treat the Vichy authorities with tact and only kept the post for a few months.

At the end of the thirties, Copeau's authority was considerable and his reputation high. He was respected by the public for having tried to make long-term changes in the standard of French theatre. He was respected by actors and directors, many of whom he had taught, for having set his standards high and having restored some dignity to the profession. But this did not prevent him from becoming caught, early in 1940, in an uncomfortably contradictory position. As director of the Comédie Française, he was expected to foster the tradition of preserving high culture for the Parisian upper bourgeoisie. But as early as 1924, his rationale for a school had included the necessity of decentralisation, so that the theatre could escape from the destructive influence of Paris. After his short term at the Comédie Française, it was this second aspect of Copeau's work that reaffirmed itself in his publication of *Le Théâtre populaire* (see chapter 2).

Copeau had many disciples, among whom he considered the most important to be Louis Jouvet and Charles Dullin. Both had broken away from the Vieux Colombier at a relatively early date, Jouvet in 1922 and Dullin in 1918. Dullin, in fact, performed for only one season with Copeau, though he afterwards claimed that he had learned more from Copeau in that year than in the whole of his previous career (Borgal, 1963: 106), and like Copeau he set up a school which functioned alongside the theatre. But it was the establishment of the Cartel in 1927 that has rightly been seen as one of the chief factors in prolonging and confirming Copeau's ideas. The Cartel was a loose association between four theatres, run by Jouvet, Dullin, the Pitoëffs and Baty. All four agreed to a common policy which was summed up in a manifesto which appeared in *Entr'Acte*, a review published by Jouvet's theatre. The values expressed in the manifesto are similar to those of Copeau's 1913 manifesto ('Un essai de rénovation théâtrale'): respect for the text, simplicity and truthfulness in staging, the search for poetic impact rather than spectacular effect. Their attitude towards the public was also similar. They asked for intelligent participation, offered lectures and other supplementary events, and insisted on starting punctually. At a time when theatres were not expected to start for at least half an hour after the advertised time, this was quite a bold step and involved Dullin in a prolonged battle with the press when a critic arrived to find the doors closed and the play begun. The four Cartel directors also pledged themselves to publish each others' programmes and so to try to extend the audience that each was building up.

In the late 1930s, Jouvet had built up almost as much prestige as Copeau. He had been a teacher at the Conservatoire since 1934, and had been offered the directorship of the Comédie Française in 1936 (he refused, suggesting that Bourdet be asked to direct, taking on Copeau, Dullin, Baty and himself as guest directors, a solution that was accepted). He was known as the director who had revealed Giraudoux to the theatre-going public and who continued a fruitful collaboration with him, but who also triumphed with classical productions, such as his 1936 *L'Ecole des femmes* and with modern comedies such as Jules Romains' *Knock ou le triomphe de la médecine*. Jouvet had more of the showman and less of the professor in him than Copeau, but he retained from his period with Copeau an emphasis on the coming together of text and performance in a united artistic whole: 'I only discover the meaning of a play through the work of staging: sets, movements, rhythms and diction are all essential elements for me in the discovery, experience and understanding of a play' (Borgal, 1963: 80).

In his partnership with Giraudoux, Jouvet had achieved what Copeau had only dreamed of: a working relationship with a writer such that writing and staging became two parts of the same creative process. Some of the plays produced by this tandem still seem masterpieces of theatrical invention – *Intermezzo*, for example – while others now seem excessively wordy. Jouvet and Giraudoux's biggest success of the 1930s, *La Guerre de Troie n'aura pas lieu* is one of those that now seem wordy. The scenic inventiveness of Jouvet helped to put across plays of the latter kind, where the dramatic action is weak. Jouvet did not regard the lack of action as a serious weakness provided that the literary qualities of the text were sufficient. He always insisted that good drama was, in the first place, good writing. But his idea of good writing included notions of rhythm, poetry, pace etc. He claimed that the theatre's job was not to make its audience understand something but to make them feel it deeply. In *L'Impromptu de Paris* Giraudoux wrote a dialogue between Jouvet and his lead actor Pierre Renoir, in which Jouvet poured scorn on the idea that the function of the audience was to *understand* and Renoir agreed: 'Luckily the best theatre audience does not respond with its intellect but with its feelings ... People who insist on understanding a play in the theatre are people with no understanding of theatre' (1982: 708). For the next generation of writers and directors the example of the collaboration between Giraudoux and Jouvet became an important encouragement.

Another aspect of Jouvet's work was also to be taken as an example by directors in the post-war period: his film career. At a time when there was almost no public subsidy at all for theatres like those of the Cartel, one way to subsidise theatre production was to take on a film role during the summer months when the theatres in Paris are closed. Jouvet, who excelled in comic roles on the stage, had an extraordinarily powerful screen presence. Where his acting style on stage was large, even grotesque, his film style was restrained, muted, with a constant hint of mystery beneath the surface. His face became extremely well known in the late thirties through taking roles in a number of films such as Renoir's *Les Bas-Fonds* (1936) or Carné's *Hôtel du Nord* (1938). His example was followed by several post-war directors for the same reasons, notably Barrault and Dasté.

Dullin, like Jouvet, had a conception of theatre that was not content to mirror reality, but that viewed it as a world apart governed by its own laws, a poetic world in which the life of the imagination took precedence. He claimed to find his models in the Commedia dell'arte and the Japanese theatre, from which he also borrowed some of the techniques fused in his school. An impression of work at the school given by Artaud: 'We act with our deepest hearts, we act with our hands, our feet, all our muscles, and all our limbs. We feel the object, we smell it, we handle it, see it, hear it . . . and all the time there is nothing there, no accessories. The Japanese are our immediate masters, our inspiration, and so is Edgar Poe. It is wonderful!' (cit. Knowles, 1972: 19).

As well as Artaud, Dullin attracted Jean-Louis Barrault, André Barsacq, Roger Blin, Jean Vilar, Maurice Sarrazin, Claude Martin, Alain Cuny, Jean Marchat, Madeleine Robinson, Jean Marais, Marguerite Jamois and many others to his school. He made it possible for Barrault to try out his early experiments in total theatre: *Autour d'une mère* (1935) and *La Faim* (1939). Through this school, and the example of his productions, Dullin influenced a very large number of the young generation of actors, directors and writers. His conception of the theatre was demanding and all-embracing. He saw it as a force for cultural and social regeneration. Not finding many modern plays that matched these ambitions, he produced many versions of plays from the classical repertoire, particularly the Greeks and the Elizabethans, with maximum use of colour, mime, music, and a rich deployment of stage resources. His most famous productions of the period were probably *Volpone* (first produced in 1928) and *Richard III* (1933).

Being interested in a global all-inclusive theatre, he naturally laid some stress on the ancient Greeks, producing two of Aristophanes' plays. Sartre gave some lectures to his school in the early years of the Occupation and *Les Mouches* was a natural choice for production by Dullin. Sartre records that he learnt his craft as a dramatist through watching Dullin rehearse. He would say to the actors: 'ne jouez pas les mots – jouez les situations' (do not act the words – act the situations. Sartre, 1969). Sartre made this his guiding principle as a playwright, as he showed by his constant references to 'un théâtre de situations' (see chapter 3).

Among the modern authors regularly produced by Dullin before the war were Pirandello and Salacrou. Salacrou also showed how much he learnt from Dullin about theatre as a total art form in the prefaces and notes to his plays. These present striking similarities with pronouncements by Sartre at the same time, demonstrating the influence of Dullin on both writers. But something shared even more strongly by all three was the conviction that the theatre could not survive without broadening the social basis of its audience. This was one of Dullin's favourite themes and in 1937 he was commissioned by the Front Populaire government to write a report on the decentralisation of the theatre. The report produced no action at the time, but was influential after the war (see below pp. 14–15).

Georges Pitoëff and his wife, Ludmila, shared with Dullin and Jouvet a belief that theatre is not best suited to the naturalist mode of representing reality. Before coming to Paris, the Pitoëffs had worked for several years in Russia (where the father of Georges had been manager of the Tiflis state theatre), had undergone and rejected the influence of Stanislavsky, and had worked as producers in Geneva for seven years. In the theatre which they directed from 1922–39 they therefore brought to the French audiences many plays by foreign authors, especially Chekhov, Pirandello, Shaw, Schnitzler and Molnar. But their stage style was characterised by simplicity and imaginative qualities closer to the work of Copeau or Jouvet than to the Expressionists in Germany or their contemporaries in post-revolutionary Russia. They held that the production of any given play had to give scenic form to the invisible forces contained in that play. A famous example of this was their setting for Shaw's *Saint Joan* (1925) which stressed the idea of saintliness by using a permanent scenic structure reminiscent of an altarpiece: a central gothic arch with two half arches on either side, and stage groupings that concentrated the audience's attention on the upward thrust, suggesting a constant movement heavenward. The Pitoëff couple also put on a large number of plays by contemporary French authors, including Lenormand, Cocteau, Anouilh and Claudel, but failed to find an author with whom to work on a regular basis as Jouvet did in Giraudoux.

The fourth member of the Cartel was Gaston Baty, whose productions were responsible for bringing the stage techniques of Expressionism to the Parisian theatre. His general tendency was away from the simplicity and dependence on the actor that characterised the other three members of the group and towards complex staging using multiple levels and picturesque settings. Like Craig, he had a life-long interest in puppet theatre and shared with him an ambitious view of the role of the producer. Unlike the other three Cartel members, he was not an actor and this perhaps explains why he paid as much if not more attention to the pictorial elements of staging as he did to the actor. He was particularly remembered for his attack on the excessive verbosity of French theatre, an attack that had something in common with Artaud's later fulminations. His choice of emphasis was expressed as follows: 'Painting, sculpture, the dance, prose, verse, song, music, these are the seven chords stretched side by side on the lyre of drama (cit. Knowles, 1967: 36).

The work of Copeau and the Cartel has been exhaustively studied by French theatre historians and large claims have been made for it. Undoubtedly, it succeeded in establishing high standards of acting, production and design, during the inter-war period. It also succeeded in broadening the outlook of the French theatre, showing that foreign plays (e.g. Pirandello or Chekhov) and foreign classics (e.g. the Elizabethans) could have a popular appeal and could be made to speak in a direct way to contemporary French audiences. These were lesssons not lost on French theatre after the war.

The Cartel directors did not wait for theatre historians; they made large claims for themselves. Dullin wrote that in the renewal of French theatre the directors had come to the rescue of the authors, teaching them the forgotten skill of writing for the theatre: 'authors seem to have lost contact with the theatre ... It is they who are responsible for the excessive, sometimes damaging importance of theatre directors. It is from this misfortune that we have the new barbarism "retheatricalisation of the theatre". To speak plainly, the directors are forced to teach the authors what they no longer know, that is to say the rules of the theatre game' (cit. Gouhier, 1943: 228–9).

This claim can probably be justified. On his own admission, Sartre learnt how to write for the theatre by watching Dullin. He had written only fiction and essays before the war; afterwards he was to become one of France's most successful dramatists. In a more general way, the tendency of authors to write plays that seem to require performance is a great deal more marked in the post-war period than it was in the inter-war period. The point can be rather sharply exemplified by contrasting Giraudoux with Genet, both authors brought to the stage by Jouvet. While Giraudoux's work always remained essentially that of a man of letters, Genet's is unmistakably that of someone who has a very sophisticated grasp of the nature of a performance art. It seems likely that by the end of the thirties the reforms and innovations brought about in the art of the theatre by Copeau and the Cartel had become sufficiently embedded in the consciousness of playgoers, playwrights and professional theatre workers to bring about that *rethéâtralisation du théâtre* claimed by Dullin.

What neither Copeau nor the Cartel could bring about was the larger cultural revolution that they had aimed at. The subsidies they received were almost non-existent, their theatres were small and depended on a regular audience of well-educated middle class Parisians. In these circumstances, it was not possible for them to become centres of social and cultural regeneration. But it is to their great credit that they understood this clearly and pointed towards the solution, especially Dullin in his report and Copeau in *Le Théâtre populaire*. The programmes of the successful decentralised theatres of the fifties were modelled very closely on the kinds of repertoire that had characterised the work of the Cartel between the wars, a fact that the directors of these theatres have been the first to recognise. Jouvet, Dullin and Baty all gave their active support to the establishment of these centres, as will be seen in chapter 5.

Less influential at the time than the tradition of Copeau and the Cartel, but equally efficient at capturing the headlines was a tradition of avant-garde theatre which looked back to Apollinaire and to Jarry. The performances of *Ubu Roi* at the Théâtre de L'Oeuvre in 1896, which had provoked Yeats' famous dictum, 'After us, the savage god', were venerated by the inter-war avant-garde as the first manifestation of a truly modern consciousness. *Ubu Roi* still retains its aggressive and subversive power. In the course of its brief parodistic action, everything is distorted, vilified, denounced. Its spirit is well summed up in Jarry's own comment: 'We must get rid of certain notoriously horrible and incomprehensible objects, which uselessly clutter up the stage, particularly the sets and the actors' (1962: 140).

Jarry died young in 1907 but his writings were admired by Apollinaire, who also wrote a Surrealist play *Les Mamelles de Tirésias*, and by the Surrealist group, who republished some of Jarry's more obscure works. Breton, the leader of the Surrealists, who maintained a dictatorial control over the movement, always admired *Ubu Roi*.

This admiration was shared by Antonin Artaud, whose first theatre project was named 'Le Théâtre Alfred Jarry'. Artaud's life and work belong almost entirely to the period before the war, and yet, by 1939, he was still a relatively unknown figure. His influence did not extend beyond a narrow circle of Parisian friends until after the war, but since then it has assumed ever greater proportions, until he is now seen as the most influential French man of the theatre this century. His work has been interpreted by innumerable critics and there is no study of the modern theatre that does not devote a section to him. It will therefore not be necessary to summarise his work here. What we shall discuss, in later chapters of this book, is how his ideas have been interpreted and used, sometimes misinterpreted and misused, by theatre practitioners since the war.

In the theatre since the war he has chiefly been known through his collection of essays *Le Théâtre et son double*. This book, almost unnoticed at its first publication in 1938, only became generally known after its re-issue in 1944. It is not a simple theatre handbook, but a visionary work, in which Artaud proclaims an entirely new conception of theatre. He shares Jarry's desire to sweep away all the trappings of the French stage as he found it in the twenties and thirties. But he goes beyond Jarry for he also has a positive vision of what should exist in its place. It is an idea of theatre that is fundamentally religious, although it does not proceed from any established religion. It assumes that the function of theatre is to group people together in order to touch and release the hidden springs of life and the dark wells of emotion that the routine of so-called civilised life normally obscures.

In order to achieve this, Artaud insists on the necessity of doing away with the rationalistic theatre of the word as enshrined in the classic French tradition. Instead (like Mallarmé in his *Crayonné au théâtre*, 1887) he stresses the ways in which theatre can release irrational forces and communicate by means other than words. In a much more violent, apocalyptic tone, he echoes Baty's call for the expressive use of sounds, lights, colours, movements and appeals to complex sign systems that would enable the actor to become a moving hieroglyph. Suffering and cruelty are never far from his preoccupations and a number of critics have suggested that although he failed in productions like *Les Cenci* (1935) to bring his 'theatre of Cruelty' to fulfilment, he achieved it in his own life. This idea was suggested by Gide, by Barrault and by many others, and given detailed expression by Alain Virmaux in his definitive study *Antonin Artaud et le théâtre*. It is summarised by Esslin, following Virmaux: 'The plays Artaud wrote and produced were far from perfect, but his own life was the perfect tragedy perfectly enacted. That is why its impact continues beyond the grave' (1976: 115).

Artaud was expelled from the Surrealist movement by André Breton in 1928. After his departure, the official Surrealist group made little contribution to innovation in the theatre, partly because of Breton's mania for poor melodrama. It is a curious fact that Jarry and Ionesco, the two major dramatists whose work would seem to qualify as Surrealist, were both active outside the inter-war years, when the impact of Surrealism on poetry and painting was so decisive. Throughout the inter-war years, the main centre of Surrealist experimental theatre was the Laboratoire de Recherches Art et Action run by Madame Akakia-Viala, Louise Lara and Edouard Autant. Their aim was:

Renewal of theatre, both form and content . . . creation of synchronism between the different forms of dramatic expression; evocation of the abstract by concrete means; use of old themes and myths, not disinterred and restored but brutally renewed . . . recourse to the fantastic and the grotesque to convey thoughts of gravity and concepts of the deepest pathos (cit. Vais, 1978: 35).

This programme suggests clear affinities with Ionesco's stated aims in the theatre and so it is not surprising to learn that his first acting role (in 1948) was in a production by Akakia-Viala and that his first play was produced by Nicolas Bataille, who had also worked with members of Art et Action. This group had a long life, beginning before the First World War, and only coming to an end in 1952, when the New Theatre was almost established.

Among the various experiments in Surrealist playwriting that took place between the wars, the work of Vitrac stands out. His *Les Mystères de l'amour* produced at Artaud's Théâtre Alfred Jarry in 1927 had been an attempt to construct a play using the principles of automatic writing. His *Victor ou les enfants au pouvoir* (1928, also Théâtre Alfred Jarry) was a parody of the bourgeois *drame* in which the sordid greed and licentiousness of the French middle class mentality was exposed by the naive view of a precocious boy genius, only nine years old but already six feet tall. This play also looks forward to Ionesco's early work and has been successfully revived a number of times since the second war. Vitrac continued to write until his death in 1952, using a farcical, music-hall style to satirise the bourgeoisie, though his plays did not at first reach beyond avant-garde audiences.

Cocteau was known as a playwright on the fringes of Surrealism but his light-hearted early works such as *Les Mariés de la Tour Eiffel* (1921) had given way to ponderous reworkings of Greek myths and so, despite his tendency to shock, and the whiff of scandal that always surrounded his activities, he was not seen as a threat to the traditions of French literary theatre. In fact it was quite the reverse: he and Giraudoux were seen as the chief standard-bearers of the new literary revival, in which poetic plays on classical subjects were once more holding the stage as they had done in the *grand siècle*. It was Cocteau's film *Le Sang d'un poète* (first released 1932) that qualified for the epithet Surrealist rather than any of his recent plays.

Cocteau's interest in adapting Greek myth was shared by other writers, notably Giraudoux, Gide and Anouilh who, along with other authors, whose reputations have not survived, were thought of as a new school of literary dramatists. It is perhaps natural that in a culture so dominated by the awareness of its neo-classical writers, especially Racine and Corneille, any literary revival should also turn back to the classical myths. They offer a chance to deal with the great subjects and an escape from the apparent mediocrity of contemporary life. For theatres appealing to the educated class they also offered something familiar, an assurance that the quality of 'culturedness' was being preserved despite occasional anachronisms, vulgarities, or hints at contemporary events, like the long scarf of Cocteau's Jocasta, so reminiscent of the one that strangled Isadora Duncan when it became entangled in the wheel of a sports car.

But by the end of the 1930s, the strains imposed on the classical material by successive adaptations were becoming too great. The only successful attempts after 1939 were Sartre's *Les Mouches* and Anouilh's *Antigone*, both of which in different ways challenge the assumption that classical material makes for literary quality (see chapter 3). However, it did not become immediately apparent to many people involved with French theatre that the classical adaptation had seen its best days. The matter was complicated by the association of classical material and the verse play. Various attempts at verse drama, particularly those of Claudel during the war and T. S. Eliot after the war (Eliot's work had a considerable vogue in France just after the war) led many people to believe that the literary/verse/classical play was in the vanguard of French theatre. This helps to explain why, when the New Theatre of Genet, Adamov, Ionesco and Beckett first appeared, it took so many people, especially the critics, unawares.

At the outbreak of war, Anouilh was just becoming known as one of the most important young French dramatists. In some respects his early plays seem very clearly a part of the inter-war literary theatre movement. His dialogue displays a debt to Giraudoux in its use of wit and whimsy, and his frequent use of a play within the play shows that he had also learnt from Pirandello. But there are other aspects of these plays that look forward to the theatre of the forties and explain why Sartre was able to claim him as an Existentialist playwright (1973: 55–67). They are partly a matter of theme and partly of style. In theme, Anouilh's early plays develop with some bitterness a protest against class distinctions and a belief that someone who has had to suffer the privations of poverty in childhood can never entirely break free from the experience. In *Le Voyageur sans bagage* (1936), Anouilh also develops the idea that we have no fixed centre to our identity, but are the victims of the images that others have of us. This theme is developed in a manner reminiscent of Pirandello but which also looks forward to Sartre.

In style, Anouilh's early plays make a clear departure from the psychological case-study drama that was common between the wars. His characters are not subtle or rounded individual case histories: they are much more like types or masks. In fact, as has frequently been pointed out, they exist by virtue of their relationship to the other characters, the young innocent girl contrasting with the corrupt old baroness and so on. Their qualities appear in their actions and encounters rather than in soliloquies or investigations and for this reason they appealed to Sartre. Above all, Anouilh's work of this period was significant in establishing a style that was dramatic, playful, poetic, able to deal with contemporary subjects without being simply mimetic or naturalistic.

For the first collected publication of his plays in 1942 he divided them into *pièces roses* and *pièces noires*, and it was his first *pièce rose*, *Le Bal des voleurs*, that made a hit with the public. It was produced by André Barsacq with the Compagnie des Quatre Saisons in 1938 and revived by him in 1940 as his first production at the Atelier theatre, where he had succeeded Charles Dullin.

The play's themes, of the division between rich and poor and the innocence of idealistic love, are similar to those of Anouilh's *pièces noires*, but they are dramatised in a comic, playful manner that never allows the social reality to intrude too much or to spoil the colour and sentimentality of the treatment. This was the beginning of a fruitful collaboration between Barsacq and Anouilh that was to continue for three decades.

Towards the end of the thirties in France there was much discussion of a mass theatre for the masses. This contrasted sharply with the practice of Copeau and the Cartel and had great appeal, especially in left-wing circles, as something radically new. In fact it was not very new: experiments in mass theatre having been conducted in both Russia and Germany throughout the twenties. In France, too, there had been a brief period when Firmin Gémier had attempted popular play production on a massive scale. In 1911 and 1912 he had already attempted an ambitious touring venture with a travelling theatre, the Théâtre National Ambulant. For the 1919–20 season he hired the Winter Circus, where he mounted two massive spectacular shows. The first was *Oedipus*, by Saint-Georges de Bouhélier, with a cast of over 200 including Olympic athletes. This was followed by a provençal nativity play *La Grande Pastorale*, directed by Baty. Gémier's stated aim was 'To create an atmosphere in which each member of the public is in communion with his neighbour and with the author in a sort of social religion' (1925: 72–3). As Gémier saw, this aim was better served by the public festivity than by the French theatre of the time. In 1920, as a result of a long campaign, Gémier succeeded in getting a Théâtre National Populaire established with himself as director, and organised a grand open-air festivity on the esplanade of Les Invalides to celebrate its inauguration. Unfortunately, Gémier had to put up with using the Trocadéro theatre, situated in the heart of the fashionable sixteenth arrondissement, so that it could never become a theatre for the masses. Even under Jean Vilar in the fifties, elaborate bussing arrangements had to be made if an audience was to be drawn from the working class areas. Furthermore, Gémier was allocated no money for a resident company, so his theatre had to function as what is now called a garage, receiving productions brought in from other theatres.

Gémier's achievement was to establish the first official Théâtre National Populaire and so lay the foundations for the successful work there of Vilar in the fifties. His failure was to confuse the theatre of massive means with theatre for the masses. The same confusion could be seen at work in the cultural policies of the Front Populaire government that came to power in 1936. For the International Exhibition of 1937 various shows were commissioned, including a composite show entitled *Long live liberty* and J. R. Bloch's play *Naissance d'une cité*, which was performed at the vast Vélodrome d'Hiver and described by Bloch as total theatre. These were inspired, to some extent, by the mass performances that had been a feature of socialist trade union gatherings in Germany in the twenties. By 1937, all such performances in Germany had been superceded by the Nazi mass rallies, and the French festivities were doubtless conceived in part as an alternative or rival form of mass celebration. The precision and power of the Nazi rallies certainly made a considerable impact on people all over Europe, who saw pictures of them on newsreel films, heard them broadcast on radio or experienced Leni Riefenstal's recreations. So hypnotic did they appear that for a long time after the war the very notion of a mass gathering seemed politically suspect.

There were many who took this view at the time of the Front Populaire but the government's commitment to mass shows was the outcome of a political struggle that had been going on among groups of the left for the whole of the thirties. There were many who favoured the promotion of agitprop work performed by small teams going out to find a popular audience in factories, streets or clubs. They argued that only in this way could hard political content be communicated and genuine two-way discussions be initiated. Others wanted to promote large-scale mass performances into which people of all classes would feel drawn, and through which the concepts of brotherhood or nationhood could be celebrated and confirmed. At first these two strategic approaches split fairly neatly into communist and socialist, the former favouring agit-prop and the latter favouring mass shows. But in the middle thirties the Soviet government put pressure on western communist parties to collaborate with the socialists and establish popular fronts, with the result that the agitprop movement was sacrificed.

This had the effect of cutting short the very promising theatre work of Jacques Prévert and the October Group. The plays performed by this group, most of which were scripted by Prévert, were characterised by a combination of playful wit and biting political satire. A good example is *La Bataille de Fontennoy* (1933) which anticipated Joan Littlewood's *Oh! What a lovely war* by presenting the First World War as a game in which lives are sacrificed in the name of hypocritical idealism while the spectator-population bays for blood. This sort of work was performed at trade union meetings, workers' halls, or in the open air. It was supported by a Fédération des Théâtres Ouvriers de France, which selected the October group to represent them at the Moscow Theatre Olympiad of 1933, where they won the first prize. But in 1936, when the Front Populaire came to power, the Fédération put all its energies into following the new fashion for massive displays of unity. Small groups like October were starved of funds and had to cease operation. It is difficult to assess the real importance, at the end of the thirties, of the political theatre movement, whether of the small agitprop or the mass festival variety. Much of the documentation was destroyed during the Nazi Occupation. What is certain is the failure, at a political level, of socialist and communist parties to prevent the rise of fascism in Europe discrediting these kinds of theatre, which had been associated with the left. It was not until 1968 that a new generation of theatre practitioners in France rediscovered the value of political theatre outside normal theatre buildings.

If the spirit of the Front Populaire survived anywhere, it was not in the theatre but in films. Already in 1936 *La Vie est à nous* had been made to celebrate the victory of the Front. This frankly propagandistic film was directed for the Communist Party, by Jean Renoir, André Zwoboda and Jean-Paul Le Chanois, and included almost all the October Group actors. The year before, Prévert had been Renoir's script writer on a film combining social polemic with brilliant dialogue, film technique and human observation: *Le Crime de Monsieur Lange*.

Renoir followed this by making a series of films with social preoccupations, among which are his acknowledged masterpieces. They include *Les Bas-Fonds* (1936) *La Grande Illusion* (1937) *La Marseillaise* (1937) *La Bête humaine* (1938) and *La Règle du jeu* (1939). Although Renoir did not collaborate again with Prévert, many of the October Group actors played small parts in these films which were animated by a broadly similar concern for the oppressed or exploited and a profound anti-militarism, although these themes were not expressed with any of the political force that had characterised October's work. Prévert established a working relationship with Marcel Carné and between them they were responsible for a number of very successful films that managed to keep alive something of the spirit of the Front Populaire during the years of Occupation. They include *Drôle de drame* (1937) *Quai des brumes* (1938) *Le Jour se lève* (1939) and *Les Enfants du paradis* (1943–44).

Alongside the left-wing demand for mass theatre or political theatre in the thirties, there had developed a trend which could loosely be described as Catholic theatre. Its most spectacular achievement was to stage Arnoul Gréban's sixteenth century *Mystère de la passion* on the square in front of Notre-Dame, an event that was to find an echo after the war in the great festival of religious drama held at Chartres immediately after the armistice, led by the Compagnons de la Saint-Jean (see chapter 2). But this trend had a more lasting influence on post-war theatre through the work of Léon Chancerel.

Chancerel had been one of Copeau's select group Les Copiaus, but did not join the Compagnie des Quinze in 1931. Instead, he began to set up a nation-wide network of theatre groups within the Boy Scout movement performing plays which frequently had a religious theme. He also formed a professional touring group Les Comédiens Routiers and a children's theatre Le Théâtre de l'Oncle Sébastien. In their repertoire the Comédiens Routiers did not concentrate solely on Catholic plays. They had a particular success with Molière's *Les Fourberies de Scapin*, developing the work that Copeau had begun with improvised farce, masks, acrobatics and the search for a modern Commedia dell'arte. Among those who worked in Chancerel's group were Maurice Jacquemont, Olivier Hussenot, Jean-Pierre Grenier, Yves Joly and Hubert Gignoux, all of whom were to become directors of Centres Dramatiques after the war.

The aims and methods of Chancerel's group were very similar to those of left-wing theatre groups, both emphasising unity, community and the importance of a combined front against fascism. Ideological motivation was considered an important factor in French theatre in the late thirties and Copeau was not the first to say that the theatre of the future would be either Christian or Marxist (see below p. 31).

The first socialist government that France had ever had, the Front Populaire, was also the first government to accept that the state had a responsibility to subsidise theatre that went beyond the Comédie Française. The Minister of

Culture Jean Zay was keen to develop a policy of decentralisation of the theatre and commissioned Dullin to prepare a report. In this report Dullin identified *la centralisation* as the chief source of the lamentable state of French theatre outside Paris. Even in Paris itself he claimed that the people had been systematically removed from the proximity of theatres, so that the theatre-going public had become restricted to a small class. The solution proposed by Dullin was the division of France into *préfectorats artistiques*. These should be 'broad enough not to degenerate into parochialism or artistic bureaucracy' (1969: 161–2). From the 'capital' of each *préfectorat*, theatre groups (as well as groups of musicians, artists, etc.) would reach out into the surrounding country by a system of arranged tours and visits.

For this to work however, he made it clear that the financial basis of theatre would have to be changed and the theatres taken out of the hands of speculators. He was convinced that the state could and should take a hand in this. He applauded the plan, already under discussion, to construct three large new theatres in the workers' suburbs of Paris, suggesting that this principle should be extended to the provinces as well. He then developed some detailed ideas on how the new theatres should be built. The major features of his recommendations were the need for a flexible stage space and for the theatre to be provided with a library and good facilities for the actors. He then went on to discuss repertoire, stressing the need for a dazzling appeal to the imagination in the early productions of the new theatres: an ideal choice would be *Le Cid*, for 'the people will instinctively follow sublime tragic action if this action is presented on the necessary scale' (1969: 172). Each theatre should have its own company, with its own touring circuit, 'that means a central establishment with an administrative staff and workshop' (ibid. 174).

This report was shelved soon after it had been written because the Front Populaire government fell from power and the political will to implement it vanished. But when, after the war, there was once again a French government with the will to act, this report was rediscovered and acted upon. Dullin's model had been well thought out; the organisation of the first Centres Dramatiques was remarkably similar in its details to what he had suggested. After 1968, there was some criticism of a cultural policy that traded on the fact that 'the people will instinctively follow sublime tragic action', but the success of Vilar with *Le Cid* and of the Centres Dramatiques with similar heroic productions of the classics showed that Dullin understood his audience. He never patronised ('above all never say: they won't understand any of that', ibid. 172) and the directors who succeeded in the post-war decentralisation movement were all characterised by a similar respect for their new theatre-going public. Dullin's comments on the best production style for such work provide a useful summary, both of what he and the Cartel had achieved and of the style that was to predominate in the Centres Dramatiques:

For new plays, a production style that is ingenious, using simple means, but profound and subtle, employing truthful performance to evoke the play; the time will come when the attraction of novelty has worn off and these new peoples' theatres (*théâtres populaires*) will once again be in competition with cinema, lavish operetta, etc. The best productions are generally the least expensive because there is more room for the spirit of the piece than for cardboard frippery (1969: 173).

The theatre at the end of the thirties was very different from what it had been when Copeau began to write his drama criticism: it had become acceptable to think of theatre as educational, even uplifting, instead of dismissing it as a corrupting influence. Three influential forces had contributed to this change: the independent directors of the Cartel, the school of literary playwrights, and the political and religious bodies that had begun to see the theatre's usefulness to them. As a result of this change in attitudes, the foundations of much of the post-war development were already in place. The organisational and artistic strategies for decentralisation had been thought out, if not yet fully accepted, the need for plays of sufficient quality to make demands on their audience had been demonstrated, and the necessity for state involvement on a large scale had been understood.

The consequences of all this were, however, far from clear to most people working in the French theatre. Very few foresaw the major split that was to occur after the war between private- and public-funded theatres or between Paris and the provinces. There was almost no hint, either, of the major intellectual currents that were to dominate the post-war theatre: Existentialist, Marxist, Surrealist. In this respect the playwrights of the ensuing four decades were to make a series of startling new beginnings. Theatre people in France at the end of the thirties were surprisingly insular: very few had travelled widely in Europe or paid much attention to developments in other countries. Pirandello's work had made its influence felt, but that of Brecht and the German Expressionists was hardly known at all. Directors of major international stature such as Meyerhold and Piscator also remained unknown outside a very restricted circle. Many of the new beginnings of the post-war period were to be fuelled by the discovery of such major precursors. The impact of foreign influences was to be all the greater for being retarded by the isolation imposed by four years of German Occupation.

2

The Occupation

During the German Occupation of France (1940–44) the Parisian theatres were fuller than ever before. Audiences were undeterred by the difficulties of getting to and from the theatre under black-out conditions, by the ban on heating in public buildings or by the interruptions (towards the end of the war) caused by air-raid sirens. The experience of living under the Occupation was one of scarcity and discomfort, brutality and fear, broken by occasional acts of extreme heroism, which often seemed as difficult to understand as the atrocities of the authorities. The absolute secrecy necessary for any political activity was well conveyed by Jean-Pierre Kessel in his documentary novel *L'Armée des ombres*. He depicts a young activist who cannot understand why his elder brother appears so passive; he abuses him for being a collaborator, only to discover, much later, that his brother was, in fact, the co-ordinator for all Resistance activities in France. In such conditions of insecurity, where even brothers kept their real sympathies secret from one another, a visit to the theatre provided, at least for a couple of hours, the experience of comradeship, solidarity and human warmth. Thierry Maulnier, a contemporary critic, wrote that the theatre 'became an asylum of relative freedom in which French people could gather together and reaffirm their national identity' (Vessilier, 1973: 25).

For the first two years after the French defeat, only the northern half of France (as well as the whole Atlantic coastline) was occupied by the German army. The country was divided into two zones and Marshal Pétain assumed authority over the 'free' zone at the head of a puppet government. The headquarters of the new Government were established at Vichy and attempts were made, by both the German and Vichy authorities, to promote the idea that life could continue more or less as usual. The theatres were permitted to reopen and the development of cultural life was encouraged.

But the freedom of theatre managers and directors was limited by a complicated system of censorship. Any play that a theatre director wished to produce had to be submitted, first to the Vichy censor and then, if approved by him, to the *Propagandastaffel* in Paris. The result of this roundabout procedure was that it took a very long time to clear a play and so, in order to avoid the risk of excessive delays, theatre producers tended to play safe. Many of the plays to which people flocked were of the most superficial kind and there was a particular vogue for historical costume dramas, the past being considered 'safer' than the present.

In such an atmosphere it is perhaps not surprising to find that many of the new plays by established authors that were performed during this period were of a frankly escapist nature. Literary figures like Cocteau and Giraudoux, who had led the poetic revival in the inter-war theatre, produced a number of plays that avoided the present, making use of the myth of the good old days in various forms.

Cocteau's *Renaud et Armide*, written in 1941 and first performed at the Comédie Française in 1943, is a good example of a play that legitimately qualifies for that rather overworked label 'escapist art'. The story is a simple fairy tale, of the kind preferred by Cocteau, about a fairy who falls in love with a warrior king and gives up her power and immortality to win his love, although she knows that his first kiss will kill her. This fanciful, rather sentimental tale is given a dramatic treatment in strict Alexandrine verses, obeying all the rules of the seventeenth century theatre: unity of place, time, subject, etc. It reads like a brilliant pastiche of Racine, not only in the metric structure of the verse but even in stylistic details such as use of image and paradox:

Olivier
Comment peut-on aimer un fantôme perfide?
Renaud
Dans ces jardins déserts tout me parle d'Armide.
Je rôde, je la cherche, et je la vois bien mieux,
Invisible en mon coeur que présente à mes yeux (1948b: 220).
[*Olivier*
How can one love a fickle ghost?
Renaud
In these deserted gardens everything speaks to me of Armide
I wander in search of her, and see her more clearly
Invisible in my heart than present before my eyes.]

But the subject-matter is so light and insubstantial, so far-removed from Racine's full-blooded catastrophes, that the resulting play has no more than the smallest curiosity value.

In the harmlessness of its subject-matter and the literary aspirations of its style, *Renaud et Armide* is typical of much that was produced under the Occupation. But it would be unfair to accuse Cocteau of always choosing safe subjects. In 1940 and 1941 he had been violently attacked, both in the press and, once or twice, in person, for writing plays like *Les Parents terribles* (1938), which suggested that family life can be vicious, and for his homosexual relationship with Jean Marais. Such things were judged by the Vichy spokesmen to be prejudicial to the official propaganda stressing *Travail, Famille, Patrie*, and typical of the kind of decadence that had undermined the moral fibre of the Third Republic. In the face of such attacks, *Renaud et Armide*, with its high-flown classical style, was clearly an attempt to vindicate his reputation as a serious man of letters.

In 1939 Cocteau had written two plays on contemporary subjects, *La Machine à écrire*, not staged until April 1941 since Jean Marais was not available earlier, and *Les Monstres sacrés*, performed in February 1940. The theme of the latter is the difficulty of separating real life from performance, especially for the professional actor of grand dramatic roles, a theme that he was to take up again after the war in *L'Aigle à deux têtes* and that was to be given thorough treatment by Sartre in his *Kean*. *La Machine à écrire* is, like *Les Parents terribles*, a family drama with a melodramatic ending in which Cocteau lambasts the hypocrisy of French provincial life. It was taken off as a result of pressure from the Vichy authorities and a revival of *Les Parents terribles* in October 1941 was also banned by the Prefect of Police because it had provoked violent incidents.

In the face of such troubles, Cocteau took refuge in the cinema, contributing to the production of a number of films and preparing himself for the important career that he was to make as a film director in the later forties and fifties. He wrote the scenario and dialogues for *L'Eternel Retour*, directed by Jean Delannoy and starring Jean Marais and Madeleine Sologne. He also befriended cultured francophile Germans, such as the official Nazi sculptor Arno Breker and the soldier-novelist Ernst Jünger. This ensured him the dislike of both left and right in France and caused him some difficulties after the Liberation. But it seems that he never actively collaborated and he was cleared of political blame at quite an early stage during the *épuration* period, when committees were set up to investigate the activities of those suspected of having collaborated.

The only new work of Giraudoux's to be produced during the Occupation was *Sodome et Gomorrhe* (1943), a play which is very much like a number of the author's pre-war works. It enacts a struggle between Man and Woman that is reminiscent of similar conflicts in *Amphitryon*, *La Guerre de Troie n'aura pas lieu*, or *Electre* and it is set, like *Judith* in the Old Testament world. The play must have been a puzzle to its first audiences, and the critics were divided. Like all of Giraudoux's work, it is wordy, even precious at times, but unlike his previous plays it is very static and quite lacking in the constant reversal of situation and play of ironic contrast that lend sparkle to even those plays whose situation does not admit of great development, like *La Guerre de Troie n'aura pas lieu*.

The main theme of the play is that Man is the embodiment of convention and of blind routine, whereas Woman is the source of imagination and the yearning for the transcendent. Lia, the woman, can fall in love with an angel, whereas Jean and Jacques remain earthbound, happy with the conventional male/ female sexual relations. The play opens with an Archangel announcing the destruction of the towns of Sodom and Gomorrah unless one married couple can be found that is genuinely happy. The obvious candidates for the happy couple at first appear to be Jean and Lia. But Lia falls in love with the angel that is sent to observe her, has a casual encounter with Jacques just to show that she is no longer part of a happy conjugal couple, and finally welcomes the destruction of her world (and herself with it) at the end of the play.

Sodome et Gomorrhe was a financial success, running for 214 performances, helped by a cast that included Edwige Feuillère as Lia and Gérard Philipe as the Angel. While not engaging directly with contemporary realities, it was less escapist than *Renaud et Armide*. It contains lines that had a corrosive resonance in 1943, especially Lia's assertions of independence from authority. When Jean orders her to stay with him, she replies: 'Your voice is loud and your gesture imperious but you cannot command me. You no longer have the power. You are commanding on behalf of others, and with them I have broken' (1982: 877). This passage has Sartrean overtones and Lia's position is constantly reminiscent of the experience, as described by Oreste in *Les Mouches*, of having been struck by the thunderbolt of liberty. Because of this she can be interpreted as a character making a general appeal for an attitude of revolt.

But Lia's gesture of revolt is not made to any purpose. Her profound desire is for some overwhelming, all-consuming experience that will offer escape from a life that has come to seem nothing but dull routine. And although it is possible to detect an anti-Vichy note in her blunt refusal to be made to feel guilty for the destruction of the towns that follows, she never offers any positive grounds for choosing to refuse the offer of happiness. Her position seems more negative than it might otherwise have done because of the way the author has portrayed Jean. Giraudoux's men are often rather pale and colourless by contrast with his women, and in Jean this tendency reaches its nadir. He has almost nothing to say that is not a response to Lia and seldom initiates any action. In fact the weakness of his character is one of the reasons why the play is so lacking in dramatic conflict.

If *Sodome et Gomorrhe* seems so inferior in comparison with much of Giraudoux's earlier work, it is for two main reasons. The first and most obvious is the absence of Jouvet during its rehearsal and production. Donald Inskip (1958) has shown that every one of Giraudoux's previous plays had been extensively rewritten (in collaboration with Jouvet) during the rehearsal period. Giraudoux had the idea for *Sodome et Gomorrhe* before Jouvet's departure for South America in 1941, but during the first years of the Occupation he contented himself with collaborating on two films, *La Duchesse de Langeais* and *Les Anges du péché*. While working on the former he made the acquaintance of Edwige Feuillère and it seems that he wrote the part of Lia for her. Perhaps if Jouvet had supervised the first production the play would have been radically changed; perhaps a stronger male part would have been composed for him to act.

There are other explanations to be found for the play's inferiority in Giraudoux's circumstances at the time. In some ways the defeat of France was a particular catastrophe for Giraudoux in person. All the warnings of his inter-war writings had fallen on deaf ears, and in Lia's attitude to the apocalypse there is more than a hint of 'I told you so'. During the first six months of the 'phoney war' Giraudoux was head of the Information Service, a post which he used to try to restore French national pride and consciousness of their heritage. After the defeat he refused the Vichy government's offer of a post as ambassador to Athens. He spent the last years of his life working on essays (only published in 1945), on *L'Apollon de Bellac*, *La Folle de Chaillot* and the uncompleted *Pour Lucrèce*. He died unexpectedly after a bout of influenza on 31 January 1944.

The essays and his last four plays show that his mental attitudes did not change under the impact of the Occupation. He remained, essentially, an idealist, interested in freedom as a spiritual and imaginative quality rather than as a concrete political reality. While the circumstances of the Occupation led many to see political issues in unusually simple black and white terms, Giraudoux's work moved, if anything, even farther away from political realities than it had been before the war. The one possible exception to this might be seen in *La Folle de Chaillot*, produced by Jouvet in 1945 after his return to Paris. In this whimsical play Giraudoux imagined a situation in which oil was discovered beneath Paris. The speculators and financiers move in and try to clear the common people out of Paris so as to begin drilling operations. Their attempts are only defeated by the initiative of the Madwoman of Chaillot, a sort of fancy-dress *clocharde* who embodies the independent spirit of French culture. The play was clearly meant as an old man's valedictory attack on all that is petty and self-seeking in the modern world. As such, it was rapturously received by audiences at the Athénée theatre, for whom the return of Jouvet was an occasion to look back nostalgically to the twenties and thirties. But the play has dated very rapidly and now seems almost irresponsibly naive in view of the very real depredations inflicted on the city by high finance.

These plays by Cocteau and Giraudoux are representative examples of the school of literary theatre that had flourished between the wars and that looked back to mythical or historical models of heroism. To contemporary observers, this school of playwriting appeared to be in a healthy state; it is only with hindsight that we can see that its apparent vigour was no more than the last spasm of movement before rigor mortis set in. The picture was complicated by the fact that, even in its dying stages, the school was joined by an author who had never written for the stage before, and whose first play was one of the big commercial successes of the Occupation: Henry de Montherlant. His first play was the result of a commission by Jean-Louis Vaudoyer, director of the Comédie Française from 1941 until the end of the Occupation. He decided that the playwrights of the Spanish Golden Age were right for the times: their plots were well removed from either France or Germany and they had already been successfully performed by German companies. Later, in November 1943, the Berlin Schiller Theater company made a visit to the Comédie Française with a performance of Calderón's *Mayor of Zalamea*.

Vaudoyer passed some Spanish plays to Montherlant with the suggestion that he might make a translation. Instead, Montherlant wrote his own play, *La Reine morte*, inspired by Guevara's *Reinar después de morir*. The play opened at the Comédie Française in December 1942 with Jean Yonnel in the role of Ferrante. It was a great success and ran for the whole of 1943. The success of the play was not surprising. Montherlant was a well-known figure in the French literary world as a result of the novels and essays he had been publishing since the twenties. *La Reine morte* was his first play, and therefore likely to arouse the interest of the Comédie Française audience for that reason alone. It is also a vigorous, colourful drama, peopled with proud, strong-willed nobles of the Spanish and Portuguese courts. This brought a breath of fresh air into the depressing atmosphere of occupied Paris, as Montherlant's preface shows he clearly intended.

The play is ostensibly about the age-old conflict between youth and maturity, idealism and experience. Ferrante, king of Portugal, has arranged a political marriage between his son, Don Pedro, and the Infanta of Navarre. But Don Pedro has already made a secret love match with Ines de Castro, whom he refuses to desert despite pressure from his father. After a period of indecision, Ferrante has Ines killed, just before he too dies, bringing the play to a fruitless end.

The two most striking characters are Ferrante and the Infanta. But both are marred by a lack of warmth, an inability to pay sustained attention to anyone but themselves. The Infanta has a truly Cornelian notion of *la gloire*, but she is devoid of the generosity of feeling that accompanies *la gloire* in many of Corneille's heroes. Ferrante is a more subtle character study, but he too lacks warmth. His opening speech to his son consists in heaping him with insults for his mediocrity in contrast to his (Ferrante's) own distinction. There is no hint in Montherlant's prose of any irony at Ferrante's expense and the whole play is weakened by his manifest failure to understand the simplest elements of a father–son relationship.

Ferrante is a character painfully conscious of his own conflicting inner tendencies. What weakens him as a dramatic character is that he has almost no human qualities with which the audience can identify. He does not appear to love anyone other than himself, nor does he have any identifiable political aims. It is quite understandable in the circumstances of occupied France that Montherlant should have wished to avoid anything that might seem too close to contemporary political reality. But even within the limitations of the situation described in the play, Montherlant shows a remarkable lack of interest in the affairs of state. No explanation is given for the political necessity of the marriage that Ferrante is trying to impose upon his son. Instead, the emphasis is all upon the interior drama of Ferrante's own hesitations: can he bring himself to take what his advisers insist is the only expedient path, killing Ines since she is an obstacle to his plans, or not? He has no firm centre or value system to which he can appeal; he calls indiscriminately upon God, whether he is planning a murder or a marriage. And when he does finally give the order for Ines' death, it is only out of wounded vanity, since she dared to take pity on him.

The result is that what at first seems to be a drama of conflict between old and young, turns out, on closer inspection, to be a drama of one man's vacillation between pride and charity, ending on a note of despair. In the final tableau of the play, two dead bodies are exposed side by side on the stage – the king's and Ines'. All the courtiers follow Don Pedro in kneeling at Ines' body, while Ferrante's is left alone and abandoned. Even the young page, in whom Ferrante had placed his confidence, abandons him for Don Pedro. The implication is that he will betray the new master as he betrayed the old. The final emphasis is on the fruitlessness of Ferrante's vacillations, the pointlessness of his action, and the corrupt fickleness of the court.

Montherlant has claimed that the only interesting theatre is a theatre of characters, but his understanding of that term relates to the psychological theatre of the early part of the century rather than to the new notions of character that were to be explored by dramatists after the war. Everything that Artaud and his followers castigated under the general title of psychological theatre is summed up in *La Reine morte*. The play appears profoundly untheatrical, and hence unsuited to performance, because of its almost exclusive concentration on Ferrante. The other characters are all only too obviously included simply to give Ferrante someone to talk to: an audience has difficulty in taking much interest in them in their own right. But there is nothing compellingly dramatic about Ferrante's state of mind or situation; the play is a character study in dialogue form rather than a piece of theatre. The same is true of Montherlant's other plays, many of which have religious themes, such as *Le Maître de Santiago* (1948) or *Port-Royal* (1954). They are conscious copies of the neo-classical model, inhabited by divided characters who do little but agonise over their inability to make a strong affirmation of selfhood. The one exception is *La Ville dont le prince est un enfant*, published in 1951, but not performed until 1967 because of the author's scruples about the subject-matter. It is set in a Catholic boys' boarding school and depicts the passions of its inmates in terms similar to those employed by writers of English public school novels from the Edwardian era. Here, preoccupations with honour contrast movingly with impulses of the heart and the restrictive setting of a boarding school is powerfully evoked.

Montherlant divides the French critics. Those who admire him do so for 'his princely style, whose broad range goes from the most classical line and noblest tones to the most baroque line and most familiar tones' (Brenner, 1978: 180). He is seen as a great literary stylist, whose finest achievement is perhaps the novel *Le Chaos et la nuit* (1963) rather than any of his plays. Montherlant's own comments on his theatre show that he was happy for his plays to be seen as exercises in *la psychologie dialoguée*: 'for me there is only one form of theatre worthy of the name – psychological theatre' (1958: 950). It is for this reason that, although Montherlant's plays had a certain success during the forties and fifties, especially at the Comédie Française, they always seemed marginal to the main developments in writing and stage-craft of the post-war period.

The interest of both *La Reine morte* and *Sodome et Gomorrhe* is that although set in a broadly classical mould, they fail to achieve either the formal or the thematic clarity of the French classical theatre. Not only do both plays lack dramatic conflict, they also lack the defiant affirmation of self that characterised the heroes of classical tragedy, even at the moment of destruction by forces beyond their control. In these plays of the Occupation we can see the collapse of confidence in the individual as a self-affirming centre. They represent a last desperate attempt, by returning to the old heroic stories, to make that affirmation. But they are incapable of doing so: Lia can find no positive statement in her defence; Ferrante, whose life has been devoted to self-affirmation, collapses in an agony of uncertainty about who he really is. This dilemma was to become clearest of all in Anouilh's *Antigone* where the heroine goes through the motions of dying for a belief but finds that belief to be empty. Long after Proust and Joyce had explored the idea in their novels, the theatre was about to experience the force of one of the most powerful and corrosive of modern convictions: that there is no God-given central essence to our characters but that we are who we are solely by virtue of our circumstances or (among more optimistic manifestations of the idea) our actions. It is for this reason that the classical models had to give way and that the plays that have shaped the modern imagination have been not these, but *Huis clos* or *En attendant Godot*.

In the rather stultifying atmosphere of German censorship and Vichy propaganda the one character that could be relied upon to please everyone was Joan of Arc. She pleased the Germans because, in her life and by her death, she had showed up both the frailty and the perfidy of Albion. She pleased the French because she could be presented as the symbol of a humiliated France fighting to regain her stained honour and self-respect. A number of performances of plays on the subject of Joan's life in various parts of France paved the way for a massive Fête Jeanne d'Arc held in all the major towns of France in May 1942. Once the subject had become established as officially acceptable, it could be used in a more frankly subversive way, as was evidently the case with the production of Claude Vermorel's *Jeanne avec nous*. This is described by Patrick Marsh as the only play that effectively communicated a message of resistance to its audience (1981: 292–4). It ran for three months in Paris in early 1942 and when published the following year was awarded the Prix de la Société des Auteurs Dramatiques.

It is perhaps not surprising that most of the successes of the Occupation were either escapist or backward-looking. More interesting are the exceptions to this rule, especially *Les Mouches* and *Huis clos* (see following chapter), and *Le Soulier de satin* by Paul Claudel. In 1943 Claudel had a reputation as a Catholic poet but his plays (mostly written between 1890 and 1920) had only rarely been produced before and were generally held to be too unwieldy for stage performance. The production was a triumph for the director, Jean-Louis Barrault, who applied to it the methods of total theatre with which he had been experimenting during the 1930s.

Claudel's work truly belongs to the first half of the twentieth century. It is in the context of that world, the world of Gide and Proust, of Rimbaud and Valéry, of Rolland and Péguy that it takes on its fullest meaning. But the plays have also enjoyed a second life, since they have been the occasion for productions, especially productions by Jean-Louis Barrault, in which the theatre of the word was transcended and a new theatre of multiple means came into existence. What is interesting is to see that Claudel, unlike Montherlant, understood and participated in this development. After his initial scruples over cutting his text had been overcome, he did not play the role of recalcitrant author defending the text, but encouraged the fullest possible realisation of the play, using all the resources of the theatre. He wrote to Lucien Coutaud, the designer of *Le Soulier de satin* to say how much he admired the way the sets fulfilled a function that was 'more dramatic than pictorial' (1966: 191–2) and went on to express his extreme delight and amazement at discovering a new dimension in his own work, thanks to the imagination of Barrault. From this point onwards, as the articles, essays and notes reprinted in *Mes Idées sur le théâtre* show, he continued to see this as an element of central importance in the stage realisation of his plays. His instructions for scenic detail and positioning are often extremely detailed and concrete, sometimes even including sketches and plans. Five more plays were to be put on before his death in 1955 and all were rewritten to some extent.

In order to understand the contribution that Barrault made to Claudel's dramaturgy, we must know something about Barrault's career and training at this point. Barrault had joined Dullin's theatre, L'Atelier, in 1931 at the age of twenty (acting his first small part on his twenty-first birthday). It was here that he acquired his training during the period that led up to the war. As well as acting for Dullin (and in numerous films), Barrault directed three plays of his own. The first, at L'Atelier, was called *Autour d'une mère* and was a loose adaptation of Faulkner's novel *As I lay dying*. The emphasis in this adaptation, as in his next two productions, was on building a dramatic action through mime and group work; there was very little dialogue. The other two were equally free adaptations: *Numance* (1937) from Cervantes' *Numancia*, and *La Faim* (1939) from Knut Hamsun's novel *Hunger*. He had trained in mime with Etienne Decroux and became a close friend and collaborator of Artaud, whose concept of the actor as *athlète affectif* he made his own. Both through the influences to which he was exposed, and through the development of his particular talents, Barrault was working towards a theatre of mixed means in which the expressive force of the actor's body is predominant, leaving little room for the verbal subtleties and witty dialogue characteristic of Cocteau or Giraudoux.

He was called up and served in the army for the 'phoney' war but as soon as he was demobilised he resumed his theatre work, joining the Comédie Française at Copeau's request during his short period as director (1940–41). In his first year at the Comédie Française he took the lead in *Le Cid* and in *Hamlet*. In the summer he produced one independent show, a double bill of *800 mètres* by Obey with *The suppliant women* by Aeschylus, at a large sports stadium – the Stade Roland Garros. Barrault's staging of both plays was reminiscent of some of the Popular Front government's attempts at mass theatre, mixing sport and drama. Honegger supplied the music and the Greek play was accompanied by mass choral movement. The choice of *800 mètres* was significant in this respect. It is a play about the mental and physical struggles of an 800-metre runner, his growing elation as he appears to be winning and his final despair as he is beaten into second place. Its performance consisted of Jean-Louis Barrault, Alain Cuny, Jean Marais and other fine young specimens pounding round the stadium track while the drama was put across by means of a commentary. It demonstrates very clearly Barrault's continuing belief in the centrality of the human physique for the act of theatre, but also his political naïvety, since the times had changed dramatically between the Popular Front and 1941: the cult of the body had acquired sinister overtones. It was this same naïvety that was to lead to his loss of the Odéon theatre in 1968. Barrault always argued that his task was to follow his inspiration and not to take account of changing political decisions. Early in the war he put his enthusiasm for physical training with youth groups at the disposal of Vichy; later he was happy to do the same for the Resistance – what mattered to him was the experience more than the context.

Through going outside the narrow confines of the theatre and interesting himself in all aspects of human movement, Barrault was to influence a large number of young people. One of the most notable was Gabriel Cousin, later an important playwright (see chapter 7), but in 1941 a young amateur sportsman who, when he went to Barrault's *800 mètres*, was attending a play for the first time in his life. He later wrote: 'The writing set up an immediate and profound resonance in me. It was familiar to me although I had not heard it before: It had been part of my upbringing. Not through school, but through the stadium. It was part of my physical experience through the practice of lungs and muscles' (Jeffery, 1980: 150).

The following year, Barrault was elected to full membership of the Comédie Française company, a position that he accepted with great misgivings since the engagement was for life. This made Barrault all the more determined to retain his artistic initiative and the production of *Le Soulier de satin* became a kind of test case in his own eyes. In order to be allowed to produce it, he had to persuade not only the other Sociétaires, but also Claudel himself. Vaudoyer was enthusiastic, but Barrault's colleagues were recalcitrant at first. The play seemed too much like hard work and some of them confessed to not understanding a word of it. Claudel was at first unwilling to cut his text to manageable proportions and Barrault was obliged to make several visits to his home in the *zone libre* before he would be persuaded. In the end, Claudel was won over by Barrault's tenacity; he came to Paris for the last ten days of rehearsal and took an important part in the process of putting the play on the stage, which included writing an entirely new version of the climatic meeting between Rodrigue and Prouhèze at the end of the third 'day'.

It might appear paradoxical that Barrault, who had worked so hard to develop a physical performance style, should choose so wordy a playwright. But Claudel's verse style is entirely unlike that of Cocteau (or Giraudoux's poetic prose). It is unlike anything before it in the French literary tradition, being based on the rhythm of the breath group, not on the number of feet in a line or the elegant balance of paradox. It builds its effects by slow accumulation, not by sudden sally, and it has an extraordinarily physical effect on the listener. Barrault regards the actor's body as an instrument (see 1975: 59) and Claudel's verse as a kind of body music; Barrault discovered that it had to be spoken with the whole body, not just with the articulatory and respiratory organs, and that movement, position, attitude were as vital to the proper rendering of each line as accent and intonation.

For all his originality, Barrault had never had the ambition to be a playwright. 'Up until then, the performances I had put on had all suffered from an inadequate text . . . mine. I wanted to apply my vision of a theatre in which the actor is able to express himself completely to a major text' (1959: 207). In *Le Soulier* Barrault discovered the 'major text' he had been looking for. But he was also attracted by its theatrical qualities. More than most of Claudel's plays, it is composed of a rich medley of theatrical styles and techniques, with the result that it may seem clumsy when read but is constantly exciting in performance. Most interesting of all, it contains, woven into the fabric of the plot itself, a meditation on the nature of theatrical representation that was unexpectedly modern in 1943 (and distinctly adventurous in 1929 when Claudel had completed the first version of the play). The theatrical quality of the text is evident from the mixture of styles and moods. Within the French dramatic tradition, the mixture of styles that is found, say, in Shakespeare, has always been censured. Interruptions of the tragic mood by grotesque scenes like that of the porter in *Macbeth* have been considered either unnecessary or downright shocking. To show the turning point in a man's life in a comic or grotesque light and then, in the same sequence of events, to demonstrate its tragic aspects, has always seemed an aberration to minds reared on Racine. The Romantic playwrights claimed that they wanted to achieve this mixture of moods, but they never really succeeded because their view of the function of performance was too solemn. Claudel succeeded in *Le Soulier de satin* because he had learned from eastern theatre how the actor can distance himself from his role and because his theme was the all-embracing completeness of God's kingdom. The two epigraphs to the play are 'God writes in curving lines' and 'Even sin serves'. Every action, whether tragic or comic, submissive or rebellious, is ultimately integrated into the divine play of God, however circuitously that integration may occur.

A good example of how this all-embracing vision was dramatised in the Barrault production of *Le Soulier de satin* can be seen in the last few scenes of the first 'day'. Rodrigue's passionate confidences in scene 7 are made to a clownish Chinaman and interspersed with characters rushing to and fro across the stage in a state of confusion. This farcical mood builds up to the point where Rodrigue decides that he must 'rescue' Dona Isabel, who desires no rescue, brings tragedy upon her by killing her lover and is himself wounded. This result will lead eventually to the proper working out of the plot, but that is far from clear at the time, and the original audience was even further surprised when, from black farce, the production moved into a mood of exoticism with the negress dancing naked in the moonlight. The plans for a meeting between Rodrigue and Prouhèze, that would seem to be of the highest seriousness, are laid by two of the most unlikely characters, the negress and the Chinaman. This scene inevitably borders on farce and it seems almost impossible to achieve the appropriate mood for the following scene, which shows Prouhèze alone with her guardian angel, drawn irresistibly towards Rodrigue, but full of doubts and misgivings. Barrault managed the mood change by introducing some mime: the thorn bushes through which Prouhèze struggles were represented by actors, and her difficulties as she tries to break through were played out by means of physical action (see fig. 1).

But the most thoroughgoing theatrical device is that of L'Annoncier. He is generally thought of as being rather marginal to the play (e.g. the Larousse Classiques du Vingtième Siècle edition leaves him out altogether) but in Barrault's production he had a key role to play. He came on at the beginning, between 'days' one and two, at the beginning of the second half (the start of 'day' three) and again to introduce the epilogue (which replaced the original 'day' four). The role of L'Annoncier is so important because he establishes the performance, from the outset, within the frame of reference of non-naturalistic theatre. It is he who raises the first curtain to reveal a second one through which he takes the audience into the different parts of the globe that the action will cover, and presents the different characters to them. He is like the fairground showman, hurrying his performers along, reassuring his audience, telling a few jokes as he goes.

But his function goes further than merely serving to introduce a particularly complicated dramatic action. It helps to alert the audience to what *kind* of dramatic action will follow and to establish the right mood so that they are able properly to understand whay they see:

Listen hard, don't cough and try to understand. The most beautiful parts are the ones you don't understand. The longest parts are the most interesting and the parts you find uninteresting are the funniest (1965: 957).

1 *Le Soulier de satin* (Claudel): the hedge represented in mime. From Barrault's 1958 revival at the Théâtre du Palais Royal.

Claudel is here warning his audience against an excessively solemn response to the show that is to follow. Like Brecht, he wants them to sit back with a detached, amused, but critical eye, to be ready to be surprised by things that they had thought obvious and to discover the unfamiliar beneath the everyday. L'Annoncier also alerts his audience to the main themes, for instance the theme of time, in his appearance between 'days' one and two:

As you know, in the theatre we can manipulate time like an accordion, as we please, the hours are made to last while whole days are passed over. Nothing is easier than to make time work in several directions at once (ibid. 1011).

His appearance at the beginning of 'day' three was the occasion for a very clever piece of mime, as the story of the letter that took ten years to travel from Rodrigue to Prouhèze was enacted. But perhaps the most arresting intervention of L'Annoncier was his introduction of the epilogue, where he went through what Claudel described as 'a regular music hall number'. His speech builds up to a Brechtian parable concerning the nature of audience participation. It tells the story of some soldiers billeted on an avaricious peasant, who manage to make him part with the ingredients for their soup despite his determination to give nothing. They do this by pretending that it's really *soupe à la pierre* (a stone soup made by boiling a miraculous stone) and that the vegetables, bacon, etc. that the credulous peasant parts with are just thrown in for the flavour. He goes on:

This stone soup, Ladies and Gentlemen, is what we have to offer you as dessert to follow our frugal banquet and your imagination will have to provide the means since the last metro prevents us from serving you the good food prepared by the author (ibid. 1103).

At one level this functions simply as an explanation of why the fourth 'day' had to be cut, as a topical joke about the scarcity of food in Paris and the need to be home before curfew. But at a deeper level it is a comment on the whole structure of the play. Its variations of tone, its rapid changes from one mood to another, from one continent to another, constitute a particular method. The method rests upon an underlying belief in the reality of God's creative energy binding together all things. But it does not attempt to give a comprehensive picture of this underlying reality. The most it can do is to provide glimpses of it, trusting that something miraculous will occur, as in the case of the stone soup. The public is presented with something that is as unreal as the soldiers' soup but equally miraculous, since its qualities are those of the Shakespearean stage, free to evoke any time or place. Gradually, as the audience has responded with its own imaginative effort, Claudel's picture of a total world order based on sacrifice and struggle but underpinned by divine love has been built up and the soup perfected. There is not so strong an emphasis as we find in many of Brecht's plays on the need to go out and change the world, but the audience is forced into a certain degree of self-consciousness; it is obliged to recognise that it cannot avoid active participation in the construction of the dramatic reality. The view of each particular person will be limited. He will not know if his struggles will be rewarded, like those of Dona Musique, who against every expectation discovers the Viceroy of Naples, or not, like those of Don Rodrigue. But he will know that every action alters the state of affairs, whether material or spiritual, for better or for worse. No action is without consequence.

Certain obvious links may be made between *La Reine morte* and *Le Soulier de satin*. Both use sixteenth century Spanish aristocrats in order to establish an atmosphere of pride and high ambition; both incorporate conflicts of a kind between love and duty. Writing with hindsight on the occasion of Barrault's 1958 revival, Roland Barthes made this comment:

Castilianism is period décor assumed by a certain variety of French culture when it wants to cast an air of nobility over the representation of an impossible desire; in Montherlant's case the device is obvious; in Claudel's the quality of 'greatness' involves fewer *words*: there is always a certain material density lending suppleness to his lines. But adultery remains the foundation (1959: 122).

What Barthes saw in plays by Montherlant or Claudel was the basic structure of the bourgeois sex comedy dressed up in fine words and period settings. In the Marxist, materialist perspective this analysis is persuasive. The story of *Le Soulier de satin* is both everywhere and nowhere. Its action takes place in settings that are scattered across the globe, but the economic and social reality of the locations is never shown or mentioned. This is because the play, for all its materiality of means, is a dramatisation of spiritual realities and conflicts. Here the world views of Catholic and Marxist inevitably part ways. For the Marxist, spiritual realities are an expression, at a complex secondary level, of economic and material realities: certain material conditions give rise, in human beings, to certain spiritual aspirations. For the Catholic (especially an old-school Catholic such as Claudel), spiritual realities express the ultimate truth of our conditions of life and so it is the spiritual conditions of an individual's or nation's life that can explain their material conditions, not the other way round.

But despite the fact that both can be classed as Catholic dramatists, the similarities between Claudel's work and Montherlant's are very superficial. *Le Soulier de satin* used the language of theatre in ways that were both creative and self-critical and left very little room for *la psychologie dialoguée* favoured by Montherlant. More important, the play ends on a note of triumphant self-affirmation in sharp contrast to *La Reine morte*. In this respect the play was very uncharacteristic for the forties and fifties and it was not until the late sixties that a similarly joyful mood of self-affirmation swept through the theatre again, though in the late sixties it was fuelled by political rather than by religious enthusiasms.

The link across the intervening decades can be found in the work of Jean-Louis Barrault. Neither religious nor political in his inclinations, Barrault's philosophy can be assimilated to the role of Deburau, the nineteenth century mime, written for him by Jacques Prévert in Carné's film *Les Enfants du paradis*. Deburau is an observer of people and a dreamer of dreams. Intensely down-to-earth in his social observation and mimetic portrayal of characters, he is also a visionary who lives for the dream of a perfect love. In the film, Deburau's love is not returned and the result is tragedy, but Barrault's two great loves, for Madeleine Renaud and for the theatre in general, have both been richly rewarded. Barrault is fond of confusing the two kinds of love, describing communication in the theatre in language normally reserved for the sexual act. As in human relationships, so in the theatre, one of his most generally appealing qualities is the combination of sincerity and spontaneity that seems to have characterised all of Barrault's work, from the earliest to the most recent. The performances of *Le Soulier de satin* in 1943 were certainly received by the Parisian theatre-goers as an extraordinary breath of fresh air in the stifling atmosphere of the Nazi Occupation.

It is tempting to put the dramatic freshness of these performances down to the work of Barrault alone. But although many of the staging ideas were entirely his, most of them had been hinted at in the first version of Claudel's play. Part of his original stage direction read:

The best effect would be just some dangling rope and a half-open backcloth beyond which the stage staff would be seen moving back and forth. Everything must look temporary, in progress, botched, incoherent, improvised with enthusiasm! With here and there a successful effect, if possible, for monotony must be avoided, even in disorder. Order is the pleasure of reason: but disorder is the delight of imagination (1965: 663).

This shows that the exuberance, vitality, colour, and the frankly theatrical nature of Barrault's production were all part of what Claudel had originally intended, although this does not diminish Barrault's achievement. It was his originality and imaginative flair that enabled him to pick on a play that had been waiting since 1929 to find a producer. In constrained, war-time circumstances at the Comédie Française, Barrault somehow managed to gather together the necessary materials for a lavish and colourful production. What he lacked was a 'total theatre' audience and interestingly enough this audience had also been defined by Claudel: 'I imagine my play being performed on Mardi Gras at about four in the afternoon in a great auditorium already hot from the previous show, which the audience invades and fills with noisy conversation' (ibid. 663). This gives a hint of the kind of audience that groups like the Théâtre du Soleil were to search out in the late sixties and seventies. They did so by playing in spaces not normally associated with theatre performance, such as a circus or a factory. But the Comédie Française audience comes to the theatre searching in a very deliberate way for cultural improvement and to partake of the cultural patrimony. Much of the impact that Claudel's play might have had was dulled by the exclusivity of its audience: Claudel became a cultural preserve, not a popular master of ceremonies.

The all-embracing, universal quality Claudel sought in the theatre also preoccupied another distinguished Catholic, Jacques Copeau, whose short treatise, *Le Théâtre populaire*, was published in 1941. It went through a number of reprintings and was influential among the men responsible for starting decentralised theatre companies in the decade following the war. In the course of his argument, Copeau returned repeatedly to the necessity of a spiritual revival, without which he claimed that no genuine theatrical revival was possible. This led him to the conclusion that the theatre of the future would be 'either Marxist or Christian. For it must be living, that is to say popular. To live, it must offer men reasons for belief, hope, fulfilment' (17). He tried to give a lead to Christian theatre by producing his own *Miracle du pain doré* in the courtyard of the Hospice de Beaune in 1943.

Copeau was most insistent that the necessary revival could never take place within the structure of the established Parisian theatres and their sophisticated, blasé audiences. There was, he claimed, a vital need for decentralisation and he placed his faith for the future in open-air festival theatre and in young itinerant companies who would perform for a public hitherto deprived of theatre. In both respects his vision was prophetic, though he died before he could see it come to fruition. He also suggested that large popular theatres should be constructed in the working class suburbs of Paris and this idea, to, was realised in the sixties and seventies. He bewailed the lack of a modern popular repertoire but argued, on the basis of his own experience, that new audiences were always eager for fresh performances of the classics and that actors who were prepared to work after the manner of the Commedia dell'arte would soon discover ways of presenting improvised work that fitted the preoccupations of a popular audience.

Although it was not until after the war that a policy of decentralisation began to be implemented by the government, Copeau's ideas were already being put into practice by small groups of actors during the Occupation. The work of such groups was an important testing ground for decentralised theatre after the Liberation. In the first two years of the Occupation, touring theatre received a boost from an organisation called Jeune France. This was set up by the Vichy authorities on the model of German youth movements as part of their nationalist propaganda campaign. Various groups of young actors received grants from Jeune France to tour the provinces. An example was La Roulotte, a group that had gathered around André Clavé. In 1941 they toured Molière's *George Dandin* and a farce by Jean Vilar, who had this to say: 'After my apprenticeship with Dullin, that was where I learnt most. What a marvellous training to act in the courtyard of an inn, or a ballroom, or a church hall, a hotel foyer or even sometimes on a stage!' (Serrière, 1959: 19).

La Roulotte continued to do similar work after the disbanding of Jeune France in 1942 until Clavé left to join a Resistance network. It regrouped immediately after the war and toured the Alsace-Lorraine region until Clavé was appointed director of the new Centre Dramatique de L'Est in 1947. Although there were a number of such touring groups, the only permanent theatre company outside Paris at the start of the war was the Rideau Gris of Marseilles. Louis Ducreux, the director, and some members of this company moved to Lyon in 1942, where they established themselves as La Comédie de Lyon. They had a considerable success with Roussin's comedy *Am-Stram-Gram* and moved the following season to Paris where they performed at the Athénée theatre for the rest of the Occupation.

More often men of the theatre moved south from Paris towards the unoccupied zone: Léon Chancerel to Toulouse, Henri Brochet to Auxerre,

Jean Serge to Aix-en-Provence (see Gontard, 1973: 89–127). Others retained their base in Paris but spent much of their time on tour. Jean Dasté is a case in point. He had established the Compagnie des Quatre Saisons together with André Barsacq and Maurice Jacquemont in 1936. In 1940 they had taken over the Atelier theatre from Dullin, who had accepted a post as director of the Théâtre Sarah Bernhardt (renamed Théâtre de la Cité by the anti-semites in power). Barsacq was to remain in charge of the Atelier theatre for the next thirty-two years. While acting part of the time in Paris, both Jacquemont and Dasté became progressively keener on working outside Paris; his longest tour was in 1943 with two farces by Molière and two improvised plays elaborated in company with the actors by a method that became known as *la création collective* thirty years later.

As the Occupation wore on, the example of such companies fired the imagination of others. A particularly interesting group was Les Aurochs – Jacques Lecoq, Gabriel Cousin and half a dozen friends – who spent the last months of the Occupation in hiding, living in caves in the woods near Nemours and developing their skills in dance, mime and sport (Jeffery, 1977: 124). This group allied itself with Travail et Culture, an organisation that had grown up during the Occupation, and that worked to encourage more creative methods in education. It arranged evening classes in song, dance, mime and movement, drawing on professionals to do the teaching (Barrault took a class; see Barrault, 1972: 155). After the Liberation it extended its activities to other parts of France, helping to form a group called Les Compagnons de la Saint-Jean and organising massive pageant-dramas in four different towns in the course of 1945: Chartres, Aix-les-Bains, Grenoble and Le Puy. At Grenoble they made contact with a group with similar aims, Peuple et Culture, which had been formed by a small team whose job had been to maintain links between Resistance groups in the south east of France. They believed that the struggle against Nazism had to be accompanied by a broad programme of workers' education: 'education seemed to us the most urgent priority if we were to continue what we had begun in the Resistance' (Cacérès, 1967: 151). Immediately after the liberation of Grenoble this group set up courses rather like Workers' Educational Association courses in Britain. A Maison de la Culture followed in their wake and an invitation to Dasté to work there with his theatre group (see pp. 88–9).

To encourage all these activities, the new government set up a national 'department of youth movements and popular culture' in 1945 and through this organisation similar courses were set up in many parts of France. Because of the involvement of progressive young theatre people such as Lecoq, Barrault and Dasté, these courses served to prepare the ground for the decentralisation of the theatre in the fifties and sixties. They also helped to articulate an ideology of popular culture as a militant political force, integral to the social life of the community and playing an active role in the preservation of freedom. This stance was adopted by many who classed themselves as part of the *théâtre populaire* movement and this too had a strong influence on the kind of plays that were to be produced in the new decentralised theatres (see chapter 5).

The German Occupation of France had proved to be of decisive significance for the development of the French theatre by encouraging a division into the two separate streams of the Parisian and the regional theatres. This division was to become progressively more important after the war, as the two streams diverged widely in the fifties and sixties. In the Parisian theatre, the pre-eminence of the literary or poetic theatre was to be successfully challenged, first by the philosophical melodramas of writers like Sartre and Camus, and then by the New Theatre or theatre of the Absurd. In the regional theatres, the main preoccupation was with the search for a repertoire relevant to a young audience coming to the theatre for the first time and bringing high expectations of the role of cultural life in liberated France.

3

The Parisian theatre I: philosophical melodrama

The commercial success of the Parisian theatres during the German Occupation helped to make the reputations of Anouilh and Sartre as well as those of Montherlant and Claudel. Post-war audiences remembered the circumstances in which they had discovered these authors, and continued to associate with their plays the spirit of defiant French cultural assertion that they had experienced in the theatres of the time. This was reinforced by the fact that both Anouilh and Sartre wrote plays about the defiance of authority. At first both seemed to be harking back to the styles of Giraudoux, Cocteau, and other pre-war dramatists who had revived the use of Greek legend; certainly both dramatists together with others, like Camus, were convinced of the need for a modern form of tragedy. Sartre gave a lecture in 1946 under the title 'forgers of myths', in which he linked the new philosophy of Existentialism with the tragic urge by saying that the plays of authors such as Anouilh, Camus and himself constituted a rejection of the realistic, psychological theatre of the inter-war period, and a search instead for a 'theatre of situations' that would present the contemporary realities of suffering and death with the force of ancient ritual. In these plays, he argued, the emphasis was all upon the moment of choice, stressing the Existentialist belief that men are not created, but create themselves through their choices: 'a small number of characters, not presented for their individual psychology, but thrown into a situation which forces them to make a choice' (1973: 65).

At first sight, Sartre's description fits Anouilh's *Antigone* (first performed in 1944) very well. The play contains a central speech, by the commentator-figure called the Chorus, in which the playwright draws a distinction between melodrama, in which everything might have turned out well, but for a series of ghastly accidents, and tragedy, in which the characters lucidly choose their own destruction. Anouilh cleverly generates sympathy for Antigone by means of his commentator, especially in the play's opening scene, where the Chorus presents each character to the audience. This technique has a powerful emotional effect in performance, as plays like Miller's *A view from the bridge* or Wilder's *Our town* also demonstrate. What it achieves is an effect at one and the same time of distance and emotional sympathy. This is particularly clear in Anouilh's prologue. His introduction of the characters one by one manages the problem of a difficult exposition of plot as well as enlisting our sympathies on the characters' behalf. The Chorus' attitude towards them all is detached, even amused, but indulgent and comprehending.

The technique is particularly successful in its appeal to the notion of role-playing: 'Antigone is the thin one, sitting by herself over there, saying nothing, staring straight ahead. She is thinking . . . She is thinking that she is going to die, that she is young, and that she would much rather live than die. But there is no help for it. Her name is Antigone, and she will have to play her role through to the end' (1946: 135). This is what is known in French as *la nécessité littéraire* – the obligation to play out a particular story simply because that is the way it has been written. For Anouilh, role-playing is synonymous with inevitability. His characters reduce the Existentialist concepts of choice and responsibility to an appeal to their role. Antigone tells Creon that her role is simply to die. But Antigone's choice is not the act of free commitment as understood by Sartre. Like Montherlant, Anouilh is here appealing to a traditional structure of experience, but emptying it of its traditional significance. The hero or heroine who discovers a role is a common feature of French tragedy. But the role is traditionally one of service to others or sacrifice to an ideal. In Anouilh's play the structure of self-sacrifice is enacted, but all the informing elements of love, patriotism, devotion, that might give meaning to this sacrifice are carefully rinsed out. Anouilh's model, the *Antigone* of Sophocles, is about Creon and the rest of the royal house of Thebes as much as it is about Antigone. Anouilh changes the focus, keeping our gaze firmly fixed on Antigone's moment of self-destruction up to the very end of the play. He achieves this by introducing a scene of pathos between Antigone and her guard, by making Haemon go through the same reactions as Antigone and by bringing the play to an end with Antigone's death.

The pattern of action in *Antigone* was repeated in many of Anouilh's subsequent plays, especially the long-running *L'Alouette* (1953) and *Becket* (1959). Anouilh's heroes and heroines need to experience the intense thrill of a moment of choice, but they do not want to pass beyond it. Antigone expresses this by saying she never wants to grow up. For the experience to be at its most intense, the choice must be a hopeless one, the diametrical opposite of commitment. Once a person commits herself to a particular course of action, her mental energies become concentrated upon this project which is outside herself and which she has to struggle to bring to fruition. The supremely self-centred desire of Anouilh's Antigone is to concentrate her energies entirely on herself. If her death was in the name of something outside herself, it would not be what it is, the act of total, if absurd, self-possession achieved by a kind of suicide.

At the time of the play's first production the structure was sufficient and the emptiness went unnoticed for the most part, since each member of the audience read into the play his own concrete difficulties – whether to resist, whether to collaborate. Anouilh's politics had always been rather ambiguous. His early plays had contained hints of social protest, but political choices were never presented in anything but the most personal terms. Creon's famous 'ship of state' speech is a good example of this: a splendid extended metaphor, but with limited applicability to a concrete political situation. *Antigone* was well reviewed in the collaborationist press and was at first assumed to be on the

Vichy side. But the progressive isolation of Antigone carries a strong emotional charge when the play is performed, leading an audience to sympathise with her much more strongly than might be evident from a reading of the play. Gradually the public came to identify more with Antigone and her uncompromising 'No!' Creon came to be seen, not as the sensible compromiser but as the opportunistic collaborator.

After the war was over, when political conflicts lost some of their very stark black and white qualities, critics began to re-appraise the play. In most cases they had harsh things to say about the extreme subjectivity of Antigone and the play's tendency to mawkish sentimentality. Hubert Gignoux, for example, dismissed the play as a 'drame psychologique en marge d'une tragédie' (1946: 115). But the central concentration of the drama on the supreme moment of choice provided a powerful link with the preoccupations of Existentialist theatre. The play's success of 1944–45 was repeated in 1947 at Barsacq's Atelier theatre. It fitted well with the mood of the times, both bitter and sentimental. Its rather racy language seemed particularly modern, with repeated use of deflation, undercutting the portentous by means of the trivial, shifting from pathos to humour, and back to pathos again. The unresolved mixture of classical and modern allusions in the text was mirrored in the costumes for Barsacq's production. These were mostly modern dress, the guards, for example, wearing black leather overcoats and black trilbies over evening dress.

In 1947 Barsacq also produced *L'Invitation au château*, a more light-hearted piece in the same mood as *Le Bal des voleurs* (1938) which had been a great success when he had revived it during the Occupation. This play uses the traditional techniques of the Commedia dell'arte plots, such as mistaken identities and comic routines, to construct a self-consciously theatrical entertainment. It draws extremely skilfully on an audience's emotions, alternating pathos with humour and never allowing the spectator to take what he is shown too seriously. The humour is either mild social satire at the expense of conventional types or traditional theatrical business around a stock situation – here the presence in the *château* of identical twins.

Anouilh declared that 'theatre is, first and foremost, characters' (Vandromme, 1965: 187), and this declaration shows that he resembles Montherlant in adopting resolutely old-fashioned dramaturgical principles. But the statement conceals the originality of Anouilh's theatre, which consists in it being neither a theatre of choice, like Sartre's, nor a theatre of character: in fact it is a theatre of mask. Anouilh cannot view social functions as anything other than falsely theatrical. In consequence, his plays are peopled by masks or types having no depth or consistency. Thérèse Malachy expressed this well with her comment that whereas in Sartre's plays the characters must choose and create their identity, in Anouilh's 'the hero is determined *a priori* by the role assigned to him, which he must play out to the bitter end' (1978: 17). Anouilh's characters do not develop in the course of a play: they simply act out their separate roles – as tyrant or dreamer, bishop or king, aristocrat or servant. A few characters (like Antigone) refuse to assume a mask and these have a kind of freedom, but it is an empty freedom because it can only be exercised to say 'no' to life. As soon as a social function or commitment is accepted, the character becomes a corrupt hypocrite and the world around him is translated into a false theatrical décor.

As a young man, Anouilh was strongly influenced by Pirandello, and his reduction of characters to masks or roles often draws on the techniques of the Italian dramatist. Pirandello's Henry IV, gradually losing his grip on his own personality as he discovers the wickedness of the world, and finally reduced to the confines of a mask, is the prototype for many of Anouilh's characters. But where Pirandello takes us through a complex exploration of the psychological and social implications of this process, Anouilh relies on light-hearted banter, setting many of his plays in the theatre, and exploiting well-tried paradoxes to do with illusion and reality. The same masks reappear in different combinations and circumstances, now predominantly comic, now cynical or bitter. The fact that they do not alter allows Anouilh to achieve some powerful dramatic effects, by playing off one mask against another. But it also limits his depiction of social realities, since the characters and their problems are exactly the same, whether the action takes place in the Middle Ages, in the French Revolution, or in the twentieth century.

This reduces the ability of Anouilh's plays to deal with the moral choices that they appear to pose. *Becket* appears to dramatise the choice between obedience to God or obedience to the secular power. In fact, just like Antigone, Becket admits that he has no love for God, only for his 'honour', and that his stand against the king is not in the name of morality, piety or obedience, but simply to defend this deliberately vague concept of 'God's honour'. Henry comments to Becket that 'Your whole morality comes down in the end to aesthetics' (1960: 182) and, like Becket, the dramatist seems content to accept the limitation implied.

Anouilh's plays have been one of the mainstays of the Parisian commercial theatre since the war. He has written over twenty, most of which have enjoyed long runs in prestigious productions by directors such as Barsacq or Barrault. In the main, they have tended to become more bitter and ironic as time has gone on, but their methods and themes have not varied greatly. This has been both their strength and their weakness. It has meant that audiences know what to expect when they buy tickets for one of his plays, but it has also made it impossible for Anouilh to develop with his times. He has remained what he was in the forties: a purveyor of stylish dramatic entertainment to sophisticated Parisian audiences.

Unlike Anouilh, Sartre rejected psychological theatre, defining his theatre as 'a theatre of situations'. In this way he expressed his belief that dramatic characters should not be distinguished by psychological traits such as greed, ambition, bravery, but by their actions within the context of particular situations. The importance of the 'situation' for Sartre was that it provided the necessary framework for action if the idea of freedom was to have any real meaning, since freedom in a vacuum is meaningless. This, broadly speaking is what he set out to show in his first major play, *Les Mouches*. The play tells the story of how Orestes returns to Argos to avenge the murder of his father by killing Clytemnestra, his mother and Aegisthus, her lover, who is usurping the throne. Orestes is seen to move from an experience of unreal freedom that is a mere absence of restraint, to a point where he accepts the restricting limitations of particular situation, and so achieves true freedom through his choice of action.

At the beginning of the play he arrives in Argos theoretically free, but it is an unrealised freedom. He has disguised himself as a tourist, Philebus, and is accompanied by his tutor, who sums up his condition, 'without family, fatherland, religion or trade; free for every commitment yet knowing one must never commit oneself' (1947a: 26). But Orestes is not satisfied. He feels lighter than a cobweb floating ten feet from the ground and longs to become involved in the situation, to become 'a man who belongs somewhere, a man among his fellow men'. He only experiences true freedom after accepting that he does belong in the situation, and committing himself to an action (the murder of Clytemnestra and Aegisthus) that defies the prevailing morality of submissiveness, and proclaims the freedom of choice that is possessed by all.

Sartre explained that in *Les Mouches* his intention had been to turn the Greek myth inside out and show it in a completely new light. Cocteau, Giraudoux and other dramatists of the pre-war years had used Greek myth to put across their ideas of tragedy and of fate, of the helplessness of man faced with cosmic forces. Sartre wished to show the opposite, while claiming that this also could be described as a tragedy, but a tragedy of liberty, since Orestes is 'a prey to liberty as Oedipus was a prey to fate' (cit. Contat & Rybalka, 1970: 88). He wanted to demonstrate that freedom was not an abstract concept, to be admired or ignored, it was an unavoidable necessity, part of our very condition of being. Towards the end of the first scene of Act II, Orestes discards his assumed identity, reveals his name and makes his decision to stay in Argos so as to avenge his father's death. In order to show the force of commitment, Sartre makes him undergo a physical transformation; Electra says:

How different you are: your eyes no longer sparkle, they are dull and sombre. Alas! You were so gentle Philebus (1947a: 71–2).

But the real change in Orestes is visible *after* his avenging murder since it is not only the act of commitment that counts but, more important, how one assumes the act and responds to others' interpretation of it. Faced with a terrifying chorus of Furies, Electra plunges into remorse and denounces the murder while Orestes takes the opposite path, reasserting his commitment by accepting the responsibility for his act, and out of this scene comes more powerfully than anywhere else in Sartre's work the triumphant assertion that 'I *am* my freedom'. Orestes leaves Argos proud and defiant with the Furies buzzing around him: the town has been purged of its guilt by the free commitment of one man. The ideas in this play must be seen, of course, in the context of the German Occupation. A similar notion was implied when Sartre wrote, soon after the Occupation, that Frenchmen had never been so free as during that period, since every thought of their own involved either the acceptance or the rejection of German propaganda. The presence of an oppressive alien force, by severely limiting their situation, gave the opportunity for freedom to be exercised more frequently.

However, it is equally clear that Sartre's thinking at this time was concerned with personal morality rather than public or political issues. Orestes' final action is open to the criticism that an effective political rebel does not assassinate and escape: he stays to help build a new society. But in 1943 (paradoxically perhaps) Sartre was not concerned with the practical politics of liberation. He was concerned with the problems of individual consciousness that he also explored in *L'Etre et le néant*, published the same year. In this treatise upon the nature of being, Sartre makes the distinction between *l'être-en-soi*, 'being-in-itself' and *l'être-pour-soi* 'being-for-self'. The latter term defined human beings, since they are distinguished from other forms of life by possessing reflective consciousness. That is to say that unlike 'being-in-itself', 'being-for-self' is conscious of the objects surrounding it; it can organise them into patterns and impose meanings; it can use them to create new objects with pre-established purposes. But most important, it is conscious of itself: inseparable from human consciousness is the consciousness of being conscious. *Les Mouches* is the drama of how one individual consciousness comes to terms with this state of affairs.

Now the world of objects, of which we are all conscious, includes other people; we perceive them as objects but we are also aware that they, too, share the reflective consciousness of 'being-for-self', that they, too, can shape external phenomena into patterns of meaning. Most important, we are aware that they perceive us as objects. Just as we have a tendency to class them objectively, so they will have a tendency to do the same to us. Other people are therefore a threat to our freedom, since they will tend to treat us instrumentally in pursuit of their own purposes. But they are also a necessary condition of our freedom, since, in the absence of God, we rely on their judgement to confirm the meaning of our acts. The dawning awareness of all this is accompanied by anguish and nausea, as Sartre's first novel, *La Nausée*, so graphically demonstrates. It is only by facing up to this anguish and accepting it that one can be true to one's freedom, and this is the meaning of Orestes' famous line, 'human life begins on the far side of despair' (1947a: 114). However, very few of Sartre's characters face up to the challenge as Orestes does. The majority refuse to face facts, taking refuge in escapism or false consciousness, for which Sartre employs the term *mauvaise foi*, bad faith.

Bad faith may be manifested in a person's insistence that his religion or his political party demands a certain behaviour from him; he may argue that he has a natural, inherited or racial superiority, which justifies him in exploiting others, he may believe that he is justified in such behaviour by social class or wealth. Another form of bad faith is to insist that one will always behave according to a certain pattern because one is 'made that way' and cannot change. 'Being-for-self' envies the unambiguous reality of 'being-in-itself' and is thus always tempted to try to become thing-like. This desire is often located by Sartre in women who are happy to be nothing but a sex object for men, and so is associated with an emphasis on the body's physical reality and power to

39

fascinate. Estelle, in *Huis clos*, has to be able to see herself in a strategically placed mirror if she is to feel quite at ease. At a more complex level this desire can be seen in the man who always plays a part or conforms to an established role – the professor who is always 'dignified', the actor who never stops acting. Within this philosophical framework the existence of other people emerges as a threat to our freedom. Our acts inevitably escape us: they put us at the mercy of others since we are only defined by our acts and our acts are defined by other people's reactions to them. It is this state of affairs that finds expression through the drama of *Huis clos*.

The play presents three people who have lived their whole lives in bad faith. Garcin has lived like a tough guy, a hero. He has played on his South American 'machismo' to impress his men friends and to seduce his women. He has argued that he can be allowed a few failings because of his fundamental courage in opposing the government. But as soon as he is placed in a tight situation he runs away. Estelle is a selfish sybarite content to be treated as a sex object. She pretends that all she wants is to be loved, and to make people happy, but after giving birth to a child by her lover she murders it rather than risk compromising her comfortable life with her rich old husband. This drives her lover to despair and suicide. Ines has been guilty of a more devious form of bad faith. Where Estelle relied on physical attraction, Ines fascinated others by sheer force of intelligence and wit. But she cannot engage in a free and open relationship, any more than Estelle, because she derives her pleasure from the suffering of others. She succeeds in separating her friend Florence from her husband and then gloats while both partners drive themselves to despair, also ending in suicide.

The audience meets these three people in hell, but it is a hell that is only progressively revealed. At first it has all the appearances of a bourgeois boulevard comedy of adultery. Sartre extracts considerable laughter from the idea that hell might consist of a Second Empire salon, and from the inability of the characters to abandon the fossilised habits of a life-time. Each expects to be able to escape from the situation exactly as they have all evaded similar problems before. Ines tries to fascinate Estelle; Estelle tries to fascinate Garcin; Garcin tries to persuade the other two that he is no fool and no coward. But each attempt is frustrated because their acts are there, in the minds of the other two characters, obstinately failing to fit the interpretation that they would like them to have. At the end of the play Garcin insists, 'I did not just dream of heroism. I chose it. You are what you want to be', to which Ines replies, 'Prove it. Prove that it wasn't a dream. Only acts can determine what the motives were ... you are no more and no less than your life' (1947a: 179). This is the meaning of the famous line that follows: 'hell is other people' (ibid. 182): because we rely on others to confirm the meaning of our acts, we are always in their power.

This play has often been interpreted in an excessively pessimistic manner. It really belongs to the more optimistic domain of *Les Mouches*. Admittedly, the characters cannot change because they are already dead. But the audience should receive a powerful reminder, almost a sermon, on the need to act freely before it is too late. In his preface to a recorded performance of this play, Sartre said:

It is a sort of living death to be surrounded by the ceaseless concern for judgements and actions that one does not even desire to change. In fact, since we are alive, I wanted to demonstrate, through the absurd, the importance for us of liberty, i.e. the importance of changing our acts by other acts. Whatever the circle of hell in which we live, I think we are free to break out of it. And if people do not break out, they stay there of their own free will. In this way they choose to live in hell (cit. Contat & Rybalka, 1970: 101).

Huis clos was published in Sartre's *Théâtre I* in 1947, with a prefatory note. Some twenty years later, Sartre was able to say: 'The other day, I re-read a prefatory note to a collection of my plays: *Les Mouches, Huis clos* and others – and was truly scandalised. I had written: "whatever the circumstances and wherever the situation, a man is always free to choose to be a traitor or not". When I read this, I said to myself: it's incredible, I actually believed that' (1974: 33–4). In the intervening period Sartre had shifted from considering human consciousness as primarily a moral and individual problem towards the view that it is more politically and historically determined. The process was a gradual one for Sartre and was accompanied by a slow disillusionment with the role of the writer in society that reached its conclusion in 1963 with *Les Mots*, a book qualified by its author as 'a farewell to literature'. In this autobiography Sartre explained that he had finally understood that he was wrong to think, like the hero of his first novel, that his salvation could be achieved by writing. The writer, he now realised, was no better and no worse than any other person and each person's actions must simply be judged on their own merits. 'Every intellectual dreams of being a man of action' says Hoederer in *Les Mains sales* (1948: 110). In *Les Mains sales* (1948) and *Le Diable et le bon Dieu* (1951) Sartre dramatised the struggles of the intellectual to break away from a concern with personal morality and to achieve instead an effective impact upon the world of social and political reality. In the first play a young intellectual, Hugo, fails to be an effective revolutionary because of his restless worries about his own worth and reality. In the second, Goetz, by abandoning such concerns, is able to break out of the vicious circle and act. Hugo and Goetz represent respectively failure and success in the quest for authentic action.

Goetz is a bastard with some of the resulting freedom that Gide saw in any child with no fixed place in society. Part-peasant, part-noble he is rejected by both camps and, when the audience first meets him, he is leading the life of an independent war-lord with a private army and his main purpose is to kill, pillage and rape. But despite the destruction he wreaks on all around him, Goetz is really engaged in a private struggle with God. In a manner clearly modelled on the experience of Jean Genet (see Sartre, 1952), Goetz has decided that he will invert the received scale of values, turning what is normally thought of as evil into his good. He is tempted to abandon this path by the taunt that anyone can hate and destroy, but no one can love perfectly. He accepts the challenge and establishes a peaceful 'city of the sun', but this leads to disaster, since neither the peasants nor the barons of the surrounding area can tolerate its existence and they destroy it. The result of the failure on Goetz is to persuade him that he was wrong in both the attempt to be thoroughly evil and the attempt to be thoroughly good. The young Genet, accused of being a thief, had adopted a similar solution, deciding that if he was called a thief he would set himself 'to be a thief'. But, Sartre argued, this solution cuts him off from real action:

he wants to act in order to be, to steal so as to become a thief, to do evil in order to become wicked. At one and the same time, the act and the freedom of the will disappear. An act that is accomplished in order to achieve *being* is not an act, it is a gesture (1952: 75).

Goetz discovers that the only way out of this dilemma is to stop trying to 'be' something and to turn his attention instead to 'doing'. In the last scene Goetz is again offered the command of the dispirited peasant army by the peasant leader who had offered him this position before. Goetz at first refuses, insisting that he wants to be in the ranks, a man among men, but in the end relents. One of the officers refuses to obey him, so he kills him, saying 'the reign of man has begun . . . I will discipline them since I have no other way of obeying, I will remain alone with the empty sky above my head since I have no other way of being together with them. There is this war to be waged and I shall wage it' (1951: 282). In Sartre's words he 'accepts the limited, relative morality that is appropriate for human destiny: he has replaced the absolute with history' (cit. Contat & Rybalka, 1970: 237). Like Orestes he makes a free choice of action, but unlike Orestes he does so within a defined political context, where he will remain.

Goetz's action brings the play to an optimistic conclusion but does not, in fact, show Goetz successfully coping with his real historical situation; the audience is left to imagine that. In *Les Séquestrés d'Altona* the audience does see history at work, but grounds for optimism have vanished. In this play Sartre attempts to present history from a Marxist perspective as a dialectical process. Both *Les Mains sales* and *Le Diable et le bon Dieu* had moved some way towards this, but as Dorothy McCall (1969: 42) rightly points out, the mode of these plays is heroic rather than dialectical. Goetz acts upon history but history hardly acts upon him. At the end of the play there seems very little reason why he should be asked to assume command of the peasant army other than the need of the dramatist to bring his hero back to the centre of the stage for his concluding speech.

In *Les Séquestrés d'Altona* however, history has pride of place. The rich middle class home in which the play is set is explained entirely by its Lutheran past and by the industrial success of its aging owner and paterfamilias, Herr von Gerlach. Gerlach has preserved his ship-building business through the Nazi period, the post-war purges and the new economic miracle. But he has ignored the dialectical process of historical change and he is alienated by his own success. The firm has grown so enormous that it has little use for the old fashioned 'captain of industry' and even less for his son who had been expected by his father to take over the firm.

Loser wins (*qui perd gagne*) is a dominant theme in the play. It can only be expressed through the historical dimension. Germany's phenomenal economic success in the late 1950s was a direct result of its losing the war and the destruction of its industry fifteen years earlier. Gerlach's industrial success and personal failure can thus be shown only in and through an evocation of the historical process. This process is made tangible for us in the shape of Gerlach's son Frantz, who lives in voluntary isolation in an upper room in the house. Frantz's sequestration is a consequence of his inability to come to terms in the present with actions he committed in the past. When fighting on the Russian front, he tortured some captured partisans. He alternately tries to persuade himself and others (a) that he did not torture them and (b) that he did so, but it was justified, since defeat of Germany would lead to genocide, so any means was permissible to avoid defeat. But the present prosperity of Germany gives him the lie, since it is founded on that very defeat he feared.

The problem of history that Sartre here evokes is the one he struggles with in *Critique de la raison dialectique*. The problem is that capital creates scarcity, oppressing men and women in society, exploiting the many for the profit of the few. But capital is only a socially created phenomenon, not a natural force, and since it manifestly works against the interests of the majority there is a problem in understanding how it is able to maintain itself. Sartre argues that it only does so because the pattern of relationships imposed by capital are relationships of serialisation: each one is obliged to use everyone else in order to satisfy his own needs, while himself being used. The possibility of free collective action disappears. In such a world, violence is endemic:

for as long as the rule of scarcity continues there will be in each and every one of us an inert structure of inhumanity . . . Nothing, neither wild beasts nor microbes, can be more terrible for man than the intelligent, carnivorous, cruel species, which can understand and outwit human intelligence and whose end would lead to the destruction of man himself (1960b: 206–8).

The final words of Frantz's posthumous tape-recorded speech echo very faithfully the ideas expounded in the *Critique*:

The century would have been good if man had not been preyed upon by his cruel enemy from time immemorial, the carnivorous species which had sworn his destruction, the malignant, hairless beast, Man himself – one and one make one, that is our mystery (1960a: 222. See Palmer, 1970).

Frantz and his father are both the victims of history. Just as the father has been alienated by the very firm he created, so Frantz has found the meaning of his acts is converted, by the subsequent course of history, from an heroic stand into a useless crime. But both are consenting victims, both accept the responsibility for what has happened. They are unable to change events but they are equally unable to deny their actions. And so they live in a state summarised by Sartre's phrase concerning *Huis clos*: 'they choose to live in hell' (above, p. 41).

In fact it is difficult to see exactly how Frantz, for example, could break out of his circle of hell. The confines of his situation no longer seem to work in favour of his freedom, as they did for characters in earlier plays. Here we are shown that the historical situation may be such as to deny any possibility of choice, unless it be a choice of one's manner of destruction. Ultimately, Frantz's position can only be understood by reference to the serial nature of relationships under capitalism: in Sartre's altered view, this can set up structures that effectively rob people of their freedom. We see this worked out in relation to three key points in Frantz's life. The first is when he attempts to rescue a Jew who has escaped from a concentration camp. His father uses his contacts with Goebbels to ensure that Frantz avoids the consequences of his action, which is thus robbed of its meaning. He is obliged, against his will, to join up and in the course of the fighting on the Russian front he tortures the partisans. Having given in to a sadistic impulse, he cannot live with the memory but tries to deny it in a variety of ways. The third point where Frantz's freedom is seen to escape him occurs soon after the war, when he is involved in a fight with an American soldier. In order to shield his son, the father again uses his contacts and Frantz once more evades the consequences of his action by shutting himself into his isolated room. The father procures a false death certificate from South America.

Each of these events makes it more impossible for Frantz to make an authentic, free authentic act. He is trapped and the windowless room with its Nazi paraphernalia becomes an image of his mental and spiritual condition. Like the characters of Sartre's early short story *La Chambre*, Frantz takes refuge in madness. He chooses to address a series of speeches to an imaginary tribunal of crabs on the ceiling of his room, thus hoping to exculpate himself by turning witness for the prosecution and condemning the whole century. Within the premises and development of the play, then, Frantz would seem to have no alternative to the path of self-destruction. He accepts the father's offer of a double suicide, saying, 'You will have been my cause and my destiny to the very end', to which the father replies, 'I made you; I shall unmake you. My death will envelop yours so that, in the end, I shall be the only one to die' (1960a: 218). Frantz's whole life has been falsified and his freedom robbed by his father's choice to devote everything at his disposal, including his own children, to the creation of a vast capitalist empire.

The picture of human relationships that emerges from Sartre's plays is one of a perpetual struggle for control; not physical control, but mental and spiritual control as each character tries to entrap the others' freedom. This is illogical, because only a judgement freely made can satisfy his or her desire for a confirmation that they are what they wish to be. Nevertheless, this struggle to 'be' for others is pursued unrelentingly by all but the very exceptional characters such as Goetz (at the very end) or Hoederer. This is why there are no happy couples in Sartre's work: relationships between the sexes are just as fraught with the struggle for mutual domination as any other relationship. Ultimately, this is a weakness in Sartre's work as a whole. It prevents him from giving any account of a satisfying love relationship between man and woman, and this diminishes him. But it gives to his analysis of false relationships a particular force and fascination, arising from an acute insight into how people present themselves to others in everyday life, that is properly dramatic.

A favourite image for expressing this is that of the actor. It appears in Sartre's philosophical works (see 1943: 98–9) and it is no surprise to find that he adapted Dumas' play about the nineteenth century actor, Kean, that his adaptation was both witty, touching and frankly theatrical, and that he undertook the adaptation as a mark of respect for the Romantic theatre. Kean is a 'monstre sacré' who behaves like a spoilt Hollywood film star. Whenever he is faced with a serious choice, he slips into play-acting. Instead of facing facts, he constantly evades them as a sort of exercise in improvisation: he adopts an attitude, strikes a pose and proceeds to act out that role as best he can. When this bores him he switches to another role. The one thing he cannot do is to drop the mask altogether and resume his own character, for he does not have one (unlike Dumas' Kean). This situation produces a series of sparklingly inventive confrontations between Kean and his various lovers, admirers or adversaries.

Sartre's image of play-acting is thus a peculiarly nineteenth century one: an important part of it is the idea that the actor must fascinate, mesmerise or dominate his audience. His actor does not show or demonstrate as a Brechtian actor might, instead he bewitches the spectator, or tries to. It is a view of the actor that owes much to melodrama and the situations of Sartre's plays are also melodramatic, dealing with murder, torture, incest, death, in fact the whole range of boundary situations that are employed to call traditional morality into question. These situations are at the opposite end of the spectrum to what are often thought of as the distinctive feature of modern dramas such as Beckett's *Waiting for Godot*, where *nothing* happens. Sartre clearly rejected this sort of minimalist approach to drama, drawing enthusiastically on the technical resources of the boulevard theatres in which his plays were performed to provide realist settings, especially within the naturalist convention of the enclosed room: both *Huis clos* and *Les Séquestrés* rely on the stage designer providing a room or rooms with great claustrophobic effect. Sartre is also capable of evoking public scenes of great power such as the day of the dead ceremony in *Les Mouches*, or a complete theatre within the theatre for the fourth act of *Kean*. But these settings, however spectacular, are always used in the manner of the nineteenth century theatre: they remain as *background*. There is never a sense that the settings or objects are there to play an active role in the drama, as, for example, Mother Courage's cart does in Brecht's play (see fig. 2).

In his theatre criticism (1973) Sartre showed a very clear understanding of the two predominant influences on the French stage in the fifties: the New Theatre of Beckett and others, and the Epic theatre of Brecht. But in his own playwriting he retained the assumptions of the naturalist playwrights about consistency of character and unilinear plot, and failed to create new dramatic forms of expression. It could be argued that *Waiting for Godot* dramatises Existentialist anguish better than *Huis clos* and that *Mother Courage* dramatises the contradictions of capitalism better than *Les Séquestrés d'Altona*.

Perhaps the reason for this failure at the structural level was that Sartre always had his eyes firmly fixed on the Ancient Greek theatre. The texture of much of the dialogue and action of his plays is racy, exciting, even melodramatic, recalling nineteenth century models, but when he himself described his own plays, he used terms such as ritual and distance, myth and collective celebration that fit the model of tragedy better.

Sartre's first experience of playwriting was the composition of 1940 of a small Christmas play, *Bariona ou le fils du tonnerre*. With this he had endeavoured to create a myth of freedom for fellow prisoners of war in a concentration camp. His last was a version of Euripides' *Trojan women* written in 1964 for the Théâtre National Populaire. In between these two attempts at modern myth, he wrote nine original plays in each of which a limited number of people confront one another in a situation that faces them with intolerable choices. They engage in rational debate before making up their minds either to seize an opportunity for action or to submit to whatever fate has reserved for them. The pattern conforms perfectly to that of a classical tragedy. As a dramatist, Sartre is ultimately on the side of the ancients rather than the moderns.

This perhaps explains why *Les Séquestrés d'Altona* is tragic in the classical

2 *Les Séquestrés d'Altona* (Sartre): a traditional naturalist set designed by Yvon Henry for François Darbon's production at the Théâtre de la Renaissance, 1959.

sense. Like the Greeks, like Racine, it presents characters faced with impossible choices. They face these choices lucidly, accept responsibility for what they are, and yet seemed doomed to destruction by actions that others took before them and over which they have no control. Within the limitations of the Sartrean dramatic vision, however, *Les Séquestrés d'Altona* is an impressive achievement. In this play Sartre came closest to integrating the various signifying elements of stage language. The house is a forceful presence, stifling the family with its monumental claustrophobia; the changes in set, from drawing-room to Frantz's room and back, follow a strictly alternating pattern that establishes the play's central conflict between father and son. Only in the final act does Frantz allow his space to be merged and lost in that of the father as he loses himself in his father's suicide. Moreover, Sartre uses flashback and madness to overlay the material reality of house, rooms, furniture etc. with the oneiric reality of the character's perceptions and anxieties. These challenge the apparently straightforward certainties of life in the commercially successful modern Germany with the result that the play presents a disturbing and complex image of life in an advanced capitalist society.

The limitations of Sartre's plays were the limitations of the commercial Parisian theatres in which they were performed. There were bound to be contradictions involved in writing plays about the problems of revolutionary politics for audiences of the well-heeled Parisian bourgeoisie. The fact that almost all his plays enjoyed long runs in these theatres is doubtless due to his skill in manipulating the familiar devices of plot and character. Sartre's career as a playwright covered the period of the forties and fifties, when the privately owned commercial theatres of Paris were more successful in appealing to a broad range of interests than they were in the subsequent decades. This was largely because of the lack of other outlets for new writing. Both the Théâtre National Populaire and the new Centres Dramatiques at first relied chiefly on revivals of the classics and there is no tradition of amateur theatre in France. Only the owners of Parisian theatres were able or prepared to take risks with a new play. The theatre's reward, if an author was successful, was often to have first refusal of the right to perform subsequent plays. Sartre became friendly with Simone Berriau, the owner of the Théâtre Antoine and offered his plays to her. In the sixties, as the state involved itself more heavily in the building and subsidising of theatres, it became more common for new or avant-garde work to be performed in the subsidised theatres. A successful revival of *Le Diable et le bon Dieu* was staged by Georges Wilson at the Théâtre National Populaire in 1968. Audiences looking for plays of this kind went less often to the commercial theatre in Paris and the owners fell back more heavily on well-known boulevard names such as Marcel Achard or André Roussin, and, later, on anglo-saxon imports such as *Hair* and *Jesus Christ superstar*.

Camus, like Sartre, was a novelist and philosopher as much as a playwright. He first attracted a wide public with *L'Etranger*, published in 1942, whose central character experiences the absurdity of life but also finds a sufficiency in the moment-by-moment sensations of existence. Like Sartre, Camus' philosophy was that men should not try to avoid or deny their sense of the

Absurd, but should accept it lucidly, creating their own values in the absence both of God and of pre-ordained purpose. During the late forties and fifties Camus and Sartre fell out over the question of revolutionary politics, Sartre moving sharply to the Left, while Camus maintained a less extreme position. But during and just after the Occupation both were preoccupied with the individual's response to his discovery of the Absurd (i.e. the absence of created meaning to be found in the universe).

Caligula, in its final version, first performed in 1945, opens just after the death of Caligula's sister. This event has opened his eyes to the futility of a life in which 'men die and are not happy' (1962: 16). Being convinced of the arbitrary nature of private experience and the universe at large, he seeks to achieve freedom by creating in his own behaviour an image of the arbitrary and the Absurd. As emperor, he has the power necessary to follow this programme with absolute logic. He outrages every convention imaginable: he offends against the laws of morality, of politeness, of justice and of piety. Above all, he attacks people's self-esteem, pride and sense of importance. He demolishes all the little hierarchies that people build up to structure their lives and to embody their sense that some things are more valuable than others. He tells his subjects that he has replaced the plague and he takes on a similar function of levelling everyone to the same state of helplessness in the face of universal disaster. He claims that by means of his programme of death, rape and pillage he can demonstrate to his subjects the meaning of freedom.

Opposed to this Dionysiac figure is the Apollonian character, Chéréa, who is calm where Caligula is frenzied, and cautious where Caligula is extreme. Chéréa accepts a hierarchy of relative values. He believes that some things are better than others, that distinctions can be established, and that the fact of death need not be seen as invalidating all human endeavour. He is not, however, entirely out of sympathy with Caligula: on the contrary, he understands him only too well since he, too, has experienced the discovery of the Absurd. But he has rejected it in favour of a more balanced revolt and an insistence on an ethic of human solidarity. Chéréa mobilises armed resistance to Caligula and towards the end of the play, as Caligula sees the approach of death, he too comes to the conclusion that his freedom was a false freedom, because nobody can make an effective response to the Absurd on his own.

The idea of group revolt as a response to the Absurd is expressed with greater complexity and emotional force in *La Peste* (1947), where the medical workers who group together as a team succeed in offering some resistance to the plague, whereas those characters who search for individual salvation fail. The scope of the novel allows Camus to contrast a great many different characters and their responses to the arbitrary cruelty of the plague. In *Caligula*, his aim was different, investigating chiefly the state of mind of the emperor embodying the Absurd. He is a man who is lucid enough to accept that life has no intrinsic purpose, but whose conclusion goes too far by accepting an attitude of despair and contempt. The play develops, with considerable psychological insight, the portrait of a man who might have become a Nazi.

When *Caligula* was first performed in 1945, Camus was known both as a novelist and as the clandestine author of the *Lettres à un ami allemand*. In these letters he had developed a line of argument similar to Chéréa's, understanding but rejecting the temptation to respond to the Absurd with 'the animal values of violence and cunning' (see Freeman, 1971: 47). Audiences flocked to see the play in the same spirit as they filled the theatres for *Huis clos* and for *Antigone*: it was a chance to celebrate the revival of independent French culture, unsubdued by the years of Occupation. The performances were also successful because of the charismatic presence of Gérard Philipe in the title role and because of its exciting, not to say sensational action. Many of Caligula's crimes are enacted on stage, not kept to the wings, as classical decorum would have demanded. The result is that the plot's progression follows the pattern of melodrama: the tyrant behaves with ever greater cruelty until the point where his subjects rise in revolt against him. This rather traditional dramatic structure is surprising in sò far as Camus had considerable experience of work in the theatre and had already demonstrated, with *Révolte dans les Asturies* (1936), that he was in touch with modern experiments in dramaturgical form. His other play of the early forties, *Le Malentendu* (1944), also follows the pattern of traditional melodrama, describing the homecoming of a son after many years absence to the hotel run by his mother and sister. He has returned with enough money to take them away with him to a new life. But they, in the meantime, are so desperate to escape that they have taken to murdering rich travellers to collect the necessary money. On the evening of his arrival, the son conceals his identity in order to surprise them the next morning, but they murder him during the night. This gloomy little melodrama is not dramatised with any of the excitement of *Caligula* and it was a failure when produced in 1944.

After the success of *Caligula*, Camus wrote *L'Etat de siège* for Barrault's company. It opened in 1948 to general critical disapproval. The play is set in Cadiz at an unspecified time and in an atmosphere redolent of the Spanish *Autos sacramentales*. In Camus' own words it is an attempt to create a modern myth, includes allegorical characters such as Plague and Death, and lacks the excitement of *Caligula*, being extremely verbose. It traces the establishing of a dictatorship by Plague followed by its overthrow, which only becomes possible when enough citizens are prepared to band together. Camus' only other original play, *Les Justes*, was more successful. It opened at the Théâtre Hébertot in 1949 and ran for more than a year. In this, he developed further the theory that revolt is the only possible response to the Absurd. The play depicts a group of terrorists in the Russia of 1905, who were to be held up as an example in *L'Homme révolté*, a historical-philosophical work published in 1951. These people were prepared to use assassination in the fight against Tsarist injustice but believed that they must pay for every political killing by the sacrifice of one of their own members' lives. The central debate in the play is the one about means and ends. Stepan, an ex-convict, has his eyes fixed only on the goal of overthrowing an unjust ruling class. He is opposed by Kaliayev who shares his goal but claims that if the tyranny is not to be replaced by another, limits must be placed on the means employed. The crisis occurs when Kaliayev fails to

49

throw a bomb into the archduke's carriage because this would entail killing the archduke's children as well. He makes a second, successful attempt some days later, killing only the archduke, and in the last act welcomes his own execution. The play is extremely static, consisting almost exclusively of discussions before and after the assassination attempts (which take place off stage).

The notion of *limits* was integral to a theory of tragedy towards which Camus was working in the early fifties. In a lecture delivered in Athens in 1955, Camus stated that he and his contemporaries lived in a 'tragic climate': 'Today, man is proclaiming his revolt while knowing that this revolt has limits, is demanding liberty while undergoing necessity, and this contradictory man . . . is the essentially tragic man' (1970: 200). But for a character to be a tragic hero, he must, as Camus says, be torn apart by his contradictions. Kaliayev, on the contrary, resolves his contradictions and succeeds in carrying out his limited protest. He can only be seen, therefore, as an exemplary rebel and not as a tragic hero. This play, like *L'Etat de siège* was too theoretical: the ideas never take on dramatic life as they did, however sensationally, in *Caligula*.

Camus continued to work in the theatre, writing six translations or adaptations, all of which he helped to stage. It remains a mystery why his own plays were so comparatively unoriginal. In 1937 he had written in the manifesto for his first theatre group, 'The Théâtre de l'Equipe will demand from the plays it performs truth and simplicity, violence in its feelings and cruelty in its action. Thus it will return to epochs when the love of life was mingled with the despair of life' (cit. Freeman 1971: 54). This suggests a programme based on the Artaudian Theatre of Cruelty, and *Caligula* or *L'Etat de siège* show that Camus had read Artaud and had been influenced by him. But Camus' work for the theatre remained very literary; he never succeeded in finding a *dramatic* style of his own.

His success as a novelist and short story writer was that of a stylist. As Sartre wrote in his review of *L'Etranger* (1947b: 99–121), the book is held together not by the reader's belief in Meursault's character – some of his actions are very inconsistent – but by the force of the narrative style which presents, as it were, the *shape* of what it is to live moment-by-moment in an eternal present. The very grammar and syntax, with its short sentences and lack of co-ordinating conjunctions, suggests an approach to life that simply experiences rather than trying to make sense of it. Barthes (1953) described this as 'le degré zéro de l'écriture' (literally: writing at zero degree) and we shall see in the next chapter that the equivalent zero degree dramatic style was not discovered until the early fifties in the work of Beckett, Ionesco and Adamov.

In the plays of Anouilh, Sartre and Camus common themes can be found: loneliness, guilt, political responsibility, the Absurd and revolt against it. These themes are also found in the plays of Armand Salacrou, who was already very well established as a dramatist by the end of the thirties, but who continued to write during the forties, fifties and sixties. He had made his name with historical plays and naturalist dramas of minute social observation, in which middle class *mores* were represented as elaborate evasions of the truth that life is meaningless. His plays are less theatrical than Anouilh's and his style more naturalistic, but he shared Anouilh's craftsmanship and skill in manipulating the established conventions of plot and character. In the immediate post-war period, Salacrou was widely admired in theatre circles as a man who had made a fortune running an advertising business before the war and then had sold up to devote himself full time to writing. He was a close friend of both Dullin and Barrault and in 1947 was offered the directorship of the Comédie Française (though he turned it down). His play about the advertising business, *Poof*, written before the war but not staged until 1950, presents some similarities with Vinaver's *Par-dessus bord* (see chapter 10), though it is neither so inventive nor so profound as Vinaver's play. Some of his plays explore themes later developed by Sartre, and his *L'Inconnue d'Arras* (1935) has been seen as a source for *Huis clos*. The play starts as the central character shoots himself and ends with his death: the action all takes place in the split seconds of consciousness between these two events. The man relives the events leading up to his death only to discover that he can change nothing. His servant Nicolas points out that 'les jeux sont faits pour l'éternité' (1943:192), a phrase that Sartre was later to make famous as the title of a film scenario. Despite certain similarities of theme and treatment with Sartre's *Huis clos* and *Les Jeux sont faits*, the play is largely a discussion piece with little of the suspense generated by Sartre's characters' efforts to dominate one another.

Salacrou suffered from the same contradictions as Sartre. His plays were put on in the commercial Parisian theatres, but, he claims in an afternote to *Les Nuits de la colère*, no good theatre is possible without a working class element in the audience: 'we do not have a true theatre public but just a collection of people who all happen to have 500 francs to spend on an evening out' (1947: 355). In a modest way he was a precursor of the social drama that was to flourish in the decentralised theatres of the sixties. Two plays from the post-war period show him struggling with how to present political problems on stage. The first is *Les Nuits de la colère*, written during the Occupation and staged in 1946 by Barrault. It was chosen by Giorgio Strehler in the following year as his opening production for the Piccolo Teatro, Milan. The play has a violent opening in which Resistance fighters and collaborators shoot one another, but then shifts out of real time as they get up again to talk about their lives and the choices that have led them to their deaths. A contrast is established between the individualists who sacrifice everything to the attainment of personal satisfaction, and the Resistance members who find a different kind of satisfaction in group solidarity. The former are led into collaboration, corruption and die lonely deaths. The latter are able to die happy because they know that the values they defend will ultimately triumph. Much of the argument and character contrast in this play recalls Sartre's *Morts sans sépulture*, or his later play *Les Mains sales*. Salacrou's play presents a similar combination of melodramatic action and philosophical discussion. It also suggests that the person who becomes too preoccupied with his own existentialist self-doubts becomes incapable of group action or solidarity, as Hoederer tells Hugo in *Les Mains sales*.

Salacrou's second play in this vein was *Boulevard Durand* (1961). It is a documentary drama about Jules Durand, a union leader of Le Havre sentenced to death in 1910 for a murder he did not commit. He was exonerated eight years later, but by then had lost his reason, and died in a mental institution in 1926. At the time of his accusation Durand had been organising a strike and the court action appears to have been a straightforward (and successful) attempt to intimidate the workforce. In Salacrou's play, the blame for the wrongful conviction of Durand is placed squarely on the shoulders of the governing bourgeoisie, who realise that they have the wrong man, but put a higher priority on industrial peace than on justice. The character of Durand is calculated to attract the audience's sympathy. He suffers, like many of Salacrou's heroes, from the anguish of feeling his existence is useless and there is no purpose in life. But through his work for the union he discovers the positive values of comradeship and solidarity. He is too honest to appreciate the machinations of his enemies and cannot believe that the court will find him guilty. He is a poor tactician, calling a strike at the wrong moment, when it is bound to fail.

The pattern of this play follows very closely the pattern of nineteenth century melodrama. Durand is poor but honest, the bosses are rich but corrupt. There are various intermediary characters who betray their own class by serving the boss's interests. Durand also has a sweetheart in the traditional manner. Salacrou employs semi-poetic imagery to reinforce the values attached to his hero. For example, he keeps racing pigeons because 'they correspond to the very principle of life. To achieve their goal, these little creatures are not afraid to fly till they drop' (1966: 166). All these qualities go to make *Boulevard Durand* a powerful play and its performance aroused high emotions, when produced by André Reybaz's Centre Dramatique du Nord. But it is also a rather old-fashioned one, suiting more the period in which it is set than the sixties when it was performed. It was left to the new authors of the decentralised theatres, such as Planchon or Gatti, to develop a dramatic form adequate to deal with the real contradictions of political struggle.

The history of theatre is, as Raymond Williams has argued (1968), the history of new sensibilities struggling to be born, new understandings of the world, new imitations of it and ways of acting upon it straining for expression. The plays discussed in this chapter were all, in their way, struggling with new images of despair, revolt, and the problem of death. But the old forms of naturalistic or melodramatic action were inadequate for the task. When the new theatre of Adamov, Ionesco and Beckett was revealed to the French public in the early fifties, it seemed to solve the problems of form and dramaturgy that had previously been so intractable.

4

The Parisian theatre II: the New Theatre

In the immediate post-war years anguish became fashionable in the left-bank literary circles of Paris. *La Nausée* (published in 1938) and *L'Etranger* (1942) both enjoyed a tremendous vogue, tempting young intellectuals to identify with Roquentin or with Meursault, which they did, displaying a similar combination of despair and excitement to that aroused by the young Werther a century earlier. It was like a second Romantic movement (Domenach, 1967: 219). The word *alienation* rapidly acquired its modern sense of estrangement from the world (as opposed to its old sense of madness) and became a touchstone of literary or artistic seriousness.

But although this fashion swept all before it in the clubs and cafés of Saint Germain, it made very little impact in the rest of France, where the prevailing mood in the cultural centres was rather more optimistic, as we shall see in chapter 5. The New Theatre began and ended in Paris. This is not to say that it had no effect at all on the provinces, but it never played a significant role in the development of the decentralised theatres. In view of the world-wide fame that this new form of theatre attracted, its virtual confinement, in France, within the ramparts of Paris is one of the most intriguing features of the post-war period.

This division between theatrical development in Paris and in the provinces can be detected much earlier than the 1950s, notably in the work of a few experimentally-minded directors such as Jean Vilar, who were to be responsible for promoting the New Theatre. During the German Occupation Vilar was engaged in two different kinds of dramatic activity. On the one hand he took part in provincial tours with La Roulotte in 1941 and 1942, performing plays by Molière, Musset, Synge. On the other, he spent time in Paris directing studio productions of lesser-known works. These were not new plays, but works by authors thought to be too difficult or risky for the provinces. Through these productions he introduced a small audience of Parisian *cognoscenti* to plays from a tradition unfamiliar in France, the tradition of Strindberg, Büchner, the German Romantics and the Elizabethans. Vilar produced two of Strindberg's plays during the Occupation: *The dance of death* and *Storm* both in 1943. Barrault's production of Gide's adaptation of Kafka's *The trial* in 1947 revealed similar qualities of nightmare, parody, frenzy and a style quite different from that of the classical French theatre. These productions and others like them helped to pave the way for the success of the New Theatre by proposing a model of drama that owed more to the tortured visions of men like Strindberg, Kafka and Artaud (whose *Le Théâtre et son double* published in 1938 was re-issued in 1944) than to the more temperate tradition of the classics revived by Copeau and the Cartel between the wars.

Vilar and Barrault were not the only directors willing to experiment. Younger men such as Roger Blin and Jean-Marie Serreau were looking for a new type of theatre: Blin, though trained by Dullin, had worked with Artaud and could see the need for a complete break with tradition. He agreed to produce *En attendant Godot* in 1950 (though he was not able to raise the funds for it until 1953). Like Blin, Jean-Marie Serreau had been trained by Dullin; like Vilar, he produced Strindberg; and he also produced the first play by Adamov to reach the stage (*La Grande et la Petite Manoeuvre* 1950). This desire for experiment was shared by the grand old man of French theatre during this period: Louis Jouvet. Having spent the war years in South America, Jouvet felt rather out of things when he returned to France. He admired Sartre, with whom he was friendly, and at his suggestion commissioned a play from Jean Genet, a writer with a scandalous reputation whose novels were passed from hand to hand in clandestine editions. The play was *Les Bonnes*, produced in a double bill with Giraudoux's *L'Apollon de Bellac* in 1947. Although this play contains many of the features of the New Theatre of the 1950s, its newness was obscured at the time by its apparent realism and by its juxtaposition with Giraudoux. Nevertheless this play introduced Parisian audiences to a new way of representing the themes of ontological insecurity and despair through a parody of traditional dramatic action. These elements were later recognised as forming part of what went to make up the New Theatre.

In 1949 Adamov was advised that the only way to get his plays produced was to get them published, so he persuaded a number of people, including Gide, Prévert, Blin and Vilar to write appreciative prefaces and published them with *La Parodie* and *L'Invasion* in 1950. At the time Vilar was attempting to raise the money to produce *L'Invasion* and he wrote, perhaps exaggeratedly, 'Posons la question: Adamov ou Claudel? Je réponds Adamov' (cit. Adamov, 1950: 16). This fervent support for a new dramatist was matched by Blin's support for Beckett. Barrault's productions of adaptations of Kafka, and Jouvet's production of *Les Bonnes* were other examples of how a climate favourable to the New Theatre was created by actors and directors in Paris.

Actors and directors, however adventurous, can do nothing without a theatre or performance space. The emergence of the New Theatre was greatly helped by the existence of a number of small 'art' theatres in the Latin Quarter of Paris (the area around the intersection of the Boulevards Saint Michel and Saint Germain). These tiny *salles* would often hold as few as 50 spectators, their running costs were low and they were able to take a risk with plays that might have spelled disaster for larger theatres. In order to try to increase their profitability they would often put on more than one play each day, the first at 6.0 p.m. and the second at 8.0 p.m. Some of these theatres have disappeared, some have been turned into cinemas (e.g. Les Noctambules, where *La Cantatrice chauve* was first performed). Only one survives as a theatre and this is La Huchette, where *La Cantatrice chauve* and *La Leçon* have been playing uninterrupted for more than a quarter of a century since their revival in the late fifties.

The plays of the New Theatre were mostly well adapted to the kind of facilities that such theatres could offer. They did not require elaborate settings or costumes and often needed only very small casts. This coincidence of plays and means of production has sometimes been exaggerated. Ionesco's plays benefited greatly from the more sophisticated productions they later received (e.g. from Barrault at the Odéon) as did those of Adamov (e.g. by Planchon in *A.A. théâtres d'Adamov*) and Beckett (e.g. in his own productions). But the essential qualities of the plays survived productions with extremely poor means (as thousands of student productions have subsequently proved). The existence of the small theatres was a crucial factor in the spread of interest in the New Theatre, since success was slow in coming. During the first three years of the fifties there were three productions of Adamov's plays and three productions of Ionesco's. Some of these were given in early evening performances or special performances outside the theatre's normal run. The audiences were small and the press was largely hostile. A few influential critics wrote appreciatively, but the majority found these plays maddeningly incomprehensible and many thought they were the victims of an elaborate hoax. Before Blin's production of *En attendant Godot* in 1953, which was an instant 'snob success' among the literati of the Latin quarter, none of these plays enjoyed a long run. Ionesco's early plays only began to be successfully revived in the middle fifties. Adamov, who began to champion political theatre in the middle fifties, never had the satisfaction of a long Paris run.

The sudden appearance of the New Theatre in the early fifties was further disguised for contemporaries, by the fact that all three of the authors mentioned were men who had already been writing for several years as novelists, critics, poets, philosophers, but not as dramatists, and so they did not fit easily into the category of 'young playwright'. In 1953 Adamov was 45 years old, Beckett 47 and Ionesco 41. Adamov had been an intimate friend of Artaud and had close links with Blin, Vilar and other men of the theatre, but his literary work had been limited to translation, autobiography, poetry and literary articles. He was fascinated by Büchner and Strindberg. He translated Büchner's play *Danton's death* for the celebrated Avignon festival production of 1948 by Jean Vilar and in 1955 he published a monograph on Strindberg. When he began to write his first original play, *La Parodie*, he was inspired by Strindberg, particularly by the example of *A dream play*. The act of writing plays, which exploited the obsessions he had revealed in his autobiographical confession *L'Aveu*, was such a liberating experience for him that he completed seven in under three years.

Beckett was writing *En attendant Godot* at the same time as Adamov was writing his first plays, although the two men did not know one another. Beckett had already written five novels of which one had been published without success. He claimed that he wrote *En attendant Godot* 'to get away from the awful prose that I was writing at the time' (cit. Bair 1980: 323). According to his biographer Deirdre Bair, he was also desperate to write something that would have popular appeal and so bring in some money. In this he ultimately succeeded, though the play was at first as difficult to sell as all his other works. It was offered to five different directors before Blin adopted it. Ionesco, the youngest of the three, was the one who most resembled the conventional image of the new young dramatist. In fact he had been writing literary criticism for many years but some of it was in Roumanian and none was well known in Paris. As a dramatist, Ionesco's strength was that of a man surprised by form: thinking that he had written a tragedy with *La Cantatrice chauve*, he discovered to his surprise that in performance its effect was that of farce. Once he had stumbled on this formula of the 'tragic farce' he proceeded to exploit it by applying it to a wide variety of situations. He wrote a large number of plays in a short space of time and the effect was, as in the case of Adamov, that of a talent which had matured slowly over the years suddenly finding expression in a flood of creativity.

The various factors outlined so far can help us to understand why the New Theatre appeared when it did appear. But such awareness cannot be expected to *explain* the phenomenon. All a study of this kind can show is what, in the work of the various writers, directors or actors who took part in it, was unexpected, pushing against the limits of ideas or dramatic forms then current. In trying to identify this, one may hope to show what the various creators of this theatre had in common and hence the justification for treating them together as a group. For although they all came before the public at the same time, the authors did not at first know one another and so could not be said to have formed a 'school' in the tradition of French artistic movements. It is all the more surprising to find that so many critics have looked for all-inclusive labels: theatre of the Absurd, theatre of derision, theatre of revolt, anti-theatre, meta-theatre, etc. The inadequacy of these, as critical terms, is that they put the emphasis on form and content. But close examination shows that the plays in question do not always share the same themes and still less do they exhibit uniformity of style. What they do all share is a radically self-conscious and self-questioning method of approach. Their plays differ from those of the traditional theatre in their most fundamental aims and intentions. In this they resemble the distinction that can be drawn between the traditional novel and the '*nouveau roman*' and this is why the term '*nouveau théâtre*', coined by Geneviève Serreau, seems the most satisfactory. A brief consideration of the achievements of the *nouveau roman* will help to illuminate the *nouveau théâtre*.

The novels of authors such as Robbe-Grillet or Butor show the development of the Modernist aesthetic to an extreme point. Modernism is that movement in literature and the arts which, from the start of the century, has become increasingly concerned with the processes of the artist's own mind rather than with the process of the society of which he is part. Novelists have become increasingly preoccupied with problems of language, seeing this as their primary material, rather than ideas or story line. Traditional elements of the novel, such as character and plot, began to be displaced, for example in Joyce's late work, by a kind of interior monologue in which many different voices could be distinguished but none precisely separated off from the others. This process reached a culminating point in the novels of the *nouveaux romanciers* who progressively withdrew from their stories, refusing to allow their readers the traditional comfort of explanations about how they should understand the words of their characters. At the extreme limit, the *nouveau romancier* supplies only a stream of discourse, leaving questions about the motives and ideas, even the identity of the speakers unanswered. Such writing transfers extremely well to radio and can also be effective on the stage or the screen. Some of Duras' novels (e.g. *Des journées entières dans les arbres*) are written almost entirely in dialogue form and hence present little difference, on formal grounds, from her plays. Robbe-Grillet has moved effortlessly from novelist to film-maker. The borderlines between the different media were to be broken down even more thoroughly in the work of the New Theatre writers than in that of the *nouveaux romanciers* since, like them, they became self-critical, focussing on the problems involved in constructing any image of the world, refusing to accept at face value any account of experience, constantly probing for the reason why the account should take this form rather than that, adopt one set of images rather than another.

The theatre of the inter-war years had seen the beginning of a self-critical trend, especially in the work of Pirandello, in which traditional notions of story and character are challenged. Pirandello was one of the authors most frequently performed on the French stage and his influence was pervasive. An example of his challenge to traditional notions can be seen in his play *Six characters in search of an author*. This play shows six 'fictional' characters breaking into the lives of a number of 'real' actors and actresses. The vivid reality of the six fictional characters imposes itself with far greater force than do the so-called 'real' characters. But because the six are only half-written characters, they are incapable of finding in their lives any of the overall consistency traditionally expected from dramatic characters. This idea was taken up and refined by the authors of the New Theatre, whose characters almost always share the same inability to make sense of their own characteristics or situations.

Among the French dramatists of the inter-war period there was a limited application of similar ideas, but it remained fairly limited. This was because, although ideas of a self-critical nature were debated, the formal preoccupations of the period remained traditional. The major playwright of the period, Giraudoux, was a self-consciously literary writer, looking back to classical myths and values for much of his inspiration. Cocteau, whose early work did include some bold formal experimentation, became more interested in the poetic image than in dramatic form, and developed to the point where his best work was done for the cinema.

Sartre too, when he began to write for the theatre, was content to adopt the structures of the theatre as he found it. But this did not make him blind to the significance of the New Theatre. He made some penetrating comments on the theatres of Beckett, Genet, Ionesco and Adamov in a lecture entitled 'Mythe et réalité du théâtre' given in 1966 (1973: 169–94). The word he used to describe the work of these writers was 'un théâtre critique' by which he meant that for these dramatists the dramatic process itself had become the subject of their plays. In order to do this they had dispensed with notions of plot and character. Being tired of the realist play, the poetic play and the fantasy play, they had chosen to make the lack of plot and the impossibility of character into the essential subject-matter of their dramas. So they took characterless characters, linked them in a plotless plot and endowed them with a series of apparently senseless movements. In this way they achieved a kind of 'degré zéro' of the theatre. The term 'le degré zéro de l'écriture' was used by Barthes (1953) to define a style of writing that offers itself as an absence of style, and to distinguish it from the usual tendency of literary writing, which is to offer the style as the constitutive quality that changes the words on the page from being mere chunks of language into 'literature'. Where the usual tendency is to filter the events described through a preconceived network of cultural, moral and intellectual references, writing at 'zero degree' would achieve a kind of transparency of language enabling the ideas and events to stand alone, without added comment or 'meaning'. An example of an author coming close to achieving this was Camus in *L'Etranger*. Barthes felt that in this novel Camus had achieved a kind of honesty, through his neutral prose style, which he used, like Hemingway from whom he learnt it, to render exactly what Meursault felt, saw, heard and thought, with a minimum of the normal literary clichés.

If we try to apply this theory in an analogous way to the theatre, the zero degree of theatre is to present characters who simply are *there*. Esslin expressed a similar idea when he wrote: 'The theatre of the Absurd has renounced arguing *about* the absurdity of the human condition; it merely *presents* it in being – that is, in terms of concrete stage images' (1968: 25). The theatre of Giraudoux, for example, was one in which the characters argued *about* the absurdity of the human condition; that of Beckett, Adamov, Ionesco, Genet and many others is one in which concrete images replace discussion. Esslin's analysis was part of his attempt to argue that what linked all these dramatists of the fifties was their conviction of the Absurd. With knowledge of their subsequent work, it is easier to see how different from one another they were in their response to the anguish of existence and that they coincide more in their use of the concrete stage images than in their metaphysical beliefs.

The reason why Beckett is the outstanding author among these dramatists of the early fifties is that his work brings to its most complete realisation this notion of theatre at zero degree. His is a theatre in which both matter and subject-matter are ruthlessly whittled away until we are left with what Geneviève Serreau has called 'le jeu pur' (1966: 90). She points out that many of Beckett's characters have affinities with clowns. What distinguishes an act between clowns is that there is no subject-matter or plot to keep them going. The mainspring of a clown act is the play instinct: its working lever is frequently a mere difference in temperament between two clowns, for example, one is sad, the other happy, and from this simple difference can spring a whole series of comic routines.

This analysis can help us to understand the action between Vladimir and

Estragon in *En attendant Godot*, since their relationship is governed by similar conditions. They are provided with none of the usual defining features of stage characters: they cannot remember where they have come from, or who they are, except for isolated fragments from the past like the fact that they once went up the Eiffel Tower. The only thing they are sure of is that they are supposed to wait for Godot, but they are uncertain about the place and quite vague about what will be the result if they do meet with him. In this situation (or rather non-situation) it is, like clowns, by displaying their slight differences of temperament that they keep the action and the dialogue going: Estragon is sleepy, forgetful, likes funny stories and dreams, enjoys a carrot the more he eats of it and has stinky feet. Vladimir is wakeful, remembers things, hates funny stories and dreams, dislikes a carrot the more he eats of it and has stinky breath. Much comedy of a traditional, clowning variety is extracted from these differences. At a verbal level, there is a very similar comedy of differences and misunderstandings which has been shown to derive from the routines of stand-up comics such as Flanagan and Allan (Davison, 1965 and 1983).

What makes the play more than just a pastiche of clown and music-hall comedian acts is partly the philosophical overtones and partly the self-conscious elements. The play is '*critique*' in the sense of Sartre's term, because the characters watch themselves act, reflect at the very moment of acting on the significance, or absence of significance, of those actions. This is particularly true of Pozzo who is incapable of even speaking without first being assured that he has an attentive audience. They are not content, like the clowns in the circus, to offer their nonsense as just nonsense, knowing that they can shortly leave the ring, remove the make-up and sit down to dinner. Instead they are stuck, like Pirandello's six characters, with nothing but the fragments that the author has written for them. They have to try to make sense of their existence within that context and that context alone. The contrast mentioned in Pirandello's play between the two worlds of fiction and reality has disappeared, swallowed up in the inexorable nightmare of the stage presentation. The audience is no longer asked to make believe but to observe the play in much the same way as it might observe a real event.

The salient fact about the New Theatre in general and *Godot* in particular is that these plays provoke reflection about the nature of theatre. Once this is clear, we can understand why their contribution towards a literature and a sensibility of the Absurd was so important. They undermined the credibility of stage presentation itself. Camus and Sartre had presented characters coming to grips with despair but had done so within traditional, often melodramatic structures. The New Theatre authors dared to do away with the reassuring structures of plot and character and to plunge their audiences into the same uncertainty that had previously been reserved for the characters in the plays. In the accepted sense of the word, Beckett's characters have no 'character'. They come from nowhere, have nowhere to go, and are sustained only by a hope that is shown to be at best a comforting illusion, at worst a cruel deception. What then is their interest? It lies in how they manage the tour-de-force of filling the space, both temporal and physical, which they are assigned. Their situation becomes a total image for existence; not just the imagined situation that they conjure up for us by the power of their acting, but their actual situation on the stage.

This, then, is the zero degree of theatre: to present people who simply *are there*. To achieve it is very difficult, since the stage is a signifying space of extraordinary richness and complexity. It is not easy to empty it of meaning. One of the most interesting results of depriving theatres of the elements that normally give meaning to our lives is that they may, like Vladimir and Estragon, end up attaining a far more extensive meaning, one that people will often describe as the universal quality of *Godot*. We shall discover that this quality of reflection on the nature and status of the stage performance was present (to a greater or lesser extent) in all those plays that we call New Theatre and therefore can be seen as an important criterion to justify grouping them together. The originality of this work was not at first understood because people could only respond to its apparent senselessness. In order to try to explain what they were attempting, Adamov, who at first appeared to be the dramatist most willing and able to explain himself, coined the term 'literality'. His explanations provide a better way in to understanding the plays of this period than the common method of starting from a philosophy of the Absurd.

For Adamov, what was meant by literality was that these plays did not operate on a symbolic level. They were not trying to point to something else beyond, they *were* that something else. For him, the play could only be considered as an event in performance, it had no existence outside that dimension. 'Theatre as I understand it is linked utterly and absolutely to performance' (1964: 13). The full force of what he meant by this can only be understood in relation to his friendship with Artaud. Adamov's closeness to Artaud in the last years of Artaud's life is apparent in the similarity between his own accounts of what he was trying to do in the theatre and the theories of Artaud. His insistence on the primacy of performance was like an echo of repeated statements made by Artaud to this effect. For Artaud repeatedly spoke of theatre as 'in fact the only real form of expression: expression in space'. This was the corner stone of his conception of theatre, the element that had struck him with the force of revelation when he witnessed the Balinese dancers at the Exposition Coloniale of 1931: 'In short the Balinese theatre, with the most extreme rigour, succeeds in giving shape to the idea of pure theatre in which everything, from conception to achievement, only has value or existence to the extent that it takes concrete shape on the stage' (1964: 80).

In the objective, palpable, physical literality of the stage event, Adamov, like Artaud, saw the possibility of expressing the intimate link between spiritual and material forces, the interpenetration of the conscious and the unconscious.

I believe that stage representation is no less than the projection, into the world of the senses, of the states and images that constitute its hidden motive springs (1964: 13).

In the plays current on the French stage at the time, metaphysical elements were not common (or where they appeared they were frankly symbolic like the character called Plague in the Barrault–Camus *L'Etat de siège*). It was thus not surprising that contemporary critics made much of the metaphysical element of the New Theatre. By making this emphasis, they overlooked the fact that the metaphysical and the physical had become one. It was not a case of the physical realm being informed or influenced by the metaphysical, but of a literal fusion.

For example, Adamov's play *La Grande et la Petite Manoeuvre* presents a central character who is gradually dismembered in the course of the action. Adamov explains this dramatic device in a passage following on from the one quoted above in which he defined literality:

What I should like to see in the theatre, and what I have attempted to put into practice in my plays, is for the manifestation of content to coincide literally, concretely, physically, with the content itself.

Thus, for example, if a man's drama consists in some form of personal mutilation, I can see no better dramatic means of conveying the truth of such a mutilation than by representing it physically on stage (ibid. 14).

This could be carried out in a crude or grotesque manner that would hardly achieve the integrated literal aim intended. But in Adamov's plays the emphasis is placed on the character's *willing* involvement in his own mutilation. He hears voices summoning him to take part in incomprehensible gymnastic routines. The voices cause him terror but at the same time exert a mesmeric, irresistible appeal. A similar fusion of physical and metaphysical is a characteristic of Ionesco's early plays. In *La Leçon* the professor is able to kill the pupil by simply using the word 'knife' and in *Les Chaises* the ontological void is experienced through the physical reality of the empty chairs in a room filled with the sound of people's voices but no people. So rather than create an imaginary story-line giving an insight into some aspect of loneliness, separation, hopelessness or aging, these dramatists present literal images, embodiments of those states.

It has frequently been claimed that the whole of the New Theatre movement was strongly influenced by Artaud. This claim is difficult to substantiate. Adamov is the only author to have known him at all well. Neither Beckett, Ionesco nor Genet (the author most often associated with Artaud) had encountered him or his work before they began to write for the theatre. It is much easier to establish his influence over a number of theatre practitioners, especially Barrault and Blin, who undoubtedly did a lot to make his influence permeate the dramatic climate of the time. But for most of the 1940s Artaud was an author known as something of an oddity, not widely accepted as a prophet until the sixties. The first publication of *Le Théâtre et son double*, in 1938, passed almost unnoticed. Gallimard reissued it in 1944 but it was not an immediate best seller and not until 1956 did they begin to publish his complete works. 1958 was the year when his reputation in intellectual circles really seemed established for the first time: this was the year of the first special periodical number – of the *Cahiers Renaud-Barrault* – devoted to him, soon to be followed by many others. It was also the year when the first English translation of *The theatre and its double* appeared.

More than a question of strict influence, the gradual spread of interest in

Artaud seems to have been a matter of critical understanding catching up with creative work. Once the new genre of 'tragic farce' had succeeded in attracting an audience, people began to notice that a new violence and a new literality had entered the theatre. It was discovered that Artaud had called for a theatre characterised by these qualities, and so his name became a kind of convenient critical short-hand for this genre.

Another point of coincidence between Artaud's work and the New Theatre was that both suggested that the theatre should exploit its uniquely rich variety of expressive means instead of relying mainly on the spoken word. At first critics were unable to perceive the richness of the New Theatre in this respect, since they were mesmerised by its bleakness and perhaps confused by the poverty of means characteristic of most of the early productions. But more recently, especially since there have been attempts to apply semiological methods of criticisms to the theatre, it has become apparent that the plays of Adamov, Beckett, Ionesco, Genet share a peculiar semiological richness. Presenting characters who were no longer the active promoters of the action, but rather passive victims, these dramatists found themselves obliged to make extensive use of lights, objects, settings to construct their stage images. Moreover, having dispensed with plot and character, they found that dialogue took on a new role. Instead of being the main carrier of exposition, values, meaning, it could become a literal embodiment of inconsequentiality, as in the chatter between Vladimir and Estragon, or of absurd anti-logic as in *La Cantatrice chauve*; it could also be stripped of all rhetoric so that the simplest phrases achieved an almost poetic power. More important still, it gave room for much of the main impact of the play to be carried, not by words at all, but by actions. The result of all this is that the audience at one of these plays will find that they are no longer concentrating mainly on the words and finding occasional additional stimulus from an action or a scene change. Instead the plays of the New Theatre present a combined assault on all their senses, sometimes all at the same time.

Some form of assault on the audience is a characteristic of all the plays of the New Theatre. To offend, shock or assault its audience is characteristic of twentieth century art in general. Music has rejected traditional harmony and fine art has overturned traditional criteria of aesthetics and composition. The theatre, relying as it does on immediate contact with a live audience, has resorted to shock tactics more frequently even than the other art forms. From the first night of Jarry's *Ubu Roi* in 1896, through innumerable scandals, such as the inter-war performances of Artaud's Théâtre Alfred Jarry, incensed audiences have protested angrily at what they considered to be an insult thrown in their faces. In 1966 at Frankfurt, Peter Handke took this tendency to its logical conclusion by presenting a play called *Offending the audience*. This consisted of actors quite literally and directly insulting the audience for the space of time that is taken by a normal evening's theatre performance.

Such assaults on the audience tend to work particularly well (and occur with particular frequency) in the theatre because of the captive nature of a theatre audience. Moreover, theatre workers have some cause to feel that revenge is due to them. For centuries the theatre has been despised by polite, right-thinking society, and yet loved at the same time for the release it gives from the constraining repressive forces of civilised existence. It has been condemned as sinful because it permitted the imaginative fulfilment of wishes that were considered sinful. In the new outspoken mood of much twentieth century innovation, these hypocrisies can be revealed and thrown back in the face of the society that is responsible for them.

The forms of audience assault that can be detected in the New Theatre are numerous. They include attacks on the spectators' sense of linguistic and moral proprieties as well as on their sense of what is important, logical or real. They sometimes even stretch to the use of physical force or at least the threat of it. Linguistic proprieties are attacked in a play like Ionesco's *Jacques ou la soumission* by making nonsense of language. The most solemn uses of language are parodied in this play by phrases that suggest only trivial nonsense. Jacques is not accepted by his family or by the family of his fiancée unless he is prepared to declare 'I love potatoes in their jackets'. The importance attached to this declaration by every character in the play, together with the triviality of its meaning, upsets our sense of the solemnity and importance of certain statements made in public such as 'I do' at a wedding.

An even more frequently used device is the inappropriate linguistic response. In *La Leçon*, when the maid discovers that the professor has murdered his pupil, she says:

And it's the fortieth time today! And every day it's the same story! Every day! Aren't you ashamed of yourself at your age too! . . . but you'll go and make yourself ill! (1954: 91).

The shocking revelation that the dead pupil is the fortieth that day makes the maid's scolding and her comments about the professor's health seem all the more inappropriate. The inappropriate language offends our sense of right or wrong, although it also provokes laughter; this kind of provocation is known as black humour.

Black humour is frequently used as a means of assault by making the audience laugh at what they would normally find tragic or horrible. The last moments of *En attendant Godot* are a case in point: Vladimir's despair rises to the point at which he is determined to commit suicide, not a moment at which one would expect hilarity. But the only method he can think of is to hang himself by the rope that holds his trousers up. As he removes it, his trousers fall to the ground and he is revealed, as Estragon insists more than once, in the classic position of ridicule – caught with his pants down. Black humour is often explained as a way of coming to terms with and ultimately dominating the horror that life (or death) may inspire in us. It may well achieve this function in some circumstances, but when presented by a performer to a live audience, its immediate effect is frequently to shock.

The hallucinatory quality of much of the New Theatre can also be seen as an assault on the audience by confusing its sense of what is real and what illusory. The effect of the literal mutilation in *La Grande et la Petite Manoeuvre* is to leave an audience in a constant state of uncertainty about what is real, what imagined. The dichotomy is never resolved in a conventional sense. A play like *Amédée ou comment s'en débarrasser* shows an equally deliberate assault upon our normal assumption that we can distinguish between the real and the illusory. The corpse that grows in the flat of Amédée and his wife can at first be seen as an imaginary or hallucinatory body representing something else, perhaps the death of their marriage or their ideals, or the pressure of passing time. But the literal, physical intrusion of the corpse into the sitting room quickly invalidates this explanation. Its concrete presence becomes the dominant factor in the play, as it grows and grows, leaving room for nothing else, and any attempts to rationalise it as a symbol of something else are further confused when it ceases to be an oppressive presence, but instead floats up into the sky like an enormous balloon, carrying Amédée with it.

The ultimate form of audience aggression, physical assault, is not so common, but it was originally envisaged by Ionesco as the climax of *La Cantatrice chauve*. Rather than the ending of the published version, which shows the play starting up all over again, he had envisaged two possibilities. One was for himself, the author, to go on stage shouting abuse at his audience. The other, even more violent, was for a couple of 'plants' to start a fight in the auditorium, which would provide a pretext for the theatre manager to insist on clearing the theatre, assisted by two actors dressed as policemen brandishing machine guns.

In all these different ways the New Theatre was a theatre of shock tactics and of audience aggression. Like most movements of its kind, its attacks were somewhat haphazard and without a clearly premeditated set of aims. But like the Dada movement that followed the First World War, its attacks were broadly on conventions and hypocrisies in the name of life and truth. And if the 'life' revealed was an agonising anxiety-ridden affair, at least it was seen to have a quality of direct experience because of the literality with which it was presented. Like most assaults, it was aimed at liberation, and what was to be liberated was, in the first place, the theatre, which was to be cleansed of its reliance on all the outworn conventions of the European cultural heritage. As often happens when all conventions are rejected, these dramatists discovered that in the process they had created a new convention. But their reliance on shock tactics put them in a dilemma: once the initial shock effect had worn off, what were they to do next? The answer was of course different for each dramatist and we shall investigate these differences.

The remarkable thing about the characteristics that allow us to class certain plays and playwrights together as New Theatre is that all of them – literality, self-consciousness, assaults on the audience – are specifically theatrical: they imply a renewed understanding of the significance and effect of an act of theatre and they relied for much of their effect on changes in the expected relationship between actors and audience. And yet they were not the work of men of the theatre or of authors who had been intimately involved in the lives of theatre companies. The concerns of Adamov, Beckett and Ionesco were all at first literary or philosophical rather than theatrical (unlike, say, Pirandello). None of them had easy access to the stage; all had difficulty getting their works performed. Their ultimate success was largely because the revolutionary implications of their plays for theatre practice were not lost on gifted directors like Vilar, Blin, Serreau or Jacques Mauclair. But, as we have seen, the directors all found that they could only afford to produce these plays on a very low budget in small 'art' theatres. Not until the sixties did the New Theatre receive a sufficient following by the public to be financially viable on a large stage. At this point these authors were taken up by Barrault at the Odéon with *Rhinocéros* in 1960 and a revival of *En attendant Godot* (directed by Blin) in 1961.

There was a natural affinity between the austere plays of the New Theatre and the small, ill-equipped stages on which they were presented. Audiences were brought into intimate (sometimes uncomfortably intimate) contact with the irreducible reality of other human beings confined in a bleak, restricted space and this bleakness, with its accompanying sense of claustrophobia, became a characteristic defining image of the New Theatre. But at the same time the small-scale productions to which Adamov, Beckett and Ionesco were condemned during the fifties did them a disservice by obscuring their scenic originality, especially their ability to evoke dream-states that could transform the conventional stage representations of reality. The production of *Le Ping-Pong* by Mauclair in 1955 is a case in point: in the tiny Noctambules theatre with its limited resources it was impossible for the director to develop the oneirical dimension of Adamov's play. Instead, it was performed in a rather conventional, naturalistic style. There was an enormous contrast between this and, say, the production of *Rhinocéros* by Barrault at the Odéon in 1960 (see below, p. 80).

Because the New Theatre was virtually confined at first to the Parisian art theatres, it became something of a cult, often appearing excessively abstract, theoretical or difficult. This perhaps explains why the authors of the New Theatre failed to appeal to many of the directors of decentralised theatres. These men had been trained in active theatre rather than in literature; they were trying to build up new audiences for the traditional repertoire and they were unwilling to endanger this by importing the latest Parisian fashion. No doubt they were also suspicious of the general atmosphere of despair in these plays, later dismissed by Adamov as 'whatever you do you'll be crushed' (1964: 21). To people of an activist political disposition this was bound to appear debilitating. Moreover there was almost no network of amateur or university theatre which might have helped to spread interest in these plays (as it did in Britain and the U.S.A.).

So far we have concentrated on what the New Theatre dramatists had in common. We shall now move on to a separate examination of Beckett, Ionesco and Adamov. A broad study of modern French theatre necessitates this selective approach, but it is worth noting that a large number of other writers produced similar work in the fifties, notably Boris Vian, whose play *Les Bâtisseurs d'empire* is a near-perfect example of the genre, or Jean Tardieu, whose short sketches published under the heading of *Théâtre de chambre* do much the same thing in miniature. Genet's plays are discussed on their own in chapter 8.

Modern French drama

Samuel Beckett

Beckett's work for the theatre consists of a long refinement on the success of his initial achievement in *En attendant Godot*. If the model for his particular type of stage action was the clown, it is far less apparent in his later plays. It is possible to perform *Godot* as a warm, almost cheerful piece about two people who preserve a dignity through tenderness for one another despite their decrepitude (though this is not Beckett's own choice of interpretation). But in *Fin de partie* the tone is altogether more savage and so it remains in all Beckett's subsequent plays. The single, inescapable defining context of the long wait for Godot by the tree, that made his first play so original, is also refined in the later plays, its stranglehold on the characters tightened. In *Godot*, some relief was provided simply by the appearance of the two new characters, Pozzo and Lucky. But in *Fin de partie* the action remains rigorously restricted to the one room in which Hamm lives with his servant Clov and his aging parents in their ashbins. All of Beckett's subsequent characters inhabit spaces that are hermetically sealed, into which only occasional memories can intrude, and their constant preoccupation is with finding a way to understand their situation, come to terms with themselves, find a language in which to express their sense of transience within stasis.

Fixed in their various prisons, whether the room of *Fin de partie*, or the mound of earth of *Happy days* or the vast urns of *Play*, these characters fill their time painfully, haltingly. Their situation on stage in all its unalterability becomes a metaphor for existence. They make reference to this from time to time, commenting on the horror of gazing out at the audience or breaking off to say 'this is awful'. When Clov asks Hamm what point he serves, he receives the literal answer 'to give me my cue!' The stage is a satisfying metaphor for an existence because, like life, it can be filled with two basic elements: actions and words. At its most basic, the metaphor can be presented through a series of actions unaccompanied by words, expressing a life in which hope is gradually defeated by the repeated experience of frustration. This is what Beckett does in his two *Actes sans paroles*. But more complex problems arise as soon as words are introduced and we shall find that the central theme of Beckett's plays is that of man's relationship with his own language (just as this is the central theme of his novels).

The recurrent theme of the Beckettian novel is the difficulty of saying anything coupled with the impossibility of *not* saying anything '. . . You must go on, I can't go on, you must go on, I'll go on, you must say words, as long as there are any, until they find me, until they say me . . .' (1959c: 418). And this is also a familiar theme in Beckett's poetry. Geneviève Serreau noticed that in a poem of 1948 Beckett seems to depict just the same situation as in *Fin de partie*. The poem is in two short stanzas, the first asking the question, the second answering it. The question is stated in the first three lines:

que ferais-je sans ce monde sans visage sans questions
où être ne dure qu'un instant où chaque instant
verse dans le vide dans l'oubli d'avoir été . . .

and is answered in the second stanza:

que ferais-je je ferais comme hier comme aujourd'hui
regardant par mon hublot si je ne suis pas seul
à errer et à virer loin de toute vie
dans un espace pantin
sans voix parmi les voix
enfermées avec moi

Beckett's own translation:

what would I do without this world faceless incurious
where to be lasts but an instant where every instant
spills in the void the ignorance of having been . . .

what would I do what I did yesterday and the day before
peering out of my deadlight looking for another
wandering like me eddying far from all the living
in a convulsive space
among the voices voiceless
that throng my hiddenness (1961a: 50–1).

The compressed, condensed, deliberately polysemic form of the poem demonstrates, in miniature, the same creative technique that is to be found in *Fin de partie*. The starting point for the play is an image: the image of a man shut in and peering out through portholes at the outside world. The character in the play who does the peering, Clov, is instructed by Beckett to do so with a stiff, staggering walk and in a manner perfectly summed up by the word in the poem *pantin*. But the image only acquires its full force in the last two lines of the poem, where the word *enfermé* for the first time suggests unwilling incarceration and the specific anguish is identified as that of being voiceless among the voices shut in with the poet.

All Beckett's characters are haunted by voices. Vladimir and Estragon talk of them:

Estragon All the dead voices.
Vladimir They make a noise like wings.
Estragon Like leaves.
Vladimir Like sand.
Estragon Like leaves (1965: 62);

Krapp plays them back on his tape recorder; the characters in *Play* are reduced to the point where they are almost nothing but voices, and this process is taken one stage further in *Not I* where the only thing visible to the audience is a speaking mouth and a dim, barely perceived, listening presence.

The voices are there because they can never be silenced. Many of the characters in the plays attempt to end, to be quiet, to achieve silence, but none succeed. *Fin de partie* is one of the best examples. In chess, it is the end game that is the most difficult and has to be conducted most skilfully, otherwise there is every probability of stalemate. In the play Hamm tries all the methods he can think of: he tells a story, but cannot bring it to an end; he tells a joke, but it falls flat; he tries to accomplish a set of actions performed in the correct order. But the longed for end does not come and he is left, in a similar state to the one he was in when the play started; a sort of suspended animation.

Like the Unnamable, he feels that his consistency is entirely composed of the words that babble in his head; but these words are not of his making. Only if he could make them his own might an ending be possible. This is the most extreme statement that can be made about the absence of character. A character in a play consists *only* of speeches set down against a given name. A novel traditionally contains a multitude of detailed description about a character's looks, clothes, parentage, upbringing, economic situation, etc. etc. In the *nouveau roman*, of course, such certainties are abandoned or, generally, just not provided. In drama, this has always been the case. In approaching a dramatic character whether he be of Aeschylus, Shakespeare or Beckett, we have nothing to go on except the lines spoken. Starting with these alone, the performer has to try to make sense of a particular character, find a consistency that will hold together all the different things written for that character to say. Beckett has pushed this state of affairs to its logical conclusion. It is part of the same process as that already described with reference to the character presentation. The process of trying to find consistency has been displaced from the performer to the character himself. Just as in the course of rehearsals, an actor must take someone else's words and try to make them his own, so, in a Beckett play, the *characters* are conscious that they take someone else's words and struggle with implications that are predominantly linguistic. If, as Clov says, there is nothing left to eat, then the only possible conclusion is: they will die. If, on the other hand there is just enough food to keep them going, a different conclusion imposes itself: they will not die (Cavell: 125).

Stanley Cavell, a linguistic philosopher, finds a quality of *literality* in the language and he is certainly right. But the literality is present also at the level of performance and character. Instead of there being, as in Stanislavskian Naturalism, a constant suggestion of 'more than' – *more* life going on off stage than is shown, *more* to the character than immediately meets the eye – there is instead a literal authority about the performance: *all* that there is to see and hear we see and hear. One of the consequences of this is that Beckett's plays encourage us not to look beyond the words and actions to their meanings, because in that sense they do not have any, but rather to experience the presentation itself as the only meaning offered. Because of this, the structural or shaping devices in the plays acquire a particular importance, and they turn out to be both many and varied. They can be examined at three main levels in the linguistic, the scenic and the active.

At the linguistic level these shaping devices range from the very simple to the very complex. At the simplest are devices like the song Vladimir sings at the beginning of Act II of *Godot*:

A dog came into the kitchen
and stole a loaf of bread
then cook up with a ladle
and beat him till he was dead

68

The other dogs came running
and dug the dog a tomb
and wrote upon the tombstone
for the eyes of dogs to come
A dog came into the kitchen
and stole a loaf of bread
[etc. ad infinitum]

The fact that Beckett particularly enjoyed this song is shown by its reappearance in *The unnamable* (1959c: 382), a rare case of Beckett quoting himself. This song is not used because of any meaning enshrined in it, but because it embodies, in a peculiarly vivid form (not without a certain mystery), a particular shape or structure: the shape of the endless cycle. A similar effect is achieved by the repetition that is a feature of Vladimir and Estragon's reflections quoted above (p. 67).

A slightly more complex example of linguistic shaping can be seen in the many jokes that enliven the dialogue of the plays and whose effect is frequently to reinforce, in literal form, the awareness of an unchangingly hopeless state of existence. For example:

Clov Do you believe in the life to come?
Hamm Mine was always that (1958: 35).

This is an example of a language joke that works rather like a riddle: the comic effect is produced by a clever, condensed form of words that says more than it at first seems to say, while also catching the listener off guard because it is not the sort of answer that had been expected.

Similar in their function to jokes are the vividly paradoxical statements that Beckett makes his characters utter at moments of extreme tension. Vladimir, filled with anguish at seeing Estragon asleep while the boy once again comes to announce that Godot will not appear that day, summarises existence in the words 'Down in the hole, lingeringly, the grave-digger puts on his forceps' (1965; 90–1). This paradoxical image, bringing together in one brutal phrase the birth that marks the beginning of a life and the death that ends it, is a striking example of one particular shape perhaps best described as the antithetical paradox. Another example can be seen in the opening lines of *Fin de partie*. The first words, spoken by Clov after removing the dust-sheets from Hamm and from the two ashbins, are: 'Finished, it is finished, almost finished it will soon be finished' (1958: 12).

Another shaping device that makes use of language can be seen in the construction of a story. Many of Beckett's characters attempt to tell stories, most notably Krapp, Hamm and Winnie. Krapp's desolate attempt to recapture, with the aid of his taperecorder, the story of one day long ago when he was happy, is perhaps the most powerful of all in its evocation of a desperate attempt to control a lost power of language, which, if once recovered, might also give access to lost happiness. Of course, Krapp fails in more ways than one. Not only does he fail to piece together his story, but there are also hints as the monologue progresses that the day in question was not such a success either.

Most complex of all, as linguistic shaping devices, are those speeches on which Beckett has imprinted the form of a disintegrating intellect. Attempts to decode the meaning of Lucky's 'think' or of the mouth's monologue in *Not I* will fail, since they are not written in the discursive rational mode. But the overall shape of their disjointed fragments conveys, in the case of Lucky's monologue, the shape of a mind that shrinks, pines and dies as a result of the failure of the world as perceived to meet the demands of the enquiring mind. In the case of *Not I* the monologue's structure is one of a constant attempt at evasion but an attempt that constantly fails. The suggestion is of a confession, reinforced by the dimly perceived presence of a hooded figure listening to the babbling of the mouth. But the repeated breaking off on the phrase 'not I' suggests a failure to evade the responsibility that is the original motive force behind the confession.

At the scenic level, Beckett constructs shapes that are strikingly expressive of confinement and endless sameness. During early performances of *Godot*, it was most frequently after the curtain had gone up on the second act, revealing the same deserted road, that spectators walked out. They could no longer bear the tension of hoping something would happen and finding that nothing did. The physical positions into which Beckett puts his characters have a vivid, condensed quality that is present at every level of his dramaturgy, but perhaps most clearly evident here. The ashbins of Nag and Nell or the mound in which Winnie is buried have taken on almost proverbial force: they are images that would be recognised very widely and not only by people who had seen these plays performed. It is this vividness and condensed power that gives Beckett his force as a dramatist.

As well as language and scenic elements, the things done on stage in Beckett's plays need to be approached with an eye to their shape. The obsessive quality with which Vladimir and Estragon return again and again to the same phrase, image or joke, finds its counterpart in action, with Estragon's obsessive pulling at his boot, or the endless changing of hats in Act II. Hamm's concern for all the actions of the day to be carried out precisely, and especially his obsession with being placed at the dead centre of his room, bear the shape of a man trying to establish his own dignity and importance, an attempt that is made absurd by his setting. The shape of the action is particularly interesting in *Play*, consisting of three characters up to their necks in urns, who are picked out in turn by a spotlight. As the light hits them they begin to speak and when it leaves them they stop. A precisely identical pattern is repeated twice so that the audience appreciates that the structure they have witnessed was no accident.

One of the most interesting features of these shapes and structures is that in so many of Beckett's plays the characters accept and confess their status as characters in a play, that is, people whose function it is to entertain an audience for a couple of hours. This is particularly true of Vladimir and Estragon whose dialogue, as has frequently been pointed out, owes much to the tradition of the music-hall cross-talk acts that Beckett had appreciated in the Dublin of his youth. The salient feature of the cross-talk act is that it elevates the aside to the level of structural principle: its humour derives from the fact that either one of the two characters can, at any moment, step outside his assumed role in order to comment upon it.

So we find that Beckett presents his audiences with a shape that is not just endlessly cyclical (like Vladimir's song) or paradoxical (like the grave-digger/midwife image) or condensed (like the grandparents in ashbins), but also a shape that is self-conscious, that comments upon itself – and that is the shape of a performance. To ask Why? What does it mean? is to commit the same error as the people to whom Winnie so scornfully refers: 'What does it mean? he says – What's it meant to mean – and so on – lot more stuff like that – normal drivel' (1962: 32). The reason why the plays call attention to their own shape is that this is another, more concrete way of warning the audience not to look for meanings behind or beyond the work, but to consider it for what it is: simply a play. Beckett himself, normally so unwilling to comment on his work, has made this plain by saying, 'My work is a matter of fundamental sounds (no joke intended) made as fully as possible, and I accept responsibility for nothing else' (cit. Reid, 1968: 33). The whole structure of *Fin de partie*, which is perhaps Beckett's most flawlessly characteristic play, can only be understood in this way. Everything that Hamm does is with an eye to the game, the performance, to how it may be played out, at last, to the longed-for end. From his first words: 'Me to play', he goes through a rehearsed sequence of events, moving on from one to the next with the perpetually anguished worry of the inveterate performer as to whether his timing is right (is it time for my tranquilliser? time for my story? etc.).

By using the means so far described, Beckett presents an image of existence as endless expectation. The dominant impression of someone who waits is of time passing slowly or coming to a standstill. Beckett exploits this experience of time. It was the *nouveau romancier* Robbe-Grillet who drew attention to this in a commentary on the question put to Pozzo by Vladimir and Estragon on two occasions in the course of Act I: 'Why doesn't he put down his bags?' Robbe-Grillet commented:

This is indeed the question that was asked a few minutes earlier. But in the meantime Lucky has put down the bags; Didi is able to convince everyone with the argument that 'Since he has put down his bags it is impossible that we should have asked why he did not do so.' Logic itself. In this universe where time stands still, the words *before* and *after* have no meaning; all that counts is the present: the bags *are* down and so it is as if they had always been (1963: 101–2).

There is a contrast between the audience's perception of minute changes, such as bags being picked up or put down, and the characters' feeling that nothing changes. It is by exploiting this contrast that Beckett achieves the dynamic force needed to give the plays their minimum necessary forward movement so as to prevent them becoming paralysed in total stasis.

And yet Beckett's characters are not totally unaware of the passage of time. Hamm asks the anguished question: 'What's happening, what's happening?' to which Clov can only reply: 'Something is taking its course' (1958: 17). Their nervous unease is echoed by Winnie, repeatedly wondering whether it is time for her song. For Beckett uses his characters' inability to grasp the passing of time as a way of expressing their inability to possess themselves. The big problem, he suggests, with self-perception is that it relies entirely on memories of the past, with all their defectiveness, or on projection into the future with all its uncertainties. If we can only live instant by instant, then it is perhaps logical to present the whole of life as merely one instant. This is what Beckett does in the second of his *Quatre poèmes*:

et vivrai le temps d'une porte
qui s'ouvre et se referme
(and live the space of a door
that opens and shuts) (1961a: 48–9).

The same perception is voiced by Pozzo: 'One day we were born, one day we'll die, the same day' (1965:89). But its most complete statement, in dramatic terms, is in the short play *Breath*. Here, in the space of 35 seconds, the passage of a whole life-time, from birth to death, is evoked.

The only possible escape from the anguish engendered by the experience of living in time would be literally out of the time dimension. This possibility is referred to allusively in Clov's opening speech in *Fin de partie*: 'Grain upon grain, one by one, and one day, suddenly there's a heap, a little heap, the impossible heap' (1958: 12). The impossible heap is the result of dividing a heap of millet in two, transferring half from one heap to the second, then again half of what is left from the first to the second and so on without ceasing. According to the pre-socratic philosopher Zeno, infinity will be reached at the point when every grain of millet is transferred from the first to the second heap.

Given the uncertainties, limitations and anguish of what little self-awareness seems available to Beckett's characters, they sometimes sense that they would be better off without it. But to escape from it is as impossible as to escape from the time dimension. Furthermore, they experience a feeling similar to that of Sartre's characters, that their existence is in the hands of some outside observer. Beckett enjoyed playing with the propositions of the eighteenth century idealist philosophers: his one film was based on Bishop Berkeley's dictum *esse est percipi* – to be is to be perceived. The film suggests that conscious existence involves a constant, anguishing sense of being observed by others and that we can never get rid of this feeling, even when entirely alone. Many of the characters in the plays demonstrate an uneasy sense that someone is watching them. Winnie has 'a strange sensation: I am clear, then dim, then gone, then dim again, then clear again and so on, back and forth in and out of someone's eye'. But although this causes her anguish, it is only an uncertain awareness. More important for her is her struggle to identify herself with her memories: 'Then . . . now . . . what difficulties here, for the mind. (Pause.) To have been always what I am – and so changed from what I was' (1962: 38). The audience witnesses Winnie's repeated failure to integrate her two awarenesses of herself, past and present. Krapp too, despite the technology of his taperecorder, is unable to join the two kinds of self-awareness, past and present.

In this way Beckett links the treatment of self-awareness to his treatment of the time dimension and in doing so shows once again the power of his plays to exploit the specific qualities of theatre. The theatre is a medium particularly apt at expressing the problem of time, since almost all stage plays rely on the audience's perception of two different time scales: that of the performance (say between 8 and 10.30 p.m.), and that of the imagined action, which can be anything from a minute to a century. The novel can, of course, talk *about* the problem of time in relation to perception and Beckett does so in *Molloy*: 'My life, my life, now I speak of it as something over, now as a joke which still goes on, and it is neither, for at the same time it is over and it goes on, and is there any tense for that?' (1959c: 36). Ross Chambers comments: 'It was this failure of language to express a certain experience of time that turned Beckett's attention to the theatre, where he was able to create that experience with a fragment of actual time' (1965b: 141). By exposing both his audience and his characters to the experience of waiting, and by denying them any hope of an outcome to that waiting, Beckett succeeded in establishing the zero degree of theatre.

Despite the success of *En attendant Godot* in the 1953 production by Roger Blin, Beckett's plays were slow to attract a large public. *Fin de partie* was not accepted by any Parisian management and so had its first performance (in French, produced by Blin) at the Royal Court Theatre in London (1957). This production transferred to the Studio des Champs Elysées, but was not rapturously received, and the play was not revived until Blin produced it again in 1968. By then, it had acquired the status of a classic and a visit to Blin's rather austere production was compared by critics to attendance at a shrine or monument. Blin's production of *Krapp's last tape* in 1960 was not very well received either. It was one of a season of new plays presented by Vilar at the 600-seat Récamier theatre by the Théâtre National Populaire in an attempt to introduce some new work into the T.N.P. repertoire. The season as a whole failed to attract a sufficiently large public and Vilar had to cut his losses.

Beckett's first large-scale commercial success was a revival of *Waiting for Godot* in London in 1957. This commercial success was repeated in France with Blin's revival of *En attendant Godot* at the Odéon in 1961, followed, two years later, by the French première of *Oh les beaux jours*, also directed by Blin. The performance of Madeleine Renaud as Winnie drew universal admiration from the critics for her almost romantic portrayal of the role, which, they felt, introduced a much-needed note of humanity into Beckett's bleak universe. In the course of the sixties, Beckett began to take a larger hand in the production of his own plays. Since then, he has been invited to direct in Berlin a number of times and has also directed new work of his in London and Paris (see Asmus, 1975 and Cohn, 1980).

His own approach to directing is to emphasise the elements of shape and structure that we have detected through studying the texts. He has complained that

Producers don't seem to have any sense of form in movement. The kind of form one finds in music, for instance, where themes keep recurring. When in a text, actions are repeated, they ought to be made unusual the first time, so that when they happen again – in exactly the same way – an audience will recognise them from before (Cohn, 1980: 231).

The account of Beckett's production of *Warten auf Godot* (Asmus, 1975) gives many examples of the rigorous patterns of movement he imposed upon his own text. He expected the actors to be able to reproduce these movements with the precision of dancers. But his additional work as a producer is not confined to movement: he also searches for the complex image that can combine a number of different elements in a condensed form, similar to the condensed images of his texts. One of the plays Beckett has produced most frequently is *Krapp's last tape*. In his production, Krapp's death is foreshadowed at the end by an anguished look over his shoulder into the void during the last playback of the tape. Krapp remains absolutely still in this position while the lights dim right down, leaving only a small beam of light on his face, reflected off the rotating spool. In this flickering image, the whole play is summed up.

Beckett's achievement is to have generated a series of many such powerful stage images which not only sum up the desperate plight of modern man, but also question the very possibility of representing that plight on stage. In his most recent dramatic fragments the clown figure has disappeared, to be replaced by ghostly shapes, only half seen, struggling to retain a feeble hold on their sense of themselves and of *That time* (the title of one such play published in *Ends and Odds*) (see fig. 3).

Eugène Ionesco

Like Beckett's theatre, Ionesco's is self-conscious and self-critical. Indeed, Ionesco was far more explicit about this aspect of his work, and produced quite a body of dramatic theory, whereas Beckett wrote none at all. Like Beckett's, too, his theatre was a theatre of shock tactics and here again he was rather more explicit than Beckett. We have already mentioned the audience aggression in his two projected endings for *La Cantatrice chauve* (above, p. 64). These violent or insulting endings were to be the culmination of a play in which our common perceptions of reality are systematically undermined and language, our principal means of apprehending and controlling reality, is pushed out of control. By the end of the play a kind of linguistic terrorism has broken out and the projected endings were intended to drive home, in terms of concrete action, the aggressive power of language that has gone mad.

Ionesco's first play seemed totally destructive, but he continued to write, discovering that by rejecting all established conventions he had created a new one. The new convention relied on a number of confusing paradoxes. Most obvious of these was their combination of hilarity and despair, summed up by Ionesco in the phrase 'tragic farce'. Equally paradoxical was the fact that while their action was literal, often very physical, their principal subject was language. Ionesco returned again and again to the treachery of language, its apparently straightforward guarantee of meaningful communication, together with its disturbing ability to mean whatever we choose to make it mean. His most memorable image of the incapacity of language to bear the weight we place on it is the orator who appears at the end of *Les Chaises*. His is the appearance for which everything in the play has been a preparation; he is the

3 *La Dernière Bande* (Beckett): one of Beckett's sad-faced clowns. Jean Martin in the production by Beckett at the Récamier theatre, 1970.

one who will deliver to the world the message composed for the occasion by Le Vieux and his wife. This is to be the moment when a life-time's wisdom and experience is distilled into language. But when the orator gets up to speak it becomes apparent that he is deaf and dumb and can only make mysterious signs on a blackboard.

This attack on language led to such plays being labelled 'theatre of non-communication', which Ionesco objected to, claiming that he believed that people communicate only too well. What he wished to suggest was that the rational, discursive use of language was not the only, nor even the most powerful means by which people communicate. *Rhinocéros* contains a passage in which Jean, who is admonishing Bérenger for his moral laxity, and the Professor, who is conducting a logical argument on another part of the stage, end up saying exactly the same lines, echoing one another in perfect unison although their intended meanings are entirely different. The effect of this device is to arouse laughter in the audience and to discredit both rational discourse and the uses to which it is frequently put. The inarticulate roars of the rhinoceroses, however, are able to communicate directly with those who are beginning to feel tempted to join them. As they listen to the roarings and trumpetings, they are drawn like metal to a magnet straight out into the street to join the herd. In *La Leçon*, the Professor is able to rape and kill his pupil by means of the simple word *couteau* and in *Jacques* an ecstasy of orgasmic dimensions is achieved by the chanting of the word *chat*.

Rather than proclaiming non-communication, Ionesco displaces our attention from rational uses of language, refusing to treat it as central focus of the dramatic action. Instead of responding intellectually to his plays, Ionesco wants us, first and foremost, to respond with our senses. We witness a dramatic action in which things occur that are by turns shocking, funny, cruel, absurd. Illogicalities are left unexplained, paradoxes unresolved, but as the action progresses the tensions that are set up by this process generate a dramatic image of a nightmare world.

The best way to understand how this works and what it may achieve is provided by Ionesco's own account of how he came to write for the theatre: 'I sometimes think I started to write for the theatre because I hated it' (1962a: 3). What he hated was a clash of realities: when he saw an actor pretending to be someone else he was painfully conscious of two realities, one flesh and blood, the other fictitious, which failed to coincide. The only kind of theatre he appreciated was the puppet theatre in the Luxembourg gardens which appeared to him brutal and rather grotesque, with no attempt at imitating 'real life'. In *Notes et contrenotes* he explained that he was genuinely frightened when he first saw actors rehearsing *La Cantatrice chauve*. He saw, not just the parodistic dialogue he had written for the Smiths and the Martins, but a presence of a particular kind: what looked like human beings turned out to be mechanical, ridiculous, violent figures from some sort of nightmare.

He suddenly understood how to resolve his painful sense of two realities failing to coincide: instead of trying to make the fiction more and more credible, he had to accept its artificiality, indeed to exaggerate it: 'to push everything to the point of paroxysm, where the source of tragedy is to be found. Create a theatre of violence: violently comic, violently tragic' (1962a: 13).

In these early attempts to theorise about the dramatic effect of *La Cantatrice chauve* Ionesco is clearly drawing on the vocabulary of Surrealism. The passage just quoted recalls both Breton's statements about the 'convulsive' quality of beauty and Artaud's emphasis on cruelty. In some ways Ionesco can in fact be best understood as a Surrealist dramatist. He has explained that his work originates, not from ideas, but from two basic states of consciousness, one of evanescence, light, release, the other of weight, opacity, confinement. His plays can all be interpreted as a struggle between these two forces, now one, now the other predominating. The paradoxical image of Amédée, at the end of *Amédée ou comment s'en débarrasser*, floating up into the sky suspended from the body that has formerly oppressed and crushed him is entirely Surrealist.

The Surrealist vision aimed to bring together unlikely objects and images in order to set up reverberations of a hitherto unknown kind. It attempted to open our eyes to a world of infinite possibilities in which anything could happen. His stage directions often suggest the use of effects pioneered between the wars in Surrealist film. In Buñuel's film *L'Age d'or* (1930) a frustrated man throws feathers out of a window which, as they emerge, go through a number of extraordinary transformations, turning, for example, first into a burning tree and then into a Bishop. Ionesco wanted the same kind of infinite transformability to be possible on stage. He faced his audiences with a world in which nothing is established or secure, anything can happen, and the only rule that can be applied is to declare every event to be an exception.

Ionesco himself has declared that, although interested as a young man in Surrealism, he is not a Surrealist. He accuses the Surrealists of having become fixated on manifestos and systems and he feels that he differs from them in his working methods (1962a: 100). But even if his methods do not always coincide, his fundamental aim, to liberate the subconscious levels of the mind from the straitjacket of logic and to achieve this by means of a dream-like style of theatre, is very similar to the programme of the early Surrealists. Although he rejects the name of Surrealist, Ionesco is a member of the Collège de'Pataphysique, a mock-scholarly gathering devoted to the science of 'pataphysics invented by Alfred Jarry, who defined it as 'the science of imaginary solutions'.

In the place of rational argument or neatly constructed plot, Ionesco relies upon dreams. He claims to have been strongly influenced by the Jungian concept that every man suffers from the separation between earth and sky. Only in childhood, during a holiday visit with his mother to the village of La Chapelle Athenaise, did he ever experience unity and harmony. This experience was like being taken right out of himself and finding the world around him totally transformed. For its short duration he experienced a feeling of indescribable bliss and total release so that even gravity seemed to lose its power over him. In many of his works he draws on memories of this experience of bliss and also of the moment when it left him. A good example is his film *La Vase*, which begins on the note of lightness and euphoria, gradually changing to the opposite. It depicts a very simple set of actions, a man getting up in the morning, dressing, writing letters, walking out along a road. These actions are repeated a number of times, first in the mood of lightness and joy, then, gradually, slowing down and becoming more and more depressed. Finally, where he had begun by bounding along the road, he ends lying, half sunk in mud, an image of inertia.

For Ionesco, this kind of sequence of dream images is not to be seen as a distortion of reality. On the contrary, it represents a truer vision than that of everyday working life, in which the inexorable logic of material things quickly takes on nightmare proportions. In a pardoxical reversal of normal expectations, he claims that dreams give us real insights whereas rational thought merely confuses.

I must tell you that when I dream I do not feel I am abdicating thought. On the contrary, I have the impression that as I dream I see truths that appear before me as self-evident, more brilliantly illumined, more sharply and more pitilessly defined than in my waking state, when everything becomes gentler, more uniform and impersonal. That is why in my theatre I use images drawn from my dreams, realities that have been dreamed (1962a: 93).

In order to maintain the 'sharp' and 'pitiless' quality ('acuïté impitoyable') of these dreamed realities, Ionesco chooses to avoid conventional dramaturgical methods: 'I attempt to relieve dramatic tension without the help of what would normally be called a plot' (1962a: 160) and he regrets that, in writing *Rhinocéros*, he allowed the story to become too prominent. He repeatedly describes his plays as 'abstract theatre', 'pure dramas', in which the rise and fall of dramatic intensity should be compared more to that experienced when listening to music than to a conventional play. Ionesco goes so far as to argue in *Victimes du devoir* that all theatre up until the present has been merely a series of detective stories, thrillers in which the whole energy of the play is directed merely towards revealing the identity of someone who has committed a hideous crime. For him the act of playwriting (described in *L'Impromptu de l'Alma*), is 'an adventure a hunt, a discovery of a universe which reveals itself to me and at which I am the first to be surprised' (1958: 13). In many of the plays the basic structure is provided by some sort of search – Bérenger's search for the killer in *Tueur sans gages* or Jean's search for himself in *La Soif et la faim*. It is a search that avoids the detective story formula since it never achieves just what it sets out to do but is pursued through a bewildering series of shifting realities. When the academic doctor asks what is its subject, the playwright is at a loss for the answer. He can only describe the creative process in which he feels he is carried along by the characters he has dreamed up, never totally in control.

In point of fact the term 'abstract theatre' is rather misleading because the force of his plays relies so much on the very concrete, literal embodiment of his stage images. But it is true that through all their variety of situations, Ionesco's plays rely on exploiting a limited number of dramatic rhythms or progressions. The experience of Bérenger in *Rhinocéros*, which has some claim to being a political play about the rise of fascism in Roumania, is precisely parallel to that of Le Monsieur in a thoroughly apolitical, surrealist piece called *Le Nouveau Locataire*. Le Monsieur moves into a nice new appartment only to be followed by a stack of furniture that grows and grows to the point where he is first walled in and then literally buried beneath the mass of invading objects. Bérenger's revolt against the invasion of pachyderms is the same as the revolt of Amédée against the body that crushes him or the revolt of King Bérenger against the onset of death in *Le Roi se meurt*. In each case we witness an individual crushed by inhuman forces from outside that threaten to invade or annihilate him. The precise nature of these forces is less important than the accelerating rhythms with which they proliferate and finally overwhelm the protagonist.

Ionesco's plays of the fifties survived their early productions better than those of Adamov or Beckett. For his vision of a theatre of paroxysm could be given adequate expression by actors who could adopt a suitably feverish style and pace of performance. This was certainly true of the original cast of *La Cantatrice chauve* and also of Paul Chevalier and Tsilla Chelton, whose movements in *Les Chaises* (1952) were reminiscent of mechanical dolls, or of the Luxembourg garden puppets that Ionesco admired. But, as in the case of Adamov, poverty of means reduced the effectiveness of the oneirical elements in *Amédée* (directed by Serreau in 1954 at the Théâtre de Babylone) or *Jacques* (directed by Robert Postec in 1955 at the Théâtre de la Huchette).

During the sixties, however, his plays were produced in the major theatres with large resources, including La Comédie Française, where *La Soif et la faim* had its first performance in 1966. In these circumstances full justice could be done to the dream-like imagery of the plays. A good example is Barrault's 1960 production of *Rhinocéros*, which emphasised the play's nightmarish progression in spectacular fashion. In the first act, life seemed relatively normal in the small town square. The first rhinoceros to be spotted did not appear on stage, it could merely be heard thundering past. In the second act, when M. Boeuf, transformed into a rhinoceros, appeared at the office, he was again not visible, but the demolition of the office staircase was quite spectacular. The transformation of Jean was also impressive, his skin gradually turning green and his forehead acquiring a horn. By the end of the third act, Bérenger's room was invaded by countless rhinoceros horns, piercing the walls like the beaks in Hitchcock's *The birds* (see fig. 4). This progressively increasing violence served to reinforce the audience's identification with Bérenger, increasing the emotional conviction of the play and disguising its political vagueness. Sadly, as his growing reputation made more resources available to him, Ionesco's plays became more static and rhetorical. Few of those written in the sixties and seventies have the imaginative or the oneirical force of the earlier works.

As the influence of Brecht became more pervasive in the course of the fifties, Ionesco found himself cast as chief opponent of political theatre. It was a role that he accepted with enthusiasm and has kept up ever since. He took every opportunity to satirise the supporters of left-wing political theatre in his plays, but did not stop there, spreading the polemic to other channels of communication wherever possible. In 1958, in *The Observer*, Kenneth Tynan accused him of writing plays that had no contact with reality. An exchange of articles followed, in which Ionesco argued that his plays did indeed have an impact upon reality, but one that was achieved through language and the artistic means of expression, not through political or historical contact. His claim was that he had enlarged the possibilities of theatre language and that this had a more revolutionary effect than plays about revolution. 'To renew the language is to renew the whole conception or vision of the world. A revolution is a change of mentality. Every new artistic expression enriches us by answering some spiritual need and broadens the frontiers of known reality' (1962a: 85).

Ionesco's claim to have renewed language, conception and vision must depend for its justification upon his exploitation of the rich resources of the stage. Every element in his plays becomes a bearer of meaning. Inanimate objects are as important as animate ones. Since they conjure up a dream reality, the plays depend a lot on atmosphere, which is generated by the use of settings, lights, colours, sounds, and on unexpected transformations, as one character dissolves into another, or some basic law of nature is denied, as when Bérenger finds he can fly (in *Le Piéton de l'air*). For their thematic content the plays are much less original, dealing with the themes that have traditionally preoccupied European dramatists, such as freedom, guilt, love, death. The most important of these themes and the one that recurs most frequently is that of death, a subject that has always obsessed Ionesco. He admits to a neurosis about death, indeed he claims that neurosis is a necessary prerequisite for literature: 'I believe that literature is neurosis. Without neurosis there is no literature' (1966a: 42). *Le Roi se meurt* provides the most sustained example of a play on the theme of death in Ionesco's theatre. The dramatic rhythm of this long play is provided

4 *Rhinocéros* (Ionesco): Jacques Noël's nightmarish set at the end of the play, with Barrault as Bérenger, at the Odéon theatre, 1960.

solely by King Bérenger's attempt to fight off the inevitable approach of death. The conflict in the play arises from his repeated attempts to restore his regal dignity which is repeatedly undercut by Marguerite and the Doctor. In *King Bérenger* is summed up the most consistent tragicomic tension in Ionesco's work: the attempts of men to assert their dignity in situations where they are merely laughable. He never appears to be more than a grotesque mockery of a king. It is as if the contrasted pair of clown and king in Ghelderode's *Escurial* had come together in one figure: he is the man who sits on a throne and yet has no power. He stands as a figure for Everyman and the play follows a similar pattern to the medieval morality play of *Everyman*. As in that play, Bérenger finds himself gradually stripped of all things that he relied on for support: his wealth, his power, even his love for the young Queen Marie, and, ultimately, his sense of selfhood. But unlike the medieval play, it does not end on a note of certainty. Rather than the soul ascending to be with Christ, we see nothing but a greyish light invading everything as Bérenger finally dies, the walls of his palace disappear and we are left with an immense, blank question mark.

This play shows Ionesco attempting to supply a rite of passage for a culture in which the power and efficacity of the traditional rites is no longer axiomatic. The public nature of the theatre and its traditional preoccupation with death make this a naturally tempting project. It has always been one of the functions of theatre to reconcile its audience to even the most unacceptable aspects of the human condition. Ionesco, in his own way, tries to do this. He offers a ritual for people who no longer believe in rituals; a passage from life to death that we can never take quite seriously, that seems to be mocking itself just when it is at its most serious, a ceremony that fully deserves the epithet grotesque: both comic and repulsive.

In the last analysis Ionesco's work must be seen as that of a mystic. A mystic for whom faith seems impossible, but for whom the traditional questions still nag with an undiminished urgency: how is it possible to explain moments of sudden joy or of unpredictable depression, the sense of being joined to the whole universe or completely separate from it? How is it possible to say that we shall die? Rather than present his audiences with stories, debates or information he tries to administer a shock to their sensibilities that will remind them of what it feels like to live and to face death. In doing this, he succeeds in creating literal, concrete images of guilt, fear, isolation and so contributes to the forging of a more direct and more effective language of communication in the theatre. But this achievement is limited by Ionesco's inability to pass beyond the expression of individual joy or depression to the social dimension. When his characters experience lightness, joy, evanescence, it is always a solitary emotion. They cannot derive joy from togetherness with others. In fact it is almost always the pressure and intrusiveness of social existence that destroys their inner sense of bliss. In other words, Ionesco is incapable of seeing the world of personal relationships as anything other than smothering and stultifying and this in turn makes it impossible for him to deal with society in terms other than caricature. Although Beckett's plays could be said to be open to the same objection, they do not invite it in the same way because of their strict adherence to the treatment of isolated, marginal characters. Most of Ionesco's plays are set recognisably in the context of society at large. Yet Ionesco the mystic cannot see society as anything other than detrimental to the soul. As he said of his first creations in *La Cantatrice chauve*, they are 'hollow, purely social characters – for there is no such thing as a social soul' (1962a: 161).

Arthur Adamov

Like Ionesco, Adamov presented a world of grotesque contrasts, both farcical and tragic, in order to shock his audience out of their easy realist assumptions. His first play, *La Parodie*, shows two contrasted characters, one bright and energetic, the other passive and supine, both coming to identically dismal ends. One of these characters spends most of the time waiting for a girl with whom he thinks he has made an appointment, and whenever he tries to discover if it is time for his meeting, he is frustrated by the absence of hands on the town clock. The experience of 'shrinking and pining' is conveyed in concrete terms as the sets close in around him and nothing seems to coincide as it should: even the dancers in a dance hall are out of time with the music. This dramatisation of the themes of time and of despair presents obvious similarities, both with the 'zero degree' theatre of Beckett and with the surreal images of Ionesco.

Adamov also shares with Ionesco the fact that writing was for him a therapeutic activity that helped him to achieve some liberation from neurosis. But the obsessive, dream-like situations and images that fill Adamov's plays are quite distinctively his own. They are associated mostly with the family: stifling mother figures, terrifying authoritarian father figures, oppressed yet strangely self-possessed sister figures. His early plays frequently centre on a male figure who finds permanent contact with anyone of the opposite sex impossible. These neuroses of sexual impotence, and of mother or father fixation, are dramatised in a series of hallucinatory images which, perhaps because of Adamov's familiarity with Strindberg, recall the Expressionist *Stationendramen* more closely than do either Beckett or Ionesco. In *Le Sens de la marche*, for example, the central character appears in a series of type situations: the home, the school, the church, the army, and in each case finds himself confronted by a paternal figure of authority in a different guise. In *Les Retrouvailles* he finds himself reverting helplessly to childhood as a dominant mother takes him over, ending up by forcing him into a pram and pushing him off the stage despite the fact that he is fully grown. In these plays we see dream and literality combining in very much the same way as in Ionesco's plays. Adamov's work showed the same struggle to go beyond what could be said in the established dramatic idiom. If anything his plays expressed with even more urgency that sense of utter despair that was dubbed '*univers concentration-naire*' or concentration-camp universe, because of its depiction of a world entirely governed by cruelty and arbitrary injustice.

At first Adamov's plays achieved this by a development and refinement of the dream play. All of his early plays present a hallucinatory, shifting reality that can never be grasped before it changes its shape. In the hands of some writers this technique can appear rather forced. In Adamov's plays, its use so clearly proceeds from obsession and suffering, that the reader or spectator is never tempted to shrug it off as self-indulgence. In two of his most interesting plays of this period, Adamov dramatises the problem of the writer and his language even more explicitly than Beckett (although he perhaps comes close to it in *Krapp's last tape*). The problem in question can be traced back to the gradual disillusionment this century with Naturalist forms.

In the Naturalist play that first flowered on European stages a hundred years ago, and that we are still familiar with as the commonest form of television drama, it is assumed that sufficiently detailed knowledge of a character's class, background, education, etc. will allow him to be fully understood. In the course of this century, this belief has more and more come under attack and the opposite belief has gained ground, namely that these facts may tell us only what is least interesting about a person. A similar change has taken place in literary theory. It used to be assumed, in an uncomplicated way, that the author, a well-defined person with a touch of something called genius, generated a stock of original characters, stories, ideas, which he then handed out for the admiring gaze of his fellows. Recent literary theory has suggested that both sides of this contract are to be re-examined. In the first place the author is 'used by' his language, cultural conventions etc. as much as he uses them and, in the second place, his readers do not simply observe, but significantly alter his stories and characters by the way they receive them, so that in some senses the reader too participates in the 'writing'.

Out of these shifting areas of debate the question that arises is who is speaking? Whose voice carries authority? To students of drama, this has always been an important question, since drama is the one literary form in which an author deliberately renounces the privilege of speaking with his own voice. He chooses, instead, to speak through a number of different characters and these characters in their turn, are interpreted by actors, so that when an audience receives the play it is in no doubt about its mediated quality. It is a major achievement of the New Theatre to have posed this question of who is speaking in dramatic terms before the literary theorists had begun to glimpse its complexities. The problem was one that received particularly clear formulation in Adamov's work. His first performed play, *L'Invasion* (directed by Jean Vilar in 1950) was about the efforts of Pierre to decipher and sort out the papers left by his friend, who was a writer. The longer they are left, the more these papers fade; already there is wide disagreement between himself and his assistant about the transcription and meaning of certain key passages. Pierre's struggle to put his friend's work in order fails; he loses his wife, his friends and even his own sense of identity in the process.

For Adamov the writer, the concrete experience of language as a dimension through which he lived, was essential. 'If I were to stop writing, everything would crumble. If words abandon me, I can no longer remain upright, I fall, I collapse . . .' (1969: 33). This is not just a metaphorical expression because Adamov saw a very close relationship existing between language and concrete space: 'Any development of thought presupposes a notion of space. Language can only be conceived and constructed in space' (ibid.).

From the familiar idea that all conscious thought necessarily uses verbal forms, Adamov built up his theory of the connection between gesture and language. They come together in the idea of literality: thought and language are inconceivable without the spatial element of gesture. In *L'Invasion*, Pierre's crisis occurs when he finds he can no longer *feel* the living force of language. All the work on his friend's manuscripts seems useless:

Everything I managed to draw from the darkness, to retrieve and set in order, remains desperately lacking in relief. Flat. Do you know exactly what I mean by flat? Flattened? Suddenly expelled from space? (1953: 86).

When he says that language has lost the quality of spatial existence he is saying that thought is no longer possible and hence that his very existence is in jeopardy.

The enormous lengths to which Adamov had to go to get his plays performed took their toll on his own sense of identity as an author. In 1953 he had a particularly vivid dream of this identity being challenged. For the next two days he wrote the dream out, as faithfully as he could, in dramatic form, changing only the status of the central character: instead of a writer, he made him a professor and named him after the Hotel Taranne, discreet but respectable, that faces coffee drinkers on the terrace of the Deux Magots in Saint Germain. The play, *Le Professeur Taranne*, shows the disintegration of a character whose claim to consistency is based on his writing and teaching as a professor. He is accused of indecent exposure, but at first seems to have an alibi and to be recognised by the people he meets. But gradually his alibi is shown to be ambiguous and the people who thought they recognised him claim that he is simply aping another professor. The final blow is a letter from a Belgian university accusing him of plagiarism. He turns slowly to the wall and begins to undress, committing the act that he perhaps secretly desired all along or that has perhaps been forced upon him by the accusations he has encountered. Here we see the writer/professor incapable of establishing his authority, his claim to originality, or even his identity. He is unmade by the doubts and ridicule of those who respond to him as much as by his loss of confidence in himself. He is an embodiment of the modern writer, who dares to expose himself to public view but whose very identity is put in question.

Le Professeur Taranne marked a turning point for Adamov. His writing and his limited recognition began to afford him some measure of liberation from the confined, neurotic existence that had been his. Accompanying this liberation was a growing impatience with the unrelieved pessimism of the New Theatre. He began to feel that there was a measure of wilful distortion involved in writing as if all human activity were condemned to senselessness. He accused himself of shaping his dream images too artfully to prove that whatever one does one is crushed. *Le Professeur Taranne* felt to him like a new departure because he had been totally faithful to his dream, not altering it to prove any thesis, and also, because, for the first time, he had mentioned a real place – Belgium. This may seem a trivial point but it was, for him, a symbolic step away from dream worlds unsituated in time and space, towards the real world that, through all our differences of perception and language, we inevitably share. In another important respect this play marked a new departure: it was not performed in Paris, but in Lyon by the theatre company of Roger Planchon. Although Adamov continued to live in Paris, most of his work after the middle fifties was performed outside the central Parisian theatre land in which the New Theatre had flourished.

Le Ping-Pong, produced in 1955 by Jacques Mauclair at the Théâtre des Noctambules, was the last of his plays to be given a first performance in central Paris for over ten years. This play, very successful in its own right, can also be seen as a transitional work, pointing to how some of the discoveries of the New Theatre were to be digested and incorporated into new departures in the years that followed. The play depicts two young men fascinated by an insignificant product of commercial glamour: the electric pin-table. They devote a life-time to getting a job in the consortium that manufactures pin-tables, then working to improve and develop the product. But they find that instead of them controlling and improving the machines, the consortium controls and uses them. The final tableau sums up a futile life as the two senile old men try to think up a new version of ping-pong. The struggles of Arthur and Victor develop into a struggle for language. They attempt to impose their ideas upon the consortium, but the language of the consortium gradually infiltrates every aspect of their lives until they are unable to conduct even the most personal transactions, such as a declaration of love, except through the language of the machine. *La Cantatrice chauve* had shown the language of social intercourse becoming reified, recalcitrant to human efforts to manipulate it. *Le Ping-Pong* showed a similar reification of language but also showed that, like it or not, we live and communicate through our language and that, as often as not, it is our language that speaks us rather than the other way round. Moreover the play began to show that the reification of language is not an innocent, chance occurrence. It may be actively promoted by groups like the consortium because of the power it gives them over a public that they can only see as consumers. This analysis was carried much further in some of Adamov's later plays, culminating in *Off limits*, but its roots and its methods are to be found in the new theatre idiom that we have been analysing as the New Theatre.

To some extent, Adamov's change of direction was not so great as he himself suggested. Many of his early plays are more concerned with the manipulation of social power than are those of Ionesco or Beckett. But a clear progression can certainly be traced from the earliest plays, in which the dominant feature is the presence of death and inexplicable cruelty, to his later plays, in which society is subjected to a much more detailed scrutiny. The difference, he said, was that in his early plays he had been obsessed by one thing, the incurable evil of death. Now he was more interested in the evils that were curable because socially created, not an inevitable part of the human condition, and therefore susceptible of change by human beings. The power of some of his later plays in this vein, such as *La Politique des restes* or *Off limits*, certainly comes, as we shall later see, from his exploitation of the discoveries and techniques of the New Theatre.

5

The decentralised theatre I: the fifties

In his book *Le Théâtre populaire*, published in 1941, Copeau had prophesied that France was already giving birth to a new kind of dramatic activity: 'I mean those young companies which the Popular Front had begun to encourage. Most have found themselves exiled behind the demarcation line [dividing the occupied part of France from the "free zone"]. Excellent point of departure: the break with Paris' (37). For Copeau, this move away from the capital was the first condition for a revival of theatre in France. At the time when Copeau was writing there were no officially recognised full-time theatre companies working outside Paris. The little live drama available to provincials was provided by tours of the previous Parisian season's commercial successes or small touring companies, often of semi-amateur status. Subsidies for such work were almost non-existent (see Gontard, 1973: 144).

The young companies to which Copeau referred consisted mostly of young actors and directors who had come under his influence or had been associated with the work of the Compagnie des Quinze. They shared Copeau's broad view that a lightweight touring company gained in dramatic vigour by having to rely principally on inventive acting and gained in social relevance by being in constant close contact with its public. Many were happy, like Dasté, Clavé, Jaquemont, Serreau and others, to take the opportunity provided by Jeune France to go on the road. Others, like Gignoux, spent the war in captivity but returned to France with similar aims. The hopes for a cultural renewal that had grown up in the Resistance movement pointed in the same direction: people were determined to take their future into their own hands rather than relying on a remote, often corrupt central government.

In this way, at the liberation of France, there was the desire for permanent regional theatre companies on the part of certain cultural and political organisations, combined with a belief in the importance of regional theatre on the part of certain actors and directors. In fact the first permanent company to be established came as the result of a specific request by representatives of Colmar, Mulhouse and Strasbourg. These towns were situated in Alsace, a province that had been disputed territory between France and Germany for the past century, and after the German defeat they were keen to re-establish their cultural links with France. The proposal met a warm response from the Ministry of Beaux-Arts, where Jeanne Laurent was newly in charge of the Spectacles et Musique sections and was looking for ways of encouraging decentralisation.

The paradox was that decentralisation could only succeed with a powerful boost from the centralised bureaucracy. Jeanne Laurent had been working at the Ministry since 1939. During the period of the Occupation, she had observed the different touring companies, had meditated on Charles Dullin's report on decentralisation and had concluded that he had been right to suggest establishing fixed companies with the responsibility of touring only round their own local areas. She therefore decided to establish a number of new Centres Dramatiques Nationaux on the basis of combined financial assistance from both central and local government. The Ministry appointed a director and provided a large part of the subsidy; the local powers provided the theatre and other facilities and contributed a fixed amount to the centre's budget. She also established a Concours des Jeunes Compagnies with a first prize of 100,000 Francs in 1946 and a special subsidy for new writing, known as 'l'aide à la première pièce' in 1947.

The Centre Dramatique de l'Est was established at Colmar in 1946 with Lucien Ducreux as its first director. As the founder of the one notably successful provincial theatre of the inter-war period, the Rideau Gris of Marseilles, Jeanne Laurent decided he was the person most likely to succeed on unknown territory. At the last moment Ducreux was unable to take up the post because of illness. He was replaced by Roland Piétri for the 1946/7 season, who was in turn replaced by André Clavé 1947–52. Piétri, who was also director of the Comédie des Champs Elysées in Paris, had adapted some of his Parisian productions for the Colmar company. Clavé declared his intention of producing a repertoire with a more provincial slant by his opening production: *L'Arlésienne* by Daudet. He remained a director until 1952 and was succeeded by Michel Saint-Denis, the former director of the Compagnie des Quinze and nephew of Copeau. Drawing on his experiences of the Old Vic Theatre School, Saint-Denis established a school and supervised the move of both the company and the school to Strasbourg in 1953. This school rapidly acquired a high reputation and within a decade had become the natural training ground for many of the actors working in the decentralised companies.

Jean Dasté, the director from 1947–70 of the Comédie de Saint Etienne, was also strongly influenced by Copeau, having lived and worked with him in Burgundy after his departure from Paris in 1924, and married his daughter Marie-Hélène. His first attempt at establishing a decentralised company after the war was not at Saint Etienne, but at Grenoble where he was invited by former workers in the cultural wing of the Resistance. A group of these, headed by Georges Blanchon, established a Maison de la Culture in Grenoble with plans for a circulating library, lectures, debates, films, exhibitions – the whole range of cultural life that had been denied them during the Occupation. A key element of the plan was for Dasté to direct a theatre company that would perform at the municipal theatre. Dasté responded eagerly for the plan fitted well with his vision of decentralisation: 'The way theatrical life was breaking away from Paris was all part of the exciting liberation after the war years' (Dasté, 1977: 33). For his first season, 1945/6, he produced Obey's *Noé*, a play originally written for the Compagnie des Quinze, which he took on tour around the region, visiting not only the main towns, but also many smaller towns and village halls. This contrasted with the Centre Dramatique de l'Est's practice which was to play only in the municipal theatres of Colmar, Strasbourg, Mulhouse, Metz and a few other large centres. Dasté's tours were a great success and encouraged Jeanne Laurent to suggest giving his company the status of a Centre Dramatique National. But the mayor and municipality of Grenoble refused to contribute and so, in 1947, the company accepted an invitation from the municipality of Saint Etienne, to become the Comédie de Saint Etienne and the second Centre Dramatique National.

Saint Etienne is a large mining and industrial conurbation south-west of Lyon. Dasté, deeply committed to taking theatre to the working class, immediately felt more at home here than he had in Grenoble. He continued a policy of itinerant theatre, travelling around the region with a single vehicle into which everything had to be fitted: scenery, costumes and props as well as actors (ibid. 34). He was accused of *boyscoutisme* but insisted that this was the only way to reach a new public. In the summer he hired a circus tent so as to be able to perform in public squares and open spaces. His repertoire was similar to that of Copeau: Molière, Shakespeare, Marivaux, Musset, Labiche with adaptations of *Nō* plays and the occasional modern classic. But his aim was more sharply defined as a recovery of popular theatre: 'To rediscover folly, festivity, the fundamental freedom of being' (ibid. 43). In these aims he prefigured the work of the Théâtre du Soleil in the seventies.

Dasté's emphasis on diffusing his work throughout the region impressed Jeanne Laurent and became a model for the three further Dramatic Centres to be established under the Fourth Republic (ibid. 15). These were the Centre Dramatique de l'Ouest, the Grenier de Toulouse and the Comédie de Provence. The first two were both cases of amateur companies turning professional with the combined support of ministry and locality and both were recognised as Centres Dramatiques Nationaux in 1949.

The Centre Dramatique de l'Ouest grew out of the Jeunes Comédiens de Rennes, a group established in 1940 that included Georges Goubert and Guy Parigot, both students at the time. The group continued to perform at Rennes throughout the forties, and travelled to Paris each year to take part in the Concours des Jeunes Compagnies. In 1946 they won second prize and in 1948 the first prize, which helped to persuade them that they should turn professional. Hubert Gignoux, who had inherited Copeau's vision of decentralised theatre through work with Léon Chancerel's Comédiens Routiers in the thirties, was invited to join the company as director. The repertoire of their first season (1949/50) was similar to Dasté's work, relying on Molière and established modern classics. Synge's *Playboy of the western world*, chosen because of the parallels it seemed to offer with life in Brittany, was not a great success with audiences; Hubert Gignoux decided that he would have to concentrate on the classic repertoire to start with, only introducing modern plays gradually.

The Grenier de Toulouse was also formed as a student group, in 1945 under the direction of Maurice Sarrazin. This company also visited Paris for the

Concours des Jeunes Compagnies, where it won the first prize in 1946 for its adaptation of Plautus' *The Carthaginian*. This production achieved such a success that they were able to take it on tour not just in France but abroad, to North Africa and also, helped by Charles Dullin, to Germany. At the same time they continued to produce a repertoire that was similar to those already mentioned, but with rather more emphasis on modern light comedy (e.g. *Am-Stram-Gram* by Roussin and *Les Sourires inutiles* by Achard), that was partly the consequence of a difficult financial situation. When, in 1949, they became a Centre Dramatique, their financial problems were eased and they were able to undertake a more vigorous programme of touring in the south-west.

The last Centre to be established was the Comédie de Provence touring from Aix-en-Provence, whose first season was in 1951/2. This company was the brainchild of Gaston Baty, the last survivor of the Cartel directors, who, after a highly successful career as a Parisian director in turn experienced the impulse to break new ground in the provinces. He died in October 1952 before he had been able to develop this work beyond a triumphant first season, but the company continued to tour from Aix under successive directors until 1968, when it transferred to Marseilles. Baty experienced the same hostility from the municipality that Dasté had found in Grenoble and the company was successfully excluded from the municipal theatre because of opposition from a wealthy local magnate.

By the middle fifties, the five companies were providing theatre performances in about three-quarters of the French *départements*. The influence of the Centres was seen as a shining light spreading outwards through a process described as '*le rayonnement*' (a term commonly used in French to designate the spread of cultural influence). The only areas not covered in this way were the north and central area south of Paris. These deficiencies were remedied in 1953 and 1955 by the founding of the Théâtre Populaire des Flandres and the Théâtre de Bourgogne, though no more Centres were established under the 4th Republic, largely because of the violent opposition to Jeanne Laurent by private theatre managers in Paris opposed to any subsidy of theatre from government funds. The general mood of post-liberation enthusiasm had evaporated, the cold war had taken its place and anything that smacked of socialism became suspect: Jeanne Laurent was removed from her post. Her policies met with opposition, not only from right-wing forces, but also from some progressive directors, such as Planchon, who believed that provincial theatre companies should establish a regular professional activity in one theatre rather than place the accent on touring. As transport and labour became more costly and as more theatre companies became established, touring by the major national companies was to become less common. Jeanne Laurent's achievement was to apply systematically the broad programme of Copeau and the Cartel as set out in Dullin's 1937 reports and to establish the practice of cooperation between central and local bodies.

Jeanne Laurent's last major initiative before losing her post was to install Jean Vilar as director of the Théâtre National Populaire in Paris in 1951. Vilar's attitude in the early fifties helps to show the courage of those who worked in the early Centres Dramatiques, for even he did not believe that a permanent theatre could succeed in the provinces. Instead he believed in the model of regular theatre festivals providing an intense diet for a short period each year. In this belief he had founded the Avignon festival in 1947. The festival had been an instant success, partly because of the brilliance of the actors Vilar could attract in the summer when all Paris theatres were closed, but also because of the new look he achieved in production style.

All performances were given on a large stage erected in the courtyard of the papal palace. No sets were used, though the shape of the stage was altered for each production to gain the maximum impact from patterns of movement. The pace was rapid, the costumes were brilliant, the lighting effects made use of strong contrasts, banners and trumpet fanfares added to the heroic style. This style had been imposed upon Vilar by the necessities of open-air performance, but it turned out to be the key to success in the huge theatre of the Chaillot Palace that was the home of the T.N.P. In the open-air, canvas flats and elaborate drapes are almost impossible to use. Not only do they look strangely artificial, they are liable to be damaged by the damp or blown over by the wind. So design at Avignon was, from the first, concentrated on geometric shapes, stage levels and patterns of movement, combined with rare decorative elements that were at home in the open-air, such as flags and banners. When he moved to Chaillot, Vilar decided that the only way to animate an auditorium of 3,000 was to try to re-create the same atmosphere. Technically it would have been possible to reduce the size of the enormous proscenium arch – this had been anticipated by the architects – but instead Vilar did away with the proscenium arch altogether so that the stage space opened out onto the auditorium with no obvious point of division. Footlights and front curtain were also abolished and a large apron stage was added, covering the whole 18 metre width of the acting space. The background was frequently left empty with nothing but black drapes at the edges, so that the actors, as they stepped into the light, appeared to materialise from a sort of no-man's land. On this type of set, what stood out in sharpest relief was the movements and the relations of the characters one to another; the tensions and connections between people that are at the heart of drama became totally visible. This was increased by extensive and rapid use of movement, filling the whole stage space and making maximum use of the different levels, steps or slopes. This vigorous movement was one of the biggest surprises to the early audiences of *Le Cid* who had come to think of a classic performance as static, not to say statuesque.

What the settings lacked in colour was made up for in the costumes which were often elaborate and designed so as to extract the maximum of suggestive force from colour combinations, types of texture, etc. Props were minimal, but where they were used, acquired considerable importance from their very isolation. Vilar's designer, Léon Gischia, had a semiologist's approach to the use of stage furniture: 'A chair should not be an object but, as it were, the sign of the object' (cit. Bablet, 1975: 300). The whole method placed strong emphasis on the appeal to the audience's imagination. Lights were used in a particularly creative manner in order to summon up a whole atmosphere or location. The forest scene in Act 3 of *Dom Juan*, for example, was conjured up by a dappled light on the stage floor suggesting sunlight filtered through branches.

These were the methods that allowed Vilar to make such an impact with classical productions such as *Le Cid* and *Dom Juan*. He did not attempt radical re-interpretations of the plays, but concentrated on making the text as clear and intelligible as possible. His faithfulness in serving the text is one of the recurring comments of all the critics (in sharp opposition to, say, Planchon, who is frequently accused of wilful distortion). In the case of *Le Cid*, he did not hesitate to present it in a heroic and lyrical manner, doubtless aided by the vigour and charisma of Gérard Philipe, who joined the company for the first time at the Avignon festival in the summer of 1951 and remained with them until his death from cancer in 1959. As Rodrigue, Philipe had one of his greatest successes; he was everything that a *jeune premier* should be: handsome, athletic, free from the rather precious mannerisms that sometimes afflict French actors and he brought with him the glamour of an already successful film career.

Although he lamented the fact that he was unable to produce the more intimate plays of the modern repertoire in the enormous space of Chaillot, Vilar welcomed the suitability of the building for the aims of *théâtre populaire*. The bare functionalism of Chaillot pleased him in contrast to the elaborate social divisions of most nineteenth century theatre buildings: 'The theatre with footlights, proscenium arch, boxes and balconies must disappear if it is not already dead. It does not reunite an audience, it divides them' (Vilar, 1975: 145).

The plan for Vilar's directorate of the T.N.P. was that it should be modelled on the Centres Dramatiques, taking theatre out to the culturally underprivileged Parisian suburbs. A government enquiry in 1951 had concluded that 'the success of the provincial dramatic centres would seem to show that the theatre must go out to the popular public in the workers' suburbs, that it is possible to interest them in either classical or modern works of a high quality' (cit. Gontard, 1973: 319). Vilar planned to achieve this by a series of 'T.N.P. weekends'. These took place in the municipal hall of one of the suburbs of the 'red belt' (so called because of their communist municipalities) and consisted of a complete programme of entertainment with two plays, a dance, a concert and meals for a single price. In this way, he was able to act upon his theory that theatre should be easily available to all: 'a public service in exactly the same way as gas, water or electricity' (Vilar, 1975: 173), while retaining the principle of a festival that united all members of a community and transcended class barriers. The unions provided publicity and support and the weekends proved a success although in the course of the fifties they became less and less frequent. As the cost and difficulty of transporting a production from Chaillot to a town hall escalated, Vilar found that better results could be achieved by using his links with unions to arrange special works outings to regular performances at the theatre.

Vilar's repertoire was more adventurous than that of the early centres: as well as Shakespeare and the French classics, he introduced his audience to the work of the German Romantics, Büchner and Kleist and put on the first large-scale production of a play by Brecht to be done in France since the war. He can thus be distinguished from directors such as Clavé, Gignoux, Dasté, Sarrazin, for whom the priority was to introduce new audiences to the traditional French dramatic repertoire. Vilar's ambition was to stimulate a civic conscience in his audiences. His view of the theatre drew consciously on the tradition of the Ancient Greeks and the Elizabethans, for whom theatre was the natural public forum for the discussion of important public events. This was in many ways a rather didactic approach and Vilar was never afraid to seem like a teacher: 'My purpose, from the very beginning, has been to provide entertainment, or even teaching, for those who are not rich' (Vilar, 1975: 205). In pursuit of this aim, Vilar showed a preference for historical plays debating man's moral and political responsibilities in given social circumstances. The repertoire of the first few seasons included *Le Cid*, *Danton's death*, *Mother Courage*, *The Prince of Homburg*, *Richard II* and a revival of *Murder in the cathedral* which Vilar had produced very successfully in 1945 at the Théâtre du Vieux-Colombier.

Financial constraints meant that Vilar was able to produce very few new plays. His contract with the government obliged him to run the T.N.P. at a profit or to accept personal liability for the loss in just the same way as the manager of a private commercial theatre. His main achievement, in the early years of the T.N.P., was in the field of audience organisation. Through contacts with unions and factories, he arranged for large numbers of workers to make regular visits to his theatre. He was helped in this by a law, promulgated soon after the Liberation, which obliged all businesses and factories over a certain size to form a *comité d'entreprise*. This committee received a percentage of the factory's annual turn-over which it had to spend on the cultural and leisure needs of its work force. Where such committees could be persuaded that the theatre was a worthwhile enterprise for its members, they became a useful source of audience recruitment. Vilar was one of the pioneers in this field and he saw clearly that new audiences would need a new theatre-going ritual. He kept his seat prices low and forbade the worst aspects of the Parisian theatre, such as the wearing of evening dress, the tipping of usherettes and the convention that the play never started until half an hour after the advertised time. Instead of expensive programmes filled with nothing but advertisements, he sold cheap texts of the plays in the repertoire and he also arranged for inexpensive meals to be available before performances. In short, he managed to turn the Chaillot theatre into as near as possible a classless space in which all would feel at home and ready to join in the process of reflection, learning and celebration of common humanity. The experience of a visit to the T.N.P. in the fifties was very uplifting. Audiences came away excited not just by the drama of the performance, but also by the appeal to their intelligence and the manifest belief of Vilar and his company that theatre had an important social role to fill. Young people and students identified especially strongly with the T.N.P., an attitude summed up in the title of the first book to appear on the subject: *Le T.N.P. et nous* (Serrière: 1959).

An atmosphere of uplifting optimism suffused the early efforts of all the directors so far discussed in this chapter. All believed that a revitalised, more relevant vision of theatre's role in society would attract a new, broader based audience and lead to a renewal of French drama in every aspect. To give a voice to these aspirations, a new theatre review was founded in 1953 by Roland Barthes, Guy Dumur and Morvan Lebesque and published by Robert Voisin of L'Arche under the title of *Théâtre Populaire*. It published play texts, articles by practitioners and articles by critics. It gave particular emphasis to the T.N.P., but also covered activities at the five provincial centres and various theatre festivals that were springing up in the regions. Its emphasis is well expressed in an early editorial: 'Theatre is our only living link with the past. Far from being a division of literary history or archeology, it calls into question the totality of man, freeing him from the conditioning to which the different technocratic forms would condemn him.' (*Théâtre Populaire* 2, 1953: 1–2). While not dealing exclusively with the new subsidised theatres, the review hoped to contribute to their search for a new public and their redefinition of popular theatre.

At first the notion of popular theatre was defined, in the pages of *Théâtre Populaire*, by reference to theatres of the past. The first issue contained an article by Duvignaud lamenting the fact that the French theatre had never given birth to tragedy of Shakespearean dimensions; the second carried a piece in which Barthes celebrated the civic dimension of Ancient Greek tragedy and complained that 'The City is almost always absent from our stage (except perhaps in Corneille) . . . our theatre has been diverted from its tragic function by the false [psychological] tragedy of the seventeenth century' (*Théâtre Populaire* 2, 1953: 22). Such definitions, relying on Athens, Medieval Europe or Elizabethan England for models of people's theatre, were not particularly new. They had been referred to by numerous theatre reformers of the twentieth century, not only Copeau and his disciples, but also Firmin Gémier, a tireless campaigner for people's theatre and founder of the T.N.P. in 1920. The result was a general movement or tendency in the theatre known as *le théâtre populaire*, grouping together people who believed in a possible revitalisation of the theatre if it could rediscover a broad mass appeal and relevance to the experience of the modern city-dweller. The turning point in the development of that movement was the visit, in 1954, of the Berliner Ensemble to Paris. By 1954 the first five Centres and the T.N.P. had all proved their value, showing that they could accomplish high quality work and attract large audiences. But their programmes relied almost entirely on works from the past. The need was widely felt for a modern repertoire that could handle large moral and political themes with the ease of the Ancient Greek or Elizabethan theatres. In the production of *Mother Courage* by the Berliner Ensemble, the *théâtre populaire* movement caught a first glimpse of the modern repertoire it had been seeking.

The first tremors of this discovery can be seen in the article by Barthes on

Mother Courage in *Théâtre Populaire* 8, July–August 1954. He spoke of having been dazzled and overwhelmed by the maturity and complexity of a theatre practice that answered all the questions posed by himself and his colleagues. Six months later the review took on a change of direction with an issue (no. 11) almost entirely devoted to Brecht, including the first publication in French of his *Short organum for the theatre*. From this point until its demise in 1963, *Théâtre Populaire* devoted itself to the elaboration of a Marxist theory of theatre practice, based on the model provided by Brecht, and to trying to stimulate the development of a similar theatre practice in France. The influence of Brecht was slow to take effect, but when it did so it was overwhelming, reaching its height in the middle sixties when no theatre company in the public sector was considered to have made its mark until it had performed 'its' Brecht.

One reason for the enormous impact of Brecht's work on men of the theatre in France was that it had been almost unknown before 1954. The only major production had been Vilar's *Mother Courage* in 1951 but his production had disguised rather than revealed Brecht's originality. Instead of presenting Mother Courage as someone who never understands how she creates her own tragedy, Vilar seized upon those elements in her make-up that suggest a tough popular heroine who survives all disasters. She became a positive character and the play became a chronicle of her indomitable optimism in the face of suffering and deprivation. Vilar's production style was diametrically opposed to Brecht's. Where Vilar's stage was austere and his production stressed heroism, passion, self-sacrifice, Brecht's stage was filled with a profusion of carefully observed detail and his production laid the stress on reason and causality rather than on passion. The Berliner Ensemble production was given in German and the foreign language doubtless also helped to focus the audience's attention on acting and production technique, the clarity and gestural quality of which were highly praised.

It quickly became apparent that the Brechtian style would not transfer easily to the French stage. The problem as expressed by Barthes and Dort was that the theatre practice of the Berliner Ensemble was essential to a full understanding of Brecht's plays. His work, as Barthes quickly saw, opened out immediately on to problems of semiology, because as well as the textual writing, it involved *stage* writing (i.e. the design of setting and action so as to convey autonomous meanings independent of the text – see p. 107). Barthes later expressed this particular quality in Brecht's work by calling him 'a Marxist who has reflected on the function of signs: quite a rarity' (1971: 95). Brecht was alive to semiological as well as to verbal communication, to the function of the gesture as much as the speech, and so his plays are only fully realised in a language whose every element (every object, every movement) is significant. To produce the play is thus to explicate it: in Dort's words, the production is a *reading*, and this was why the performances of the Berliner Ensemble made such an impression of clarity and intelligibility.

The production of these plays is, properly speaking, their *realisation*. Written and planned specifically for the stage, with the intention of arousing a particular relation between that stage and the public, his work only achieves its true existence in the theatre

– but in the theatre it can equally well be compromised, its meaning obliterated or completely falsified. By its very structure, Brecht's dramaturgy is *unstable* like certain chemical compounds which, in given conditions, are in danger of *transmutation*, producing a reaction which is the opposite of what was expected (Dort, 1967: 228).

Dort stressed the fact that Brecht's was the opposite of 'poor theatre': in order to demonstrate the poverty of Mother Courage, a great richness of signs was employed and this meant high production expenses. Theatres like the T.N.P., or the Comédie de Saint Etienne, which did the first French performance of *The Caucasian chalk circle* in 1956, did not have the money to match the work of the Berliner Ensemble. More important, perhaps, they identified with the traditions of austerity associated with Copeau and the Cartel. In such plays as *Mother Courage* and *The Caucasian chalk circle* it is not simply the actions of the characters that are important, but the actions of the characters in response to their changing circumstances. For this reason, great weight must be given to the depiction of these circumstances so that the contradictions of the characters emerge clearly. For example, when Anna Fierling is urged by her daughter to sacrifice shirts to bandage soldiers' wounds, we must understand that she cannot afford to be kind-hearted or she will lose the trade that is her precarious means of livelihood. In the productions by Vilar and Dasté, the elements against which Anna Fierling or Grusha have to struggle were not presented in sufficient detail and as a result the plays lost their dialectical quality. The 'transmutation' occurred: Anna became a heroine instead of a blind dupe and Grusha became a natural mother instead of someone who learned motherliness by hard work and education in the ways of the world.

Such difficulties, combined with the lack of translations, meant that productions of Brecht's plays were slow in coming to the French stage. Dasté's *Caucasian chalk circle* was the most influential production of the fifties. For Dasté, the attraction of Brecht lay not so much in his politics as in his vigorous deployment of elements of folk literature; he described him as '*the* popular dramatic poet of our time' (cit. Hüfner, 1968: 112). His production extended Brecht's use of masks, played up the humorous aspects of Azdak's scenes at the expense of their didactic function, and generally stressed the folk-tale quality of the play (see fig. 5). It was well received by audiences and was revived in 1960. Other productions of the fifties included *The good woman of Setzuan* and *Fear and misery of the Third Reich* by Planchon (see following chapter) *Mother Carrar's rifles* by Cyril Robichez at the Théâtre Populaire des Flandres and *The exception and the rule* by André Steiger at Bellac, for which his company was disbanded by the mayor on the grounds that they were a subversive influence.

But the sixties brought a wave of Brecht productions to the decentralised theatres. L'Arche rapidly brought out translations of his plays and other writings and *Théâtre Populaire* published Benjamin's commentaries. A list compiled by *Atac Informations* of all the plays performed in decentralised theatres between 1947 and 1972 shows Brecht in third place after Molière and

5   *The Caucasian chalk circle* (Brecht): Jean Dasté in the role of Azdak (centre) in the 1956 production at the Comédie de Saint Etienne, directed by John Blatchley and Jean Dasté.

Shakespeare. Forty-eight separate productions had been mounted, all but four since the beginning of the sixties. Such a massive concentration of effort on a single contemporary author was bound to exert an influence on every aspect of decentralised theatre, not only on acting, directing and stage design, but also on new writing in French. It is thus important to understand the principles of Brechtian dramaturgy and the aspects of it that seemed particularly important to French theatre workers and critics. The enormous impact of Brecht can chiefly be explained by the fact that the discovery of his theatre practice extended beyond his own work to a whole tradition of theatre going back to the Elizabethans, a tradition that is periodically 'discovered' in France and then rapidly forgotten again.

This tradition was defined by Brecht himself when explaining what he meant by 'Epic' theatre: 'The line that seems to lead to certain attempts of the Epic theatre runs from the Elizabethan drama via Lenz, early Schiller, Goethe (*Götz* and both parts of *Faust*), Grabbe, Büchner. It is a very strong line, easily followed' (cit. Willett, 1967: 105). As we have seen, Vilar had already been turning to works in this tradition, albeit with a rather more romantic emphasis, and so to some extent the climate was ready for Brecht's own Epic theatre. It is perhaps difficult for British readers, reared on Shakespeare, to understand the scale of mental re-adjustment required of the French if they were to assimilate Epic theatre. In France the theatre has almost always acknowledged the classical canons derived from Aristotle. For Brecht, Epic theatre stood in direct contrast to Aristotelian theatre. By Aristotelian theatre, he meant not just classical plays conforming to Aristotle's rules, but the whole 'ranting and pretentious German classical stage', of his time, where 'noisy declamation tries to blanket the emotions of the character with the emotion of the actor' (cit. Willett, 1967: 165). These descriptions by Brecht of over-emphatic acting would have been equally applicable to the French theatre of the forties and fifties, where noisy declamation and forced emotional tones were only too common. In place of such emotional self-indulgence, Brecht proposed *Epic* theatre.

Epic theatre has been defined in various ways, both by Brecht himself and his commentators. It is a somewhat elastic term, part of its usefulness lying in the recognition that something as elusive as a theatre performance cannot easily be tied down by precise formulae. The essential qualities of Epic theatre can, nevertheless, be set down clearly enough. All have their roots in the relationship that is established between an actor and his audience. The Epic actor's job is not to bewitch the spectator, to plunge him so deeply into a tale of passionate emotion that he follows the performance like a somnambulist, hardly aware of himself, his surroundings, or the art that has gone into creating the illusion that absorbs him. Instead, the Brechtian actor aims to show the spectator how a particular action came about, and in doing so he maintains the same respect for the spectator's freedom of judgement as he would if he were recounting the details of a road accident he had witnessed to an impartial bystander. The various techniques employed in Epic theatre are all designed to facilitate this new relationship. 'The task of Epic theatre, Brecht believes, is not so much to develop actions as to represent conditions' (Benjamin, 1973: 18). From this basic task follow the peculiar features of Brechtian dramaturgy: its method of story-telling, its untragic heroes, its use of alienation and interruption, its didactic and gestural qualities.

Brecht's understanding of how to 'represent conditions' was very different from anything in practice on the French stage of the fifties, distancing itself from both classicism and Naturalism. First, it involved taking a story that was not sensational or novel. Most of Brecht's own plays employ folk tales or historical characters. Secondly this story was not told in order to stress the psychological dilemma of its protagonist. Classical French drama relies so heavily on brilliant 'case-studies', in the pattern of Racine's *Phèdre*, that it has always been hard for French critics to see the value of a play in which the main force of the drama derives from anything other than the heroic individual's experience of anguish. Brecht's characters are untragic: they are carefully presented so as to arouse as little terror and pity as possible. Instead they provoke a response of sympathy, interest, even surprise. The spectators understand the characters' dilemmas, sympathise with their difficulties and are surprised to find that the hero's situation closely resembles their own. They do not identify with the hero so as to forget about themselves; instead they consider him with emotion and sympathy but also with reason and judgement, as they would a friend asking for advice about how to cope with difficult circumstances.

Using these kinds of story and character, Epic plays aim to represent familiar conditions in a new light: they have to be revealed in such a way as to seem strange and surprising. This is achieved by a variety of alienation effects (*Verfremdungseffekte*), the most important of which is the device of interruption. 'Take the crudest example: a family row. Suddenly a stranger comes into the room. The wife is just about to pick up a bronze statuette and throw it at the daughter. The father is opening the window to call a policeman. At this moment the stranger appears at the door. "Tableau", as they used to say around 1900' (Benjamin, 1973: 18–19). Instead of developing the family row to its exciting climax, the Epic dramatist or director interrupts the movement of passion to reveal the conditions through the eyes of a stranger. What had been merely a private drama becomes a public event and hence its nature alters. The imitation of real life on stage should never become an end in itself, argues the Epic dramatist. The demand of audiences for something that 'seems real' often becomes a demand for blinkers, an insistence on limiting our view of an event to one viewpoint only. When the scene is interrupted our single vision or identification is broken: we lose the dreamy pleasure of the somnambulist but gain the maturer pleasure of a multiple viewpoint, seeing the event through the eyes of several different characters.

To interrupt the story of the play in this way is to introduce an element of self-conscious artifice very similar to that associated with the Modernist writing of novelists like Joyce and it was this self-conscious quality that attracted the displeasure of Lukács and led to Brecht's condemnation as a 'formalist' for many years in Eastern Europe. But Benjamin saw this self-consciousness as one of the most productive aspects of Epic theatre and this is the way it has struck many French writers and directors.

The naturalistic stage is in no sense a public platform; it is entirely illusionistic. Its own awareness that it is theatre cannot fertilise it; like every theatre of unfolding action, it must repress this awareness so as to pursue undistracted its aim of portraying the real. Epic theatre, by contrast, incessantly derives a lively and productive consciousness from the fact that it is theatre. This consciousness enables it to treat elements of reality as though it were setting up an experiment, with the 'conditions' at the end of the experiment, not at the beginning. Thus they are not brought closer to the spectator but distanced from him. When he recognises them as real conditions it is not, as in naturalistic theatre, with complacency, but with astonishment (Benjamin, 1973: 4).

The artful revelation of real conditions described above is achieved in Epic theatre by a reliance on gesture as much as on word, and on contradiction more than on smooth progression. Brecht used gesture or 'gestus' to mean both the fundamental attitude or point of a story or relationship and also the concrete, material expression of that attitude. Words *and* actions together could be used gesturally, so that emphasis on gesture did not necessarily mean a scorn for text. But the gestural emphasis involves the actor externalising all feelings, and so in Epic theatre the words cease to be the privileged central location of a character's 'true' feelings. Sometimes the purpose of gesture is, in fact, to undermine and contradict the words spoken by the character. In a number of Brecht's plays, particularly *A man's a man*, the characters are not written as consistent, unified personalities but as a string of contradictory impulses moving abruptly from one attitude to its opposite. Each separate moment must be appreciated in and for itself, a concept difficult to grasp for minds brought up to think that the essence of playwriting is to knot up a crisis and then unknot it with a skilful *dénouement*. In Epic dramaturgy it is the *déroulement* (process) rather than the *dénouement* that is important (see Demarcy, 1973: 282).

In some ways this conception of character was not excessively strange to those familiar with the New Theatre and it is perhaps not surprising that the first production of a Brecht play after the war had been *The exception and the rule* in 1947 by Jean-Marie Serreau, a director shortly to become famous for his productions of Adamov, Ionesco and Beckett. But it was very alien to the more traditional French stage, where the character (*le personnage*) was sacrosanct and the very word for a speech, *une tirade*, implied almost a piece of recitation for which an actor would take up a fixed position. The new acting and decorative style required by Brecht's more concrete dramaturgy was not available in early productions such as Vilar's *Mother Courage* or Dasté's *Caucasian chalk circle*, as we have seen. It took about ten years for French actors and designers to discover how to meet this challenge (see next chapter).

In the long term, the influence of Brecht's Epic theatre filtered through to have its effect, not just on acting and staging in France but on playwriting as well. This influence is found almost exclusively in the decentralised and 'popular' theatres and so it is interesting to see that Brecht's underlying aim was always to communicate with a popular audience (see Bradby & McCormick, 1978: 116–17). He was a great admirer of Luther's style, trying, like him, to capture the rhythms of popular speech, its gestural qualities and its absence of smooth transitions from one thing to another. In answer to a question about how to treat the rhythm when speaking the verse of his *Antigone*, Brecht answered: 'By applying the syncopation common to jazz. This brings an element of contradiction into the flow of the verse, and allows the regular to prevail against the irregular' (cit. Willett, 1967: 101). This whole emphasis on dialectical, gestural language that did not move smoothly with elegant syntax, but progressed abruptly by leaps and bounds was the very antithesis of what was normally accepted as good writing in France and thus pointed to a whole new territory that had not been explored by French dramatists. We shall be examining examples of the writers who attempted to follow him, writers like Adamov, Planchon, Vinaver, in chapters 6, 7, 9 and 10.

Because Epic theatre was so unlike the accepted dramaturgical forms familiar in France during the fifties, it was some time before an appropriate critical vocabulary was available to discuss it. This accounts both for the delay in Brecht's own plays being appreciated and also for the relative slowness with which Epic plays began to be written in France. Even as late as 1981 Jean-Pierre Sarrazac, writing about the dramatists of the seventies, still found it necessary to devote his first twenty pages to demonstrating that the traditional Aristotelian criteria of the unities cannot be applied to Epic plays. French artistic life is perhaps more dominated by orthodoxies than is common in other countries. For Epic theatre to be a form that was taken seriously, a new orthodoxy had to be established. This achievement, largely the work of Bernard Dort and the *Théâtre Populaire* team was not without its drawbacks. In order to preserve Brecht's work from incompetent productions in the uncomprehending climate of French theatre they exerted a tight control on all would-be directors. They were able to do this because Robert Voisin, as publisher of Brecht's plays in French translation, had also acquired rights over performances in French. When Dasté did the first French production of the *Caucasian chalk circle*, he was subjected to an examination of his methods and motives by Voisin, Barthes, Dort, Dumur and others associated with *Théâtre Populaire*, and only public pressure persuaded Voisin to lift a ban on performances (see Dasté, 1977: 47–9). This kind of attempt to exert control produced an atmosphere of the witch hunt and soured relations between the supporters and detractors of political theatre for more than a decade. It was satirised by Ionesco in his *Impromptu de l'Alma* and denounced by Planchon in an article entitled 'Orthodoxies' published in 1962 (see following chapter).

In the long term it was the actors, directors, and designers of the decentralisation who, by their persistence, imposed a taste for Brecht on the French public. For many of them, the discovery of Brecht was experienced as a sort of liberation. For the first ten years after the war, as we have seen, to work in this sector of the theatre meant to coax new audiences into seeing that the great peaks of the French repertoire were not simply academic texts for the classroom, but could come to life on the stage if given the right treatment. In Brecht, they discovered not only a modern popular author who spoke in a gritty, twentieth century voice about matters that interested the people, they discovered also an alternative tradition of plays going back to Shakespeare, whose principles of construction seemed far more 'modern' than those of the French classics. Instead of an emphasis on unity, they found a drama of contrasts and rapid changes; instead of a small cast of aristocrats, they discovered a cross-section of people drawn from all classes of society. Even more liberating was the discovery that the French classics, too, could be produced in a manner that approximated to the methods of Epic theatre. The first director to work in this way was Roger Planchon, who will be assessed in the next chapter.

Apart from Planchon's theatre, Brecht's influence showed only a slow encroachment for the remainder of the fifties. The only productions of his plays were *Mother Courage* by the Grenier de Toulouse in 1959 and *The resistible rise of Arturo Ui* by Jean Vilar at the T.N.P. in 1960. The production of *Mother Courage* was by Jacques Mauclair, who had made his name in the New Theatre and who used Maurice Sarrazin's invitation to direct the play as an opportunity to school himself in Brecht's work and methods. He stated that he had tried to follow the *Modellbuch* faithfully, although the restricted means and small stage of the Grenier made this a difficult task. The production met with some success but did not receive comment in the national press (see Hüfner 1968: 124–5).

Vilar's production of *The resistible rise of Arturo Ui*, with himself in the title role, showed a considerable change of emphasis from his *Mother Courage* in 1951. Writing of the earlier production, Dort noted that 'pathos triumphed over statement; we were shown not an action but a passion' (1967: 234). With *Ui*, Vilar was making a clear public statement. 1960 was the year of the signing of the Manifeste des 121 against the war in Algeria and the establishment of Salan's fascist O.A.S. (Organisation de l'armée secrète). For a time it looked as though de Gaulle might countenance a take-over in Algeria by the right wing of the army, determined to maintain 'l'Algérie Française'. In these circumstances Vilar's choice of Brecht's play was pointed, and he reinforced the point by declaring to the press: 'I am showing you not Hitler but the fascism of yesterday, today and tomorrow. I am showing the danger which concerns us every day' (*France–Observateur*, 10 November 1960). But although the general statement was clear enough, the production style did little to give it concrete contemporary relevance. The setting was spare and generalised, in the T.N.P. tradition, with extensive use of lighting to create atmosphere, and the result was to give the message a general, even a universal significance. In the same year, the Berliner Ensemble made a third visit to Paris with their production of the same play which was full of circumstantial details clearly locating the play in the historical circumstances of Weimar Germany.

In 1963 Jean Vilar resigned as director of the T.N.P. His relations with de Gaulle's government had become progressively more strained and he wished to devote himself full-time to the ever-expanding Avignon festival. In a sense, also, he had achieved what he could at Chaillot. The heroic period was over: the great peaks of the classic repertoire had been reconquered and heroism was out of fashion. Furthermore, Vilar had failed in one of his most cherished ambitions, which was to stage the work of new playwrights. He had made an attempt in the first T.N.P. season, with *Nucléa* by Pichette and *La Nouvelle Mandragore* by Vauthier, but both had failed disastrously at the box-office. He had concluded that new work could not be presented in a theatre of the size and scale of Chaillot and his next venture had been in the 1959/60 season, when he hired the Récamier theatre for a special season of new plays. There were guest productions of plays by Beckett, Pinget, Vian, Obaldia, Brecht, and Vilar himself directed the first production of a play by Armand Gatti (see chapter 7), but this season, too, was a financial failure and the frustration he experienced may have influenced his decision to resign soon afterwards.

In his last years at the T.N.P., Vilar seems to have made up for his inability to produce modern plays by choosing his repertoire for the comment it was able to make on contemporary political events. Certainly the critics interpreted his productions as political allegories. *Antigone* was seen as a comment on the trial of the Réseau Jeanson – a group of intellectuals who had organised an underground support system for the Algerian Liberation Front. Antigone's revolt was presented, not as a mystical self-fulfilment in the style of Anouilh, but as the only logical response to tyranny. *The Mayor of Zalamea*, a play about whether the normal demands of justice can be suspended for generals in time of war, coincided with the acquittal of three officers convicted of having tortured a young Algerian woman to death. Perhaps the most obviously political of Vilar's productions in this period was Aristophanes' *Peace*, a straightforward condemnation of the tendency to deify a strong leader at times of national crisis. The production was clearly aimed at de Gaulle, and this particularly enraged the pro-Catholic press, which had been using terms like *présence divine* to describe the general. Jean-Jacques Gautier, the influential theatre critic of *Le Figaro*, came out with the statement that Vilar should be prevented from doing such work in a subsidised theatre, and Mauriac wrote a particularly poisonous article to the same effect. Vilar accepted this challenge and replied that he considered it his duty to put on plays like *Peace* at that time. In 1951 his duty had been to perform *Le Cid* for audiences who had no conception of what French theatre represented. In 1961 his duty was to do everything in his power in favour of a peaceful settlement of the Algerian war.

In retrospect, his achievement is that of an *animateur* as much as that of a director: he had an extraordinary gift for stimulating a demand for theatre where none existed before. Not only did he establish the first and most successful of all the summer festivals; he also created a demand for theatre in the workers' suburbs around Paris with the result that there are today more than a dozen fixed theatres operating in the 'red belt' and many additional cultural centres in which plays are frequently performed. He also established a pattern later followed by many other decentralised theatres by forming an association of audience members, publishing a regular news-sheet for them entitled *Bref*, and supervising other associated publishing such as the texts of the plays and a series on directors entitled *Le Théâtre et les jours*.

The strength of Vilar was in his utopian vision of the theatre for all and the patient intelligence which he brought to the realisation of this vision. In the first ten years after the war, his contribution to revitalising the theatre, especially in the Parisian region, was tremendous. His insistence that theatre had a noble function – that of providing a space where order could triumph over chaos and human beings could unite in the getting of wisdom – was the strongest link with the moral seriousness of Copeau, helping to promote a conception of theatre that became a solid foundation for the expansionist policies of the sixties. Vilar preferred to see himself as the heir of Gémier, the founder of the T.N.P. Like Gémier, he had spent time with touring theatre and open-air theatre. Just as Gémier had spoken of people's theatre as a civil religion, Vilar expressed the desire to establish a bond of communion and common celebration in his audience. Those who have written about the first twenty years of the Avignon festival have had recourse to the language of mysticism – the sacred, the liturgical, the celebratory and the ritual – in order to describe the experience. For the first generation of workers in this field he became the standard-bearer in the struggle for people's theatre and, as a figure of national prestige, a moral support to all those in the decentralised theatre who were working to give concrete meaning to the concept of *le théâtre populaire*.

The Resistance, as we saw in chapter 2, had acted as a most powerful force for unity and cultural democracy. Vilar's rather euphoric declarations of his desire to unite his public and make them forget their social differences in the enjoyment of high art is quite logical within this perspective. But in the sixties, and especially after 1968, this came to be seen as a contradiction – either a contradiction to be accepted as it was by Planchon, or to be rejected, in the style of Benedetto, who hardly performed any plays from the accepted repertoire. After Vilar's departure from the T.N.P., those interested in political theatre began to ask whether its task *should* be to unite its audience. Perhaps, they suggested, an effective political theatre should not unite but divide its audience, and if unity was not possible at a political level, because of the state of class war, then it should not be the aim of the theatre, where it could only play into the hands of the ruling powers. These questions were to become the preoccupation of the second generation of *théâtre populaire* workers, beginning mostly in the sixties.

6
The decentralised theatre II: Planchon and Adamov

When Barthes described Brecht as 'a Marxist who has reflected on the function of signs: quite a rarity', he might have been expressing just what it was that Planchon had found so exciting about Brecht (Barthes, 1971: 95). Planchon's interest in Brecht could be expressed differently by saying that it was founded on the combination in Brecht's work of two apparently contradictory qualities. One was Brecht's concern for concrete, material detail, his repeated insistence that 'truth is concrete'. The other was Brecht's equally vehement anti-naturalism and his opposition to illusionistic theatre because of the way it generates sympathy rather than surprise. Like Brecht, Planchon has struggled to create theatre that respects the concrete texture of lived human experience but also seeks to surprise its audience, not presenting them with familiar images but discovering new signs and meanings in performance.

Planchon is the most successful and most influential representative of the new social and historical theatre which has established itself in France since the fifties. It is a theatre that borrows little from the inter-war Cartel or from the New Theatre of the fifties. It identifies much more with an older tradition, going back through Brecht and Büchner to the Elizabethans, of a theatre combining a fluid, epic style with a broad range of reference, at once personal, social and historical. While it may employ grotesque techniques, these are more likely to be influenced by Jarry than by Beckett. But as well as the influences already mentioned, it is a theatre profoundly marked by the influence of Artaud. The one point Brecht and Artaud had in common was their interest in the theatre of the Far East. Planchon was the first of the many directors and playwrights we shall discuss to have taken an interest in Japanese theatre because of its elaborate gestural language, owing nothing to illusionism but converting everything into specifically theatrical signs.

Planchon was attracted by Artaud long before he had discovered Brecht. As a very young man immediately after the war, even before he had decided to form a theatre group, Planchon haunted the literary cafés of Lyon, reciting Rimbaud and Michaux and discovering piecemeal the work of Artaud, Bataille and Genet. A part-time job at the Westminster Foreign Bank provided him with enough to live on while he explored the worlds of poetry and theatre. He did not come from the educated classes. His father, who ran a café, had grown up on a peasant farm in the Ardèche where his grandparents still lived. He was educated by the Christian Brothers, who sensed his exceptional qualities, and one of his teachers, when it became clear that he had no academic vocation, encouraged his interest in modern poetry and the cinema. Coming from this background the discovery of 'poètes maudits' such as Rimbaud and Artaud was a revelation that marked him deeply. The influence of Artaud can be seen particularly clearly in the tortured protagonists of Planchon's own plays.

His other major interest was the cinema. He went as often as he could to see whatever was available. In the late forties American films were once again available in France after a gap of five years. The effect of seeing the big Hollywood spectacular song and dance films was to give the young Planchon a taste for fast moving musical entertainment. But he also took an interest in other kinds of film and in film theory as well. He followed the work of *Les Cahiers du Cinéma* from its 'first appearance in 1951, becoming aware of semiological approaches to performance well before semiology became fashionable in academic circles. He adopted a famous aphorism of the *Cahiers*: 'tout travelling est un problème de morale' (every travelling shot involves a moral problematic) and made it his own, transferring it into stage terms and claiming that every production entailed a similarly global responsibility on the part of director and actors (Copfermann, 1977: 161). Unlike Barrault, he does not believe that it is possible to be a mere servant of the play, but insists that the act of production is itself an act of criticism.

His career in the theatre began in 1950 when he put on a burlesque show entitled *Bottines, collets montés* with a group of friends. This consisted of a collage of scenes from Courteline and Labiche produced in such a way as to comment on a variety of comic traditions: American burlesque films, the French mime tradition (at that time being vigorously revived by Barrault, Marceau, Lecoq etc.), the Surrealist humour of Jarry and Vitrac and the popular comic verse of groups like the Frères Jacques with their roots in music hall. The play won a prize of 25,000 francs for the group in a local amateur theatre competition and became the first of many burlesque productions, being followed by *Rocambole* in 1952, *Les Trois Mousquetaires* in 1957 and many others. With the prize money, the group established itself as a small semi-professional company called Le Théâtre de la Comédie. They went on to perform Marlowe's *Dr Faustus*, and *Hamlet* adapted from an eighteenth century German text attributed to Kyd with inserted texts by Rimbaud and dedicated to the memory of Antonin Artaud.

In 1952 the company moved into a disused printing works in the centre of Lyon where they built a small auditorium of 110 seats. This remained their home until 1957 when they moved into the large municipal theatre at Villeurbanne. From 1952 onwards they were determined to work as a professional theatre, performing throughout the week, even though this brought enormous financial difficulties and members of the company were often obliged to take extra daytime jobs. They succeeded in this ambition, which made them the only permanent producing theatre company existing outside Paris apart from the five newly established Centres Dramatiques.

The theatre's repertoire during this period included more work from the Elizabethans, *Twelfth night* (1951), *The merry wives of Windsor* (1952), Marlowe's *Edward II* (1954) and two plays by Calderón, *Life is a dream* (1952) and *The Mayor of Zalamea* (1955). But they did not confine themselves to burlesques and the classics. They also put on an impressive number of new plays. These included the work of the New Theatre, Ionesco's *Amédée* (1955), *La Leçon* and *Victimes du devoir* (1956), as well as Adamov's *Le Sens de la marche* and *Le Professeur Taranne* (1953). The encounter with Adamov was particularly significant, since Planchon discovered that the older playwright shared his admiration for Artaud and his attitude towards the traditions of Elizabethan theatre. Adamov was impressed with the quality of the company's work and wrote versions of Kleist's *Broken jug* and Marlowe's *Edward II* for them in 1954.

1954 was the year of the Berliner Ensemble's first visit to Paris with *Mother Courage*. Planchon did not see the production because he was at the very same time engaged on the French première of Brecht's *The good woman of Setzuan*. They returned a year later and Planchon went to see them: 'I presented myself to Brecht with my production photographs of *The good woman* as my only recommendation. I spent five hours with him. He told me what he liked and what he didn't in our work, and we discussed it. From this interview, and from the productions of the Berliner Ensemble, I was seized with the conviction that here was truth and that I should not hesitate to copy boldly' (cit. Bataillon, 1982).

Brecht had just completed an adaptation of Molière's *Dom Juan* and the discussion turned on the uses of the classics in the modern theatre, especially of Molière, Shakespeare, Lenz. For several years after this meeting, Planchon's work became a sort of dialogue with Brecht the author, Brecht the theoretician and, above all, Brecht the director. Discussing the work of Brecht with Adamov and Allio in 1962, Planchon explained what he had learned from Brecht in the following terms:

The lesson of Brecht is to have declared that a performance combines both dramatic writing and scenic writing; but the scenic writing – he was the first to say this and it seems to me to be very important – has an *equal responsibility* with the dramatic writing. In fact any movement on the stage, the choice of a colour, a set, a costume, etc., involves a total responsibility. The scenic writing has a total responsibility in the same way as writing taken on its own: I mean the writing of a novel or a play (Adamov, 1964: 214).

Planchon's response to this lesson was characteristic of his peculiar mixture of humility and self-confidence. He decided that the only sensible thing to do, in the face of such mastery of stage language, was to work an apprenticeship: to copy the master perfectly so that one day he would be able to better him. Accordingly, he did a fresh production of *The good woman* in 1958, attempting to follow exactly the Berliner Ensemble's production and described his work as a 'modest copy'. He also produced *Fear and misery of the Third Reich* (1956) and *Schweyk in the Second World War* (1961). But the impact of Brecht is most clearly visible in his adaptations of the classics, especially *George Dandin* (1958) and Shakespeare's *Henry IV* (1957), and his approach to new writing such as Adamov's *Paolo Paoli* (1957).

Planchon was not as overwhelmed by Brecht as has sometimes been thought.

In 1956, when the influence of Brecht was at its strongest, he produced *Aujourd'hui ou les Coréens*, the first play by a young author, Michel Vinaver. This play, about the experience of a group of young soldiers in Korea who lose their platoon and discover an 'enemy' just like themselves, does not resemble a Brechtian parable. It presents a real encounter between real people, for which the propaganda of war cannot account. Planchon provided a scenic image of the immediacy of the experience by covering his stage with sand and planting it with a forest of rushes and bushes. The play impressed even the Parisian critics by means of its very physical acting style, realistic sound effects and palpable materials. For the first time, Planchon's work received notice in the national press and attracted interest from people outside the region.

Adamov states in his autobiography that it was a visit to *Les Coréens* that made him decide to give *Paolo Paoli* to Planchon rather than to a Parisian theatre. (Vilar had wanted to produce the play at Chaillot and decided against it on the grounds that it required a smaller theatre.) In fact Adamov had maintained close contact with Planchon since 1953. During this period Planchon was clearly influenced by Adamov. In 1970 he recalled the excitement of hearing him talk: 'Why did we never film or tape-record those hours together? Kafka, Büchner were there, brought to life for us on the edge of the void' (1970: 5). The years of their collaboration (1953–60) coincided with the years when both were most deeply influenced by Brecht and it is clear that the way each of them responded to Brecht was influenced by the same process in the other. Planchon could see in Adamov an insistence on defending the place of the oneirical as well as the political realities of life: Adamov learned from Planchon the importance of scenic writing as well as of dialogue writing.

Paolo Paoli, heralded by the critics of *Théâtre Populaire* as the first truly Brechtian play to be written in France, was the product of this shared development. *Paolo Paoli* is a play about feathers, butterflies and buttons. But this lightweight subject-matter is used to give an account of the origins of the First World War in France. The starting point for the play occurred to Adamov when he was 'ghosting' the memoirs of a famous entomologist. This man had built up a profitable trade in rare South American butterflies using convicts escaped from the hulks at Cayenne as cheap labour to hunt for new specimens. Adamov found himself 'seduced by this image, at once burlesque and tragic, of the convict armed with a butterfly net' (1964: 47). The two principal characters of the play are Paolo Paoli, a butterfly trader, and Hulot-Vasseur, a feather industrialist. Behind the apparent frivolity and insignificance of the feather business, Adamov discovered the startling fact that for most of *la belle époque* feather products had great economic significance, forming the fourth largest of France's exports. Starting with familiar images of luxury and frivolity, Adamov constructed a play about the cycle of trade in a capitalist system. The plot shows all the relationships in Paolo's small circle of friends progressively dominated by commercial considerations. At first only objects change hands but soon wife and mistress, servant and worker are bargained and exchanged. The plot becomes a frenzied spiral of self-interest through which Adamov examines the conflicts characteristic of a capitalist society, in which people lose the ability to live for anything but objects, and their moral values become synonymous with trade values.

The force of the play lies in its humour. This grew from the techniques employed in Adamov's earlier plays (see chapter 4) and relied on a particular application of derision, as Barthes pointed out: 'the disproportion between the subject and the use to which it is put in the play, between the general objects of capitalist conflicts and the world of butterflies and feathers' (Adamov, 1964: 76). This humour had been a feature of, for example, *Le Ping-Pong*, in which two men devote their whole lives to the improvement of an electric pin-table. But in that play the pin-table was symbolic: it stood for the whole world of capitalism. In *Paolo Paoli* the objects had a real commercial value and were not treated symbolically but set in their real historical context. For the first time in writing this play, Adamov had recourse to documentary research, a method that he was to use in most of his subsequent plays. He explained that he found, in historical reality, 'a poetry so extraordinary that any strictly personal invention seems feeble by comparison' (ibid. 66). Poetry, for Adamov, meant words and images that are 'at a crossroads of meaning' (1955: 14), so that they have a different impact or significance at different levels. The most effective dramatic technique, he believed, was one which combined events of a fantastic quality with hard historical realities, switching his audience's minds from one to the other by means of the humour of disproportion. In this way a theatrical transposition could be achieved that was far more effective than simple documentary drama. So in *Paolo Paoli* he held up to ridicule, not the grand manoeuvres of the imperialist powers, but the sordid circuit of barter in the feather and butterfly trades: 'the motive force of a useless trade being the same as that of a useful one, the commercial operation appears in its true light, unmasked' (Adamov, 1964: 58).

If this unmasking was not to appear schematic or facile, Adamov's play had to present credible characters with sufficient complexity for the links between their private lives and the public events of the period not to seem strained. His skill in achieving this was particularly admired by Martin Esslin: 'The characters are most ingeniously chosen to represent a whole microcosm of the political, religious, national and social forces involved in the origins of the First World War. Adamov's brilliance as a dramatist is shown by the astonishing ingenuity with which he has condensed all this – and extremely convincingly – into a cast of only seven characters' (Esslin, 1980: 118). Each character is defined by social situation and by bargaining power vis-à-vis each of the others. But even more importantly, they are defined by their language. The play presents a fascinating study in rhetoric as each character attempts to deceive or fascinate the other. This very use of language becomes a comment on the public life of *la belle époque*, since it betrays a constant disproportion, or even contradiction, between words evoking eternal values and actions motivated by immediate self-interest.

The denunciation of the rhetoric of false idealism is something that Adamov had learned from Brecht and he expressed his debt on many occasions (e.g. Adamov, 1964: 216). But even though such techniques of demystification were not original, *Paolo Paoli* was one of the earliest and most effective plays to exploit these techniques in France. It shows that the use of high-flown rhetoric to delude other people about one's true motives is ultimately self-destructive, for it results in the delusion of the characters themselves so that they end up not knowing who they are or what they believe. Their rhetoric also becomes a kind of defence against history. They talk endlessly of the progress of historical events, giving themselves the impression that they are in control of the situation, but the ending of the play shows the gap between their inflated words and their real situation. As Bernard Dort wrote: 'They have spoken for too long, events have been at work and now they must submit to them, words are superfluous. *Paolo Paoli* therefore ends on a silence' (1967: 259). Escape is impossible and they are all dragged into war for having hidden their heads in the sand like Hulot-Vasseur's castrated ostriches. Paolo is unable to express his sudden disgust: language literally fails him because it has been misused for so long.

In order to emphasise both the links and contradictions between the small world of Paolo and the larger realities of European history, Adamov employed the Brechtian technique of projections between scenes. These served to remind the audience of the salient events of the year in which the ensuing scene was set and used documentary extracts from contemporary journals to demonstrate the importance of such things as feather products. The alternation between allusion to historical events in these projections and the scenes of private life in each tableau suggested a society defined by the pressure of external events without ever recognising this to be the case. These projections also had the effect of interrupting the flow of the action, as in Brecht's own plays, so that each tableau was presented as a self-contained unit.

However the essential structure of the plays is not strictly Brechtian, consisting of a repetitive, spiralling movement, in which the futile circuit of trade and exchange turns ever more frenziedly inward upon itself. Only at the very end does Paolo make a half-hearted attempt to repair some of the damage he has done by giving the proceeds of the sale of his rare charaxes to Rose, his exploited servant. The play is Epic in its structure, but it is largely fatalistic, offering a description of a corrupt society, not an optimistic programme of action. As Adamov himself said, 'the difficulty of writing a positive character remains terrifying' (1964: 59). It was a difficulty he was to attempt to overcome in his next major play *Le Printemps 71* published in 1960 by *Théâtre Populaire*. Meanwhile Adamov had broken out of his nightmare world of hallucination and obsession into the real world of history and had shown that Epic theatre could flourish on French soil. Planchon's production emphasised the concrete quality of the characters' situation, with stage sets incorporating vast numbers of the special drawers and cases used by entomologists or, in the case of Stella's hat shop, the whole paraphernalia of hat boxes, hat stands, etc. This was necessary, he felt, to lend real historical weight to what might otherwise appear as merely fantastic or whimsical. *Paolo Paoli* marked a decisive turning point in the careers of both men. For Adamov it brought the liberation of discovering that he could write about the real world and did not have to remain entirely locked within his own neuroses. For Planchon it was the occasion of his company's first visit to Paris and was instrumental in persuading the mayor of Villeurbanne to accept Planchon's proposal for a permanent producing company in the municipal theatre of this industrial suburb some three miles from the centre of Lyon. He renamed the theatre Théâtre de la Cité to express the idea of a theatre in the heart of the city providing a source of reflection on the conditions of life of its citizens. In order to emphasise his view (shared with Jean Vilar) that theatre should be a public service, Planchon arranged for a questionnaire to be distributed among the people of Villeurbanne to find out what they would most like to see. The two most popular authors to emerge were Shakespeare and Dumas. The theatre's first production, on 31 October 1957, was *Henry IV*, Part I renamed *Le Prince* and Part II *Falstaff*.

The play was seen by Planchon as a vast reflection on the problems of power and its legitimacy, of order versus disorder and of ideas of national unity. The production emphasised the political aspects of the play by presenting the nobles as fundamentally self-interested, using the high-flown renaissance rhetoric only to cover their grasping motives – an interpretation that was all the more unexpected in that it flew in the face of the accepted T.N.P. heroic style. Planchon encouraged his actors to emphasise the discontinuities evident in Shakespeare's characters and not to try for a carefully unified psychological study in the traditional French manner. The effect of this was to lay stress on the social conditions governing the characters' behaviour. The settings were entirely constructed from huge maps, which situated the shifting changes in the action, and the costumes established a precise differentiation, not only between the nobles and the clients at Mistress Quickly's tavern, but also between the different grades of nobility: the nobles with potential power, the leaders of clans, the military men.

On 13 May 1958, the very day when the events in Algeria precipitated de Gaulle's return to power, *Les Trois Mousquetaires* opened. This production, full of exuberance, puns, gags, tricks of all kinds, used Dumas' plot as pretext for the construction of a 'joke and dagger' show that formed a burlesque counterpart to the serious meditation on power politics in *Henry IV*. The method was parody and no current style was spared, from Westerns to puppet shows, from Brechtian history to high-flown epic. The watch-word was Dumas' own comment: 'The rape of History is permitted, but only if you give her a child' (cit. Bataillon, 1982).

In October 1958 Planchon produced his first play by Molière: *George Dandin*. In choice and method he was more influenced by Brecht's thoughts on the contemporary uses of the classics than by the directors of the Cartel, whose aesthetic values were based on notions of taste, beauty, skill. Brecht had insisted on a particular perspective on the world, moreover he had shown that the director's work or 'scenic writing' carried a responsibility equal to that of the author's textual writing. *George Dandin* is a farce about a rich peasant who wants to marry above his station. Traditionally, it had been played in the italianate style. Planchon, together with his designer René Allio, decided to break with tradition, to present the truth of the social and economic situation out of which such a comedy arose, to aim for realism as opposed to stylisation.

The set was an imposingly realistic farm building of the type frequently depicted by the seventeenth century painter Le Nain. The activity on stage evoked the workaday reality of a busy, successful farming establishment on one typical day, lasting from morning till night. Beneath the farce of a cuckolded husband, audiences discovered a cruel social comedy about class. The successful farmer is ridiculous because he turns his back on everything he knows in order to marry a Lady, and his social pretensions are all the more ridiculous since the behaviour of the aristocrats is shown in such a poor light. The roots of the plot were seen to reach deep into the realities of French provincial life. Adopting a notion of Charles Dullin, Planchon wrote that what he appreciated in Molière was that his plays were not so much studies of characters but of situations. The same approach was later applied to other classic texts, creating the social situation for the play by means of a realist, critical presentation immensely rich in detail. The most notable were *La Seconde Surprise de l'amour* by Marivaux in 1959, and *Le Tartuffe* in 1962.

The sixties were the years in which Brecht became the single most pervasive influence on the theatre in France. Planchon was generally thought of, by admirers and detractors alike, as the leader of the Brechtian faction. But 1961 was marked by Planchon's last production of a play by Brecht: *Schweyk in the Second World War*. Allio and Planchon perfected a revolving stage which was used to give the effect of a cinematic movement. When in motion it could be used almost like a travelling shot and the fixed elements of scenery around it were like framing devices. The colours and materials used in costumes and sets were all chosen to contribute to the particular rapid, episodic rhythm of the play, drawing the audience into an interplay of opposites. The composer Hans Eisler, a friend of Brecht since the late 1920s, came from East Berlin to work on the production and was delighted by Planchon's incisive, irreverent interpretation of Brecht. The play was one of the company's great popular successes and also a personal triumph for Jean Bouise, who had played Falstaff and now took the role of Schweyk. But for the Brechtian critics, especially those writing for *Théâtre Populaire*, Planchon was guilty of a production that owed more to Planchon than to Brecht. He responded to this criticism by publishing an article in *Théâtre Populaire* entitled 'Orthodoxies'. In this, he argued that two exactly similar readings or understandings of a play may provoke quite different scenic ideas. He claimed that his use of special effects allowed for the superimposition of two distinct realities, pointing out that Brecht's own notes for the play had demanded this kind of effect.

During this period, the influence of Brecht was principally apparent in Planchon's revivals and adaptions. Marivaux's *La Seconde Surprise de l'amour* was the big surprise of the 1959 season for the critics, as Planchon subjected the play to the same kind of treatment as *George Dandin*. Instead of the frothy, light-hearted *marivaudage* to which audiences were accustomed, he presented a performance filled with the concrete, material details of life in an eighteenth century household. Most revolutionary of all, he kept the servants of the household on stage as silent presences throughout the action. Marivaux's text took on an entirely new dimension when it was spoken, not by isolated couples but in front of working people who had to go about their business while the aristocrats frittered their time away. The text was not altered at all but simply set in its complete social environment with a devastating effect on the audience's response to it. The critics were, on the whole, very positive about this experiment and its success helped to pave the way for his production of Molière's *Le Tartuffe* in 1962.

The following season, Planchon produced an adaptation of Gogol's novel *Dead souls* by Arthur Adamov. Gogol's novel tells the story of Chichikov's journey across the vast space of the Russian countryside, visiting the landowners and buying the title deeds to their dead serfs. The reason for this bizarre transaction is that he has discovered he can raise large sums of money on the evidence of possessing many serfs. Once they are dead, the owners are prepared to part with them for very little but, the Russian bureaucracy being very slow, Chichikov can rely on them remaining on the public records, as if they were still alive, for many years. Through Chichikov's quest, Gogol painted a picture of Russia that was spiritually dead and produced a comic masterpiece in the literature of protest against slavery. For Adamov, the story provided a brilliantly effective image of the inhumanity of all exploitation. He wrote an adaptation that compressed the events of the novel into fifteen scenes each constructed around a bargain of a different kind. Chichikov had to discover the weak point of each new landowner and then play on that to persuade him to part with his serfs. Through each of these scenes, Adamov brought out a different aspect of the economic and political exploitation employing a deadly irony that at first seems simply rather cool but ends up as a devastating indictment of a whole social system.

Planchon applied Brechtian staging methods to this play, using film projected onto screens to particularise each place visited on Chichikov's travels. The sets were realistic but only occupied a part of the stage, with gaps round the sides, so that the constructed nature of the performance was visible. In order to achieve an acting style that was both sufficiently comic and sufficiently detached, Planchon decided that each character should have a false nose of a different shape. He was encouraged by Gogol's own fascination with noses, but Adamov felt that the whole production had become too fussy. He and Planchon fell out and the break in their relationship was not repaired until the late sixties shortly before Adamov's death.

Between 1958 and 1961 the company made five separate visits to Paris and became established in the minds of the national critics as the most outstanding young theatre group in France. But for the company a more important battle was being fought during these years for acceptance in Villeurbanne itself. In 1959 a regular news-sheet, *Cité-Panorama*, was launched which carried news of exhibitions, discussions, subscription arrangements for factory groups, the provision of special public transport for visits to the theatre, etc. Planchon and other members of the company went out to youth groups, union meetings and even got up on the tables to talk during the coffee breaks in works canteens.

Precise figures for the class composition of theatre audiences are always hard to come by, but it seems that the success of these attempts was only partial. The Théâtre de la Cité's audiences were very similar to those of Vilar's Théâtre National Populaire, consisting mostly of young people, teachers, etc. with a good smattering of works outings from both white- and blue-collar establishments.

Whatever the composition of its audiences, the Théâtre de la Cité played to full houses and earned the confidence of the mayor of Villeurbanne. André Malraux promised that the theatre should have the status of a Centre Dramatique National, which was finally conferred in 1963. He also proposed that Planchon should head a new Maison de la Culture, but Planchon resisted this suggestion on the grounds that the structure of the Maisons put too much power in the hands of a Conseil d'Administration, leaving insufficient freedom to the artistic director. During the sixties, Planchon was beginning to spend more time writing his own plays and he became more preoccupied with artistic creation than with his administrative functions. At this stage the theatre was run by a dual directorate of Planchon and Robert Gilbert, one of the earliest members to join the group, who had by this time given up acting to be the full-time administrative director. The company still grouped together the friends who had been together since the early fifties: Robert Gilbert, Claude Lochy, Georges Barrier, Jean Bouise, Isabelle Sadoyan, Henri Galiardin, Julia Dancourt, Alain Mottet, Jacques Rosner, Colette Dompiétrini (Planchon's wife), and others who had joined in the course of the fifties like Gilles Chavassieux and Armand Meffre. In the course of the sixties, Jacques Rosner took over some of the new production work (including Gatti's play *La Vie imaginaire de l'éboueur Auguste Geai* in 1962) and Planchon began a policy of hiring well-known actors, especially film actors, for particular productions. Michel Auclair, for example, played Tartuffe in 1962 and Richard II in 1961, Bernard Fresson played Troilus in 1963 and Sami Frey played Titus in the 1966 *Bérénice*.

Planchon had always approached production work with a very free and creative attitude, filling out a text with innumerable scenic details or even, in some cases, inventing words as well as action (e.g. *Les Trois Mousquetaires* adapted from Dumas). In 1960, for a new production of *Edward II*, he abandoned Adamov's translation and made his own version. In 1961 Planchon wrote his first play, *La Remise*, since when he has written more than twelve others. Ten of these have been performed at Villeurbanne, but only four have been published and so it is on these four that the following discussion will focus. They are *La Remise* (1961), *L'Infâme* (1969), *Le Cochon noir* (1972) and *Gilles de Rais* (1976). They have sometimes been seen as a cycle of peasant plays exploiting Planchon's first-hand experience of life in the rural communities of the French provinces. All take as their starting point a genuine historical event of a particularly violent nature. All attempt to reconstruct that reality but in the process aim to achieve much more than a simple reconstruction of events. They show, in addition, how those events were lived through and understood on an imaginary and spiritual plane; how the conflict between individual fears and desires and social and ideological pressures can drive someone to madness or infamy. They are all based, to some extent, on the pattern of an investigation: the moment of violence is not shown but the play probes and searches for an adequate explanation. In *La Remise* this pattern was very obvious, since the play's basic structure is that of a police investigation after a murder. In the later plays it is not so crudely obvious, but nonetheless present.

Coming from so accomplished a director, one might have expected the texts to include detailed stage directions; instead they are spare and condensed, each divided into about a dozen scenes and containing almost nothing in the way of instructions about acting or production. The French is not literary but very powerful, even violent and crude, borrowing much of the verve and condensed quality of proverbial peasant wisdom. Planchon has stated that with *Le Cochon noir* certain key images like the open-air wedding came first, and once these were in place the plot almost seemed to construct itself. This account can help us to understand the characteristic movement of these plays, which is through a variety of highly coloured images each of which catches up different strands of the complex social, psychological and spiritual forces that precipitated the central event.

Through the police inquest in *La Remise*, Planchon traced a semi-autobiographical account of his family going back three generations and covering the period from the end of the First World War to the fall of Dien Bien Phu in 1954. The play is perhaps too 'clever' with its superimposition of different time scales and attempts to move between the domestic drama of the Chausson family and the larger canvas of world events, explaining each by reference to the other. But it has considerable qualities which were to become more apparent in the later plays: the meticulous and subtle depiction of everyday events in such a way as to link them to broad historical events, and the equally sensitive depiction of the relations between what is inexplicable or mysterious in human beings and what *can* be explained, such as their social, ideological or economic conditioning. The staging, in which reality underwent a subtle transformation, changing from reality-as-lived to reality-as-dreamed, was not understood by contemporary critics, nor was the poetic violence of the language. In his subsequent plays, Planchon was to refine and simplify this technique of superimposing and confronting different time scales or perceptions of reality or the differing outlooks of differing characters and classes.

In *L'Infâme* we witness an attempt to understand the crime of the curé d'Uruffe, a case widely reported when it happened in 1956 of a parish priest who murdered his pregnant mistress, cut out the foetus and baptised it in her blood. Planchon's abbé Duverger is depicted with a kind of sympathy, showing him not just as a man who was foolish, ignorant and lonely, but also as someone capable of illumination. It was an attempt to follow a fellow human being along a seemingly incomprehensible path that he was to repeat with *Gilles de Rais*. The structure of the play is clearer and simpler than that of *La Remise*, but Copfermann is certainly right to suggest that there is a great similarity between them (1977: 256). In both cases the murder results in an inquest that does not really answer the question it sets itself. In both cases the audience itself becomes the investigator and judgement proceeds as much from the tortuous mental processes of the characters involved as from the due process of the law. In the case of the abbé Duverger, as with the old Emile Chausson of *La Remise*, we witness the unleashing of a fundamental life force which cannot be integrated into the social or religious structures of the society in question. In each case we see a character who destroys what he cannot control or understand which, in the last instance, turns out to be himself.

In *Le Cochon noir* it was the harsh violence of a mountain village environment that came out most clearly. The play is set in 1871 and its story is of a girl raped on her wedding day. But the rape is not depicted on stage nor does the victim bemoan her fate or make speeches about her feelings. Instead, the play shows how her social position within the village alters. The combination of fear, pity and disgust aroused by this event is such that it affects the life of the whole community. It becomes the focal point for the last power-struggle between the dying curé and the hermit, a white magician on the fringes of the village community who makes a living as a deviner and herbalist in the folk tradition. Because the hermit is prepared to be harsher and because he can play more subtly on the collective sense of guilt, he is able to persuade the whole community to go through the ritual of exorcism. This process in turn makes us think about how the peasants of the Versailles army were able to believe in the necessity of an exorcism by blood to get rid of the Paris Commune in the 'semaine sanglante' of May 1871.

This connection between the suppression of the Paris Commune and an obscure exorcism in the provinces was at the origin of Planchon's conception of the play: 'as the grandson and great-grandson of peasants, I wanted to investigate the mechanisms that could lead country people into becoming the death-squads on the Commune. . . My great-grandfather was in the ranks of the Versailles army. I can say that that has haunted me' (cit. Copfermann, 1977: 312). The play opens with a prologue spoken by some young Communards who are collecting for the widows and orphans, and there are various references by characters in the play to the news of events in Paris. The mechanisms identified in the play were similar to those that led to Duverger's crime in *L'Infâme*: fear of authority, both that of parents and of God; fear of one's neighbours and of the inexplicable disaster that occurs like a thunderbolt; superstition, ignorance and the constant struggle to scrape a precarious living in a harsh environment. The play was set on a stage with an extremely steep rake, so steep that it literally made it difficult for the actors to stand and move about, and this very concrete, physical difficulty became, in performance, an image of the difficulty and precariousness of life in the mountain village (see fig. 6). The text contains many scenes of violent physical contact which the performance made the most of. During the rehearsals Planchon made the comment: 'What matters is flesh. My plays are written for the body' (cit. Burgess, 1974a: 61). This emphasis on physicality found embodiment in a particularly vivid image repeatedly placed between scenes, in which Violette and her fiancé strain to reach one another from opposite sides of the stage.

They are linked by a cord onto which is tied a fuse. The fuse is lighted and the fire runs between their outstretched arms, burning them so that they drop the link.

The villagers of *Le Cochon noir* are poised between two worlds: the old world of primitive folklore and the new world of ruthless violence. *Gilles de Rais* again presents a superimposition of two different ideologies. Gilles is a man trapped between two worlds, the one in its dying spasms, the other not yet born. The Medieval Age, dominated by the inextricable combination of Catholic Church and feudal system is drawing to a close but has not yet been replaced by the Renaissance. Gilles is both a powerful baron – the richest man in France and a warlord who has deserved the King's protection by his support in the wars against the English – and also a man struggling to develop new values that will replace the decadent, decomposing church order. His child-murders are partly the expression of a death-wish, partly an attempt to summon the devil. The devil is the only alternative he can see to the divine order; no third way is apparent. But he finds that the devil is elusive: he exists only in opposition to the prevailing values. This dilemma is presented in the trial scene, whose setting and action mirror the performance of a medieval mystery play. God obliges Gilles to play over and over again the restricted repertoire of roles open to the rebel in feudal Catholic France: first the warrior

6   *Le Cochon noir* (Planchon): model for set by Luciano Damiani showing steep rake; stage set for wedding scene with sky cloth in lowered position; T.N.P.-Villeurbanne, 1973.

knight fighting the English army of occupation, then the two great rebel roles in the Bible story, Cain and Judas. Here, in an image of great complexity, are drawn together the social conditions of the time, the imaginative and ideological structures they gave rise to, as well as the impact of these things on the mind of a particular individual.

These are difficult plays, not easy to grasp from the text alone without the benefit of Planchon's own production ideas. They are best understood as a modern attempt to create a dramatic form with some of the qualities of Shakespearean drama. This may be seen in their episodic structure and discontinuities of plot and character, so foreign to the French tradition, in their profusion of images frequently calling for emblematic staging and their ambition to present a whole world, the real world of history on stage. To begin with the characters, these often contain unresolved contradictions: actions apparently taken against their own best interests or that cause the audience to question the view or judgement that they have taken to the character. Copfermann is fond of talking of the 'margin of mystery' that Planchon allows his characters. This stems from a deliberate choice on Planchon's part to avoid the neat psychological case-studies of Naturalist drama. With his subject-matter drawn so extensively from peasant life, it would have been all too easy to sink into a pastiche of Zola. His starting point is not the invention of a character whose behaviour can be explained given a particular combination of heredity and conditioning, desires and frustrations. Instead, he begins with a given aspect of historical reality, so that the plays can be seen as imaginative attempts to understand these characters and why they did what they did. Because of the necessary otherness of these characters such attempts can never be exhaustive or definitive. The two plays in which Planchon explores his own roots show this particularly clearly, but so also do the other two. Planchon described his action in writing *Gilles de Rais* as like trying to tread in the footprints of Gilles up to a certain point, to discover the point at which he had to break off or sink into madness and crime.

Planchon has been criticised for picking characters who are violent, but of course in doing so he is following a time-honoured tradition which goes back to Shakespeare and the Greeks, as Sartre had already pointed out when he had to face this criticism. And like Sartre, Planchon tried to draw people's attention away from the tendency to examine psychology towards a view of a whole scene or situation: 'people read the words of a play, they do not read the whole situation; they read moment by moment, in fact they should read each scene as a whole' (1969c: 62). This implies a practice of playwriting in which characters do not explain themselves to the audience, as do the characters of Racine, Claudel or Montherlant, but in which the characters are explained by their situation in all its aspects. Violette, in *Le Cochon noir*, is a good example of this. Her character is not just explained, it is constructed by the struggle in her society of which she becomes the focus. Her suicide expresses the final sterility of this struggle.

It should not be thought, however, that Planchon's dramas neglect the psychology of individual characters. The power of the subconscious is an essential factor in their behaviour. Duverger's crime (in *L'Infâme*) can only be admitted to his mother but the murder was itself a misplaced attempt to free himself from the stifling maternal power. He cannot grasp this but grapples with a partial understanding: 'It's incomprehensible. And don't imagine that I see in this the hand of God, I am talking of other forces, more terrible, closer, inside me. Forces of which I know nothing, which subjugate and bind me. But, mummy, whose hands tie the bonds?' (112). Gédéon, in *Le Cochon noir* is driven by an obsession with the return of the Emperor, who dominates his dreams and imaginings in the shape of both father and mother figure. In the dream sequence of Scene VI, first Violette brings him a live pig, announcing that she has given birth to it after Gédéon's rape, and then Gédéon is reprimanded by the Emperor who changes into the shape of his daughter Eulalie and forces him to submit to his/her sexual advances. The scene hints at the psychological trauma behind Gédéon's treatment of Eulalie and Violette: he is fighting his own fear of authority, impotence and death.

The original quality in Planchon's treatment of his characters' psychology is that the social and psychological frames of reference are treated in the same manner, whereas we are used to plays in which they are contrasted. In most historical plays the social/historical and the private scenes alternate: every so often we penetrate behind the façade of public events to observe the characters in their private lives and examine their motives in depth. Planchon has claimed that his plays 'have no *depth*. It's all on the surface. There's nothing hidden behind' (cit. Burgess, 1974a: 67). What this means is not that the characters are superficial, but that the social and the individual aspects of their lives co-exist as functions of one another.

Unlike Sartre, it is not the political or social ideas alone that principally interest him, but the way in which people respond personally, emotionally, imaginatively to the political and social circumstances of their lives. He explained that in *Le Cochon noir* 'the hermit uses the disaster for his own ends, to increase his prestige in the same way that Pétain used the French defeat in 1940, which wasn't explained but mystified. By a sort of magical thinking it became the fault of the Front Populaire, of immortality and loose living. Pétain could then promise to "restore true values"' (cit. Burgess, 1974a: 80). Magic crops up in one form or another in most of Planchon's plays and Bernard Dort described their world as being 'caught between magic and history' (1974: 49). Magic is a way of denying or controlling the concrete, often painful experience of living. These irreducible physical realities are emphasised in the plays while they also demonstrate the opposite tendencies of magical thinking. Planchon's dramatic writing emphasises the concrete, material realities of life while at the same time showing how these are mediated, interpreted, built into the imaginative responses of the individual's life.

The structure of these plays also contributes to such a depiction of reality. The structure is Epic in the Brechtian sense. That is to say that each scene is self-contained and its relationship with the scenes before and after tends to be one of juxtaposition or contradiction rather than of unilinear development. Since all of the plays are built around a particular crisis, the function of each scene is to reveal a different aspect of that central crisis. The relationship of the authorities with Gilles, for example, appears quite differently in different scenes. The various attitudes they display include: disgust at his murders, fear of his power, greed for his lands, opposition to his heresy. The change from one to another may take place from one scene to another, or more abruptly, as in Scene iv, where the Duke of Brittany first refuses to rescue the bishop's man captured by Gilles only to announce, two lines later, that he *will* rescue him. Planchon justifies these contradictions by arguing that they allow a more dramatic and more life-like representation of human behaviour, and points to examples from Shakespeare. Like Shakespeare, he also mixes the comic and the tragic, particularly in the depiction of political life.

In *Gilles de Rais*, even more than in the earlier plays, these methods produce dialogue of a poetic, multi-layered quality in which almost everything said has meanings on more than one level. An example of this can be seen in the account by the Duke's mistress of cutting up a boar after the hunt (23). At one level the scene is a simple description of hunting which was the major pastime of the feudal nobility. At another, the girl's speech seems to take on a pagan delight in the killing and skinning of the animal – she becomes a sort of Huntress Diana for whom there is no place in the world of medieval Christianity. The Duke's response to her speech is to ask the Cardinal Inquisitor if he thinks she is possessed by the devil. At a third level she echoes the behaviour of Gilles, who takes a similar delight in killing children. This kind of poetic texture does not rely on language alone but is constantly reinforced by action. In this instance we are ready to make the link between Gilles and the image of the hunt because the previous scene has shown him hunting children as game.

Each scene is constructed so as to bring out the different interpretations of events by different characters. This is complemented by Planchon's rehearsal technique, which is to work through each scene a number of different times, each time treating it from a different character's point of view. 'The rehearsals work over the scene in successive layers rather like colour printing – first the red, then the black, and so on – until the whole picture is built up' (Burgess, 1974a: 67).

Like Shakespearean drama, this kind of dialogue demands a rich, emblematic style of staging. At the level of production, Planchon clarifies and emphasises the images, while making each piece of action or stage setting stand for truths beyond itself. The staging of the trial, Scene ix, in *Gilles de Rais* was a particularly impressive example of this. For most of the play, the action took place on a ramp some twenty-five feet square. For the trial, in John Burgess' words,

the stage explodes in all directions. The canvas drapes at the side fly out to uncover two subsidiary stages which roll forward to join the main playing area. The gauze sky peels away to reveal a bright new backdrop, all blue and gold, and a further range of landscaped hills, this time with gilded peaks. From one side there rolls the Virgin Mary's tower, while God the Father descends from the flies on a sort of platform representing paradise garden. The *pièce de résistance* occurs half way through the scene with the arrival of the Tower of Despair – a huge Bosch-like contraption which wheels on and lowers its drawbridge for Prelati to enter (1976: 21).

The stage floor also opens up so as to allow Gilles to descend into the pit underneath. The inspiration for this impressive composite image was a medieval manuscript illumination in the *Très Riches Heures du duc de Berry*, and its purpose was to convey an image of the world as the medieval writers and painters saw it (i.e. the only image available to Gilles). It was a world which was complete, whose beginning and end were known from the Bible and from which there was no escape, since the heavens, the earth and even the regions under the earth were ultimately in the power of God. Some of the actors became spectators while others were involved in the performance of the mystery play. The play within the play effectively conveys the trap into which Gilles has run. The parts he has to play work against him: he cannot escape, but must play out, of his own free will, the role of condemned rebel to the end. The dialogue manages to convey three distinct actions occurring simultaneously: the trial itself, the performance of the mystery play and the asides commenting on both (ibid. 16).

Part of the extraordinary excitement of seeing a production by Planchon is in the richness of his stage imagery which is evident throughout the plays, not just at the climactic moments like the one described above. The scope and size of the images will vary greatly from scene to scene, making for an effect of constant surprise, holding the spectator's attention. Scenes of movement and vigour will alternate with scenes of calm. Planchon's aesthetic is, in fact, one of surprise. He aims to surprise the public with an unexpected image of itself. In the long term he hopes that this will achieve a political goal, by changing the way people view society and one another. But it is not an aesthetic of immediate political efficacy, and he insists that for his images to be able genuinely to surprise and disconcert he must spend the time and the money necessary to convey the materiality and texture of life with the maximum of complexity. This is what he means when he says that his plays are written for the body, and it is certain that he achieves, by different means, something of the quality that Esslin admired in the theatre of the Absurd when he wrote that 'it has renounced arguing *about* the absurdity of the human condition: it merely *presents* it in being – that is in terms of concrete stage images' (1968: 25). But at the same time, of course, these plays are also very much *about* something. Their subjects might be summarised as firstly, life in a rural or peasant community and secondly, life in a post-Christian world. Both might be subsumed under the broader subject-heading of man's relations to history.

Perhaps surprisingly, Planchon is the first French dramatist of stature to attempt a serious treatment of peasant life. Despite the major contribution of French novelists to the Naturalist movement, no major plays appeared taking the life of peasants as their main focus before the appearance of *La Remise* in 1962. Such plays were sometimes seen on the French stage, but they were translated from other cultures, like Hauptmann's *The weavers*. Planchon's originality in finding a stage idiom that can adequately handle this range of experience has not always received the recognition it deserves. In the life of peasant communities, Planchon discovered a strong element of paganism which interested him as someone who had experience of living in a post-Christian age. The ideological battle ground between paganism and Christianity fascinated him as an area in which alternatives might be sought and found. He saw the theme of *Gilles de Rais* as a contemporary theme because 'We're living in the ruins of the cathedrals and in the ruins of the Greeks. It's interesting to recognize in Gilles the first man who saw a cathedral as a ruin' (cit. Burgess 1976: 23). If Planchon's work appears obsessed with death it is partly because this is perhaps the major unanswered question in a society where religious belief has crumbled. Drawing these themes together is Planchon's passionate interest in history. This is what links him with Brecht and Shakespeare and explains why he has been particularly attracted to Shakespeare's history plays. His plays are successful not only because of their original approach to characterisation, structure and subject-matter, but because they are written with an acute awareness of how theatre communicates: not through words and the intellect alone, but through the emotions and the senses. Planchon's plays leave us with intense images of a world torn between conflicting ideologies which turn out, on closer inspection, to present us with a mirror of our own time.

It is as a maker of images that Planchon seems most impressive and so there is a natural continuity between the concerns of the plays and the concerns manifested in his productions of the sixties and seventies. In these we find the same political and psychological preoccupations that are expressed in his own plays. A convenient case in point is provided by *Le Tartuffe*, the best known of Planchon's Molière productions, and the one to meet with greatest approval from the critics. The first performance was given at Villeurbanne in the Autumn of 1962. Planchon chose to present the play against the background of a society undergoing a process of transformation. The young Louis XIV has successfully played off the new bourgeoisie against the feudal nobility, brought the civil war to an end and founded the modern French state, unified beneath his absolute power. The ideology of Catholicism is an efficient regulator of his subjects' behaviour in every aspect of their lives.

In Planchon's reading of the play, it became both a bourgeois comedy and a political thriller. A bourgeois comedy because, as Planchon pointed out, it is the first play of its kind in the French repertoire based on adultery. The fact that Orgon's infatuation is not with another woman, but another man, provides the play with its cruel ambiguity. In Orgon's blind attraction for Tartuffe, emotional feelings and religious beliefs are combined and confused. A political thriller because it tells the story of a criminal who almost succeeds in ruining a rich bourgeois household. The fifth act, often held to be a mere piece of sycophancy by Molière, became in Planchon's production a terrifying demonstration of the all-pervading tentacles of the police state. If Orgon is saved, at the last minute, from the clutches of Tartuffe, it is only because he has proved useful to the king in the past and may do so again in the future, especially since he has put himself in the king's debt.

The set, constructed by René Allio, consisted of a highly polished marquetry floor, and walls made up entirely of paintings from the period depicting swooning saints. Most were naked or in various stages of undress and there was a repeated ambiguity as to whether they were swooning in spiritual ecstasy or physical agony (see fig. 7). At the end of each scene one of these walls of paintings flew up until, at the end of the play, the decorative elements in the house had been stripped bare and the audience was left facing bare stone walls. The process of stripping bare enacted in the play had found its scenic equivalent at the level of the settings.

This production was revived in each of the five subsequent seasons. The new version had its first performance in the summer of 1973 at Buenos Aires. The new version retained some of the features of the old, especially the gradual stripping bare of the set to reveal harsh, prison-like stone walls at the end. But all the details of both set and performance were recast in a much more physical, concrete form. The social transformation was mirrored in the literal transformation of Orgon's house. He has the builders in: each successive room in the house reveals a half-finished fresco, a new piece of marble ornamentation, an equestrian statue still under wraps (of the king, presumably). The impression given was of a rather comfortless renaissance fortress being transformed into a showy Louis XIV mansion. The intrusion of the King's representative at the end was made even more violent than in the first version:

7 *Le Tartuffe* (Molière): René Allio's set for the first production, Théâtre de la Cité, Villeurbanne, 1962. Left to right: Dorine (Françoise Seigner) Marianne (Collette Dompiétrini) Cléante (Gérard Guillaumat) Elmire (Anouk Ferjac) Orgon (Jacques Debary).

he was accompanied by armed men who herded the family into a sort of pit or semi-dungeon, while Tartuffe was gagged and his servant bound and strung up.

The costumes were rather different from those used in the first production. In 1962 all the characters wore the formal dress of the period. In the 1973 production, grand clothes were worn only for public occasions. The rest of the time, when the family was seen talking amongst themselves, they wore informal dress – shifts, shirt-sleeves, dressing gowns. This greatly enhanced the audience's awareness of the intimate nature of the family drama – Tartuffe's penetration into the most secret aspects of family life became almost tangible. Similarly the acting style was extremely physical. The ambiguous body movements of swooning saints had shifted from the pictures of the first production into the physical positions and gestures of the actors themselves, especially of Planchon in the role of Tartuffe and Guy Tréjan in the role of Orgon (see fig. 8). By the brilliant use of these elements of 'scenic writing' Planchon succeeded in superimposing different realities: the experience of both religious faith and of feigned devotion; the process of individual character development and of social transformation; the means by which power is established both within the family and in society at large.

8 *Le Tartuffe* (Molière): Hubert Montloup's set for the 1973 production, T.N.P.-Villeurbanne, Planchon (right) in the role of Tartuffe, Guy Tréjan (left) in the role of Orgon.

The decentralised theatre II: Planchon and Adamov

During the 1960s, Planchon produced one other classic from the French repertoire: Racine's *Bérénice* (1966) and two more plays by Shakespeare *Troilus and Cressida* (1964) and *Richard III* (1966). On the occasion of *Richard III* he stated:

I cannot live without Shakespeare . . . in his world I feel completely at ease . . . I find in his plays the two things that excite me and that seem worthy subjects for the theatre: politics and love. In Shakespeare the social analysis never crushes the individual psychology of the characters while at the same time the characters do not mask the general view of the society that is being described (cit. Bataillon, 1982).

Both plays were performed in a style that could be described as physical. Unlike most French directors, Planchon expects his actors to take risks and to be physically agile. Having come to the theatre with almost no training, he is scornful of the conventions governing what an actor can and cannot do. The battle scenes in *Troilus and Cressida* particularly included moments of violence when the actors really put themselves at risk. What appealed to Planchon about *Troilus and Cressida* was its fierce demystification of the twin myths of the glory of war and the power of love. His production emphasised the physical reality of war and love, showing how the fine words that are associated with both serve only to mask the unacceptable aspects of their reality. The set, by André Acquart, was an enormous pivoting, folding structure suggesting both the tents of the Greek camp and the walls and gates of Troy. In the course of performance it was shifted to make a whole variety of shapes so that the battle scenes, played like wrestling matches, took on a variety and excitement that they seldom have (see fig. 9).

Richard III is a play about the seizure of power. Here Planchon's production provided a meditation on murder considered as a fine art, a psychoanalytical study of refined duplicity at the service of overwhelming ambition. Through the play of alliances, double-dealings, ploys and betrayals Michael Auclair performed Richard not as a hunchback devil, but as a schemer among schemers, sharper, swifter, more insensitive to the sufferings of others than his less successful opponents. He was attractive, even fascinating, but his was the fascination of the abyss. *Richard III* was the first production by Planchon's company to be given at the Avignon festival. Like *Troilus and Cressida*, the production was full of movement, with bodies of men manoeuvring on an almost geometrical pattern. The most important elements of the set were a number of frightening machines evidently designed to kill or torture. The manoeuvring of these machines by the actors became a powerful stage image of men forced to service the machine of war and political ambition.

During the period of the 1960s the company performed new plays by Gatti, (*La Vie imaginaire de l'éboueur Auguste Geai*) and Arden (*Armstrong's last goodnight*) as well as revivals by Goldoni (*La Villégiature*) O'Casey (*Purple dust*) and Vitrac (*Le Coup de Trafalgar*). Those were all directed by Planchon's assistant Jacques Rosner. Planchon was devoting more and more time to writing and then to directing his own work both tragic and historical (*Bleus, blancs, rouges ou les libertins*, 1967; *L'Infâme*, 1969) and burlesque or satirical (*Maman Chicago*, 1963; *Dans le vent*, 1968; *La Mise en pièces du 'Cid'*, 1969).

During the sixties Malraux's policy of grouping regional cultural events into a network of Maisons de la Culture had been gradually taking shape, but Planchon continued unresponsive to suggestions that he should head a Maison, fearing the diminution of his artistic freedom and dissolution of his carefully nurtured links with unions and workers' groups in the Villeurbanne area. In 1968 he felt he had been proved right when many directors were summarily dismissed from their Maisons for having allowed students and workers to hold debates or political meetings. In 1969, since Planchon was clearly determined to stay, the Villeurbanne municipality agreed to an ambitious rebuilding and re-equipment of the Théâtre de la Cité. The last productions before renovation began in the summer of 1969 were *L'Infâme* and *La Contestation et la mise en pièces de la plus illustre des tragédies françaises 'Le Cid' de Pierre Corneille, suivie d'une 'cruelle' mise à mort de l'auteur dramatique et d'une distribution gracieuse de diverses conserves culturelles* (a mocking reminder of the full title of Peter Weiss's *Marat/Slade*). *La Mise en pièces* was a response, part serious,

9 *Troilus and Cressida* (Shakespeare): André Acquart's designs for Planchon's production, Théâtre de la Cité, Villeurbanne, 1964.

part ironic, to the cultural ferment that had accompanied the wave of factory occupations and demonstrations of discontent throughout France in May 1968. In the summer of 1968, the Villeurbanne theatre had been the scene of a congress of theatre workers from all over France, who met together for several weeks to discuss the implications of the near-revolution for their work. A serious attempt was made to re-assess the cultural policies of the sixties. One of the main conclusions was that they had accepted too willingly the subsidised Gaullist structures of Maisons de la Culture, etc., and that this had led them into a cultural ghetto, cut off from broad political developments. They declared that the theatre should, in future, aim to attract the 'non-public', i.e. those who would never normally think of setting foot inside a theatre.

Planchon's play showed three members of this newly identified 'non-public' setting off in search of meaningful popular theatre. In the course of their journey, every current theatrical technique or style was reviewed and satirised, from the Living Theatre to *Hair* and from Vilar to Grotowski. But Planchon went beyond mere pastiche to include a serious consideration of the impasse of post-structuralist thought. For, as Terry Eagleton has argued, post-structuralism was at this time emerging as a convenient way for Leftist intellectuals to overcome the disappointments of 1968 by evading political questions altogether.

If meaning, the signified, was a passing product of words or signifiers, always shifting and unstable, part-present and part-absent, how could there be any determinate truth or meaning at all? If reality was constructed by our discourse rather than being reflected by it, how could we ever know reality itself, rather than merely knowing our own discourse? (1983: 143–4).

And, if this was the case, how could anyone hope to act upon reality? These were the questions that had been raised by the writers of the New Novel and the New Theatre and were being followed up with enthusiasm by critics such as Barthes and Derrida. Planchon's *mise en pièces*, or 'deconstruction' of *Le Cid* was an attempt to show that behind the excitement and the slogans of 1968 there was a dizzying abyss of self-contradictory theory that questioned the very ability of art to make statements about reality.

Meanwhile, in Paris, the T.N.P. had been lurching from crisis to crisis and the Minister was desperate for something to restore its fortunes. The solution was to offer the directorship to Planchon. He refused to leave Villeurbanne but suggested that he and his administrative director, Robert Gilbert, should take on a new young artistic director, Patrice Chéreau, and that this team should constitute the new T.N.P., based in Villeurbanne but touring more than previously. The suggestion was accepted and when the theatre reopened after the rebuilding, it was as the Théâtre National Populaire. The first production, in 1972, was an adaptation of Marlowe's *Massacre in Paris* directed by Chéreau and set on a stage that gradually filled with water so that by the end of the play the characters seemed literally to be wading in blood. Chéreau proceeded through the 1970s to produce a mixture of classics (*La Dispute, Peer Gynt*) and modern plays (*Toller*, by Tankred Dorst and *Loin d'Hagondange* by

Jean-Paul Wenzel). Planchon also returned to productions of contemporary writers other than himself: Vinaver with *Par-dessus bord* (1973), Pinter with *No Man's Land* (1979) and Adamov (who died in 1970) with *A.A. théâtres d'Adamov* (1975).

Planchon's invitation to Chéreau to join him as co-director of the Théâtre de la Cité was provoked by the departure of Jacques Rosner, who had been a member of the company since very early days, had taken on half the production work in the sixties and who left, in 1971, to become director of the Centre Dramatique du Nord at Tourcoing. Chéreau, born in 1944, the son of a painter, had already made a considerable reputation as a director of outrageously unusual treatments of the classics. His *Richard II* in 1970 provoked the same reactions of extreme dislike or enthusiasm that his *Ring* cycle provoked at Bayreuth in 1976. But he was also a declared partisan of *théâtre populaire* and had spent 1966–69 setting up a permanent theatre company at Sartrouville, one of the predominantly communist workers' dormitory suburbs of Paris. His attitude towards people's theatre was similar to Planchon's: he believed that the artist must never compromise in order to 'be popular', that true popular culture was not attainable in a capitalist state, but that the artist must make his work accessible to the mass of the population.

His productions have been chiefly remarkable for their extraordinary visual qualities. He has worked mostly with the Italian designer Richard Peduzzi and, like Planchon, gives the stage sets a very active role in his productions. Particularly striking was his version of *La Dispute* by Marivaux, designed by Peduzzi, a play which recounts an experiment in human engineering: two children are brought up in utter seclusion from the world, separate and behind high walls until adolescence. They are then introduced to one another and their behaviour observed. At the point when the adolescents began to discover a world of possibilities stretching beyond the walls that had always confined them, the walls themselves began to move and a terrifying sequence followed in which they took on a life of their own, almost like additional characters. Another example of Chéreau's visual brilliance was his production of Wenzel's play *Loin d'Hagondange*, a Pinteresque piece about a retired couple, which he set in an immense desolate landscape running quite counter to the rather realistic setting specified in the text (see below, chapter 10).

Planchon's own production work in the seventies represented something of a return to the preoccupations of his earliest work at the Théâtre de la Comédie reviewed in the light of the fifteen years during which Brecht had become the major influence on the French stage outside Paris. In the aftermath of the upheavals following 1968, many people pointed out that even the best productions of plays by Brecht had had no political effect on their audiences: the revolutionary message of the plays had been neutralised and absorbed by turning them into cultural values, a process for which the word *la récupération* was coined. In this situation it seemed something more than Brecht's appeal to reason was required. At the same time there was a renewal of interest in Artaud and his call for theatre to assault the senses of its audience, to play on its deep fears and confront them with a crisis of the whole personality. For some time it became a critical commonplace to evoke a theatre that would combine both Brecht and Artaud, thus uniting the two broad influences of Marxism and Surrealism.

Planchon's own plays made this link after their own fashion. A very different way of achieving it can be seen in the plays that Adamov wrote during the sixties. When Planchon returned, in 1975 to production of work by Adamov, it was a form of tribute to the master from whom he had learned and the fellow author who had been aiming at similar goals. The tragedy for Adamov was that none of his plays since *Les Ames mortes* had been produced by Planchon. Some were not produced at all in France, others were given inadequate but well-meaning productions that did nothing to help the reputation of an author who had been written off by the same critics who had previously praised him. As an absurdist, they said, he had been original; as a committed dramatist he was no more than a pale imitation of Brecht.

Adamov brought these accusations upon himself by claiming that *Le Printemps 71* had improved upon Brecht's *Days of the commune*. Although the play is built on a very interesting contrast between scenes of caricature and scenes of realism, Adamov was perhaps unnecessarily keen to create positive characters and the result is at times simplistic. He was more successful with a short neurosis play, *La Politique des restes*, in which he superimposed an individual's persecution complex on a general political situation. The action is set in a white racist state: South Africa or one of the southern states of the U.S.A. where, in the early sixties, there was still a mass of legislation discriminating against blacks. It employs a courtroom setting, with a number of flash-backs, to develop the story of Johnnie Brown, a white, who is being tried for the murder of Tom Guinness, a black. At first the court is disposed to let him off, despite the machinations of his wife and his brother who both want him safely confined to an institution. It is only when he announces that he is just as ready to kill whites as blacks that the court finally condemns him.

Johnnie Brown is afflicted with an obsession that all the rubbish in the world is being reserved for him to eat. This neurosis is drawn directly from a clinical account by Dr Minkowski of a patient who held this belief. He saw it as a deliberate policy – 'the rubbish policy' – on the part of the authorities, and those parts of the play in which Johnnie expresses his fears possess that extraordinary poetic power of reality to which Adamov alluded when talking of *Paolo Paoli*. For Dr Minkowski's patient, the profoundest terror was caused by the *proliferation* of rubbish, the belief that more and more nail clippings, razor blades, cigarette ends, chicken bones, fruit pips, etc. etc., were being piled up ready to be forced into his stomach. It only required a small extension of this persecution complex to reach the point where Adamov's Johnnie Brown felt the proliferation of human beings, first black then white as well, to be a threat. The atmosphere of a repressive totalitarian régime had been a feature of almost all Adamov's earlier New Theatre plays. In *La Politique des restes* it was again skilfully built up so as to make the transposition of Johnnie's neurosis from things to people quite acceptable.

Just as *Paolo Paoli* had exposed the rhetoric and self-deception of *la belle époque*, so in this play the hypocritical language of apartheid is dissected and unmasked. The courtroom setting is particularly appropriate for this purpose, since it involves the repeated revelation of false justifications on the part of the various witnesses. Not only do we see the terror of an individual, Johnnie Brown, when threatened by external objects, we also see the fear of a whole society that the blacks they have dehumanised and treated as objects may become a threat to them. By juxtaposing the two fears, Adamov shows apartheid in its true light as a kind of mass mania. Johnnie's terror at the multiplication of blacks is shared, at a more or less repressed level, by every white who appears during the trial. His madness is only different in degree, for when his lawyer pleads that innumerable whites have killed blacks with impunity, his fear of blacks suddenly changes into a fear of proliferating white racists. This puts him outside the limits of 'acceptable' madness and so the court must sentence him to confinement in a mental institution.

During the middle sixties Adamov went through a long period of illness and alcoholism as a result of which his writing suffered, both in quality and in quantity. But towards the end of the sixties he recovered sufficiently to write a remarkable autobiography, *L'Homme et l'enfant* and a major play, *Off limits*, in which he succeeded in applying the techniques he had used in *La Politique des restes* to a full-length play of great power and complexity.

Off limits was set in America and enabled Adamov both to draw on his own private obsessions and also to set them in a precise social and political context. His masochism, alcoholism and self-destructive urges all had their counterparts in the show-business and university worlds he discovered on his two visits to America in 1959 and 1965. The commercial side of the show-business world, especially in commercial television, offered a dramatic example of distortion and false rhetoric; the anti-war stance of some students and academics attracted him, especially their preoccupation with how a gesture of revolt could be made effective.

It was the period in America when 'happenings' were becoming fashionable. Adamov structured his play around a sequence of parties, each of which was punctuated by games or 'happenings'. The characters are divided into two camps: the young and the middle-aged. The latter exploit the entertainments industry and all, in different ways, live by the exploitation of images. The young people are not yet enslaved to the industry but are tempted by it. The middle-aged drink, the young take dope. All live with the anguish of the Vietnam war, seen as a principal cause of the disintegration of American society. Somehow Adamov had to introduce the war as an element of central importance within an affluent society apparently far away from it. In a masterly stroke Adamov accomplished this by means of war-games: Jim and Peter attempt to interrupt the parties by playing out violent agitprop sketches, but, however violent, these can never be more than games, and so their very nature admits their impotence.

As well as the war-games, Adamov introduces 'happenings' that are like parlour games – for example each guest at the party has to answer the question 'What is reality for you?'. Through such games, Adamov reveals the fundamental attitudes of his characters behind the masks that they habitually wear. But he also contrives a distancing of the play-instinct and an examination of its functions. He shows how it can act as a gesture of defiance or as a mere defence against boredom. He shows at the end of the play how it can be exploited and turned to profit. In order to dodge the draft, Jim and his girlfriend Sally have crossed the frontier to Mexico but have been shot before they reached safety. Humphrey decides to make a film of this, turning it into a touching episode of two young star-crossed lovers who finally meet in death. The political thrust of Jim's protest is entirely *récupéré* by playing it back with minor distortions.

The form of the play perfectly embodies its subject-matter, moving with great fluidity from one action to the next, from one game or conversation to another, just as at a party. But there is no tendency to create an excessively realistic party atmosphere: the change from one action to another is too abrupt (like cross-cutting in the cinema) and so the audience retains a critical attitude. In between each *tableau* there is a brief *récitatif*: blank verse modelled on the American beat poets adding a different viewpoint on what has been revealed or, as in Dorothy's final outburst, showing an awakening of political consciousness. While undoubtedly one of Adamov's most original plays, it also exhibits a number of Brechtian features, culminating in the brilliantly satirical funeral elegy for Humphrey O'Douglas, in which all the television magnate's vices are presented as great American virtues.

The play as a whole is successful because it brings together private anguish and public disaster, showing how each serves to explain the other within the context of a real society. It is a play of great complexity not built around a single character like *La Politique des restes*, but presenting a dozen or so characters in equal depth so as to achieve a microcosm of a whole society, as in *Paolo Paoli*. It is also successful because of its considerable economy: Adamov called it 'my favourite play because it is the most abrupt' (*Journal* 24 January 1969). It is a difficult play to read because it leaves so much to the producer's imagination and makes large demands in terms of action. The first two productions were, not surprisingly, quite unlike one another. Gabriel Garran's production for the Théâtre de la Commune at Aubervilliers stressed the manipulative functions of modern television, with monitors dotted around the auditorium, but did not achieve a sufficient ferocity in the acting style. Klaus-Michael Grüber's production at the Piccolo Teatro of Milan set the play on a vast pink plastic décor, vaguely suggesting a luxury lavatory on some ocean liner adrift in the middle of a golf green (see fig. 10). The images in this production had a quality that was both literal and dream-like and it was the combination of these two things that characterised Adamov's last and most mysterious play *Si l'été revenait*.

This play is made up of four dreams in which each of the major characters dreams about the other three. In it, Adamov sacrifices the precise political commentary of a play like *Off limits* but achieves a quality that can only be described as extreme literality (see chapter 4). Adamov wrote that there should be no objective version; 'everything is both subjective and objective' (1970: 9).

This play develops beyond the literality of Adamov's early plays. In those, the literality often contained an allegorical overtone: when Le Mutilé lost his limbs in *La Grande et la Petite Manoeuvre*, his literal amputation explained his mental and spiritual condition, separated from everything that once gave meaning to life. In *Si l'été revenait* each person's dream stands for itself alone.

When Planchon returned to work on Adamov, it was with the aim of presenting the man himself, in this literal manner, with no special pleadings or general explanations. Planchon felt that in Adamov's life, as in Artaud's, the most moving conflict had been in his own person rather than in any one of his plays. He therefore presented the man as well as the works. His production, entitled *A.A. théâtres d'Adamov* was in two parts. The first part was played in the foyer (cancelled at Villeurbanne because of fire regulations but reinstated at the Chaillot theatre in Paris). This consisted of snatches from Adamov's early plays, performed in a style that recalled the early fifties, and used to build up the climate of anguish and treachery, misunderstanding and mutilation that is characteristic of those plays. Throughout this part, the audience (all standing or milling about) was surprised to see Laurent Terzieff, in the role of Adamov, interrupt the action to denounce or criticise his own work, using the words of Adamov's preface to his second volume of collected plays.

For the second half, the audience moved into the auditorium proper where

10 *Off limits* (Adamov): Piccolo Teatro, Milan, directed by Klaus-Michael Grüber, 1969.

they were confronted by a high fence, marked PRIVATE PROPERTY, running around an enormous pile of phosphorescent blue granules planted with miniature oil derricks. To one side was a shining chromium railway line running into another dune of sand rising up behind. On that and behind it was a real railway line on which a real revolutionary train, decked with flags, rolled in and out at certain points in the action. In this setting, evoking both the easy childhood of Adamov and the treacherous difficulties of acting on shifting sand, as well as the demands of larger social movements breaking in from outside, was played out the story of Adamov's own interior divisions, using largely the texts of *Le Sens de la marche* and *Comme nous avons été*.

Le Sens de la marche depicts a central character, Henri, with clear autobiographical overtones, placed in a series of situations: the home, the army, a church, a school, in which he repeatedly comes up against the authority of a father figure, who is always the same. A group of Henri's friends who are going away to form a revolutionary party break in a number of times and urge him to join them, but although he wants to, and tells them he will join them in a while, he never manages to do so, and ends up betraying one of them. The other play, *Comme nous avons été*, depicts an even more obviously autobiographical figure simply named A., asleep in bed; a character called the Mother and another called the Aunt appear, and wake him up, asking if he hasn't seen 'their little boy' who was playing with his ball in the passage. They don't seem at all put out not to find a little boy but to settle down to talk. Before long A. begins to play the part of the little boy and by the end, the Mother is tucking him back into bed in a sequence that recalls the putting of the strait-jacket on the Father at the end of Strindberg's play.

Planchon mixed together scenes from these two plays, but did not alter anything in them at all, simply allowing them to counterpoint one another and build up an image of the repressive family background. Alongside this he was able to show the impulse towards the social and political action that Adamov experienced but did not fulfil. Planchon claimed that his show was even more didactic than Brecht in that it showed the family, the psychological pressures exerted by father and mother and repressive social institutions all subtly linked, so that to achieve liberation from one it was necessary also to be free of the other.

The message, as Planchon himself pointed out, was not particularly new; it was one of the slogans of the May 1968 student riots. But he claimed that Adamov was the first to have found an adequate stage language in which to express this: one that is not naive or simplistic. In order to illustrate this, Planchon showed the kind of creative visual work that is necessary on an Adamov text. For example, taking his cue perhaps from the title of *L'Homme et l'enfant*, he would include both the child Adamov and the adult in the same scene. The opening scene from *Comme nous avons été* shows the Mother desperately asking A. where her little boy is; A., rather irritated, tries to control himself and tells her he hasn't seen the boy while at the back of the stage in a weird dream light the child-Adamov appears with an enormous pistol which he shoots at the Mother before disappearing. The production was filled with such images, images with the precision and clarity yet dream-like hallucinatory quality of Surrealist paintings.

An entry in Adamov's journal dated 29 January 1969 reads, 'Men, whose unconscious remains archaic, live imprisoned in modern life'. This tension between atavistic human needs and the alienating terrain of modern life was a constant theme of the plays of both Planchon and Adamov. The production of *A.A. théâtres d'Adamov* was the occasion for Planchon making the following assessment of Adamov:

Adamov is one of the rare authors whose theatre is essential for any playwright . . . We have much to learn from him. Here is a single example: for Adamov every speech had to fulfil four functions: to be almost an everyday phrase, at the same time to contain a latent psychoanalytic content, to open out onto social problems and, simply by its expression, to describe a character. Four demands to be made of each speech: that was Adamov's ambition (1977a: 34).

Undoubtedly Planchon is right about the importance of Adamov as a model for the development of French theatre among the practitioners themselves. He is one of the few authors to have been followed equally keenly by those in the Parisian theatre as by those in the decentralised sector. A remarkable number of important directors or groups worked on his plays at an early stage in their career. They include Vilar, Planchon, Blin, Mauclair, Serreau, Théâtre du Soleil, Théâtre Populaire de Lorraine. Among the reasons for this are the fact that Adamov provided a living link with Artaud, both by his friendship with him and by his search for a drama of gesture and literality. At the same time he was an erudite and very literary writer whose use of language became an unusually sensitive instrument for depicting the crisis of twentieth century man, as Barthes demonstrated (1957). Above all, at a time when many playwrights were driven into opposing camps, either dealing with the private anguish of individuals or the public crises of parties and nations, Adamov succeeded in creating a dramatic form flexible enough to deal *both* with the complexity of the human subconscious *and* with the confusions of modern capitalist society.

In the latter respect a play like *Off limits* is perhaps a greater achievement than any of Planchon's recent plays which have tended to become more historical. But Planchon's achievement is to be seen in his production work as well as in his play writing. In particular, his contribution to the *théâtre populaire* movement has been enormous by simply refusing to go to Paris and seeing the title of Théâtre National Populaire come to his theatre in Villeurbanne.

Planchon's other productions of the seventies are almost all expressions of the preoccupations he shared with Adamov: fear of death, political impotence and the fatalistic sense of the denial of simple satisfactions by powers beyond one's strength to influence. The production of *No man's land* treated Pinter's bleak text with a kind of visual literality that has never been seen in Britain, where his plays are usually performed on very crowded sets, filled with the bric-à-brac of a naturalist middle class interior. The set, designed by Ezio

Frigerio resembled a Magritte painting and presented the audience with a strange sensation of floating in space because the floor was made up of luminous plastic segments coloured blue and white. In addition, the frozen calm of this Magritte-like picture was constantly threatened by the breaking in of quite different images. Each half of the performance began in darkness, the only visible thing being a small perspective model that began to move in a hallucinatory fashion, so that for a while one could not be sure if it was moving or not. At various points in the action curtains covering a large window on the upstage wall parted to reveal a desolate country scene. And at the end of the play the whole box set rose slowly into the flies accompanied by a strangely frightening noise, which was at first impossible to identify, but then revealed itself as thousands of empty bottles, piled up against the backstage walls of the set, being released as the walls moved up, and rolling out onto the floor of the stage, leaving an image of an empty alcoholic waste land.

Throughout this period the company was performing *Le Tartuffe*, both at home and abroad (it came to London's new National Theatre in 1976) and Planchon also returned to Shakespeare in 1978 with productions of *Antony and Cleopatra* and *Pericles* played on alternate evenings. But the grand sum of his work at this time is to be found in his linked productions of *Athalie* and *Dom Juan* in 1980 and 1981 both designed by Ezio Frigerio. These brought together his preoccupation with love, politics and death, with the powers of ideology, superstition and belief, and they expressed these themes through a scenic language of a rare richness and profusion. *Athalie* is a play seldom performed in France. It tells the story of how the high priest Joad hid Joas, the last remaining representative of the line of David, from the murderous grasp of Athaliah, queen of Judah, until he was old enough to be annointed king. His coronation provides the occasion for a rebellion by the Levites which leaves the queen dead, the young king enthroned in her place and Jaweh victorious over Baal. Although its subject-matter is drawn from the Old Testament, the tragedy is constructed along classical lines, even including a chorus (of the daughters of Levi) on the ancient Greek pattern. And although ostensibly about the just purposes of God in history, the play derives its power from its very Jansenist presentation of a God whose purposes can never be fully known or understood but who demands blind faith and total obedience, a God who, as Joad points out in a famous speech, reveals his power in bloody deeds of death and violence such as the downfall of Jezabel, her body devoured by dogs.

The drama of the play is provided by a power struggle between Joad and Athaliah. Joad is usually pictured as a worthy Hebrew patriarch, Athaliah as a dignified if anguished queen. Planchon's performance as Joad made one think more of the Ayatollah Khomeini than of Moses. He was a man illuminated by faith. He spoke rapidly, with laughter in his voice and a characteristic confidence that God was on his side. Athaliah also emerged rejuvenated: she was presented as a reasonable, pragmatic politician. Her every action had been taken for the good of the kingdom, her goal had been stability and tolerance. But such worthy aims did not have the force to withstand the determination and fanaticism of Joad. The play interested Planchon, he said, as a commentary on the totalitarian ideology of the age of Louis XIV. Not content with having established absolute control in secular terms, Louis' ambition was to govern the private morality and even the spiritual life of his subjects.

Planchon's production was rich in images of Catholic triumphalism, the cross and the canon not so much opposed as mutually reinforcing. He encouraged the audience to reflect along these lines by introducing a tall male angel, dressed in shining golden armour, resembling the young Louis dressed as Apollo for a court ballet. One of the difficulties of performing *Athalie* is that the 8-year-old Joas has to deliver a fair number of lines, all in a tone of pious wisdom. Planchon made the boy mute, but had the angel stalking the stage behind him and speaking his lines. Slightly distorted through a system of amplification, these speeches came across as the divine voice itself. Racine's text amply justifies such a device by alluding frequently to the disturbing impact of divine intimation through dream or prophecy. Athaliah says she is tormented by a dream in which the young Joas strikes her dead and this dream sequence was also enacted in the course of the production.

Racine's work is normally performed in France in a rather statuesque, declamatory fashion, following what seems to have been the practice in Racine's own time. Planchon introduced an enormous amount of movement and physical action into the play. Instead of having the chorus appear only at the end of each act, he kept them on stage almost throughout the play so that their actions and reactions became an important element. Like the villagers of *Le Cochon noir*, they were helpless, the pawns of other people's power struggles. Their presence on stage enabled Planchon to situate the play, from the very beginning, on two different imaginary planes. The words told us that this was the temple and these the daughters of Levi, but the image of the girls lined up at table, enclosed by the seventeenth century neo-classical cupola, suggested the young ladies of Saint Cyr, for whom the play was originally written, and their vulnerability in the political circumstances: as Mathan enters they run, screaming from the menace of his lieutenants.

On alternate evenings to *Athalie*, performances of Molière's *Dom Juan* were given, using the same actors and certain elements of the same set (the cupola, for example, was used in both productions). There were some interesting combinations of roles. For example, Gérard Desarthe, who played the role of Mathan in *Athalie* was cast as Dom Juan; the two peasant girls of *Dom Juan*, Charlotte and Mathurine, were both members of the chorus of *Athalie*. In this way the two plays emerged as two sides of the same coin: where *Athalie* conveyed the triumph of a totalitarian Catholic ideology, *Dom Juan* expressed the spirit of dissidence that insists on questioning everything. But Dom Juan's challenge to authority was enacted in a stage setting where every element threatened to overwhelm him, from the violence of the chivalric code, presented in the scene in the forest, to the monstrous death's head of the commander's tomb, from the pathos of Dona Elvire's appeals, to the very elements themselves: the monumental waves on the seashore, frozen in a movement that seemed about to engulf him (see fig. 11).

For both plays the set included a short platform, projecting into the auditorium, that was shaped like a black marble tomb watched over by a skeleton. This ever-present reminder of death provided a scenic echo to the constant warning, in the texts of both plays, of impending doom and destruction. For both Athaliah and Dom Juan are characters who dream about their own deaths. Both attempt to make a stand on the set of values they have chosen, but both are haunted and ultimately destroyed by the power of God. The experience of seeing these productions was a particularly satisfying and complex one because, as well as their ideological and social aspects, they projected a powerful psychological portrait of individuals attempting to face up to the ultimate question of death. The main characters of both productions were shown to be people who were not just constrained by external pressures but who experienced these pressures as interior psychological and spiritual struggles. Years before, Planchon had expressed his admiration for Shakespeare by saying that in his plays social analysis never crushes the individual psychology of the characters, while at the same time the characters do not mask the general view of the society that is being described. In his productions of *Athalie* and *Dom Juan*, Planchon achieved just this balance and richness, so that the spectator's mind was constantly moving from

11 *Dom Juan* (Molière): the waves on the beach, designed by Ezio Frigerio, as Dom Juan (Gérard Desarthe) tries to seduce both Charlotte (Cathy Bodet) and Mathurine (Dominique Messali). T.N.P.-Villeurbanne, 1980.

the plight of the individual to the social or ideological context and back to the individual. The result was a powerful statement about the struggle of human beings for a sense of their independent existence, haunted by death, surrounded by powers that they cannot control, able to define themselves only by means of the mental structures of their age and community, frequently failing to understand their own or other people's motives.

The complexity of the images and actions in a Planchon production places great demands on an audience. He is sometimes accused of producing theatre that is over-subtle considering his desire for broad popular appeal. His answer to this is to deny that there should be any discrepancy between popularity and quality: 'I've always said that to bring people from outside culture into the theatre, one must present the best things in the world, and then see how it works out. Of course one explains and comments in a production; but I've never believed in making a theatre to attract "the masses" with comprehensible plays or acceptable stories' (1972: 46). The fact that his theatre has not attracted a huge working class following, he says, is not really surprising: 'I don't believe that theatre can make much impact on a state of affairs that only a change in civilization could modify. I hope to live to see the dawn of this change, but in the meantime what a theatre like the one I run can do is to go on making people aware that there is a violent cultural divide. Our job is to keep the wound open' (1977b: 33).

7

The decentralised theatre III: the sixties

Planchon has been studied in some detail because he is an exemplary case: both for the quality and range of his work and for the official government recognition of it, he stands pre-eminent in the decentralised theatre. The fact that he is also one of the outstanding modern playwrights makes him a particularly appropriate subject for a book of this kind. But the need to single out one example for detailed treatment should not obscure the enormous expansion in the decentralised theatre that took place during the sixties. In many areas this was the work of young people, who became known as the second generation of the decentralisation. They were people who, growing up during the fifties, had been inspired by the work of Vilar, Planchon or one of the Centres, had in many cases attended the theatre school in Strasbourg and had then decided to set up their own theatre company in a deprived urban area or provincial town which had never had a resident theatre company before. This was both new and surprising. Previously, young actors or directors had always gravitated to Paris and, once there, had joined one of the established companies. The spawning of new young companies in the course of the sixties brought intense new life to the decentralisation movement, although this also involved an element of instability as was to be shown in 1968. It also helped to make up for the lack of amateur theatre in France, since many such groups started with semi-amateur status.

The most frequent pattern was for a group to establish itself in a place where it could attract a small subsidy from the municipality and then to approach the Ministry of Culture with a request for additional money. The Ministry created a theatre section, with inspectors, whose job it was to assess the standard of work being done and weigh up the relative merits of the grant applicants. A category was invented with the title *animateur culturel*. If a theatre company's work was judged to be of a sufficiently high standard, its director became an *animateur* with a small subsidy and his company was given the status of Troupe Permanente. At the same time, a number of new Centres Dramatiques were established with much larger subsidies and the *animateurs* were encouraged to expand their activities to the point at which they might be eligible for the status of Centre. For the director of a Centre, the glittering prize at the top of the ladder was to be promoted director of a Maison de la Culture. The Maisons were the brainchild of Malraux, de Gaulle's Minister of Culture from the start of the Fifth Republic in 1959 until 1969. He saw them as the modern counterpart of the gothic cathedrals: glorious centres of excellence scattered across France which would attract the biggest and best of the orchestras, exhibitions and theatre companies away from the capital. The Maisons were to be jointly funded by the Ministry of Culture and the local municipality and administered by a director responsible to a board of local councillors, industrialists and representatives of special interest groups.

This conception of the Maison de la Culture did not fit well with the idea of *théâtre populaire* that men such as Planchon were working for, which explains why he was unwilling to be involved in running a Maison. In some cases adroit directors were able to use their position in charge of a Maison to create a resident theatre company of the highest standards devoted to work of local and contemporary relevance. Gabriel Monnet achieved this at Bourges until he was dismissed in 1968. But more often the prestige and cost of these ventures was so enormous that they became political footballs, kicked back and forth between the local authority and central government. In the process, as Planchon had rightly foreseen, the artistic freedom of the director went by the board, the budget was earmarked for prestigious visiting shows and it became impossible to establish a permanent local company.

By the middle of the sixties half a dozen Maisons were open and a similar number close to completion, but only those at Caen and Bourges included a permanent producing theatre company. In general, the administrative structure of the Maisons made it difficult for full-time theatre companies to operate. Where the theatre companies were dynamic, they often came into conflict with the board of management. This was the case of Jo Tréhard, brilliant director of the Comédie de Caen, who was dismissed from his post as director of the Maison in 1968. He withdrew with his company to a converted parish hall, leaving the theatre of the Maison free for the more commercial tours favoured by the municipality. The Ministry took Jo Tréhard's side and continued to fund his company, so that the Maison ceased to exist and there was war between the municipality and its former theatre company. An even worse case was that of the Maison at Saint Etienne. The Ministry had deliberately chosen Saint Etienne because of Dasté's long-standing work there. He was consulted throughout the process of designing and building so that the stage and workshops of the Maison could be tailored to his company's needs. But as the building neared completion Dasté fell out with the local board of management. The Ministry did its best to put pressure on the board to install Dasté in the Maison that had been built for him, but without success. It opened without the Comédie de Saint Etienne or any other permanent producing theatre company.

But despite the disappointing record of the Maisons de la Culture, in terms of theatre, the new Centres and Troupes Permanentes established during the sixties represented a very considerable expansion. By 1966 there were eight Centres and nine Troupes Permanentes; by 1972 this had risen to twenty and seventeen respectively. The repertoire of the new young theatre companies established at this time was, in some ways, similar to that of the first five Centres in the fifties. The main difference was in spirit and style. Where the early pioneers had turned to Molière and the classics in the spirit of Copeau, these plays were now performed in the spirit of Brecht, borrowing the ideas and techniques pioneered by Planchon. This new wave of directors was excited by the polemic between the supporters and detractors of political theatre. Almost to a man, they placed themselves on the side of political theatre and delighted in experiments with materialist productions of plays hitherto assumed to be devoid of political content. The classics still proved the main box-office draw, but the new directors were more inclined to experiment than the first generation and gradually a number of contemporary authors were introduced into their repertoires. In a number of cases these new authors were local writers who benefited from a close link with the theatre company and who enjoyed the advantage of seeing their successive plays performed by the same company. Among these were Pierre Halet who had four plays produced by the Comédie de Bourges between 1963 and 1968 and Armand Gatti, a Southerner, three of whose early plays were performed at the Grenier de Toulouse. Not all companies found their 'house author', but many proved strikingly adventurous in their choice of authors. The survey of plays in decentralised theatres carried out for *Atac informations* in 1972 shows that more than 400 different authors had been performed, and although Molière, Shakespeare and Brecht were considerably ahead of the rest, the range of different authors was extremely wide, including a large number of contemporary French writers as well as a great many foreign plays, both moderns and classics.

Towards the end of the sixties, many of those involved in the decentralisation movement were beginning to feel that they had lost their sense of direction. By bringing live theatre to culturally impoverished areas, they had imagined that they would be stirring people up, encouraging them to think for themselves and to question the benefits of the consumer society. But they found that in fact their actions had often had the opposite effect. After the instability of the last years of the Fourth Republic, much of the population was grateful to de Gaulle for presiding over a period of expansion. His presidency became synonymous with the rebuilding of national pride and the new theatre companies found that they were treated as part of this larger enterprise in recovering *la gloire*. Far from encouraging their audiences to question the status quo, they had become the museum guards of a showcase for French cultural prestige. And the harder they struggled to assert their artistic independence, the more lavish the praise that was heaped on them and the more completely they were absorbed by Malraux's cultural imperialism. They felt that they had been cheated, that instead of achieving an effective protest, they had become the sugar on the pill of the modern capitalist state, the 'supplément d'âme' or dash of soul designed to make the rest acceptable.

This feeling had been fuelled by influences from outside France, particularly by the Living Theatre, which made a number of visits to France in the course of the sixties, and by Grotowski's Theatre Laboratory, which brought its production of *The constant prince* to the Odéon in 1966. In the work of both these companies, French theatre workers felt they had discovered a revelation of a theatre of immediacy and gut reaction, which possessed an emotional force that had sometimes been lost by excessive attention to Brecht and to the theatre of reason. When the student riots of spring 1968 broke out, the protestors often occupied the local theatre as a suitable debating forum. In an almost penitential mood, many theatre workers accepted the charges of elitism and irrelevance thrown at them by the students and agreed to try to change their strategy. In some cases they put this into immediate effect, interrupting their programmed performances in order to take agitprop shows out into the streets and the occupied factories. The mood of penitence and new resolve quickly turned to shock as a number of directors were dismissed on the grounds that they had misused their positions to engage in political activity.

During the summer, a large number of those responsible for decentralised theatre met at Villeurbanne to discuss the crisis. They concluded that the events had shown that there was a strong working class opposition to the Gaullist vision of France and that their main failure had been in not attracting sufficient numbers of this oppositional class into their theatres. They christened them the 'non-public' and resolved to make every effort to orientate theatre towards them. The main difficulty, as they saw it, was that no substantial working class repertoire existed that would be suitable for approaching the non-public. The solution to this dilemma was to construct their own material in the light of the interests of the particular sector of the non-public that they were aiming at. This method of work helped to answer another criticism which held that the director had acquired excessive power and tended to behave like a dictator. In this new working method, every member of the company had an equal right to voice his opinion, to suggest a line of research or dramatic construction and to criticise the work of any other member. The method became known as *création collective* and was successfully practised by a few groups throughout the seventies. It will be discussed in chapter 9.

Of course, the methods of *création collective* were not favoured by everyone: many believed from the outset that it would only lead to indifferent 'committee' writing and others were more concerned with a radical reassessment of the whole concept of theatre as a public service that had been popularised by Vilar's generation of directors. Broadly, the younger generation was concerned to develop a clearer set of political objectives. Since the new decentralised theatres had depended for their success mainly on revivals of the classics, there was now a running debate on their political relevance in the pursuit of people's theatre. This was a debate that had played an important role in the cultural movements of the 1930s, but had lain dormant during the fifties and early sixties. Now, as young theatre workers began to rediscover agitprop and the theatre of direct political action, they also rediscovered the controversies and contradictions that go with it. Hard-line communists in the thirties had insisted that the classic repertoire was alien to the people, being tainted by the aristocratic and bourgeois classes who had brought it into being. The Popular Front spokesmen, on the other hand, had insisted that art of every tradition belonged to the people and that the people would respond to it if given the chance. Men like Vilar had adopted the Popular Front line. Now the young militants took the opposite view, considering that only performances directed at their particular political and social circumstances could be of any use to working class audiences. A first contradiction, of course, lay in the small percentage of blue-collar workers attending even the most 'popular' theatres. So they adopted the only possible alternative: they went out into the streets to recruit new audiences. A good example of this approach can be seen in the work of the Théâtre Populaire de Lorraine. After 1968 this group abandoned its earlier practice of performing the classics with plays by Brecht and Adamov. Instead it adopted the practice of picking a theme such as the steel industry of the Lorraine basin or immigration in the area. Its members then approached appropriate sections of the local community, talked with them, tried out ideas, even showed them specimen scenes. Finally, when their new play had been put together, they performed a special short 'trailer' for it to groups of workers as they came out of the factories and made sure that the full performances were at times that fitted with the shift system and in places, like union halls, that the workers did not find alienating. The form taken by such shows is discussed in chapter 9.

Such work was more likely to flourish in urban than in rural areas and it is significant that many of the new decentralised companies of the sixties had chosen a different strategy from the touring model of Dasté at Saint Etienne or Goubert and Parigot at Rennes. Instead they had tried to identify with a particular urban community, establishing themselves as a permanent presence. But not all groups operated in the manner of the Théâtre Populaire de Lorraine.

The theatres that were, in some ways, the least affected by the prevailing sense of a need to rethink from first principles were the theatres that had already been pursuing a more overtly political policy before 1968. This was mostly true of the theatres that had grown up in the workers' suburbs around Paris, at Aubervilliers, Nanterre, Villejuif, Saint Denis, and Sartrouville. These are chronicled in some detail by Philippe Madral in his book *Le Théâtre hors les murs*. A convenient example is the first of these to be established, Gabriel Garran's Théâtre de la Commune at Aubervilliers. Garran's early productions were not of the French classics but were drawn from a more recent tradition of political theatre classics like Vyshnevsky's *Optimistic tragedy*, O'Casey's *The star turns red*, the work of Brecht. He did not produce Molière and his only Shakespeare was *Coriolanus* in a production that showed the influence of Brecht's version of that play. He also produced new plays with a clear political orientation such as Weiss', *The investigation* and Cousin's *Opéra noir*. An immense amount of energy went into organising small local discussion groups among people interested in the theatre, contacting all manner of societies and individuals with no previous experience of theatre, and arranging events outside the theatre proper, such as readings by Gatti of his *Chant public devant deux chaises électriques*. This work was able to extend over a long period in a consistent manner because of the support, both financial and moral, of the communist mayor, Jack Ralite. Since the theatre was paid for entirely by the municipality, Garran did not have to contend with the contradictions of performing Marxist theatre in a building financed by the capitalist state. In this

143

way, unlike many directors and companies, he was able to rely on a homogeneous community, clearly defined cultural aims and a policy of dialogue with unions and workers well established before the turmoil of 1968. Like other directors of the Paris suburban theatres, such as Raymond Gerbal and José Valverde, he had taken part in some of the few militant or agitprop productions of the fifties, and had a clear view of the usefulness of theatre in a Marxist perspective as a raiser of political consciousness. With the advantage of these clear political objectives, these directors tended to take over the leadership of the *théâtre populaire* movement in the late sixties and it was to the theatres of the Parisian 'red belt' that people came to look for the latest experiments in a relevant, politicised people's theatre.

At the same time there were other directors who became impatient with the sharp divisions that were polarising the French theatre into opposing camps, the one trumpeting political relevance and the other claiming artistic or metaphysical profundity. The outstanding example was Jean-Marie Serreau, who had directed early productions of Brecht (*The exception and the rule* in 1947 and *A man's a man* in 1954) as well as plays by Adamov, Ionesco and Beckett. For Serreau, as for Planchon, the tendency to set Brechtian theatre and New Theatre in opposition to one another was both unnecessary and limiting. In the course of the sixties, he conducted a number of experiments in multiple staging and multi-media events. One such experiment involved the simultaneous staging of Michel Parent's play *Gilda appelle Mae West* on four separate stages in a sports club at Dijon in 1962. The play attempted an account of the dropping of the first atomic bomb from the different viewpoints of the pilot, the victims, and subsequent history. Other experimental performances, often combining film, music and drama were conducted in the Pavillon de Marsan in Paris. Through these experiments, Serreau was searching for a new form of theatre that would 'attempt a synthesis between scientific knowledge and poetic knowledge' (cit. Masson, 1966: 13).

He discovered this synthesis in the work of writers from the former French colonies. He was the first director to introduce French audiences to a number of new playwrights, including the Algerian Kateb Yacine and the Martiniquan Aimé Césaire. His attempt to stage Yacine's *Le Cadavre encerclé* in 1958 during the Algerian war nearly provoked a riot by right-wing groups, so he had to transfer the performance to Brussels. In 1964 he successfully produced it at the Récamier theatre and followed this with the same author's *Les Ancêtres redoublent de férocité* at the T.N.P. in 1967. His productions of Césaire's works are discussed below (pp. 148–51). He was the first director to recruit black actors in a systematic way, not only to perform work by African and West Indian writers, but also to act in plays by Brecht, Genet and other European writers. Through this work, he acquired a strong influence over a whole generation of young actors and playwrights from third world countries who, as students in France, had attended his productions or worked with his company. Until his unexpected death in 1973, he did everything he could to persuade those concerned with political theatre in France of the vital importance to them of developments in the third world:

The major event of our time, is that the third world is breaking free from its historic ghetto.

The theatre of the third world, which is both political and poetic, calls into question our whole western civilisation, within which the idea of humanism has always been identified with the idea of the West.

That is what I call euro-centrism. To be a Brechtian today is to speak of the third world (Serreau, 1974: 31).

In 1971 he had established a theatre alongside the Théâtre du Soleil (see chapter 9) at the Vincennes Cartoucherie; it was named Théâtre de la Tempête and was to be dedicated to multi-media work in continuation of his earlier experiments at the Dijon festival and the Pavillon de Marsan in Paris.

Playwrights of the sixties: Césaire, Cousin, Gatti

The expansion of decentralised theatre in the sixties led a great many authors to write plays for the first time. Sometimes they were responding to commissions, sometimes they were simply motivated by the exciting possibilities that were opened up by the growth of theatre companies outside Paris. From the many interesting playwrights of the period I have selected three whose work is broadly representative of their social and stylistic concerns. All three were known as writers before they became playwrights, beginning to work for the theatre only in the late fifties or early sixties. All three have used the theatre to confront political questions of world-wide dimensions such as neo-colonialism or the nuclear threat, and all three have experimented with forms of Epic theatre. All three had written poetry before turning to the theatre and we shall find that, in different ways, all of their plays rely on poetic effect as much as on social or political analysis. Finally, all three have a conception of theatre in which song, movement and gesture are as important as dialogue – their texts are written so as to make unusual demands on the creativity of the performers.

Aimé Césaire

Aimé Césaire is a playwright who makes a mockery of critical attempts to categorise. His plays are poetic but quite different from those of Claudel, political but quite different from those of Brecht. He has never been associated with a particular decentralised theatre, although his plays exemplify the aims of the decentralisation movement particularly well. But to analyse his theatre solely in these negative terms is to obscure its real power and originality. For Césaire's two major plays, *La Tragédie du roi Christophe* and *Une saison au Congo*, achieve a unique renewal of dramatic style, both through their use of language and through their dramatic construction. With these two plays, and with *Une tempête*, adapted from Shakespeare, Césaire administered a shock to the French theatre world very similar to that produced by Soyinka's work in England.

Césaire began his literary activity as a poet, historian and politician. His most famous poem *Cahier d'un retours au pays natal* was first published in 1939. In this he expressed the difficulty he had in shaking off the prejudices of his European education, which had implanted deep in his unconscious an image of himself as necessarily inferior because of his colour. The poem works through his humiliation towards a conclusion which affirms his will to identify with his exploited fellow countrymen, resisting the temptation to become an 'honorary white'. He was elected mayor of Fort-de-France (Martinique) and communist deputy to the French parliament in 1945. By the time he came to write *La Tragédie du roi Christophe*, he had already published six volumes of poetry as well as a number of political and historical studies.

His first play, *Et les chiens se taisaient*, appeared originally as an extended poem in the collection *Les Armes miraculeuses* (1946). Ten years later Césaire expanded and rewrote it as a separate play, but it has not been performed in French and although it contains many of the themes of Césaire's later plays, it has none of their theatrical brilliance: it remains first and foremost a poem. Césaire's three plays for the theatre were all written in the course of the sixties *La Tragédie du roi Christophe* (1963), *Une saison au Congo* (1966) and *Une tempête* (1969). During this period the West African states formerly part of the Belgian and French Empires all achieved their independence and Césaire plainly wrote with them in mind: both his chosen dramatic form and the subjects he dealt with were deliberately directed at an African audience. But his methods and intentions echoed those of workers in the French decentralised theatres.

He chose to write plays rather than poetry for two reasons: he wanted to reach a broader audience and he wanted to deal more directly with politics. Both of these ambitions were in response to the new situation he saw developing in Africa. 'My theatre is political because the major problems in Africa are political problems. . . I want a theatre in direct contact with our problems' (cit. Mbom, 1979: 26). 'In Africa, theatre is an essential means of communication. Because of this it must be directly accessible to the people' (cit. Laville, 1970: 240). In fact his plays have not been widely performed in Africa, perhaps because, like Soyinka's, they are too critical of newly independent black governments, but the above statements show how much he had in common with the *théâtre populaire* movement. His plays were all produced by Jean-Marie Serreau and had a considerable impact in France.

Stylistically, too, they take their place in the decentralisation movement, being influenced by Brecht and described by the author himself as 'Epic'. 'My theatre is not an individual or individualist theatre, it is an epic theatre for it always presents the fate of a whole community' (cit. Harris, 1973: 126–7). The plays present all the characteristics that we have identified for Epic theatre: they tell their story by means of contradictions, present their characters in fragmentary form and rely on strong didactic and gestural qualities. Above all, they are plays which aim to arouse the critical reactions of their audiences: 'It seems to me that the underdeveloped countries will only be saved when their inhabitants have got beyond their present lack of consciousness' (cit. Laville, 1970: 240). As he showed in the *Cahier*, Césaire believed that the most important liberation was the liberation of black men's minds from the image of themselves implanted by centuries of white imperialism. The most damaging effect of the colonial period was the success of the white man in making the black man see *himself* through the white man's eyes. No self-respect was possible for the black races while they still considered themselves to be uncivilised failures, 'boys' who could only hope to rule themselves if they followed the lead of their white masters. This was the thesis developed by Fanon (a former pupil of Césaire's) and dramatised for white audiences by Genet in *Les Nègres*. Césaire attempted to put the idea into dramatic form for black audiences using a French of great stylistic subtlety which draws on the language as spoken in Caribbean and African countries as well as the French of France.

La Tragédie du roi Christophe presents a brilliant dramatisation of the problem of black identity because of its use of multiple viewpoint. Christophe, and his efforts to create a truly independent Haiti, are seen through the eyes of the peasants, the mulattos, the church, the foreigners, the army, the rebels. Each view of the king and of the national situation is made to contrast with another, so that the story is developed by contrasts and contradictions in true Epic style. The play begins with a prologue in the form of a cockfight between two cocks named after the two political leaders, Pétion and Christophe. This suggests the theme of the popular contest in much the same way as Brecht's prologue to *In the jungle of the cities*. Here we are introduced to the mood of the common people of Haiti, a mood which Christophe sees as his principle enemy. It is a mood of noisy gaiety, undisciplined, excitable, ready to see everything as material for a joke or a wager.

This gives way to a scene in which Christophe and Pétion confront one another in the Senate, where Christophe has been isolated as a dangerous negro by Pétion's influential group of mulattos. Pétion tries to neutralise Christophe by offering him the post of president, but Christophe sees through the manoeuvre, refuses the offer and establishes a separate kingdom in the northern part of the island controlled by his forces. The rest of the play covers the period from 1811 to 1820 when Christophe ruled in Haiti as King Henry. Through his dramatic reconstruction of this period in Haitian history, Césaire was able to present the conflicting views of African liberation during the period of the fifties and sixties. According to the different viewpoint presented, Christophe appears as either hero or tyrant, visionary or madman.

In his own eyes, he is the father of his people and all Haitians are his family. His paternalism is clearly modelled on the West African *Oba* or King. He insists on having a court, with suitable ceremonial and religious observances. He insists on administering justice himself and severely punishes any of his lieutenants who exceed his orders. He refuses to share out the land among his courtiers, arguing that all the land belongs to him and through him to the people of Haiti. He insists on the need for work and discipline but is magnanimous in victory, refusing to take Port-au-Prince by force when it lies within his grasp, preferring to spare the people and hope for peaceful collaboration.

But against this vision of himself as the wise *Oba* is set the experience of living under his rule. His triumphant march on Port-au-Prince is interrupted by the scene of the death of Metellus, a rebel general. In a lyrical but terse style, Metellus denounces the struggle between Christophe and Pétion, claiming that neither is really working in the interests of the Haitian people. At the height of Christophe's powers, in the middle of Act II, Césaire introduces a grotesque scene in which Christophe forcibly marries off all the unattached young peasants he can find because, he claims, he is worried by loose morality and anarchy. This scene, together with others where the peasants are presented on their own, show us how Christophe's ideas of liberty became, in practice, a kind of tyranny for the Haitian people. The scenes in which Christophe is on stage alternate very cleverly with those from which he is absent, so that a dialectic is established between Christophe's vision of his country liberating itself by its own heroic efforts and the people's view of Christophe as a man suffering from *folie de grandeur*.

The play's structure is thus eminently Brechtian, since every judgement that appears to be made about the king and the political situation is then undermined by a different judgement in the following scene. The audience is not provided with a definitive view of Christophe, or of his achievements, but with a number of conflicting views which it is up to them to reconcile. This method is made into a vivid means of portraying the post-colonial struggle, since most of Christophe's contradictions stem from his desire to combat racist images of the black man. Because the negro had been considered primitive, Christophe insists on a court, sanctified by courtiers, ceremonial and religion. Because the negro had been written off as a lazy good-for-nothing, Christophe insists on the discipline of hard work. His tyrannical behaviour is not shown as the inevitable result of the corruption brought by power, but as the unfortunate consequence of his lucid understanding of the real problem: he has seen that negroes must liberate themselves from the *image* that they have allowed colonial civilisation (mulatto power as well as white power) to impose upon them. The play is called a tragedy because Christophe is not a tyrant but a Promethean figure. When his efforts to maintain his heroic programme reach fever pitch, he suffers a stroke and dies some months later amid the disintegration of his kingdom. But his death is not seen entirely as a failure. The play closes on a ceremonial praise chant and an invocation to Shango to carry the king back to Ife, the spiritual heartland of Africa for the Yoruba religion and a link back to their homeland for the negroes of the Caribbean.

The power of the play lies in the way that these problems of liberation from colonial rule are expressed in a dramatic idiom of such richness and variety. The scenes range from the market place to the court, from the battlefield to the church; the characters are drawn from every level of society and their different speech idioms are brilliantly characterised. There is a Shakespearean breadth and power in the evocation of this society in a state of ferment. The portrait of Christophe is enhanced by a device drawn straight from Shakespeare: that of the court jester. Hugonin fills this role, constantly intervening with songs and dances, frequently criticising Christophe, contrasting the heroic image with a picture of monumental folly. All of this gave enormous opportunities to the first director of the play, Jean-Marie Serreau who, during the sixties, became identified with the young African and Caribbean theatre, building up a team of black actors and producing works by a number of black writers. He and Césaire collaborated closely on the production, and the play was considerably altered in the course of rehearsals.

What emerged from Serreau's production was the profoundly gestural quality of Césaire's play. Although written in a language that has frequent recourse to poetic metaphor, the text is never verbose because the speeches imply action. A good example is the metaphor of the river. In the *intermède* between Acts I and II we see two rafts bringing timber down the river to the sea. The rafters discuss briefly the difficulty of the last stage of the journey when a rope is thrown from the bank: miss it and your raft floats irretrievably out to sea. The river journey, with its associated hard work and practical difficulties, becomes a metaphor for the task of liberation. At the end of the act the metaphor is recalled when Christophe announces that Haiti is in the *raque* of history – the *raque* being that part of the river bank too muddy to cross. It is this impossible, treacherous mud that they must slog through if they are to find liberty. But the reply of the old peasant is that the *raque* is a trap. It must be avoided by taking another route, following either the river or the higher ground. The image of the river catches up a number of the play's themes – Christophe's defiance of tradition contrasted with proverbial wisdom, the hard work needed to rebuild the country – and expresses them in a concrete, natural image implying physical gesture and social attitude with great economy of means.

Serreau could not get French backing for the play and so its first performance was at the Salzburg festival in 1964. Here it was a huge success, but arguments with the German backers held up a French production until 1965, when it opened at the Odéon before touring round the Maisons de la Cuture and decentralised theatres. Césaire's second play *Une saison au Congo* also opened outside France at the Venice Biennale of 1967, after which it transferred to the Théâtre de l'Est Parisien. Here again Césaire collaborated closely with Serreau and rewrote sections of the play during rehearsal (see Laville, 1970). The play presents some similarities with *La Tragédie du roi Christophe*: it centres on Patrice Lumumba and his attempts to establish an independent Congolese Republic and it shows him failing through trying to achieve too much too soon. But there are also important differences. The tragedy of the Congo in the early sixties was at least in part the result of interference by outside forces, notably the investors in mineral resources. Their involvement meant that the odds were bound to be heavily against Lumumba and so he appears as more of a victim than Christophe.

Where Christophe presented a fascinating mixture of the grotesque and the admirable, Lumumba is almost wholly admirable and so the play becomes more of a saint's life than a tragedy. The grotesque note is reserved for the chorus of bankers, instead of being used disconcertingly in the depiction of every level of society. For many critics, the play was a disappointment, not matching the power and subtlety of *La Tragédie du roi Christophe*. Bernard Dort, for example, while recognising the very considerable interest and merit of the play, argued that its characters remain too individual, not assuming the destiny of the whole nation. He considered that the power struggles in the Congo looked so different when placed in one historical perspective (the European) from the way they appeared in another perspective (the African), that Césaire should have decided which audience to write for. (Dort, 1971: 281).

Césaire himself was quite clear about which audience he wrote for: 'I write theatre for underdeveloped countries because I come from one myself' (cit. Laville, 1970: 240). With *Une saison au Congo* he wanted to move from the historical reconstruction of his previous play to direct dramatisation of contemporary reality. He chose to do this in a manner that owes much to traditional African models and conforms less to the Shakespearean–Brechtian model than *La Tragédie du roi Christophe*. The reason for the change of dramatic method is to be found in the change of subject-matter. The question discussed in the earlier play was how the mentality of a whole nation might be changed so as to enable it to assume real independence. In *Une saison au Congo* this theme is still present, but it is subordinated to the major theme of the fragility of the newly liberated African states in the face of the neo-colonial powers (see Mbom, 1979: 71). Not that Césaire's play presents a profound economic analysis. The realities of the situation that he depicts are brutally simple: western investors are determined to stop at nothing to protect their investments. Rather than allow Lumumba control of the rich Katanganese mining areas, they encourage secession and foment civil war. Because of their intervention, Lumumba is defeated and killed.

Christophe's downfall possessed the traditional tragic characteristics, stemming from the *hubris* and *hamartia* that were part and parcel of his greatness. But Lumumba's death failed Aristotle's test of the tragic since 'a good man must not be seen passing from happiness to misery' (Aristotle, 1920: 49), so Césaire looked back to the tradition of the African hero play or legend that had informed his first play *Et les chiens se taisaient*. In their broad outlines, these hero plays are remarkably similar to the Arthurian legends of medieval France and Britain. They present a god, king or leader who is identified with the fertility of his country. This hero emerges in a time of trouble, faces the hostility of his own people but wins them round to his cause, triumphs for a time but is overthrown by rival factions and is killed through the treachery of his own lieutenants. However, his death is not the end but is followed by the affirmation of his continuing spiritual life.

Césaire's play about Lumumba follows this pattern, appropriately adopting a tone of celebration. The high points of the play are Lumumba's speech on independence day, in which he rejects the semi-dependence offered by the Belgian king and proclaims the need for full independence immediately, or the episode in which he meets a delegation of mutinous troops and transforms their opposition into delirious support. The heroes of African legend are always representative figures rather than individual case-studies, and Césaire was most insistent that Lumumba the man was not the centre of his play (and hence did not figure in the title). He is to be seen as 'an individual representing a community' (cit. Harris, 1973: 125) just as the Sanza-player is 'the incarnation of the people' (ibid.). So the play is not mainly concerned to investigate a series of political choices, but rather to celebrate the survival and strengthening of an idea, the idea embodied by Lumumba. By including a final scene in which Mokutu (albeit hypocritically) acknowledges Lumumba as hero and martyr, and by presenting the whole period as a *season*, Césaire suggests that as the seasons change and return, so Lumumba's vision of independence will one day flourish.

By adapting a traditional African model to his own requirements, Césaire was able to write a play that went beyond a negative account of Lumumba's defeat. The popular and celebratory aspects of the play were strengthened during the rehearsals with Jean-Marie Serreau, and the part of the Sanza-player was amplified. In the original version, he had simply provided interludes between the scenes. Now he took on a more integrated role, passing judgement on events as well as describing them. The part was performed by Douta Seck, an actor of great presence who had performed the role of Christophe. He became a sort of answering voice in dialogue with Lumumba, representing between them the awakening political consciousness of the Congolese people. For the Sanza-player's interventions, Césaire drew heavily on African proverbs and jokes.

These elements of traditional literature had also been present to some extent in *La Tragédie du roi Christophe*, though the frame of reference was more clearly Caribbean in that play. Hugonin, in the role of court fool, had appeared at the end as Baron Samedi, the Haitian messenger of death. Such devices show how Césaire turned traditional elements to his advantage in the creation of Epic theatre. For the Sanza-player's songs and interventions are used to interrupt the action and provoke reflection in just the same way as Brecht used songs in his plays, and although the structure of *Une saison au Congo* is less clearly dialectical than that of Césaire's previous play, there are other Epic devices that the two plays share. Both proceed by short, disjointed scenes and although Césaire divides these up into Acts, the plays would lose nothing if these divisions were ignored. Both plays alternate between comic and serious episodes and both contain moments when the action is brought to a halt by heightened, poetic speech. Both contain scenes of grotesque social satire. In *Une saison au Congo* this tone is reserved for the European bankers, terrified for their investments, who talk in an approximation of Alexandrine verse.

Césaire has stated that 'the theatre should evoke the invention of the future' (cit. Laville, 1970: 240). In this play, his principle characters are made to embody the old and the new ways of thinking. Lumumba says to M'siri, who is about to kill him: 'You are the invention of the past, I am the inventor of the future' (109). Lumumba's vision of an integrated, self-reliant African state is contrasted with two different attitudes, both outdated. One is that of Mokutu, Tzumbi, M'siri and others, who claim to be working for the nation but in fact promote the old tribal rivalries for personal gain. The other is that of Hammarskjöld, the Secretary General of the United Nations, who claims to be neutral while in fact allowing the Belgians access to transport planes and weapons. Hammarskjöld is given a sympathetic treatment: he arrives in the Congo confident in his power, as a neutral observer, to find a solution. But he gradually discovers that there is no such thing as a neutral stance, his attempt at neutrality serves the Belgian financial interests and destroys Lumumba. He ends up a despairing figure because instead of promoting his Christian principles of peace and reconciliation, he sees that he has simply been a tool of old established interests and has contributed to the sacrifice of an innocent.

With *Une tempête*, Césaire confirmed his celebration of black creativity and his denunciation of bankrupt European ideology. The play retains Shakespeare's plot in most of its details, but radically alters its ending and its whole meaning. Césaire's fundamental innovation is to divide the characters of the play according to the colonial class-structure. While Prospero and the shipwrecked party are all Caucasians, Ariel is a Mulatto slave and Caliban a negro slave. One extra character is introduced, Eshu, the trickster god of West African religions. Caliban is quite unlike Shakespeare's monster, although the scenes with Stephano and Trinculo are cleverly written to provoke reflection on the idea of the monstrous in Shakespeare as the product of arrogance and ignorance. Césaire's Caliban is a man who knows his own mind. He is a follower of Shango and implacably opposed to the works of Prospero. He despises Ariel, the half-caste who happily does his master's bidding. His one aim is liberty and the repossession of his island. He is aware of the extent to which Prospero's 'magical' (or technological) powers have only been developed by means of his own enforced cooperation and he is determined to oppose further exploitation of himself or of his island. Prospero, too, is rather different from the serene magus of Shakespeare. His control of the island's spiritual powers is not complete, and the masque he conjures up of Ceres, Juno and Iris to celebrate the betrothal of the lovers is interrupted by Eshu in obscene and humorous mood.

Caliban's attempts to overthrow Prospero by force are doomed to failure but in a final confrontation he tells Prospero that time is on his side since the lies of white 'civilisation' about the 'underdeveloped' world are gradually being exploded. Rather like Garcin in *Huis clos*, Prospero finds he is unable to leave the island while Caliban has still not accepted his right to mastery: 'I too hate you! For it is through you that, for the first time, I have doubted myself' (90). He elects to stay on the island, continuing his struggle to dominate Caliban and the forces of nature. Time passes, and in a final epilogue we see Prospero old and tired. The climate has changed, he feels cold, and from the distance we hear Caliban's song of liberty.

Gabriel Cousin

Cousin's work falls very clearly inside the main stream of post-war decentralised theatre, both in terms of its structure and its themes. His plays have been produced at Saint Etienne, Marseille, Auch, Arras, Chatillon-sur-Chalaronne, and although some of these productions have visited Paris, none of his plays has been premièred in the capital. Cousin has remained loyal to the ideals of *le théâtre populaire* as defined in the immediate post-war period: a commitment to making theatre more widely available and to promoting social drama in the context of a broad humanist struggle for liberation against all that is oppressive in the modern world. He claims to have drawn inspiration from the discovery of Brecht, and his plays must certainly be classed under Epic theatre, but his inspiration appears more Catholic than Marxist and his work has not appealed greatly to the more radical generation of post-1968 men of the theatre.

Born into a working class family in 1918, Cousin left school at 13 to work an apprenticeship as an electrical fitter. During the Second World War, after capture and repatriation, he trained as a sports instructor and was attached to various factories in the northern suburbs of Paris. Soon after the war he moved to Grenoble where he has continued in physical education work ever since. He began to write poetry in the late forties and plays followed in the fifties and sixties. Sport was his major interest in life and it was in the sports stadium that he encountered theatre: the first play he saw was Obey's *800 mètres* produced by Jean-Louis Barrault at the Roland-Garros stadium in 1941 (see pp. 24–5). Since then, he has claimed that human movement is, for him, the foundation of drama: his own plays are imagined first in terms of movement and only secondly as texts. The Occupation years were a period of discovery and self-education for Cousin. He attended the theatre frequently and was particularly impressed by Barrault's *Soulier de satin* (1943) and Vilar's *Murder in the Cathedral* (1945). During this period he became friendly with Jacques Lecoq, whose famous mime school was established in Paris in 1954 and who had a hand in directing many of Cousin's plays.

Thematically, Cousin's plays deal with the major world-wide problems of our time – hunger, racism, exploitation, the nuclear threat. But these subjects are approached at an ordinary, everyday level and the characters depicted in his plays all belong to working class or peasant communities. The settings are very varied, including Japan, France and Brazil, and his methods are influenced by Eastern and South American forms. All of his plays proceed from an attitude of goodwill towards his fellow human beings and moral indignation at the persistence of injustice. He does not always escape Gide's dictum: 'C'est avec de bons sentiments qu'on fait de la mauvaise littérature'.

When Cousin began to write, it was not drama, but poetry that attracted him. His first success, *Le Drame du Fukuryu-Maru*, began life not as a play but as a long poem, which Gabriel Monnet persuaded him to translate into dramatic form. His theatre retains the marks of its origins: every one of his plays includes passages of poetic writing which bring the action to a halt and are delivered in oratorio style. His major poetic work is *L'Ordinaire Amour*, published in 1958. It celebrates a love relationship with nothing wild or exceptional, just an 'ordinary' love, whose joys and sorrows are found in a heightened awareness of the simple activities of every life. A similar approach is manifest in the plays. Each one is constructed around a love story and each attempts to show how this relationship can transform the vision of 'ordinary' life. But the paradox of Cousin's plays is that they depend on physical expression as much as on verbal poetry. Cousin believes that the practice of the ordinary physical skills associated with the maintenance of everyday life can, like the love relationship, acquire a transforming quality, changing even the most oppressive conditions into a circumstance for the affirmation of life. This can be seen particularly clearly in *Le Cycle du crabe*. The inhabitants of the shanty town on the outskirts of Recife live in conditions of extreme poverty and despair. Mortality is high and hardly a day goes by without a burial in the marshy land over which the shanty town is constructed. The only source of food is from the crabs that infest the marshes, growing fat on the corpses of the dead. In these appalling conditions, Cousin repeatedly shows us both the movements and the songs of a 'chorus' of crab fishers. The skill of their movement and music is beautiful, despite the horror of their surroundings. Cousin explains the importance of these sections by saying that his characters live a life of physical exertion and that music and dance, even in the worst conditions, are at the origins of 'the individual's vital impulse' (1969: 188). The skill of the crab fishers is demonstrated in scene three by contrasting them with the clumsy movements of two new arrivals in the shanty town, who discover the difficulties of wading through mud and seizing a crab at speed.

Cousin's plays are filled with songs and movement which he sees as integral to the action because he considers the essence of *le théâtre populaire* to be festivity and celebration: 'Although the subject is austere and tragic, it must not be boring . . . there must be alternation of rhythms, of acting styles and of audio-visual means' (ibid). Cousin rightly identifies popular taste in theatre as a taste for variety. He is helped by his use of techniques drawn from Eastern theatre, the most important of which is in characterisation. Cousin's characters are established not by means of psychology and environment, but by costume, mask and movement. Most of his plays present a whole community, with a consequent diminishing of emphasis on the individual, and he sometimes employs a narrator on stage. All of this helps to reduce the tendency towards naturalism and makes it easier for the play to be broken up into a variety of sections with contrasting rhythms. Much of *Le Drame du Fukuryu-Maru* takes place on the fishing vessel affected by the hydrogen bomb test at the Bikini atoll in 1954. The men express first their involvement in the normal tasks at sea, and then their reactions to the bomb and fall-out, in a kind of group voice in which the individual's motives and desires become submerged within the group experience. In his 1962 programme note, Lecoq wrote that Cousin's achievement was to have found a modern equivalent for the ancient Greek chorus: 'The language of his characters, which changes abruptly from an everyday style of lyricism creates a text rich in dissonances which calls to mind the freedom of jazz or of modern dance'.

In the notes to the text of this play, Cousin quotes Einstein's remark after the dropping of the first atom bombs, to the effect that everything had changed about war except our way of thinking about it. The need for a new way of thinking to cope with the changed conditions of late twentieth century living became Cousin's major theme. In the *Fukuryu-Maru* this is conveyed through the character of Matsuyama, a once beautiful girl who had been disfigured and rendered sterile eight years before by the Nagasaki bomb. She is in love with one of the fishermen but the shame of her disfigurement is too great to allow her to accept his love. She goes away for a complicated operation to remove the facial disfigurements. In the meantime the fisherman is caught in the fall-out from the bomb test. When she returns, her beauty restored, she finds him dead. She is tempted to despair but instead agrees to join with the villagers in mobilising anti-nuclear opinion. Her renewed beauty will be 'the beacon in the night voyage towards the high seas of peace' (Cousin, 1964: 252). The play ends on a 'Cantata to peace'. The play is a good example of both the strength and the weakness of Cousin's writing. Its passionate sincerity is admirable and in its treatment of love it avoids the trap of sentimental individualism. On the other hand, it assumes an idealistic picture of relations within the fishing community so that the message of peace is rather too naïve to carry conviction. A second play on a Japanese theme, *Le Voyage de derrière la montagne* went some way towards correcting this fault by depicting a village community where love and self-sacrifice did not necessarily pay off, and where selfishness and cunning were a surer guarantee of survival.

But naïveté again marred Cousin's next two plays *L'Aboyeuse et l'automate* and *L'Opéra noir*. The former attempts, like Adamov's *Ping-Pong*, to use the 'New Theatre' vision of alienation and absurdity to comment on the reality of modern urban life. It starts from a wonderfully bizarre newspaper item Cousin found about a woman who could produce perfect imitations of the barks of different breeds of dog. He imagines such a person being used by a zealous municipality to catch unlicensed dogs and to prosecute their owners for the licence fee. The play contains some good scenes evoking the loneliness of a crowded city for someone who feels isolated. In the production of 1961, the members of the crowd wore masks designed by Amleto Sartori and were choreographed by Lecoq to great effect. But there is a parallel plot about a young man who wants to be an actor and can only find work demonstrating brassières. This carries less conviction and the play seems to sit rather uneasily between parody of commerce and indignation at its harmful effects. Moreover it is hard, in this grotesque world, to believe in the love which flowers between the barker and the demonstrator, since every other emotion has been shown to be cynically manipulated. In *Le Ping-Pong* where Adamov also tried to apply techniques of the grotesque and the absurd to real life, love was experienced by the protagonists as yet another mystification. In Cousin's play a rather clumsy scene in which the lovers are psychoanalysed side by side fails to persuade us that their love alone in the surrounding absurdities is not grotesque or hopeless. *L'Opéra noir* is a less complex piece attacking the theme of racism head-on and relying for much of its effect on negro jazz music. As a musical about the tragedy of racial violence it achieves a strong emotional effect, though it does not go further than a straightforward statement of moral indignation.

Cousin's most accomplished play to date is *Le Cycle du crabe*. In this the themes so far mentioned are all integrated into a moving story about poverty and exploitation. The sequence of scenes has an epic spread, moving from the arid planes of the sertão to the swamps of the coast. The struggle to maintain dignity in degrading circumstances is presented with an eye for the telling detail, like the wonder of a tiled floor to people who live perpetually up to their knees in mud. The message of the play is more militant than any of Cousin's earlier pieces, building up to the point at which we see the young radical priest, Joazeiro, announce that 'in certain cases the only dignified action left to man is to take up arms' (124). It is Joazeiro who, in this play, articulates Cousin's theme of the need to find a new mode of thought. The result is, significantly, connected with a popular festivity. Under cover of singing and dancing, the inhabitants manage to extend the boundaries of their shanty town, thus depriving the authorities of the excuse of overcrowding which was to have been their pretext for destroying it. But Cousin recognises the utopian quality of this vision: in the last part of the play the authorities find it only too easy to trick the shanty-town dwellers and it is destroyed after all.

The structure of this play is not fundamentally different from a piece of agitprop theatre: it aims to manipulate its audience's feelings to the point at which they will condemn outright the established governing powers of Brazil. As in much agitprop theatre, the authority figures are guyed (Cousin specifies that they may even be played by puppets) and only the downtrodden peasants are presented with any depth. But the agitprop structure is filled out with movement, music and scenes of individual human interest that are sufficiently well observed to lend conviction to the overall message. Cousin has never made any apology for his didactic approach: 'To show up and to help destroy the alienation brought about by the new myths or gods (news and publicity, techno-mechanisation, ideological dogmatism, collective fears that induce people to accept fascism or war to preserve freedom or peace) this seems to me the major role of the poet or dramatist' (Jeffery, 1980). Occasionally this leads him into the trap of stating the obvious rather too fervently, or expressing a rather naïve belief in the power of love to change the world. But the power and interest of his plays in performance, because of the mixture of dramatic means he employs, has made them successful in the theatre. Cousin continues to subscribe to the vision of *le théâtre populaire* as articulated by Gémier: 'a means of uniting all men'.

Above all, he believes that poetry and playwriting are part of a larger, essentially *practical* creative activity that is available to all and that is the only effective answer to oppression and alienation. In 1972 he put this belief into action by founding C.R.E.F.A.T.S. (Centre de Recherche d'Entraînement et de Formation pour l'Animation Théâtrale et Socio-éducative) in Grenoble. In his centre he arranges short courses to demonstrate the liberating effect of creative physical activity for members of any trade or profession. He tries to reveal to people the pressures that society puts on them to compete and to show off rather than to collaborate and to *be*. He then suggests creative activity that can help them recover a renewed sense of wholeness. In the work of the centre one can see a logical outcome of Cousin's plays both in their ideological assumptions and in their practical aspects.

Arman Gatti

Like Cousin, Gatti believes in the value of the individual's creative response to his environment. In recent years he has taken this idea much further than Cousin, rejecting all established conventions for artistic expression and trying to promote an entirely new conception of art in which there are no spectators, only participants. At an earlier stage, in the sixties, he wrote a large number of political plays and became the leading figure among political dramatists in the decentralisation movement. All of the plays written during this period were concerned, directly or indirectly, with revolutionary politics and many are set in countries that he had visited in the fifties as a journalist, mainly South and Central America, and the Far East.

Born into a poor immigrant family in 1924, Gatti was only 17 when he was captured in a round-up of Resistance groups and deported to a labour camp in Germany. This experience of the camp was to mark him for the rest of his life. He said that:

For the survivors [of the camps] only two attitudes were possible: systematic amnesia to avoid reliving something which, deep down, one never ceased to relive; or else, for those who continued to be obsessed by the experience, to rid oneself of it, not by keeping quiet, but by talking (Gozlan & Pays, 1970: 19).

Gatti was a survivor who talked. Much of his work was an attempt to exorcise the ghosts that haunted him from this period. Gatti had always written poetry. After the war he took up a career in journalism, achieving considerable renown before abandoning it at the end of the fifties in order to write and direct both plays and films. Since then he has produced over twenty plays, a number of cine-films, a great many video-films and has arranged or provided the impetus for an enormous variety of cultural/political/artistic events bearing little resemblance to theatre or film as they are normally understood.

His plays written and produced during the sixties depend on an optimistic and somewhat naïve belief in the power of theatre to change the world. He had turned to theatre because he was convinced that the problems of the world were essentially collective and political and that a collective art form was therefore needed to take proper account of them. By writing plays with political and historical themes he was also following the same path as writers like Adamov and Planchon, who had turned their back on the dead-end of the Absurd. Like them Gatti was to use the perceptions and techniques of the New Theatre in order to create a new form of Epic theatre that could cope with real historical circumstances.

The main similarity between the methods of Gatti and those of New Theatre lies in his fragmentation of character. Gatti's characters are always in crisis. Neither they themselves nor the people around them are clear as to their true identity. But this is not, as in Ionesco's plays, for example, because everything is absurd and there are no fixed points of reference. It is because, for Gatti, the unified image always falsifies. If one wants to grasp a human being in his totality, then one must understand his contradictions, especially the contradictory ideas and feelings that he may hold at different ages. In other words, Gatti searches not for what holds together and unifies a character but for the way in which his past and his future do battle. Just as Césaire attempted to show, through Christophe's contradictions, 'the invention of the future', so Gatti dramatises the struggle for the birth of a new consciousness.

A convenient example of how this is done can be seen in his autobiographical play *La Vie imaginaire de l'éboueur Auguste Geai*. In order to depict his father, Gatti presents him at five different ages: at 9, 21, 30, 46 and ageless. Each role is played by a different actor so that it is possible to have all five on stage simultaneously interacting with one another. In the play's first production (by Jacques Rosner in 1962 at the Théâtre de la Cité), the stage was divided into three different areas, but Gatti's stage directions specified seven different spaces. These different playing spaces were to be identified not with place but with time. The action of this play is all composed of the memories and dreams of Auguste Geai during his last hours of life and so the central space is the hospital bed in which he lies dying at the age of 46. His most vivid memories relate to three moments in his life. The time when he was nine years old and a fire destroyed the shanty town in which he lived, killing his parents. The time when he was called up to fight in the First World War. The time when he married and got a job as a street cleaner. Now, at the age of 46 he has been clubbed by a C.R.S. riot policeman while taking part in a strike. The fifth time-space shows him as he imagines himself at retiring age with a son who has become a professional film director.

The reality of the character Auguste Geai is to be found in the interplay between these different time-spaces. This allows Gatti great flexibility in showing how private, psychological factors are woven together with external realities to create one man's life. For example, the child aged nine is terrified of an old tramp known in the shanty town as the black baron; when, as a 30-year-old, he can laugh at such fears, his life is no less under threat, this time the threat of exploitation by the boss of the dustcart company, known as the white baron. He succeeds in throwing off his fear and standing up to the boss, but pays for it with his life. Another example of the rich interweaving of psychological and social pressures in this play can be seen in the sequence of the dance marathon. It was through winning the prize at such a marathon that Pauline, Auguste's first love, had been able to leave the shanty town. In Auguste's mind the dance marathon becomes an image for his whole life, a grotesque image in which he is constantly struggling to keep in time with a band composed entirely of C.R.S. riot police (see fig. 12).

For anyone with revolutionary aspirations, time is experienced eschatologically: Auguste Geai looks forward to the time after the revolution yet meets failure and death in his own life. His compensation is to imagine his son making a film about his life that will show its struggles and demonstrate that the life of a dustman is worth as much as that of any man. The imaginary filming is presented on stage in the same way as the scenes of past events and so we see Auguste Geai's future influencing our view of his past, just as his past has influenced our view of his present. Of course his future is in one sense only imaginary and yet the events it refers to have their referent in history since Armand Gatti, the son, *has* been able to recreate his father's life on the stage if not on the screen. The revolutionary consciousness of A.G. annihilated by a blow from a police baton lives on in the person of his son, A.G.

Many of Gatti's other plays from this period approach the birth of revolutionary consciousness in a more direct manner, telling the story of an episode from the Chinese Civil War (*Un homme seul*) or the independence struggle in Guatemala (*La Naissance*) and others display a similar technique of temporal superimposition. His first play, *Le Quetzal* (published in 1960), was also set in Guatemala and shows two episodes in the resistance of foreign domination separated by four centuries. The play presents its different episodes in such a way as to suggest that present resistance can only be understood by reference to the original conquest and, vice-versa, that the story of the conquest only makes sense as the first incident in a process of continuous resistance over the centuries. The common pattern of these plays is similar to that of *Auguste Geai*: a defeat is shown, but a defeat which has unexpected repercussions at different moments of history.

Gatti's other main theme in the sixties was the concentration camp experience. This was the point of departure for *L'Enfant-Rat*, *Chroniques d'une planète provisoire* and *La Deuxième Existence du camp de Tatenberg*.

12 *Auguste Geai* (Gatti): the scene for the dance marathon, directed by Jacques Rosner, sets by René Allio. In the background, the dance band of C.R.S. riot police; to left and right, photos of Auguste Geai at different ages. Théâtre de la Cité, 1962.

Rather than confronting Nazi brutality head-on, these plays concentrate on the long-term effects of the camps on the survivors. The concentration camp experience is something they cannot put behind them. However far they travel away from their camp, they still bring their period of incarceration with them as a memory more vivid than their current experience. The second existence of the Tatenberg camp, to which the title makes allusion, is its continuing existence in the minds of its former inmates. The two main characters, Ilya Moïssevitch and Hildegarde Frölick, might be able to make a new life together were it not for their earlier experiences which continually break in and disrupt their present. Moïssevitch is haunted by the systematic extermination of his race and by the people he knew in the Tatenberg camp. Frau Frölick, a puppeteer, tries to relive through her puppets the death of her husband, a German officer shot for desertion on the eastern front. These two characters are unable to make a relationship in the present because one is trying to use the present to recreate the past and the other finds the past constantly invading his present.

A similar group of haunted survivors appears in *La Cigogne*, whose characters sift through the ruins of Nagasaki after the atomic explosion. Each finds an object through which he or she catches echoes of the dead person to whom it once belonged. Like the death-camp survivors, these people share the experience of living a 'future in the past'. As Richard Coe has commented:

Anyone who has shared the experience of absolute catastrophe is, in a memorable phrase, 'sur l'autre versant de la montagne' (on the other slope of the mountain) . . . seers and prophets living ahead of time . . . their vision is that of the logical implications of our 'reality'; but they live 'now' in the dimension in which those logical implications have already been worked out. For them, not only the present, but even the future is already historical (1983: 77).

What the group of atomic survivors shows us, as they struggle to comprehend their own intolerable reality, is the consequences of man-made catastrophe – a warning and an appeal to audiences who have not yet had to suffer a similar fate.

During the period of the sixties Gatti and his plays were in heavy demand throughout the expanding decentralised theatre system: twelve of his plays were produced, six directed by himself. But despite his apparent success, this was a period of disillusionment for Gatti. His plays all depend on the assumption that theatre can influence life. Their fragmented form and their careful accounts of the growth of political consciousness in a character or a group were calculated to surprise an audience, to jolt it into a new awareness and to provoke a similar political awakening. Instead of this happening, he found that his work was becoming a marketable cultural product. He felt that the shock effect of its challenge to traditional ways of thinking and of playwriting was neutralised by the programming policies of theatres which would include his work in an otherwise conventional repertoire as a concession to ideas that they normally ignored. The turning point for Gatti, as for so many others, came in the course of 1968, although his misgivings had been building up during the preceding years, coming to a head for the first time in 1967 over the performances of *V comme Vietnam*.

This play had been thought of by Gatti as the chance to make a direct political statement. It was commissioned by a political body, the Collectif Intersyndical Universitaire who arranged for it to tour France after its opening at the Grenier de Toulouse. The play contrasted the mechanistic, computer-dominated strategy of the Pentagon generals with the Vietnamese people's simple will to resist. It attempted to show that the Vietnam war was not fundamentally a struggle between communism and capitalism but 'between the human spirit and the robot spirit' (Knowles, 1976: 186). The Americans in the play are all military strategists, imprisoned by modes of thought and analysis that can predict with extreme accuracy just how much it will cost to kill each Vietnamese soldier, but which cannot account for the human spirit's will to independence.

But Gatti found that the production of this play presented its own difficulties. The actors of the Grenier were unhappy about performing, especially as the play was put on in place of a previously advertised *Twelfth night* (for which many tickets had already been sold). Gatti tried to make a virtue out of their opposition by casting them as the Americans while his own group of actors played the Vietnamese. This naturally created tensions which were magnified by the attempts of those organising the tour to use it for propaganda, according to their own view of the war (see Long, 1979).

The tensions and disagreements produced by this experience led Gatti to the belief that too many contradictory interests were at work in the established theatre for it to be a satisfactory political medium. Amidst all the squabbles and the institutional inflexibilities the fundamental aim of communication between people was being lost. The simple act of a writer/actor/producer addressing an audience was becoming impossible. He felt that the most satisfactory part of *V comme Vietnam* was the discussion with the audience that followed each performance. He used this as a point of departure for his next experiment, *Les Treize Soleils de la rue Saint-Blaise* performed at the Théâtre de l'Est Parisien in the spring of 1968.

Some months beforehand, Gatti and Rétoré (the director of the theatre) had invited regular audience members to come and help write a play. About thirty people volunteered, and met a number of times: 'they discussed town planning, militancy, horse racing, women's problems, computers, the Resistance, workers' frustrations, holidays . . . For me it was dizzying' (Gozlan & Pays, 1970: 250). Gatti constructed his play around the situation of an evening class for adults. The teacher asked the members of the class to imagine that their street was to be cleared for redevelopment: they had to imagine what should replace it. Through their dreams and aspirations Gatti attempted to depict the social reality of contemporary France. But the experience was marred by squabbles over political 'correctness' among some of the 'authors' and the resulting play seems banal and disorganised.

This led Gatti towards his campaign of the seventies for a 'theatre without spectators'. He had already shown an unusual sensitivity to the part played by an audience in creating a show. His *Chant public devant deux chaises électriques*, performed at the T.N.P. in 1966, had presented the execution of Sacco and Vanzetti in the U.S.A. in 1927, not in its own right, but through the reactions of four audiences in different parts of the world – Boston, Hamburg, Turin and Lyon. This made for a very unwieldy play, with little dramatic action, best described as an oratorio without music. Moreover it was another example of an experiment that did not offer a very positive role to its real audience, although there was plenty of excited participation by the four on-stage audiences. It was the experience of another T.N.P. production in 1968 that convinced Gatti he had to turn his back on established theatre.

The production in question was of *La Passion du Général Franco*. The play, one of Gatti's best, portrays Franco through the experiences of those he had forced into exile, either by political persecution or by economic pressure. The play shows four groups of people on their journeys: from Madrid to Frankfurt, from Kiev to Krasnoyarsk, from Havana to Mexico, and from Toulouse back to Madrid. This device allows Gatti to fragment time and space, as in his other plays, but without entirely sacrificing the suspense of story-line, since each group of travellers is anxious about the journey's outcome. Their present worries and uncertainties overlap with their memories, since they live in the curious 'double space' of refugees, strangers both to their motherland and in their adopted country. Once the four journeys are established, Gatti can allow what happens in one to influence the spectator's view of another, and so a complex evocation is built up of the traumas of Franco's Spain. The play gradually reveals itself as an 'anti-passion' since 'It is not Franco who dies on this Calvary. Franco is nothing, nothing more than a bad habit. He was the product of rifles. Rifles are dead substances. They kill, but create nothing. It is not Franco who dies in this passion, neither is he resurrected' (1968a: 127). Instead, a spirit of resistance is brought to birth by Franco's savage repression, and the end of the play shows the different people, separated by the time and space of their exile, joining together in expressing their will to resist. The play was already well into rehearsal when the government, anxious about trade negotiations with Spain, imposed a ban on the production in all subsidised theatres. Gatti was finally convinced of the need to take theatre outside the theatre. He was not able finally to produce the play in France until 1976, after the death of Franco.

The experience of working on *Les Treize Soleils* had convinced Gatti that the most powerful weapon of repressive governments was their ability to lock people into a deadening daily routine in which everything is taken for granted and the power to question, or suggest alternatives, is neutralised. From the end of the sixties to the present day the main thrust of Gatti's work has been to force people to question their everyday experience, abandoning normal assumptions and articulating feelings that are normally repressed by 'civilised' life. Of course, Gatti was not the only person to make such attempts at this time. The slogans daubed on Paris walls in 1968, such as *L'Imagination au pouvoir* expressed a widespread feeling that changes of an altogether unprecedented kind were necessary. A flood of films appeared in the early seventies, pleading for release from the constraints of modern industrial life, like Claude Faraldo's *Themroc*, in which language disintegrated into grunts and roars and primitive instincts were liberated. But for Gatti such experiments were unsatisfactory, first because they did nothing to change the passive role of the public and 'the public is a shameful notion. It's the voyeur, the consumer. I'm for a spectacle without spectators, where each person participates in the creation, where each learns from the other. I don't want the voyeur' (Champagne, 1981: 29). Secondly, Gatti distrusted attempts at psychological liberation that ignored the historical dimension. His own work had always taken as its point of departure a person or event open to historical documentation. This continued to be his method in his work outside the theatre.

At the beginning of the seventies Gatti spent some time directing his plays in West German theatres before returning to French-speaking territory for *La Colonne Durruti* (1974). Durruti was an anarchist leader in the Spanish Civil War, but Gatti was less interested in recreating his life than in finding what his ideas might mean to people in a distant part of Europe four decades later. He found a disaffected factory on the outskirts of Schaelbeek in Belgium and threw the workshops open for anyone who cared to come and participate. The result was an event in which the creative process itself became the show. The walls of the factory were covered in posters; there were discussions, demonstrations and other events, often with no *a priori* link to Gatti or his work. This was followed by an experiment in the Belgian countryside involving 'about 125 pieces of farm machinery, trailers and wagons, a motorised stage stretching across the countryside' (Gatti, 1982: 76). The project was based on the story of a local farmer named Adelin 'who had had enough of seeing his land chopped up by super-highways, dormitory communities . . . finally he took his animals and walked all the way to the Dordogne in the south of France' (ibid.). The project succeeded in involving some 3,000 people as it moved from hamlet to hamlet: 'Everybody gave his own interpretation of Adelin, how they saw him, etc. Each person used the fiction to say what he personally had to say' (ibid. 77).

In Gatti's subsequent projects the emphasis became more and more on getting people 'to say what they have to say'. To assist them, he and his team (known as 'the tribe') acquired a portable silk-screen printing workshop and video equipment which they used to show how the dominant habits of the pictorial media may be subverted. Some of these projects led to the creation of television programmes subsequently broadcast on O.R.T.F. This was the case of *The lion, its cage and its wings* (1975), six programmes in which the immigrant workers at the Peugeot factories of Montbéliard expressed their view of France. Another series of programmes entitled *La Première Lettre* was made in L'Isle d'Abeau in 1978. For this project the catalyst was the history of Roger Rouxel, an obscure Resistance fighter shot by the Germans in 1944 on the eve of his eighteenth birthday. But the main purpose of such projects is not the production of television programmes. Broadcasts take place long after the event and are considered by Gatti to be a mere 'spin-off'. The main purpose of each project is to prod people into creating something for themselves and thus to experience the liberation of moving from the position of the consumer to that of the creator.

In order to do this, Gatti constantly puts himself at risk, refusing to shelter behind institutional roles or buildings. The best example of this was his project at Saint Nazaire in 1976, for which he proposed the image of the wild duck that needs to fly against the wind on its arctic migrations, in order not to be frozen stiff in mid-air: its feathers are set at the wrong angle to protect it if it flies *with* the wind. By means of this image, Gatti wanted to tackle the subject of Vladimir Bukovsky and other Russian dissidents forcibly confined in psychiatric hospitals. The choice of subject enraged the local branch of the French Communist Party, who launched a smear campaign against Gatti. But Gatti was able to use this turn of events to reinforce his assertion that institutions and ideologies kill. After an initial period of hostility to his project, Gatti was able to persuade large numbers of people to take part and the result was the production of a journal, countless posters, a large number of small plays, video-projects, kite-dramas, exhibitions and a gigantic model of a wild duck outside the Maison des Jeunes et de la Culture (see Campos, 1978). At the height of the project, Bukovsky was released and came to speak at Saint Nazaire. No further programmes or films were drawn from this project but it had shown what Gatti wanted to show – for each person in the world there is a choice between independent thought that flies against the prevailing current of opinion or passive acceptance of what the state and its institutions offer. Moreover it had shown that there is a link between the level of political participation by people in France and, say, the course of political repression in Russia. Gatti's latest project has been in Northern Ireland, which he perceived as a society divided by two different languages, by two different modes of perception: the British army operating through the language of high-technology surveillance, closed-circuit television and computer print-outs, the population in the streets countering in lapidary form with graffiti. Part of the project involved teaching unemployed youths in Derry how to work in video and film, how to plan, organise and execute a shooting script.

Gatti's position as a revolutionary dramatist is a contradictory one. On the one hand he insists that theatre must divide rather than unite its audience since its function should be to reveal the hidden reality of the class war beneath the apparent order of the capitalist state. On the other hand, he does not advocate violence. He has repeated throughout his life that his interest lies not in 'la prise du pouvoir' but in 'la prise de la parole'. In this respect his projects of the seventies are the logical outcome of his earlier plays. The plays depict people who struggle, amidst the confusion of their social roles and private fears, to express themselves, and so to create a reality for themselves. In the plays, Gatti frequently employs metaphor or heightened poetic images to underline this vital function of self expression. To demonstrate the dignity of a street sweeper, Auguste Geai makes him master of the dawn: 'Ce sont les balayeurs qui font naître le jour' (1962: 83. It is the street sweepers that bring the day to birth). Frequently he has recourse to blank verse in order to intensify an experience, the verse is direct, uncomplicated, often employing animal imagery. Tan, in *Le*

Poisson noir, evokes the collapse of will power among his caste with the words

We are a herd of buffalo
fleeing in serried ranks beneath the rain.
Beneath the rain the buffalo
have lost their outline, lost their colour ... (1958: 52).

Gatti was always fascinated by the images which people employ to describe themselves. *Les Treize Soleils* acquired its title from one person's response to Gatti's question: 'what would you like to be?' The answer came back: 'a sun'. He continues to search for this kind of intense image, but as much by liberating expression in others as in himself. He has not ceased writing in the seventies, but inspiration for his plays is now drawn largely from the project work and they are seen as subordinate to it. An example is *Le Cheval qui se suicide par le feu*, presented as work in progress at the Avignon festival in 1977. Neither this nor others of his recent plays has been published.

Gatti cannot be considered solely as a playwright. His achievement is to have found the means to create a new role for himself, in which his function is more than just to be an *animateur*: it is the function of the folk artist translated into modern terms. He is the poet who stimulates others to acts of poetry, craftsman who shares his skills with all who care to work with him. The money he requires to live and to purchase equipment comes from a variety of sources. Some comes from broadcasts, some from grants for particular projects, made either by central government or by local associations, some comes from his own earnings as an author and director. But he has so far avoided the temptation to settle down in an institution, always moving on to a new place and never repeating the same project. The influence of his example on young theatre groups of the seventies has been considerable, since his very existence was proof that original work did not need to shelter beneath the roof of a Maison de la Culture or a Centre Dramatique.

Together with that of Césaire and Cousin, Gatti's work has done much to promote the idea of participation. All three dramatists are concerned with liberation and all demonstrate that this is not something that can be handed out, but will only come if those in need of liberation are able to participate in the process. All three dramatists employ a form of Epic theatre, stressing the concrete reality of history-as-lived, and all three use poetry to show how minds, as well as bodies, must be free. There are very obvious differences between the plays of these three authors, stemming from their ideological positions, Césaire promoting a form of Negritude, Cousin a form of Humanism and Gatti a form of Anarchism. But their reasons for choosing similar subject-matter, drawn from the struggles of the oppressed in the third world and in Europe, is the same: to express the deep conviction that the old frames of reference, both literary, philosophical and political, are inadequate to cope with the realities of today. In their different ways, each one is reaching out for a new way of *thinking*.

8

Total theatre

Jean-Louis Barrault achieved his first large-scale directorial triumph in 1943 with Claudel's play *Le Soulier de satin* (see above, chapter 2). Since then he has continued, both as an actor and as a director, to exert a powerful influence on the French theatre. His name has become identified with a certain conception of 'total theatre', which he has developed and refined in response to the changing state of his fortunes and of the cultural orthodoxies of his day. From his earliest days in the theatre, Barrault had established himself as an avant-garde actor and director. Before the war, while still under Dullin's tuition, he had directed three experimental shows of his own, all adaptations depending more on the expressive use of the actor's body than on speech for their effect.

He had consorted with Artaud, from whom he acquired a taste for metaphysical speculation about the philosophy of performance. Artaud praised the first of Barrault's experimental productions very highly. This was *Autour d'une mère*, adapted from Faulkner and performed four times at the Atelier theatre in June 1935. Artaud wrote that this show was a victorious demonstration of the importance of gesture and movement in three-dimensional space:

The theatre, which opens up a physical space, demands that we fill this space, that we furnish it with gesture, that we make it come alive in itself magically, that we enable it to release an aviary of sounds, that we discover in it a new set of relationships between sound, gesture and voice – that is true theatre and that is what Jean-Louis Barrault has created (1964: 216).

What appealed to Artaud was Barrault's attempt to use the actor's body, voice and movement to create a theatre of rich expressive means but which did not rely on the traditional apparatus of illusionist scenery and costume. There was a celebrated moment in this performance when Barrault had to mime the breaking-in of a wild horse. His performance, as both horse and rider, had such a powerful effect on Artaud that he wrote that with this *cheval-centaure* Barrault had achieved the same magical force that was visible in the Balinese theatre.

Barrault was also influenced by Etienne Decroux, the most famous teacher of mime in the inter-war period. Photographs survive of Barrault and Decroux, stripped off, demonstrating the interplay of muscle and balance in a series of complex movements. Barrault welcomed the demands of strict physical discipline, was fascinated by athletes and by the urge to compete. He found the idea of the mass, open-air performance attractive and went along with the doctrine, prevalent in the late thirties, that popular theatre and popular sport were intimately linked, as demonstrated by his production of Obey's *800 mètres* (see chapter 2).

As he developed his idea of total theatre, he continued to see the actor and his body as the central means of expression. But he shocked and surprised his contemporaries at the Comédie Française by rejecting the French traditions of the statuesque pose and the uniform gravity in serious plays. Total theatre was to be a theatre of mixed means, employing jokes, acrobatics, singing and dancing, in fact all the characteristics of the popular theatre tradition. It was the combination of these elements that made *Le Soulier de satin* such an extraordinary production. Barrault continued to present hitherto unstaged works by Claudel during the decades that followed the war and this long association with a difficult author certainly helped him to develop and refine both the acting and production methods that had triumphed in *Le Soulier de satin*. *Partage de midi* was the first, in 1948 (revived in 1961), then *L'Echange* in 1951; *Christophe Colomb* in 1953 (revived 1960); *Tête d'or* in 1959 (revived in 1968) and *Sous le vent des Iles Baléares* in 1972. All of these productions proved attractive to audiences and to some extent Barrault became identified in the public mind with grandiose productions of Claudel. When Malraux appointed him director of the Odéon in 1959, he chose to open with *Tête d'or*, an early play which Claudel, who died in 1955, had refused to allow him to produce during his life-time. Out of Barrault's nine seasons as director at the Odéon, five contained a major Claudel production (or revival).

Through his work on these plays, Barrault came to lay stress on the active participation of every element of theatre language, not just of the actor's physical expression: 'Sometimes a production ceases to be merely a frame and rises to the level of essential theatre: it becomes, in a way, humanized, integrated with the characters and participants in the action; then the production *signifies the play* in harmony with the actor's work' (1973: 3). These comments were made by Barrault about his production of *Christophe Colomb* in 1953. He went on to explain how the various scenic elements contributed to the signifying process, e.g.: 'As for the music, it behaves like the men of the troupe: by turns actor and commentator' (ibid. 4). Through descriptive passages like this, Barrault evokes a picture of the richness and complexity of signifying systems at work in one of his productions. But it should not be thought that he brought these methods to bear on Claudel alone. His period as director of the independent (unsubsidised) Marigny theatre 1946–56 and of the (state-owned, subsidised) Odéon 1959–68 included a considerable range of work. Although he produced some plays from the classic repertoire, more than half of Barrault's productions during this period were of new plays or adaptations.

His particular interest continued to be in experiments with mime, dance and other expressive means. Sometimes the experiments were applied to a classical text, as in his production of the *Oresteia* in 1955. Barrault's theory of art and his metaphysics of the actor were both founded in ternary systems (see e.g. 1949: 65–7). The trilogy structure of the *Oresteia* was irresistible to him, as was the challenge to a modern director of ancient Greek chorus passages. The *Oresteia* was greatly admired by Claudel and it may have been because of this that Barrault was drawn to it; he did not return to Greek tragedy after 1955 although he produced an adaptation of Seneca's *Medea* (1967). More often his experiments were applied to adaptations of non-dramatic material: *Le Procès* (1947) and *Le Château* (1952) from Kafka; *La Tentation de Saint-Antoine* (1967) from Flaubert; *Rabelais* (1968) and *Jarry sur la butte* (1970). The last two were celebrations of their authors into which were woven large sections of their work. *La Tentation de Saint-Antoine* was chiefly the work of Béjart and his modern dance company, but it included Barrault in the central role which demanded the use of both speech and movement. As well as this, Barrault's theatre became identified with the New Theatre though, as we have seen, he did not produce plays by Beckett and Ionesco until the sixties, when their reputation was already established.

In 1968, during the political upheavals of May and June, students occupied the Odéon and used it for a debating chamber. Instead of calling in the police, Barrault talked to the students, rather plaintively asking why they should pick on him since he had always sympathised with them and opposed authority. For

13   *Rabelais* in a wrestling hall. The open-stage set for Barrault's production, designed by Matias at the Elysée-Montmartre.

this, he was dismissed from his post by Malraux. He moved his company to a wrestling hall near Clichy, where he produced a montage of texts by Rabelais which he had been planning since before May 1968. He used *Rabelais* to make his protest against the high-handed methods of the authorities, and audiences flocked to see it out of sympathy for him. But the success of the show can also be attributed to the fact that it drew together elements from all the currently fashionable performance styles and brought them together in an invigoratingly new, open space, freed from the constraints of the proscenium arch, the boxes, the red plush, and other paraphernalia of the auditorium at the Odéon (see fig. 13). An actor who performed in the English version at the Roundhouse two years later described the mixture as 'elements of La Mama and Bread and Puppet theatre, pantomime, circus, political cabaret and discotheque' (Wallis, 1971: 84). The performance generated excitement and a sense of liberation, at least at the level of style.

But although each separate element of the show was colourful, skilful, exciting, its total effect was rather disappointing. It lacked the firm dramatic framework of a Claudel play, and the Renaissance breadth of Rabelais' world view was boiled down to the slogan 'fay ce que vouldras' which, in the fashionable idiom of the time, became 'do your thing'. The experience of attending the wrestling hall provided Barrault's regular audiences with the thrill of intellectual slumming, but he did little to attract an audience of locals, and the ultimate impression created was of vast amounts of energy in search of an aim. The bold mixture of styles, fascinating in itself, was not used to explore any significant idea or situation. This was also true of his 1970 production at the wrestling hall, *Jarry sur la butte*, and continued through similar shows based on the work of La Fontaine, Restif de la Bretonne, Nietzsche, Diderot and Voltaire. These were all presented between 1972 and 1980 at the Orsay theatre, an auditorium of variable shape and size installed in the disused Orsay station, on the left bank of the Seine opposite the Louvre. Here he also continued with revivals of his great Claudel productions (including *Le Soulier de satin*), as well as occasional productions of new plays, and he also made the space available to other groups such as the Grand Magic Circus. His most recent montage was *L'Amour de l'amour* (1981), a symposium of texts on love through the ages, with which he opened his new Théâtre du Rond Point in an old ice-rink just off the Champs-Elysées. During his period at the Orsay and Rond Point theatres, he has been seen as a living legend: audiences have come largely to marvel at the performances, both of himself and of his wife, Madeleine Renaud. This is only fitting, since no other French acting couple can claim to have been taking leading roles with such success since before the war, and all of Barrault's most memorable achievements have been essentially those of a great actor and mime, as Jean-Jacques Gautier remembered in his account of *Rabelais*: 'How, with eight stretched-out pieces of rope, lighting which suggested the reflections of moving water, the enchanting music of Polnaroff and the concerted movement of a dozen men undulating to the rhythm of the waves – how Barrault out of nothing, created a ship surging forward on the high seas . . .' (O'Connor, 1971: 98).

Roger Blin shares the same training and influences as Barrault. He, too, trained with Dullin and was familiar with Artaud. But his personality is entirely different. Where Barrault is passionate, outgoing, enthusiastic, Blin is more retiring. In view of the influence both men have had on theatrical image and acting styles, it is no doubt significant that both came to the theatre with an interest in painting. Barrault quickly discovered his true vocation as an actor and director but for Blin this came more slowly. He only began to act because he found that the stage was the one place where he could speak without stammering. Blin was very active in the early New Theatre productions. Barrault, who was always attracted by a densely structured poetic text, produced new plays by Christopher Fry, Georges Schéhadé and Jean Vauthier during the 1950s. Blin responded to the less flowery violence of texts by Adamov and Beckett. He acted the part of Le Mutilé in Adamov's *La Grande et la Petite Manoeuvre* directed by Jean-Marie Serreau in 1952 and directed the first production of *En attendant Godot* in 1953. His persistence in the face of difficulties earned him the respect of Beckett, who entrusted him with the productions of his next plays – *Fin de partie* (1957), *La Dernière Bande* (1960) and *Oh les beaux jours* (1963).

Yet despite this close identification with the work of Beckett, Blin's reputation rests even more on the remarkable productions of plays by Genet: *Les Nègres* with a black cast partly composed of amateurs (Lutèce, 1959) and *Les Paravents* with Jean-Louis Barrault and his company (Odéon, 1966). This is partly due to the extraordinary letters written to Blin by Genet in the course of the production of *Les Paravents*, which make it possible to achieve an unusually precise insight into the collaborative work of writer and director. From this correspondence it is clear that Blin's conception of theatre fitted particularly well with that of Genet, as we shall see. It also had much in common with Barrault's total theatre. The chief points of similarity emerge well from an interview with Blin published by *The Drama Review* in 1963. Blin explains that for him there is no separation between the work of direction and the work of design in the theatre: they are simply aspects of the same creative process. He takes care to specify that he prefers to work with a sculptor or an architect rather than a painter because the design must produce a working space and working objects that serve the play, not just a pretty background. He has a strong sense of design and is proud of having designed the original tree for *En attendant Godot*. But his main emphasis is on the participation of every item on stage in the signifying process: 'Take a telephone, for example, place it on a table on stage. That's all right, but I want that telephone to be able to eat, to talk, to have a life of its own. It must be an animate object' (1963: 117).

The theoretical basis upon which statements of this kind depend incorporates a particular view of realism in the theatre. In England, a naïve view of realism has tended to dominate the theatres this century. More often than not, telephones have been accepted as simply telephones. They have not been called upon to manifest a life of their own. But in France it has long been an orthodox position to say that realism in the theatre must be different. Cocteau, in 1922, had written: 'instead of trying to diminish the absurdity of life, to attenuate and rearrange it, as you would rearrange your account of an incident in which your own role did you no credit, I accentuate it, I develop it, I attempt to depict *more truly than the truth*' (preface to *Les Mariés de la Tour Eiffel*). The idea that the art of the theatre had to be in some way 'truer than truth' was familiar to the directors of the Cartel and to writers such as Giraudoux or Anouilh. Blin's statement above carries echoes of Jouvet's assertion:

A table belongs to a certain place, a certain owner. But a table abandoned in the middle of a field takes on an entirely new expression; that is theatre. An object which is a true object but also false, that is the true truth, the truth of theatre (Jouvet, 1952: 135).

Such statements imply a view of dramatic realism conditioned by the knowledge that any object, once it is placed on stage, undergoes a transformation: it is immediately perceived as a sign and hence acquires significance. Moreover, the significance attributed to it will depend as much on the attitude of the observer as on any inherent qualities of the object in question. In this way a cardboard dagger may appear to be a terrifying weapon of death, but a real room with real furnishings may equally well appear to be quite illusory. Blin expresses this idea in the following terms:

Take a street. The street most frequently placed on stage today is the street you see every day. If you reproduce it on the boards as such . . . well, I call this stupid realism. But the street you see at night when you are drunk – you see it in a different way. You are wobbly. The street turns, it assumes weird shapes, its alive. What do you see in the street now? How do you see the street? This is true discovery. You are perceiving reality; for the first time all bonds and restrictions have been broken. Objective reality has been dislocated. You now perceive a far deeper reality. That street has become flesh and blood for you (1963: 118).

A director with this view of how reality should be presented on stage enjoys a special kind of artistic and representational freedom. At times he may choose to depict a street, a table, a telephone, by conventional means. At others he may employ only the actors, as in Barrault's *Soulier de satin*, when a hedge of thorns was presented in mime by a group of actors (see fig. 1). Or again he may invent a fresh sign system embodying elements drawn from both real and imaginary worlds. In his productions of Genet's plays Blin exemplified the last approach most distinctly and this is what gives them their particular interest.

It is difficult to separate the texts of Genet's plays from the production style of Blin. Genet himself acknowledged this when he noted, in the Arbalète edition of *Les Nègres* that Blin's production was inimitable, having reached perfection, and that no future edition of the play would be permitted unless it included his production photographs. Blin's production of *Les Nègres* in 1959 was the first occasion on which Genet felt that his work had been satisfactorily presented on stage. The next occasion was Blin's *Les Paravents* in 1966. More than any other dramatist of our period, Genet writes dialogue that is incomplete until it is placed in the context of performance. While this is the basic condition of all play texts, Genet exploits it more thoroughly than most, and the ideas expressed in the letters to Roger Blin are as relevant to the earlier plays as they are to *Les Paravents*.

Genet's plays derive their special theatrical richness from the fact that they all depict people who are oppressed struggling for liberation at a mental, spiritual and imaginative level. The prisoners, maids, rebels, blacks, Algerians, are all subject to constraint and tyranny of one kind or another, to which they respond on an imaginative rather than an objective plane. Ideas, images and mental states confront one another and struggle for control. But this struggle of conflicting subjective states is theatrically exciting because it is expressed through the most concrete stage language, appealing to all the senses and especially to the common love for ceremony and ritual.

In accounting for the way Genet's characters apprehend the world, some account of his own experience is inescapable. As a young child, fostered because his mother had abandoned him, Genet acquired the sense that he was an outsider. 'I learned it in a very silly, foolish way like this: the teacher had asked us to write a little essay; each pupil was to describe his house. I described mine and it turned out that my description was the best and the teacher read it aloud and everyone made fun of me saying, "but it's not his house, he's a foundling." Immediately I felt so empty . . . so empty. I became such a stranger' (1977: 12). Once you have been branded an outsider with such finality, there is no hope of appeal; it is useless to try to argue or to reason. Genet chose a different way, the only way he considered to be open to him. He accepted the condition of outsider, making it into a virtue. He joined the Foreign Legion only to desert soon afterwards, he cultivated a hatred for everything that was French and an admiration for everything that seemed opposed to distinctly French values. In other words, he accepted the insult that his classmates had thrown at him and turned it into a value, a principle to be followed.

In his essay *Saint-Genet comédien et martyr*, Sartre recounts a similar anecdote from Genet's youth: his foster parents, who realised that he was helping himself to things, described him as a 'little thief'. At this point, argues Sartre, Genet made the existential choice of character: rather than try to exculpate himself, he accepted the accusation with joy. A quality had been conferred upon him, the quality of villainy. Very well, he would accept the description and seek as his means of personal salvation, to live up to it as thoroughly as possible. In this he seems to have succeeded, spending most of his youth in reform schools and prisons. It was in prison that he first began to write: *Notre-Dame des fleurs* at Fresnes in 1942 and *Miracle de la rose* at the Santé prison in 1943. These are novels of homosexual eroticism written in sumptuously poetic prose. They are theatrical novels in the sense that they portray people constantly preoccupied with appearances, both their own and others.

They are also theatrical in another sense: a very special sense that Genet was to develop of what is the essence of theatre. The characters in these novels are put into a strict hierarchy according to their actions, the more terrible the crime the more splendid they appear. The most magnificent of all are those who have committed the ultimate crime – murder. But their actions only account for part of the impression they make. The other part is supplied by the admiration of the beholder. It is necessary to view them with an attitude that can only be described as that of faith. When this condition is fulfilled, a mystical transformation of outward appearances occurs in such a way as to reveal another reality, visible only to the eye of the believer. *Miracle de la rose* contains a celebrated scene in the courtyard of Fontevrault prison in which a notorious bandit steps out from the condemned cell under the admiring gaze of his fellow prisoners and suddenly his chains are transformed into a garland of roses. This principle of the need for *belief* in order to provoke a transformation of appearances became a central principle of Genet's theatre, as we shall see shortly.

Genet's novels were published in the forties, some in clandestine editions in order to avoid government censorship. His first two plays, *Haute Surveillance* and *Les Bonnes*, were also written during this period. In 1952 Sartre's essay appeared and Genet has admitted that this crushing homage made it very difficult for him to write anything new for several years (1981: 21). Since then he has written three major plays: *Le Balcon* (1956), *Les Nègres* (1958) and *Les Paravents* (1961) and nothing more. In the sixties and seventies he championed the causes of various urban terrorist groups including the Black Panthers, the Fedayeen and the Baader-Meinhof gang. He has described himself as 'a black whose skin happens to be pink and white' (1977: 12) and his early identification with the criminal classes has shifted to an identification with the oppressed, the dispossessed and the coloured. His plays are not really plays in our accepted sense of that word; they are ceremonies designed to exorcise and transform. They are strategies for overcoming the oppression of their characters, all of whom have been deprived in some way of their subjectivity and forced to live only through the eyes of others. The maids live only through the mistress' image of them – a strange mixture of her children and her slaves. The blacks live only through the image that is projected upon them by the white colonisers.

In his prefatory note to *Les Nègres*, Genet explains that the play is written for white audiences and that if, by chance, it were to be presented one night in a theatre where the audience was made up entirely of blacks, someone would have to put on a white mask and be ushered into the front row of the stalls so as to mark clearly the nature of the play. The reason why this is so important to Genet is that the sense of what is to take place on stage is created by the spectators as much as by the actors. The play does not have a story in the conventional sense. Its action consists of a sequence of carefully planned rites whose purpose is to undermine and dissolve the status of the actors as 'blacks', i.e. people whose being is defined by 'whites' as being black, non-white, other, alien, inferior. When they are among themselves, Africans behave differently, as Frantz Fanon points out: 'The black has two dimensions; one when he is with a person of his own race, the other when he is with a white. A black behaves differently with a white and with another black' (1952: 13). *Les Nègres* is a ritual ceremony for dissolving the second of Fanon's 'two dimensions'. If the play were performed with no whites present, then this dimension would not exist, would not be experienced as a difficulty and so the play would lose its chief function.

The status of theatrical reality for Genet is thus similar to the reality of religious ritual. It depends on a quality of belief and comes into being through the combined forces of the players who evoke it and the audience who assist them. (The French for attending a performance is *assister à un spectacle*.) In his preface to the 1954 edition of *Les Bonnes*, Genet explained this quality, that was, for him, the condition of theatre, by writing that 'the loftiest modern drama has been expressed daily for two thousand years in the sacrifice of the Mass'. He went on to recount a story of boys playing war in a park:

They were divided into two troops and were preparing to attack. Night, they said, was coming on. But it was noon in the sky. They therefore decided that one of them would be Night. The youngest and frailest having become elemental, was then the Master of the Fray. 'He' was the Hour, the Moment, the Ineluctable. He approached it seems, from far off, with the calmness of a cycle, though weighed down with the sadness and pomp of twilight. As he drew near, the others, the Men, grew nervous and uneasy . . . But the child was arriving too soon to please them. He was coming before his time. By common consent the Troops and the Chiefs decided to eliminate Night, who again became a soldier on one of the sides . . . It is on the basis of this formula alone that a theatre can thrill me (Préface à Pauvert, 1954: 16–17. Trans. Frechtmann).

Genet's plays strive for a ritual or ceremonial action that will create the conditions for belief to be first evoked, then questioned, and finally subverted. But Genet's plays do not present images of religious practices whether saintly or satanic. This is because he does not want to write plays *about* ritual or transcendence. Instead he requires a generalised belief system sufficiently widespread and uncritically held for him to be able to assume a number of basic attitudes in his audience. This belief system he finds in politics, especially in generalised inherited beliefs about structures of power and authority. *Les Bonnes* and *Le Balcon* provide good examples of this, relying as they do on the notions, seldom questioned, that rich people need servants or that society requires figureheads such as judges or bishops. It is even more effectively demonstrated by *Les Nègres* and *Les Paravents*, which exploit the most basic stratum of inherited political prejudice in France: the natural superiority of the white coloniser, his history, culture and language, over anything that the indigenous African societies can offer. The language itself bears the imprint of this profound belief (as Fanon also points out) since the word white carries connotations of moral worth and black is the colour of evil.

It is therefore at the level of language, image, metaphor that Genet's plays operate. The figures of state, the maids, the blacks, do not represent the reality of power or slavery, but its image. They are reflections of the images in the minds of their audience, and, in so far as they present the social hierarchies, they become figures onto which the audience projects its own image of social roles and power relations. Having been excluded from real society, Genet sets up a dream society which he can possess through play. In this way he can subvert images of reality, though he cannot have a direct effect upon it.

The function of much religious ritual is, in fact, to change reality. For example, a rain dance has the very concrete purpose of changing climatic conditions. It is important to see that Genet's rituals do not function in this way. On the contrary, they all end in some sort of self-annihilation. One of the maids commits suicide and Roger, the revolutionary leader in *Le Balcon*, castrates himself. The plays do not aim to alter or master reality, neither do they try to criticise it. Genet is most emphatic, in his note prefacing *Le Balcon*, that the stage should not be a vehicle for resolving social problems or for criticising social reality. He insists that the problems set out on the stage should never be resolved on the imaginary plane because this will leave an audience with the comforting sense that the problem has been abolished and requires no further action. 'On the contrary, let evil explode on stage, let it show us naked, leave us hagard if possible, and with no other recourse than to ourselves' (1968: 35). He wrote the same thing in his notes on how to act *Les Bonnes*, 'this is not an apologia on the lot of domestic servants. No doubt there exists a trade union for them – that does not concern us' (ibid. 269). The consequence of this is that the plays are not satirical in the common sense. Rather than cutting their characters down to size, they exalt them. 'This play (*Le Balcon*) must not be played as if it were a satire of this or that. It is – and must be played as – the glorification of the Image and of the Reflection. Only then will its significance – satirical or not – appear (ibid. 276).

Because they are required to glorify the image, Genet's plays demand a particular acting style, one that is extremely difficult to describe. It is based on underlining and demonstrating the contradictions of the actor's activity on stage and for this reason it has rightly been seen as having certain points of contact with Brechtian acting styles. In order to achieve the glamorisation required by Genet, and to accommodate the complex speech patterns of his poetic prose, the actor has to adopt the grand rhetorical manner. Since Genet has emphasised so strongly that *Les Bonnes*, for example, is not a social protest play about the hardships of domestic staff, it is obviously important not to have actresses giving carefully studied naturalistic performances that will convince us we are watching 'real' servants. On the contrary, the roles of Claire and Solange require grandiose stylisation, fascinating but false, and this is where the chief contradiction lies: the actress must *also* be able to indicate the falseness. As well as exuding glamour, and fascinating her audience, the actress must underline her rhetoric in such a way as to show that she *could* act differently and that she is only an actress underneath. Genet's famous comment that 'if I were to put on a play with women's roles I would insist on them being performed by adolescent boys' (1951: 140) clearly points in this direction, especially since he goes on: 'I would notify the public of this by means of a sign nailed to the set' (ibid.). In his last three plays the dramatic illusion is frequently broken or brought into question, only to be re-established even more forcefully. Archibald comments at the beginning of *Les Nègres* on the fact that he and the company are only actors; towards the end, when Ville de Saint-Nazaire announces that the real, off-stage murder has taken place, the actors who represent the white court remove their masks. They only put them on again in order to enact their own destruction and as they do so they remind us once again that they are only actors:

Village For us to get rid of you, must we massacre you?
The one who was the queen No need. We actors, and our massacre will be lyrical.
(To the four blacks of the Court): Gentlemen, your masks! (1960: 165).

The contrast or contradiction sought after in acting style mirrors the contradiction between the imaginary worlds and the real worlds evoked by Genet's plays. These two worlds are brought, rather obviously, into conflict in *Le Balcon*, where a revolution is defeated not by bullets but by the powers of imagination and the glamorous appeal of theatrical images of power. In *Les Nègres* the players constantly remind themselves that the ceremony on stage is merely a 'front' behind which is taking place the trial and execution of a traitor. But the contradictions are most thoroughly present in *Les Paravents*, whose basic structural principle is in the contrast of real and imaginary objects or patterns of behaviour. The mobile screens that make up the set for the play allow for this contrast: 'Near the screen there must always be at least one real object (a wheelbarrow, a bucket, a bicycle etc.) which can confront its own reality with that of the objects drawn on the screens' (1961: 10). Imaginary objects are created in many ways. The farmyard is established simply by use of the actors' voices (as was the malevolent jungle in *Les Nègres*). The authority of Sir Harold is established by the presence on stage of an enormous peccary glove, suspended in the air with a life of its own.

The effect of these staging methods is to make the presentation of uncomplicated, self-evident reality impossible. The presence on stage of each and every reality, the particular shape that it takes, is conditioned by the mind through which it is passed. To take a simple example, the episode in which the Arabs set fire to Sir Harold's plantations is conveyed by the Arabs drawing flames on the screens while a loud noise of burning trees comes from the wings. Sir Harold, who is on stage at the time, notices nothing. The audience sees an act of arson depicted so as to show what that act means to the Arabs.

In order that there should be no mistake about the nature of this form of stage presentation, Genet made frequent reference to the notion of *décalage* in his notes to the play. There was always to be a gap, or dislocation in the presentation of reality so as to prevent the audience from taking it at face value. In the manner of acting, Genet specified that this meant picking a gesture not normally suited to the word. In his last letter to Blin he suggested finding gestures that contradicted the words: 'for example, to go with a sad inflexion of the voice, a gesture of hand and foot that is gay, this operation rejecting the imitation of the natural, must not be done haphazardly: its aim, among others, is to show and reveal what passes unnoticed *habitually*' (1968: 262–3). The idea expressed here is very similar to that of Blin describing the view of a street (see above p. 171). Their ideas are so alike that it is not surprising to find Genet, in his letters, heaping praise upon Blin's production.

In his productions, both of *Les Nègres* and of *Les Paravents*, Blin appears to have achieved the acting style required by Genet. In *Les Nègres*, the use of masks contributed towards the sense of *décalage*, but more than this, the fact that the cast were partly amateurs seems to have helped. They achieved a quality described by Barthes as 'a sort of intelligent gaucheness, which maintained Genet's work in that state of metaphysical *dépaysement* which is its justification' (1960: 96). In *Les Paravents* the actors also used exaggerated, mask-like make-up. Their movements were often contradictory, for example talking to one another while looking in opposite directions, and they created or destroyed the various objects or settings that they required by drawing them on mobile paper screens. By contrast, Peter Brook's production of *Le Balcon* at the Gymnase in 1960 failed utterly to achieve this quality of dislocated reality. Both the acting styles and the use of décor suggested a conventional sleazy brothel with heavy drapes and dim red lights. Marie Bell, a powerful tragic actress, performed Madame Irma with rhetorical authority but no accompanying falseness or *décalage*.

The collaboration between Genet and Blin was at its most complete in the Paris production of *Les Paravents*. This production has rightly been seen as exemplary in its achievement of a total stage language, in which the objects,

14 *Les Paravents* (Genet): the opening scene in Roger Blin's production, Odéon theatre, 1966, with Amidou in the role of Saïd and Maria Casarès in the role of the Mother.

screens, costumes and actors all played an equally important expressive role (see fig. 14). The most original element in this achievement was the screens themselves, which played a complex role, being at one and the same time both a rejection of the conventional, imitative stage setting and also a means by which the actors could materialise anything they wanted, from a simple object, like the clock stolen by Leila, to the emotional responses of the characters or the consequences of their actions (e.g. the burning plantation). By means of the screens and the way the actors played with them, Blin was able to bring into being Genet's vision of the complex interdependence of image and reality. His preoccupation with death as the only deliverance from, or final consecration of, the image was conveyed by the actors bursting through the screens when they died. In the course of the play a very large number of screens is necessary. Blin's production did not entirely solve the technical problem of how to prevent these from encumbering the action, especially on André Acquart's stepped set, and he also had difficulties with some of the actors' inability to draw clearly. But these were minor problems beside the brilliant creation of a performance in which every element called into question both its own reality and the reality of everything else around it. This quality in the production was summed up in the elaborate costume of Warda the prostitute. She was adorned with layer upon layer of sumptuous clothes and poured scorn upon the familiar function of the prostitute's costume which is to reveal and to be removed. Her hair was pierced with enormous pins which she used, not to fix her hair, but to pick her teeth.

Behind all this lies Genet's particular vision of how theatre performance functions and has its effects. For him, the stage is a *de-realising* space. That is to say, it denies the reality of everything that appears within its confines. The idea is stated by Archibald, the master of ceremonies of *Les Nègres*, 'An actor . . . A black . . . if he tries to kill, destroys the reality of even his knife' (1960: 164). The idea that what the stage presents is mere illusion, or shadow play, without substance is a familiar one, especially in twentieth century writers following Pirandello. Genet takes the idea further than most and turns it into a principle. He insists that the job of the stage is not to imitate life and recommends the abolition of anything that might tempt an audience to see play performance as an imitation.

If Genet turns his back on life, then he cannot avoid facing death and this is a prospect he seems to welcome. All of his plays culminate in an enactment of death. This is taken to its extreme in *Les Paravents*, a play which Genet described as illustrating the world of the dead and, in some sense, being played *for* the dead rather than for the living. He explains that the reason for his particular staging techniques is because the de-realising effect of the stage space makes it very close to the realm of death.

Our reason for setting life and the stage in opposition to one another is that we sense that the stage is a space bordering on death, where every liberty is possible . . . The actors' make-up, by making them 'other', will allow them every liberty: they will no longer have social responsibilities but will have different responsibilities to another Order of things.

Their costumes will not clothe them, stage costumes being a means of parade in every sense [French 'parer' – to decorate]. You understand what kind of beauty they must have. Not a fashionable beauty, but a necessary beauty (1968: 222).

This kind of passage is often quoted as evidence that Genet was influenced by Artaud. In fact Genet appears to have read very little Artaud (see Blin, 1981) and although the idea of a theatre facing ultimate realities and characterised by necessity has similarities with what Artaud desired, there is one crucial difference. For Artaud the theatre was always to be seen as a place where life would be revealed. It was a terrifying even a cruel experience. But it was always to be the means of drinking at the well-springs of life. For Genet it is a void, a nothing opening only onto death. In the same letter to Blin he makes this plain concerning *Les Paravents*: 'Most plays, they say, have a meaning: not this one. It is a festivity whose elements are disparate, it is the celebration of nothing' (1968: 223).

This celebration is achieved by the construction of plays presenting an unusually complex interdependence of form and content. It is well-nigh impossible to separate these two things in the traditional manner, especially since Genet has stressed that his play is about nothing. The standard question: 'But what is this play *about*?' thus loses its relevance. Of course it is possible to separate off particular techniques for discussion, but comments about technique cannot avoid being also comments about content. The performance style we have been examining could be described paradoxically as both anti-theatrical and excessively theatrical. It runs counter to all traditional expectations of what theatre can offer us but it also confers significance on even the minutest action or object appearing on stage. The same is true of the plays' content. All Genet's plays present us with anti-societies. The worlds of prison, brothel, blacks or rebels are all defined by opposition to traditional, habitual, right-thinking society. The people inhabiting these worlds are all aware that their existence and, more profoundly, their very consciousness is conditioned by the contempt of others. But Genet's plays do not therefore, like some absurdist dramas, dissolve all social distinctions in a vision of nightmarish horror. Instead, they investigate with precision the levels of interdependence that link the oppressor to the oppressed and they present ceremonies of metamorphosis in which the oppressed, by accepting and exaggerating their condition, hope to turn their shame into pride, to change the rules of the game so as to turn the tables on their oppressors.

The events presented on stage in these plays do, therefore, have a very real connection with what occurs in the world outside. But each event is clearly an image, not a substance. Any sense of the substantiality of what confronts the audience is repeatedly reduced by the use of mirrors or of sliding sets that fold away into each other like Chinese boxes (*Le Balcon*) or of mobile screens that can act as vehicle for any image (*Les Paravents*). The central event of *Les Nègres*, the murder of a white woman, which is elaborately recalled and re-enacted, turns out to be only the image of an action when the catafalque, in which the woman's body supposedly lay throughout the performance, is shown to be empty. The ceremony of alternating hatred and adoration played out between maid and mistress in *Les Bonnes* is shown to be pure image, since both maid and mistress are played by maids. When the real mistress does appear, the maids behaviour towards her reverts to the normal submissiveness.

It is because the events of the plays all share this essential status of image that they are so wordy. For someone reading Genet's plays for the first time, the first impression is of excessive wordiness and of scatalogical indulgence. The reason why they are wordy is that language is the most powerful means of conditioning somebody else's image of himself. By imposing a language upon a colonised people, the colonisers force the natives to adopt all the hidden value judgements enshrined in the colonisers' language and to abandon their own inherited value systems as they cease to use their own language for important transactions. *Les Nègres* dramatises a struggle between two languages, two sets of cultural associations and value systems. The court appeals to Racinian purity, metaphoric whiteness, spotlessness, the splendour of light and the demonic powers of darkness. The blacks respond with a 'litany of the livid', exploiting the unpleasant associations of pallor, and then develop a new set of value associations in which positive values are associated with notions of blackness. This strategy is quite unlike the poetry of negritude as practised by Senghor. Senghor writes in praise of the beauty of all that is black, but uses metaphors that are traditional such as fertility or mysterious shadow. Genet, on the other hand, picks on those things that have traditionally been used as insults by whites: odour, cannibalism, thick lips, savagery. This is the language through which the white colonisers oblige the blacks to represent themselves; this is the only self-consciousness that is available to them. And so they develop and extend it, they celebrate it to a point of extremism that no white man would ever contemplate and thus achieve a kind of freedom by becoming responsible for the first time, for their own images of themselves.

Le Balcon shows a different variation of this strategy. Here the audience sees a number of very ordinary people who, by dressing up as a bishop, a judge, a general, but even more by appropriating their languages, manage to experience the reality of living those social roles. The play shows, in Genet's words, that 'power cannot do without theatricality . . . Power shelters behind some kind of theatricality, whether it is in China, the Soviet Union, England or France . . . There is only one place in the world where theatricality does not hide power and that is the theatre' (1977: 14). What Genet means by this is that political power derives its legitimacy from the force of the images it manages to implant in the minds of people. If you want to know how power operates, you should study the behaviour of images, and especially of theatrical images. *Le Balcon* opens with a sequence of tableaux in which the nature of certain key images is probed. Each of the images represents an accepted figure of authority in most societies: the bishop, the judge, the general. In each case these roles are played not by a real bishop, judge or general, but by men whose ordinary occupations are unexceptional who come to Madame Irma's house of illusions in order to indulge their fantasies by playing these roles. Each one is assisted by one of Madame Irma's remarkably versatile team of prostitutes. Through the interplay between prostitute and customer Genet conducts a demonstration of social roles.

The judge provides a good example of how this works. In his case the prostitute is dressed as a thief who has to admit to a number of crimes. Once the judge is convinced that she really has committed the crimes in question, he passes sentence. For his satisfaction to be complete, the 'thief' must not only make out a convincing case for having committed the crimes in question, but must also accept the sentence meted out. In other words, it is a condition of the judge's existence that the criminal should acknowledge him as such and accept his right to pass judgement. It might seem, if this is the case, that to change the social order would be a simple matter of refusing to accept the rights of judges, bishops, generals to exercise their authority. But this turns out to be less easy than it seems. Outside the walls of Madame Irma's brothel a revolution is in progress which at first seems likely to topple the existing powers. But it turns out that revolutionaries cannot do without images either. They have picked on a charismatic singer named Chantal and made her into the symbol of their struggle for liberty. The leader, Roger, is opposed to this process. He sees that it will never lead to a genuine break with the hold of the existing power structures on people. 'In order to fight against an image, Chantal has allowed herself to be turned into another image. The struggle is no longer taking place in reality . . . we have lost sight of the reasons for our revolt' (1968: 94–5). But he can do nothing to stop the army's fascination with her. When the false bishop, judge and general parade on the balcony, with Madame Irma dressed as a queen at their head, their power of attraction is irresistible and the revolution is quelled.

An additional authority figure who makes frequent appearances at the brothel is the Chief of Police, the real one, who comes to ask, anxiously, whether anyone has yet asked to play out his role. He is always disappointed and this upsets him because he knows that unless he can project a suitably fascinating image his hold on power will never be secure. His ultimate satisfaction comes at the end of the play when Roger, the defeated leader of the revolutionaries, comes to the brothel for the first time. Having failed to lessen the grip of existing power by armed force, he hopes to undermine it from inside. He asks to play the role of police chief but instead of playing out the established scenario, cuts it short by castrating himself in the middle of the ceremony. He fails in his aim, just as the maids fail in *Les Bonnes* to alter the existing power relationships between mistress and servant by offering their mistress poisoned tea. The Chief of Police who is spying on Roger's ceremony has a moment of worry but then realises jubilantly that he is intact and much more powerful than before because his image is now consecrated and he has entered the pantheon of accepted authority figures. The way that power operates, Genet suggests, is similar to the theatre in that both demand a special quality of belief and depend on fascinating a public.

The relationships between those who fascinate and those who are fascinated change in Genet's last two plays and the change illustrates the constant reversal of expectations and challenge to established positions that marks these plays.

The interplay of fascination in social relationships as it is presented in *Le Balcon* could be assimilated to the classic Marxist analysis that proceeds by asking who depends on whom. At first sight it may seem that the penitent depends on the bishop, the criminal on the judge, the soldier on the general. But closer analysis reveals that it is really the other way round: the general only owes his position to the obedience of his troops, the bishop to the penitence of the believers, the judge to the criminal's acceptance that he deserves punishment. In this way, then, the judge depends on the criminal, and so on.

In *Les Paravents* this relationship is again reversed. The judge, who appears in Scene 7 is of a different kind from the judge of *Le Balcon*. In this poor muslim village the judge is Le Cadi who administers religious rather than secular justice. He can only give judgement when he is in a suitably inspired state and once he has achieved this state it is God who speaks through him. When Saïd comes up for trial, his inspiration is already fading and he tries to put off the case. But Saïd is insistent that he must be sentenced and locked up. In order to become more thoroughly the criminal and outcast that he is, Saïd has to earn the disapproval of society through the courts and undergo the accepted punishment: imprisonment. For him the judge is merely a means to a necessary end, a fact of which he is dimly aware: 'I can see vaguely what you achieve with each new sentence and I understand your aim more or less, but what about me? Where does each new sentence lead us? My usefulness to you is to thrust you even further down in your desired direction, but you, you, you, what use are you to me? And who worries about the poor judges. Who?' (1961: 80). So here the equation has been reversed. Instead of the judge depending on the criminal to consecrate his image of himself and to justify his function, it is the other way round. The criminal who desires to maintain and perfect his status relies on the judge (and behind him the whole force of right-thinking society) to pass sentence. Otherwise his criminality has no guarantee of authenticity.

Part of the fascination of *Les Paravents* comes from its persistent questioning of the conventions normally held to govern relationships between individuals and social groups. In performance the most spectacular example of this was the presentation of the brothel and of the prostitute Warda, played in 1966 by Madeleine Renaud. Warda does not solicit the favours of individual men. Instead she keeps a whole group of men at a distance, fascinated by the complexity of her costume and by the charisma of her personality as she attempts to turn her position outside accepted society to good account by achieving almost the status of a goddess. She does this, paradoxically, not by accepting only men who are rich or handsome, but by accepting only those who like Saïd, are thoroughly crapulous. In this way she accepts shameful conditions, transforming them into the instruments of glory.

Les Paravents, like *Le Balcon*, presents an armed revolt – that of the Arabs against the French colonial army. But once again its manner of presenting the rebellion is very different from that of *Le Balcon*. In *Les Paravents* the traditional symbols do not win the day as they do in *Le Balcon*. In fact there is no ultimate victory in the play, unless it be the victory of death. But the struggle is still presented in terms of conflicting images. On the one hand are the French soldiers, whose uniform is glamorous rather than practical. They are taller than the other characters, with costumes that are padded out in some cases and with exaggerated features. They are in all respects larger than life. Genet recommends the costume designer to 'Invent uniforms that are very war-like in which the colours, insignia and symbols give expression to the idea of Force' (1961: 193). He also recommends that their guns should be made of wood painted blue and pink, and that their first entry should be made backwards with their legs kicking in unison like a chorus line of Bluebell girls. In the combination of these things, Genet is seeking for the expression of an image of the French soldier in Algeria, possessing all the colourful glamour of Beau Geste and all the cruelty of an occupying force. In the course of the action, the soldiers' glamour becomes tarnished as their image is pitted against the images invented by the Arabs and drawn on the screens. Gradually we see that the image of the soldier as Bluebell girl is no longer powerful enough to withstand attack. The missionary, who understands such things since he too deals in symbols of power, is the first one to point out that the rebels are acquiring their own beauty. He also points out that the rebellion is caused, initially by the Europeans rather than by the Arabs, since they have provided the examples of cruelty and images of force.

Through all the plays, then, Genet develops a meditation on the relation between symbolic imagination and political reality. He shows that political events are presented through drama and that they are both perceived and lived through as drama. In other words their power is derived from an imaginary level of reality. Even more important for a revolution than having the right ammunition is to have the right dramatic symbol. The charismatic singer on the barricades was a powerful symbol a century ago, but has not survived the enduring power of the established authority figures. The symbol of the handsome legionnaire has become similarly superannuated.

In the view of some critics, this imaginary clash of symbolic realities concludes in the form of a purely negative suicidal ceremonial from which nothing positive can be drawn. Bernard Dort argues persuasively that Genet's plays must be seen as a kind of battle against theatre itself in which the conventions of European theatre are undermined and pushed to an extreme point where they negate their own ability to act as vehicles of meaning (1971: 173–89). Genet himself has written unambiguously of his view that western society and its theatre are both in the final stages of decay.

I do not know what the theatre will be like in a socialist world; I can understand better what it could be among the Mau Mau, but in the Western world, which is increasingly marked by death and turned toward it, it can only refine in the 'reflecting' of a comedy of comedy, of a reflection of reflection which ceremonious performance might render exquisite and close to invisibility. If one has chosen to watch oneself die charmingly, one must rigorously pursue, and array, the funeral symbols. Or must choose to live and discover the Enemy. For me, the Enemy will never be anywhere. Nor will there ever be a Homeland, whether abstract or interior. If I am stirred, it will be by the nostalgic reminder of what it was. Only a theatre of shadows could still move me (Préface à Pauvert, 1954: 16. Trans. Fechtmann).

In this perspective, the constant preoccupation with death in his plays can be seen as almost a will to theatrical suicide and the ultimate image of the theatrical universe can be located in the final scenes of *Les Paravents*, where the dead are not those that have died physically but those that have burst through the screen and become identical with their own image, become purely reflections of themselves.

Dort suggests that the point of the references in *Les Nègres* to a 'real' act of rebellion, supposedly occurring off-stage, is more than just to suggest that somewhere else in the world effective rebellion is possible: it is to show that whatever happens in reality is forever beyond the reach of the western theatre-goer's grasp. All the theatre can do is to translate reality into its own images – and this translation fatally involves betrayal of that reality. He is able to point out that betrayal is itself something frequently alluded to by Genet. It is raised to the level of principle by the central couple, Saïd and Leïla, in *Les Paravents*. These are the only characters to avoid becoming fixed as effigies of themselves. Although the other characters who have broken through the screens to the realm of death constantly expect their arrival, they never appear. Their escape is due to their success in constantly negating any image of themselves. As the outcasts of the village, they are seen as rebels, but they negate this by betraying the rebellion. As criminals, they are seen as attempting to evade justice, but Saïd insists on being sentenced. But in this constant betrayal are the seeds of suicide, since it renders rational revolt meaningless. Revolt of this kind against established norms cannot be made in the name of any other principle, since that principle is itself reversed and negated at the earliest opportunity.

Dort's conclusion is thus that Genet ultimately destroys any possibility of meaningful communication through the conventions of western theatre. To begin with, Genet had accepted its challenge, had indeed revelled in it, had refined its traditional preoccupation with illusion, with the self-reflecting play within a play, with the confusion between mask and face. But where, traditionally, these devices are used to secrete an ultimate truth, Genet pushes them to an extreme point where, far from secreting their own special kind of truth, they reveal only a nothingness of destruction and death. His theatre charms, fascinates and traps its spectators, but once it has enticed them into its imaginary world, it destroys the ground under their feet, leaving them with their disguises destroyed and an intuition of only one thing: that their lives are a living death.

But to look at it this way is perhaps to accept too narrow a view of what Genet has achieved in the theatre. Alone among the major playwrights of post-war France, Genet has devoted an important part of his work to Africa. Or, to be more precise, he has constructed plays from the collision of African and French mentalities, and has provided powerful images for the mentalities imposed upon the colonised. This is a considerable achievement and particularly so because in doing so he manages to blur the simplistic division of the contemporary French theatre into either absurdist plays or political dramas. He does this by showing the close interdependence of image and reality, especially as encountered by people and nations attempting to free themselves from neo-colonialist oppression. After the literal oppression of white government in African territories has been removed, oppressive mentalities linger for generations. By addressing his last two major plays to this problem, Genet has engaged more closely with political reality than many of his comments would suggest. Genet's plays, at a dramatic level, present an extraordinary refinement of the visual possibilities of theatre language, while at the same time glorying in a rhetorical linguistic style. This is because both images and language are employed by people to re-present themselves, to construct a version of how they see themselves in the world which then becomes a basis for action. Ionesco talked of the playwright's job to create a revolution in our way of seeing the world by extending the idiom of theatre. Genet certainly achieved this and exerted a considerable influence on subsequent French theatre.

We should not be put off by acts of suicide or self-castration with which most of the plays conclude. The plays' relationship with reality is not a simple one. The activities that occur on stage may sometimes be held up for admiration sometimes not. The responsibility for making the links with common reality is made to rest with the audience. When Madame Irma, at the end of *Le Balcon*, tells the audience to go home but to be aware that everything there will be even falser than what has happened on stage, she is doing much the same thing as Brecht. She is insisting that in the lives of each audience member there are processes no different in kind from what has been shown on stage. The only difference is that none of the problems evoked can be solved on stage: the stage can only glamorise. Therefore it must push glamour to its utmost. The solution of real problems is for real life.

Vauthier, Audiberti, Arrabal

These three playwrights, though dissimilar, all have points in common with Genet. The words 'ceremony' and 'ritual' recur in the accounts of their work and all three deal in the private worlds of fantasy and neurosis. The plays of Audiberti and Arrabal suggest images of sumptuousness and of evil; those of Vauthier and Audiberti have considerable poetic force, though this sometimes degenerates into mere verbosity. But although these characteristics suggest parallels with Genet, the plays of these authors are mostly rather naïve in their use of theatre; certainly they do not display the same brilliantly self-questioning use of dramatic conventions that is to be found in the work of Genet. Neither do they achieve the same disturbing analysis of the interplay between the fantasies of the individual and the fabric of society at large.

Jean Vauthier, born in 1910, first became known for *Capitaine Bada*, directed by André Reybaz in 1952 at the Théâtre de Poche, but his major success was with *Le Personnage combattant*, a two-and-a-quarter-hour monologue performed by Jean-Louis Barrault in 1956 at his studio theatre, the Petit Marigny. This performance was an astonishing tour de force by Barrault: he turned Vauthier's very wordy play into a sort of ballet, performing it at breakneck speed with constant movement around the stage. The play recounts the last night in the life of a writer who returns to the hotel room where, many years previously, he had tried to compose a story. Throughout the night he struggles with the words he has written and with his treacherous memories in a vain attempt to recapture his youth, at times reminding one of *Krapp's last tape*.

But the play lacks the clarity and precision that mark Beckett's confrontation of different moments of self-awareness. In this play, any such intuitions are drowned in a tidal wave of justifications, explanations, ratiocinations and appeals to grandiose notions, in the words of Barrault's preface: 'a sort of redemption of the individual through the total gift of himself. Man, after a night of suffering, rediscovers the faculty of transfigured life. He rediscovers the poetic gift of the metamorphosis of things' (1955: 11). In the end, the hotel waiter, who has made occasional appearances throughout the play, becomes so exasperated that he knocks the writer down and drags him off by one leg.

For Barrault, the production was a triumph. He revived it at the Récamier in 1971 in alternation with Madeleine Renaud's most famous one-woman performance: *Oh les beaux jours*, and the critics once again applauded the virtuoso display. Meanwhile, *Capitaine Bada* had been revived by Marcel Maréchal in 1966 at his Théâtre du Cothurne, Lyon. Maréchal, an actor of much heavier build than Barrault and less of an acrobat, performed at a less feverish pace, but brought an interpretation of great lyrical power to the play, without losing its derisive force. In this, and the additional *Badadesques*, that he had performed two years previously, Maréchal received high praise from the critics. Georges Neveux considered that he had revealed Vauthier's hero as having the same derisive, puppet-like relation to the interior life of the modern individual as Ubu has to the exterior life of modern society.

This judgement seems somewhat inflated. In *Capitaine Bada* we see another writer struggling with his inability to control his own words, but here he is accompanied by Alice, his wife. Her alternating moods, first chasing after him and then refusing to satisfy his desires, add a dimension of the sex war to the futile struggles of the failed writer. But here, too, the language is so confused, so interminably digressive and so uncontrolled, that the audience is exhausted rather than enlightened. The published text has an original format, being printed in two columns, with stage directions down one side and text down the other. Alas, this only helps to reveal more clearly the lack of necessary link between the actions suggested and the dialogue.

Vauthier's most recent play is *Le Sang*, commissioned by Maréchal and performed in 1970 at his new Théâtre du Huitième in Lyon. In this play, Bada reappears as Angelo-Bada, a playwright-director, attempting to produce a revenge tragedy filled with corpses and blood. On the night of the first performance, he decides to change everything, to the fury of the actors, who are terrified of having to improvise. He ends up by forcing all of the players to recreate their roles and the play culminates, not in a blood bath, but in laughter and dancing.

Angelo-Bada wants the theatre to be constantly called into question, he wants his creation to be in a state of constant movement, a perpetual revolution, both by himself and by others. It is a stirring subject. It's revolutionary (Maréchal, 1974: 148).

In this play, Vauthier comes nearest to escaping from the world of private fantasy. Unlike the earlier plays, it contains much that is authentically dramatic and the device of the play within the play is deftly handled. But the location in real time and space of Angelo-Bada remains uncertain. As he and his actors step in and out of role, they are not responding to pressures of a social, psychological or ceremonial kind like those that impose themselves upon Genet's blacks in *Les Nègres*. Instead, they are simply functioning as part of an autonomous, fictional world in which all power lies with the author-producer. The elaborately theatrical Elizabethan setting also seems strangely gratuitous, possessing neither great fascination for what it is, nor any clear relevance to the world outside. Geneviève Serreau's comment applies to this as to his earlier plays:

Vauthier possesses an undeniable power which is most effective when used, in burlesque style, for calling into question the self or the world. He establishes on stage an exasperated, exasperating language, hungering for the unreal and the absolute, and which has the disturbing force of a baroque object whose purpose cannot be guessed (1966: 142).

Jacques Audiberti, like Vauthier, was 'discovered' by Maréchal in the early sixties after being performed in the small 'art' theatres of Paris during the forties and fifties. With productions of plays by these authors, Maréchal was consciously trying to bridge the gap between the Parisian and the decentralised theatres. He admired Audiberti even more than Vauthier for his poetic and imaginative power. He remembers his production of *Le Cavalier seul* in 1963 as the moment when he truly discovered himself and his vocation: 'I had a sort of veneration for Audiberti . . . I saw in him a brother, or rather a father' (1974: 42). *Le Cavalier seul* ranges across the whole Mediterranean world, from France to Byzantium and Jerusalem, and develops a poetic meditation on the struggle between the forces of good and evil. It tells the story of a young French peasant who sets off on a crusade, discovering all the fascination of the East and ending up at Jerusalem, where Christ appears and begs him to prevent the imminent arrival of the crusader armies. He fails to act, joins in the sack of Jerusalem, and realises too late that he has recrucified Christ. The play is largely static, relying for its effect on a multi-layered poetic text filled with verbal invention and linguistic jokes, ranging from the delicate to the scatological. The texture of the writing is not unlike that of Christopher Fry and, like Fry's work, it requires grand oratorical delivery rather than a great deal of action in performance.

Audiberti's first play, *Quoat-Quoat*, had been a great success when produced by André Reybaz at the Gaîté-Montparnasse in 1946, despite the fact that he had not written it with performance in mind:

When I wrote *Quoat-Quoat* I did not distinguish theatre from any other literary genre – the sonnet, for example. I wrote dialogue exactly as I might have written a story or a poem. The idea that it might one day be performed on stage, quite sincerely, never crossed my mind (1965: 93).

187

The following year Georges Vitaly scored an even greater success with *Le Mal court* at the Théâtre de Poche, a production that he twice revived, in 1955 and 1963. In the course of the next two decades, until his death in 1965, more than a dozen new plays by Audiberti were staged, most of them by Vitaly. They became a mainstay of the small Paris 'art' theatres, along with those of Ghelderode, Schéhadé, Dubillard, Billetdoux, during the period of the fifties when the New Theatre was struggling to establish itself. Their verbal pyrotechnics and poetic force made them more easily acceptable to critics and theatre-goers brought up on the avant-garde of Cocteau and the Surrealists. Indeed they employed some of the Surrealists' techniques for revealing the dark forces of the unconscious beneath the ordinary surface of everyday life, and appeared to provide a more promising pointer to the looked-for dramatic revival than the bleak, colourless worlds created by Adamov, Ionesco and Beckett.

For his own part, Audiberti never laid any claim to dramatic originality: 'my theatre has nothing new about it . . . I have always dealt with a single subject, the conflict between good and evil, between the soul and the flesh' (cit. Serreau, 1966: 30). *Le Mal court* exemplifies this statement very clearly. It shows Alarica, the princess of an imaginary country, Courtelande, who begins the play full of innocence and purity, is then humiliated and betrayed, learns the ways of evil and embarks on a reign of vice and tyranny. The plot and the themes are deliberately conventional, bathed in a glow of fairy-tale magic. The characters mostly bear functional names: Le Roi Parfait; Le Cardinal; Le Maréchal; and are devoid of any psychological substance. They tend to talk in abstract terms of *la puissance, le bonheur, la beauté, le désir, l'honneur, la raison*. But their make-believe world is never troubled by doubts or questions from outside. The nearest Audiberti came to confronting the real world was in *La Poupée*, a rather confused play on the theme of the futility of all revolutions, that was made into a film by Jacques Baratier in 1962. Maréchal chose this play to open the Théâtre du Huitième in Lyon in 1968, giving the ending a more optimistic thrust by adding an extra speech and by the spectacular unfurling of red flags, but this went against the drift of the play and of Audiberti's work as a whole.

Fernando Arrabal's life and works are dominated by the traumas of his childhood in Spain. He was born in 1932 and was only four years old when, in 1936, his father, an army officer known for his Republican sympathies, was arrested and sentenced to death by Franco. His sentence was commuted to a thirty-year prison term but his wife, a pious and repressive Catholic, behaved as if he had died shamefully. She cut his head out of all the family photographs and made sure that the young Arrabal never made contact with him. So from an early age the dramatist's loyalties were torn in two directions. The discovery of letters from his father convinced him that his mother had betrayed him; he left home, arriving in Paris in 1955 with severe tuberculosis.

It was during this illness and long convalescence that many of his first plays were written, in Spanish, as a means of liberation from fear: 'I write down anything that comes into my head . . . I write for myself, as one takes drugs' (cit. Aslan, 1970: 311). These plays were then translated into French by his wife. Their language is simple, even rudimentary, and their appeal lies not in poetic language but in their strange sado-masochistic images of suffering and desire: 'as I cannot conceive of love without violence, the more tenderness there is in my theatre, the more violence there is by contrast' (ibid.). One of his early plays, *Fando et Lis*, illustrates this statement by presenting a young couple who are going on an incomprehensible journey to a place called Tar. Lis is paralysed, chained to a cart; Fando alternately caresses and tortures her in a succession of childish games which end when he kills her. They have no consistency as characters outside their alternating roles of master and slave, existing in a hallucinatory world which bears little relation to anyone or anything else. The figures in Arrabal's plays all resemble Fando and Lis: they are capable of extreme childlike naïvety but also of extreme cruelty and appear as the embodiments of fundamental Freudian drives shorn of all the normal constraints of daily life. Their actions all tend towards rituals involving the familiar props of repressed sexuality: chains, cages, whips, coffins, etc. Angel Berenguer (1977) has argued quite persuasively that the structures of political repression in Spain underlie these plays, but they are hidden structures, not immediately apparent to the average theatre-goer who, in the sixties, tended to respond to the sensational and prurient aspects they display.

Arrabal's first plays were published in 1958 and his *Pique-nique en campagne* produced by Serreau in 1959. But it was not until the sixties that he achieved notoriety, thanks to some spectacular productions of his work by Victor Garcia, Jorge Lavelli and Jérome Savary, and thanks also to a happy coincidence between his ideas of sexual liberation and the new permissive atmosphere of the 'swinging sixties'. For Arrabal, 'once my play is written, I should like a producer of wild genius to handle it with absolutely no respect and to use it as the pretext for his show' (cit. Aslan, 1970: 313). His wish was first fulfilled by the Spanish producer Victor Garcia, who composed a montage from four plays: *Le Cimetière des voitures, Oraison, Les Deux Bourreaux* and *La Communion solennelle* (one of the short pieces grouped together as *Théâtre Panique* in his *Théâtre V*). These were performed in 1966 at Dijon in a large warehouse as part of the fourth and last experimental festival run by Michel Parent to develop forms of simultaneous staging (see p. 144 and Knowles, 1971). The spectators were seated on revolving chairs which surrounded two of the six acting areas and were themselves surrounded by the other four. The only elements of décor were the shells of six old cars, suspended from the ceiling, and cunningly jointed and hinged so that the actors could move over, under and through them. The movements of the actors did not always relate to the lines spoken, but attempted to convey their atmosphere of arbitrary violence. In the text of *Les Deux Bourreaux*, Dorothy Knowles recalls that:

at one moment one of the two brothers slammed the lid of the boot down on the other who had taken refuge there; at another moment his brother was stretched as if crucified on the bonnet of the car during the torture of the brothers' father inside the car. Garcia here applied to the full his particular theory of movement, that is to say movement born of the heat of the moment and completely divorced from realistic acting. The search for a new type of specifically *theatrical* movement, for a series of self-contained, mobile, human hieroglyphics which Garcia pursues along with other Latin-American producers and artists, was here carried by him into the realm of inanimate objects (1975b: 532).

Garcia's work on this production revealed a mastery of pure theatrical imagery that he was to repeat in later productions, notably Genet's *Les Bonnes* in French, and Lorca's *Yerma* in Spanish with the Nuria Espert Company. In its exploration of multiple staging and its free associations of unusual images, the production helped to prepare the ground for the group theatre experiments that will be discussed in chapter 9.

Similarly free treatments were given to Arrabal's plays by the Argentinian director Jorge Lavelli, notably *L'Architecte et l'Empereur d'Assyrie*, and by Jérome Savary with *Le Labyrinthe*, both in 1967. During the period of the sixties, Arrabal was elaborating the notion of *théâtre panique*, defined as 'a manner of being, presided over by confusion, humour, terror, chance and euphoria' (cit. Aslan, 1970: 314). On the one hand this has led to some interesting film work, such as *Viva la muerte*, directed by Jodorowski; on the other it has resulted in several volumes of dramatic fragments which are almost indistinguishable from the then fashionable happenings, celebrating liberation from repressive authority, whether sexual, religious or political.

Arrabal's claim to recognition as a dramatist must depend on his longer works, such as *L'Architecte et L'Empereur d'Assyrie* in which two men, marooned on a desert island, play a succession of sado-masochistic games, changing roles, imitating one another, until finally one devours the other. On the fringes of this play there hovers the familiar Modernist theme of the disintegration of the subject into infinitely variable discourses. It is a theme that we shall find explored more rigorously in the work of Vinaver and other playwrights of the seventies. But Arrabal prevents his audience from seeing his characters as anything other than the projection of his fantasies and so the necessary sense of engagement with reality is sacrificed for the satisfactions of the voyeur. At first the combination of eroticism, cruelty and perverted ritual in his plays led critics to invoke the name of Artaud. But with hindsight it is clear that Arrabal's self-indulgent treatment of his fantasy world ignores the essential element of Artaud's vision:

Theatre of cruelty means first of all a theatre that is difficult and cruel for myself . . . It is not a matter of sawing up our personal anatomies but of the much more terrible and necessary cruelty that the external world can exercise upon us. We are not free. The sky can still fall on our heads. And the theatre's function is first of all to teach us that (Artaud, 1964: 121).

Ultimately, the plays of Vauthier, Audiberti and Arrabal are all locked within worlds of private fantasy. They may be read with pleasure but the essentially public and social element of theatre performance is not fundamental to them. Where they have proved successful in performance, this has been because a gifted director, such as Barrault, Maréchal or Garcia, has used them as a springboard for his own scenographic imagination.

9

La création collective

'The adventure of the Théâtre du Soleil is the most important adventure in the French theatre since Jean Vilar and his T.N.P.' (Bablet, 1979: 88). This is the judgement of Denis and Marie-Louise Bablet, both members of the theatre research team at the prestigious Centre National de Recherches Scientifiques. The company's work and history from 1964 to 1977 is the subject of their *Diapolivre*, the first of its kind to be published, consisting of a book, a set of eighty-four slides, descriptive analyses of each separate slide and a sound record of part of the company's most famous production, *1789*. Film versions have been made of *1789* and of the more recent *Mephisto* and the company has also made a film for television, *Molière, ou la vie d'un honnête homme*, which has been broadcast throughout Europe and America. It is rare indeed for such a quantity of visual documentation to be available for a contemporary theatre company, offering a unique opportunity for study of its work, which is among the most exciting and influential to have appeared on the French stage in the last three decades. Its importance is due to the fact that it has repeatedly called everything into question: the status of the play text, the role of the various theatre workers, the shape of the performance space and the actor–audience relationship. Most remarkable of all, the company has enjoyed a string of popular successes, despite its resolutely experimental stance and its location in a distant and unfashionable suburb of Paris.

Although the membership of the company has not remained exactly the same in the course of its thirty years' existence, continuity has been provided by its director, Ariane Mnouchkine. She is a most unusual director in that she has always worked to diminish the power of the director, moving instead towards a pattern of collaborative creation and shared responsibility rather in the manner of Brecht, at the Berliner Ensemble, describing himself as *Probenleiter*. In a discussion held in April 1975, she was asked to explain how her practice differed from that of most theatre directors. She replied that the main difference was that she had no foreknowledge of what would happen in the rehearsal and improvisation sessions of the Théâtre du Soleil. Instead, her role was to explore and create in company with the actors, designers, etc. 'Remember', she said, 'that the director has already achieved the greatest degree of power he's ever had in history. And that our general aim is to move beyond that situation, by creating a form of theatre where it will be possible for everyone to collaborate without there being directors, technicians, and so on in the old sense' (1975: 12).

This rather utopian attitude is combined with a lively sense of history and its bearing on the present to create the distinctive quality of the work of the Théâtre du Soleil. The company first formed under that name in 1964, choosing not to be known by a utilitarian-sounding set of initials, such as T.N.P., T.E.P., but by the more suggestive word *soleil*, which they picked 'as a tribute to certain film makers associated with light, generosity and pleasure such as Max Ophüls, Jean Renoir, George Cukor' (Bablet, 1979: 7). A few members of the group had known each other since 1959 when they had formed a student theatre group, the Association Théâtrale des Etudiants de Paris. As well as putting on shows (directed by Mnouchkine), this group had sponsored lectures, including Sartre's 'Epic theatre and dramatic theatre' given in the Sorbonne in 1960 (reprinted in Sartre, 1973). During the early sixties Mnouchkine worked in films and travelled in the Far East, where she discovered at first hand the expressive power of the highly stylised Asian theatre, a discovery that only began to have a clearly identifiable effect on the group's work in the middle seventies, but was always an important influence.

In the early sixties a considerable number of new theatre groups were being formed and at first the Théâtre du Soleil did not seem to differ greatly from many others. Their early repertoire displayed a common tendency towards left-wing playwrights and revivals of the classics: Adamov's version of *Les Petits Bourgeois* by Gorki was followed by *Le Capitaine Fracasse* adapted from Gautier's novel by a member of the company, Philippe Léotard, then Wesker's *The kitchen* and Shakespeare's *A midsummer night's dream*. Like most other groups of this kind, they were constituted as a Société Coopérative Ouvrière de Production. No doubt they took the idea of the cooperative more seriously than some: all important decisions had to be taken by majority vote and every member had to take his turn at the menial jobs such as sweeping the stage. But it was not until after 1968 that they decided that every member of the company should take the same salary and began to devise a play of their own by the method that came to be known as *la création collective*.

Like Planchon's company, the Théâtre du Soleil combined social concern with an ebullient sense of the special delight to be had from a theatre of celebration, good humour, gags and *lazzi*. *Les Petits Bourgeois* was followed by the explosive *Capitaine Fracasse*. Both plays were performed at the Maison des Jeunes et de la Culture in Montreuil and then in other halls or theatres around Paris and its suburbs, but neither met with mass success and the members of the company found it difficult to live without daytime jobs. But in 1967 they had their first big success with *The kitchen*, the first play of Wesker's to be performed in France. Not wanting to have to move around from hall to hall again, they hired the disused Cirque Médrano in Montmartre for a small rent since it was due for demolition. The ring was turned into an arena stage, with the audience seated in a semicircle on some of the old circus benches. In Paris, novelty accounts for a lot, and the excitement of going to the circus to see a play certainly accounted for some of its success. But it was not just the novelty that audiences responded to, nor was it just the work of an important new English dramatist. They discovered a young, vigorous company, whose acting style seemed to fit with the atmosphere of the circus ring: it was an ebullient, physical style, achieving its effects by patterns of orchestrated movement that became almost acrobatic at times. It was a long way from the rather wordy, static style often seen at London's Royal Court Theatre, the cradle of new English dramatists like Wesker.

This style was founded on two distinct determinations, rarely found together in the same theatre company. One was to take seriously the working life of ordinary working people, those who seldom go to the theatre, to find a way of dramatising the conditions in which they work and the relationships they establish in those conditions. The second determination was to discover an adequate theatrical transposition for those conditions so as to avoid the trap of naturalism or 'kitchen sink drama', as the writing of Wesker and his colleagues was dubbed in England. Wesker's text fitted perfectly with the first determination but presented problems with the second, which were only overcome by the use of heightened gesture and movement. Every member of the company spent time as an observer in a restaurant kitchen so as to be able to present on stage an image of the frantic rhythm and growing tensions produced in the kitchen of a big restaurant. Then they returned to the rehearsal room and turned what they had observed into mimed gesture. The result was not an illusionistic reproduction of the working day in a kitchen so much as a theatrical metaphor for a working life of any kind (see fig. 15).

15   *The kitchen* (Wesker): Mnouchkine's production at the Cirque Médrano, with designs by Roberto Moscoso, 1967.

The success of the production enabled the members of the company to abandon their daytime jobs and won them three awards, but it did not please everyone. Their request for subsidy was turned down by the committee of 'Aid to Young Companies' and the production attracted some criticism in left-wing circles. The critics argued that the play made a negative political statement since it showed the kitchen workers as oppressed and underprivileged but having no choice other than submission to the boss. A year later, during the wave of student protests and factory occupations, the company took the play into the factories and found that these audiences grasped immediately what they had tried to show: not a rather negative play about the catering trade, but a more generalised play about all factory work (there is a helpful assonance in French *cuisine/usine*) and the negative ending was taken not as a cry of despair but as a powerful protest. The performances gave rise to lively debates in the factories and works' committees about what *could* be done in such circumstances.

At the same time as performing *The kitchen* to workers in occupied factories, the company was performing *A midsummer night's dream*, again in the Cirque Médrano. It was a violent, elemental production, played on a vast slope covered in animal skins with the fairies played as dangerous, satyr-like creatures, dressed in nothing but goatskin trousers, with blood daubed on their naked torsos. It anticipated Brook's 1970 production at Stratford to some extent, placing emphasis on movement and acrobatics; this was strengthened by casting two dancers from Béjart's company in the roles of Oberon and Titania.

The Théâtre du Soleil felt that the events of 1968 had revealed inadequacies in their work and opened up new directions in which they ought to develop. On the one hand they drew the logical conclusion of their cooperative company policy by adopting absolute equality of salaries and resolving not to employ actors from outside the group again. On the other hand they wanted to respond through their art to the problems raised in the heat of the events of 1968 concerning the political function of the artist in general and of the author in particular.

The group felt strongly that, like Artaud, they wanted to use the whole range of expressive means in the theatre. It was vital for them to discover a properly theatrical language and not to rely solely on the methods of political, historical or sociological analysis and debate. As a group, however, they had experienced the full force of Brecht's influence and were determined that the search for a new theatrical language must lead to the discovery of an idiom that would make it possible to deal with political process as well as private drama.

The first result of this new approach to their work was *Les Clowns*, which the group presented in 1969. *The kitchen* and *A midsummer night's dream* had both, to some extent, been productions in which the actors were struggling for a style of theatre in which the spoken text was not the only important means of communication. These productions were first steps towards a theatre relying on movement, sound, voice and a total, defining environment (rather than a stage set or décor). *Les Clowns* took them much further in this direction, since it started, not from plot or story, but from character or, rather, from mask. Now, in the wake of 1968, the company felt that they must re-examine the premises on which their work was based and, above all, question their social function. They came to the conclusion that the best figure they could find as a picture of the actor or artist in society, was that of the clown. Accordingly, each member of the group worked on a series of autobiographical sketches that would explain who he was, how he came to be a clown, how he considered his own function, and why he had chosen one particular clown costume and mask. Once the actors felt secure, each in his particular role, they came together to perform group improvisations. What was shown to the public was simply a series of these costumed improvisations with music, songs and gags thrown in.

Looking back on *Les Clowns* a year later, Ariane Mnouchkine explained how it had been characterised by one major failing, but also by a major success. The failing was the lack of real group work: '*Les Clowns* was essentially a set of individual creations by each member of the company. There had been no collective creation and this was perhaps the show's major defect' (Mnouchkine, 1971a: 6). But the success of *Les Clowns* was that it enabled the actors, for the first time, to find their own language. The three major improvised plays that followed (*1789, 1793* and *L'Age d'or*) were all made possible because of it: 'It is through the language formed by work on *Les Clowns* that we are trying to speak of the Revolution' (ibid. 14). This statement was made while work on *1789* was still in progress but it expresses clearly what the group believed it was achieving: a means of expression that worked richly and effectively, without over-simplifications, on either the individual, the political or the theatrical level.

In the autumn of 1970, at the Piccolo Teatro in Milan, the Théâtre du Soleil gave the first performance of *1789*. It was not until early 1971 that performances began in France, in the disused *cartoucherie* (cartridge-factory) at Vincennes. The play was an enormous success and performances continued there until 1973 with brief visits to other places (e.g. to the Roundhouse in London where it played to capacity audiences for four weeks). During the last few performances of the play's run a film was made under the direction of Ariane Mnouchkine. Copies of this film are in distribution and may be requested through the French Embassy's Cultural Services.

1789 achieved something of the same effect on the theatre of the seventies that *Waiting for Godot* had had on the theatre of the fifties: it established in the eye of the theatre-going public a new dramatic form, *la création collective*, and brought a flood of critical and explanatory writing in its wake. The theatre review, *Travail Théâtral*, that had been founded in 1970 by Bablet, Copfermann, Dort and Kourilsky, seized on the company's work with enthusiasm, printing 35 pages of interviews, analyses and photographs in its second issue. Other theatre groups were keen to copy the Soleil's methods and it became all the rage to put on collectively scripted shows, to such an extent that the playwrights began to complain that no author could have his works performed.

Above all, the experience of the quarter of a million spectators who flocked to see the show was of liberation. *Waiting for Godot* had impressed audiences in the early fifties through an unprecedentedly bleak image of life as one long approach to death. At the Cartoucherie, the experience was more like a resurrection. From the moment when the audiences first entered the performance area and discovered to their surprise that there were no numbered seats, let alone any *ouvreuses* who had to be tipped or other deadening paraphernalia of Parisian theatre, the mood was electric. The production built on this mood to establish an unparalleled sense of joy and festivity. As the account of the first year of the Revolution built up to the taking of the Bastille, a carnival mood broke out, sweeping everyone along in a common celebration of the overthrow of tyranny. Even the portrayal of the subsequent repression by La Fayette's militia could not damp the audience's sense of joy and release. Many simply did not want to leave at the end but remained in animated discussion with the actors and with one another until the early hours of the morning. It was the sort of thing one might associate with a religious celebration or peace festival, but not normally with a theatre performance. Coming at a time when the excitements of 1968 had faded, and any gains in social terms were being rapidly eroded, the play seemed to offer a revival of that fiery enthusiasm for social justice and rejection of inherited constraints.

The form of *1789* was unlike that of any other play being performed at the time. It can be seen to draw on a variety of influences but owes most to the company's own internal organisation, its original working methods and its growing political awareness. The move from *Les Clowns* to *1789* had not been easy. At first an attempt had been made to devise a play about the Paris Commune of 1871. Here again the influence of Brecht and of Adamov could be seen. But the work did not satisfy the members of the company and they turned their attention instead to the French Revolution. There were a number of different reasons for choosing this. In the first place, they wanted a simple story that would be familiar to all and as free as possible from cultural accretions. Their first thought was to use characters drawn from folk tales, but they concluded that today even folk tales are received as 'cultural products'. The Revolution was chosen as something that every member of the audience would at least be familiar with however disparate their interpretations of it might be.

It was also a solution to the company's desire to speak in its plays about the modern world. For Mnouchkine 'The French Revolution marks the appearance of capitalism' (1971a: 4). The political analysis contained in the play suggests that the effect of the Revolution was to replace the aristocracy of the nobles by the aristocracy of the rich. By dramatising the events of the Revolution, they were thus presenting an explanation of the modern world and not just engaging in an attempt to revive a lost historical period.

Moreover the problem of historical knowledge was one that interested the company in its own right. They wanted to attempt a portrayal of the Revolution that circumvented the need to choose between the history of great men or of little people – *Danton's death* or *Mother Courage*. Instead they were interested in contrasting visions of the historical characters and the historical process: what Raymond Williams calls 'complex seeing'. A good example of this is the presentation of Louis XVI, who is played by a number of different actors in the course of the play, some portraying him more sympathetically than others. This process becomes even more extreme when Louis is played by a puppet. In the episode when the women of Paris bring the king back from Versailles, he is portrayed as a gigantic carnival figure who is carried in triumph over the heads of the crowd. An earlier episode, representing the meetings of the three estates, is portrayed as a marionette show in which Louis, like all the characters, is presented in the ridiculous guise of a hand-puppet.

The problem for the group was that these aims could not be served by performing ready-made plays; they had to construct their own. But it was not so simple a matter as the work on *Les Clowns* for which they had needed simply to work on their own skills and imaginations. Here they were confronted with real historical characters and a period which they had to get to know in great detail. The task of research and documentation was divided up between the different members of the group and the results then pooled. A number of different historians gave lectures on the different aspects and interpretations of the period, and showings of films like Gance's *Napoléon* and Griffiths' *Orphans of the storm* were arranged. This was followed up by improvisation work. The actors would divide up into groups of four or five and search for ways of presenting the various events of the period (1789–91). At the end of a day's work anything between ten and thirty improvisations would be demonstrated for the judgement of the whole company. Many would be abandoned; some would be retained for further elaboration. The final play consisted of eighteen improvised scenes, some extremely simple and some very complex, some relying entirely on the recorded words of historical characters, others using highly theatrical and metaphorical means of presentation.

It is clear from the descriptions of work on *1789* that the process of constructing the play was a source of great excitement within the group and that it reinforced their sense of team-work and solidarity. The actors felt not only that they were discovering a new theatrical style that would enable them to avoid the usual traps of historical or political dramas, but also that this discovery was intricately linked with their new-found method of work in which every member of the group was expected to contribute something to every stage of the play's preparation. They contrasted this with the social organisation in a capitalist economy, where people were encouraged to become specialists, acquire qualifications, and then sell those specialised qualifications to the highest bidder. In the work on the play no one member of the company of thirty-five had a privileged say in the creative process. Everyone did at least some work on the fabrication of the stage structures, the construction of the props and the design and making of the costumes. Naturally, the technical director put his special skills, for example, at the disposal of the group. They did not pretend that everyone was equally gifted in all departments of theatre activity. But the notion of the specialised 'department' into which nobody else is allowed to trespass had been broken down.

It was the new form, the unusual playing space and the refusal to act in a conventional theatre that, in Mnouchkine's view, constituted the real strength and originality of the play. By contrast with 'les spectacles qui pensent à gauche' (i.e. plays with a revolutionary message, but that are put on in a conventional way), the original form of the play lent it a profounder effect than is often achieved by left-wing rhetoric. As proof, she cited the hostility of government funding bodies. Despite a subsidy of only 240,000 francs in 1970 and 300,000 francs in 1971 the company clung to the importance of their special style and playing space, sure that they had discovered what they were searching for during the work on *Les Clowns*: 'a form that is clear, direct, luminous' (Mnouchkine, 1971a: 4). One of the vital elements in achieving this was the actors' sense that what they were doing was a part of themselves and engaged them totally as people. To be an actor in the sixties was frequently to have a profound sense of being alienated and exploited; he or she was often expected to simulate violent or brutal behaviour, to undress on stage or to be put through various painful contortions. Especially in dramas following the 'absurdist' vogue, the personal responsibility of the actor was severely reduced and he often felt no more than a puppet moved by the inscrutable forces of author and director. In contrast to this experience of alienation, the actors of *1789* experienced a total commitment to what they were doing. One of them expressed it by saying that he wasn't just hired to act, he was expected to learn to contribute. '*1789* also encouraged me to study; I read a lot and thought a lot ... Not only do I now feel happy as an actor, I am also in personal agreement with what I perform professionally; along with my thirty-five comrades, I am a part of what I do, both on stage and off stage' (Soleil, 1971b: 15).

For Alfred Simon (1976) this attitude on the part of the performers was crucial, since the resulting play became an *acte* in Artaud's sense rather than a performance. It achieved the status of a genuine rite of celebration, since it engaged the collective beliefs of the whole group and provoked the particular type of audience response mentioned above. This was achieved by a special theatrical style that combined a variety of different performance techniques. The broad all-inclusive style was that of fairground theatre which aims for big, often farcical effects, and which relies on an immediate contact with its audience with none of the standard conventions for keeping them at a distance such as the proscenium arch, the orderly rows of seats in which the audience is forced to be passive, or the whole mystique of theatre which gives the actor an untouchable prominence. For *1789* a set of stages and bridges was constructed running around four sides of a square and *enclosing* the audience so that the audience was surrounded by the action. The spectators were not seated but standing and would move in one direction or another according to the shifts in the action. Sometimes the action could overflow from the stages and pass through the audience, reducing the gap between spectators and actors (see fig. 16). This process was taken to its logical extreme in the scene of the taking of the Bastille. Here each actor positioned himself at a different point in the central area, gathering a small knot of spectators around him and described the taking of the Bastille as if he was describing it to his fellow citizens. The audience members' sense of identity with the Revolutionary citizens of Paris was completed as a *fête populaire* broke out with the final announcement of the taking of the Bastille. It included acrobats, a wrestling match and a number of fairground amusements in which the public could take part. *The entry of the gladiators* blared out and everyone was drawn into the carnival, which lasted long enough for each spectator to move around, enjoying all its different elements.

But the broad fairground style did not lead, as it might have done, to general demagoguery, because of the variety of other theatrical techniques that were worked into the play for specific purposes. These were all introduced as part of a self-conscious meditation on the question of how history can be re-told: at various points of the play, alternative views of the same event were suggested and the use of devices such as puppets had a distancing function which prevented the public from an oversimplistic identification of themselves with the Paris mob. Costumes and make-up were applied within full view of the audience, romantic music was added to certain scenes as an ironic counterpoint. Many such devices were used to show that everything in the play was the result of hard work and careful artistic choice and that this version of history was being offered for the audience to probe and question. The costumes were broadly in period, but with deliberate anachronism: the nobility's clothes suggested feudal excess and contained elements drawn from the dress of earlier centuries. Those of the bourgeoisie in the final auction sale, lining up to bid for expropriated church lands, suggested the middle of the nineteenth century: they were grotesquely flamboyant, clearly modelled on Daumier, and displaying conspicuous wealth in a manner as excessive as the nobility had done.

Audiences were introduced to this self-conscious approach to the problem

16 *1789* (Théâtre du Soleil): ground plan showing arrangement of five small stages linked by runways and steps, Milan, 1970. Designs by Roberto Moscoso.

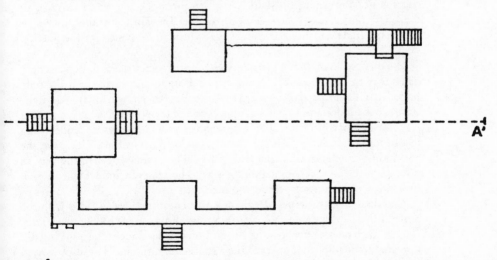

A A'= 35 m

of historical reconstruction in a prologue of great simplicity and clarity, depicting the flight of the King and Queen to Varennes in July 1791. This episode was chosen because it is one of the best known but equally one of the least relevant to the history of the Revolution as seen by the people. It was presented with all the sentimentalised dignity that the Hollywood costume drama has perfected, and the story was told in tones of sad nostalgia by an actor-narrator. But this was soon interrupted by the narrator who changed his tone with the words: 'This is one way to recount history; we have chosen another.' From this point onwards, the audience was constantly aware that what they were seeing had been chosen by the actors in deliberate contrast to other, more traditional ways of describing the period.

By viewing the film and studying the text published by Stock, it is possible to recreate these performances. Their enduring value lies in their extraordinary richness and variety of narrative method and sociological function. Different methods were employed to achieve different effects. Certain scenes aimed to provoke a gut reaction: in one of the opening scenes we see a peasant woman flanked by a nobleman and a prelate, each demanding his tax or tithe. Getting no response, they seize the only thing in front of her, a cooking pot, and the short scene ends on her screams of anguish, helplessness and revolt. Contrasting with this straightforward depiction of poverty and oppression is a scene entitled 'The King's Betrayal', in which the power of court intrigue to change the King's mind is suggested by portraying Cagliostro as a magician, who whips up Marie-Antoinette and two of her ladies into a sort of wild dervish dance. Here the dance of possession works, not as a literal picture of how the court ladies behaved, but as a metaphoric representation of court intrigue, its methods and effects. Other episodes are given similar metaphorical treatment. The relinquishing of privileges by the nobility on the night of 4 August 1789 is depicted by a group of nobles stripping off their feudal costumes to the strains of Mahler, with gestures of exaggerated narcissism; the final confiscation ('récupération') of the Revolution by the powers of bourgeois trade and finance is conveyed through the image of the auction sale.

The play closes on Marat warning that the aristocracy of the nobles has only given way to the aristocracy of the rich and urging that civil war is the only hope. This is reinforced by a speech by Gracchus Babeuf read out by one of the actors. Babeuf declares that in the oppression of the poor by the rich a state of war already exists, which will only be resolved by a total overthrow of existing institutions in order to achieve the perfect happiness of all. This gave the concluding moments a polemical thrust which naturally opened the way to discussions of how perfect happiness was to be achieved and whether a total overthrow of institutions could produce such a result.

The phenomenal success of *1789* left the Théâtre du Soleil faced with the most difficult question for any theatre group: how can we follow that? They wanted to go on to show how the Revolution had developed after 1791 but did not want to be trapped into repeating a successful formula. They also worried that their extraordinary success in discovering a new theatre language had occupied their audience's minds so completely that they had been unable to focus on the substance of the play: the old fear of formalism. At first they went back, as they had done before, to exercises on clowns and the Commedia dell'arte. They attempted improvisations in which the great powers were shown playing cards for the partition of Poland in the parodic style of *1789*. But such experiments did not seem to bear fruit and after further work the key to progress appeared to lie in the method used for the Bastille scene in *1789*. This was the scene in which each actor had told the story to a small knot of spectators as if he or she had been a Parisian present at the event and were now recounting it to others. In one of the rehearsal sessions an actor performed an improvisation employing the same story-telling device: to explain what the politicians were thinking in 1792, he imagined that he was a servant in a Girondin household who was off duty, giving his friends an account of discussions he had overheard.

Encouraged by Ariane Mnouchkine, the actors worked more and more on telling a story or giving an account of an event. Just as they had done in the work leading up to *1789*, each member of the company selected a particular aspect of the years 1792 and 1793 for research. The results of this work were presented in the form of accounts given by one member of the 'petit peuple' to another. The fairground barker style, which had made for much of the showmanship and excitement of *1789*, was abandoned in favour of a much more sober, rational and unified level of discourse. In this way it became possible to show the common people of Paris developing a political vocabulary and language. The play, named *1793*, became a celebration of this *prise de la parole* by people who before the Revolution had not been allowed a voice in public affairs at all.

But the problem of an appropriate playing space remained to be solved. Abandoning the fairground style also meant discarding the multiple stages surrounding the audience. The historical period and the desire to present that history through the lives of the common people led to the solution, which was to set the play in one of the sectional meeting halls of the *sans-culottes*. The events evoked in the play run from the demand for the death of the King in July 1792 to the suppression of the sections in September 1793. This was the period when the influence of the *sans-culottes* was at its highest, when the structure of the monarchy was finally dismantled and when the ideal of direct democracy came closest to realisation. The aim was not so much to excite the spectators, carry them away with enthusiasm as in *1789*, but rather to appeal to their critical faculties and to more reflective emotions.

For the first few moments of the performance it seemed that the style would be no different from that of *1789*: spectators were faced with a long stage and a lurid backcloth. Operatic music by Bizet accompanied a brief, parodic evocation of the years 1791–92 with the actors dressed to represent the powerful nobility. But like the opening scene of *1789*, this was revealed as a false start. The announcer proclaimed: 'Ladies and Gentlemen, we have just shown you the struggle of the powerful against the people, now we shall show you how the people organised for their struggle against the powerful.' As he finished, the backcloth rose and the audience flooded into the section hall beyond. Here they found somewhere to sit, mostly on the floor in the middle, and remained in one place for the rest of the evening, although they had to turn from time to time, as the action took place on three sides of the hall, which occupied one complete wing of the Cartoucherie (18 m × 45 m) (see fig. 17).

As the performance developed, each spectator was able to experience something of what it was like to be a *sectionnaire* in 1793, to follow the discussions, hear news of the major political events, and share the excitement of discovering how to participate in the democratic process. The subtitle of the play (*The Revolutionary city is of this world*) expresses the emphasis of the play. It aimed not just to evoke an historical period, but to present an image and a process: the image and the process of direct democracy at work. It wanted to show people busy with the most humdrum, ordinary occupations, living through a period when, with all its contradictions, they came closer than before or since to having a direct impact upon national events.

The elements of set were extremely simple: three huge wooden tables, purpose-built using eighteenth century techniques of joinery with wooden pegs rather than nails. These were used for eating, for gatherings and discussions, but could also do duty as improvised stages on which various places could be evoked, such as the communal cistern for washing clothes used by the women of the *quartier*. The most powerful scenic effect was in the use of lighting. This was entirely concealed in the roof or behind window panels, but by a clever use of fluorescent tubes was able to suggest an astonishing range of different atmospheres, from a bright winter's morning to a warm summer's evening. The lighting somehow enhanced the sense of delight in the new revolutionary age that was expressed by the characters as a feeling of living more intensely. It was not a rosy glow of nostalgia, but a sharp, invigorating luminosity in harmony with the name and aims of the company.

For a play of this kind, the practice of having one character played by a number of different actors was not appropriate. In the course of their improvisations and work of historical documentation, each actor developed a particular character with a particular occupation – e.g. baker, blacksmith, washerwoman, porter – and the section itself was identified as that of Mauconseil in the *quartier* of Les Halles. As they improvised and rehearsed, it became clear that groupings were as important as individuals and they worked, among other things, on chorus scenes from ancient Greek tragedy to investigate group performance. One of the most successful and moving elements of the play was the group of women who at times achieved something very close to a choral speaking voice, while still maintaining a sense of their individual humanity. Lengthy work was needed to find the right tone of voice and vocabulary for each character, but because they had decided not to enact directly any of the well-known figures, such as Robespierre or Marat, they did not have the usual problem of historical plays which is to overcome the preconceived images in the minds of the audience. The considerable reliance on story-telling also helped to shape a particular acting style similar to Brecht's

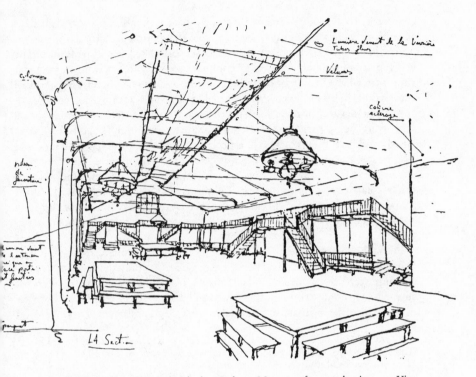

17 *1793* (Théâtre du Soleil): sketch by Robert Moscoso for production at Vincennes Cartoucherie, 1972

model of the actor as someone who tries to present, not to 'incarnate' his character. When Gérard Hardy, as citizen Lebreton, a postal worker, gave an account of his participation in the battle of Valmy, the spectators were clearly conscious of both levels: Hardy was showing them how Lebreton had behaved and Lebreton was showing his fellow *sectionnaires* how the revolutionary army had behaved (see fig. 18).

In the course of the evening the audience became familiar with the occupation and opinions of each individual, and also with his or her manner of relating to the different groups and tendencies, so that the whole fabric of the political life of the *section* was evoked. This aspect of the Revolutionary period is one not emphasised very much by the history books on either side of the Channel. If one thinks of the early years of the Revolution, images of the Terror spring to mind but not much else. The play therefore had an undeniable pedagogic function and part of its excitement lay in this discovery of a neglected aspect of history. In a more closely reasoned manner than *1789*, it showed how the force of business and of military power worked inexorably against the interests of the mass of the population and why, despite the extraordinary political progress of the *sections*, they were powerless to prevent their own suppression in September 1793.

In order to give more force to this account, considerable appeal was made to the rationalist fervour of the Enlightenment, that period in cultural history that immediately preceded and in some senses provoked the Revolution. The centrepiece of the play was a civic banquet in which the hymn to Reason was sung with what can only be described as profound piety, as much on the part of actors as of the characters they portrayed. The result was rather too emotional, so that the sense of historical perspective was lost and spectators tended to feel they were being preached at too much. But other, simpler emotions were clearly and forcefully portrayed, especially the ever-present fear of starvation. For most of the play the mood was not as solemn as this suggests. The continual use of the story-telling device, with each citizen passing on news and views to others, carried an in-built theatrical dimension so that opportunities for humour were frequent. If an attendance at *1793* involved one learning something, it was certainly, in Brecht's phrase, 'cheerful and militant learning'.

Perhaps the greatest emotional force of the play stemmed from another of Brecht's favourite qualities: friendliness. The most moving moments of the evening were those when the characters overcame their mutual fears or suspicions to come to one anothers' help and discovered in the process both the joy and the suffering that can be found in a shared commitment. These were not

18 *1793* (Théâtre du Soleil): Serge Coursan (Jean Choux) foreground and Gérard Hardy (Citizen Lebreton) standing left during the sequence telling the story of the battle of Valmy. Note on-stage band. Cartoucherie, 1972.

fashionable sentiments in the seventies but the Soleil company members were able to express them with peculiar conviction because of their philosophy and practice of cooperative living and working. This philosophy is made instantly apparent to every member of the public by the way he or she is received at the Cartoucherie. The building consists of three wings. While the second and third are used for performances, the first is kept as an exhibition and bar space staffed by members of the cast who all take their turn at selling food and drink, posters and programmes. In this situation any member of the public is able to get into conversation with them. They also prepare for the performance in the open so that their costuming, make-up, warming up routine etc. are all visible to the spectators. The traditional paraphernalia of the artists' dressing room are all there – trays of grease paint, mirrors, unshaded lights – but instead of being shrouded in mystery behind closed doors, the preparations for the performance are open to scrutiny. They describe this approach as *artisanal*, meaning craftsmanlike in the sense of exhibiting the processes that go into the creation of the work of art so that the finished work may be better appreciated.

1793 was again a great success with the public but the critical response to it was more varied. Those who had come hoping for a repeat of *1789* were disappointed, not finding such an exciting variety of stylistic resources. But others took the opposite line: Gilles Sandier, for example, wrote that *1793* contained, in a different form, every element that had gone to make the success of *1789*: 'the political analysis, the inventive staging to express it, the power and beauty of the images and the relationships established between performers and spectators' (cit. Bablet, 1979: 72). *Travail Théâtral* also devoted a great deal of space to it, focussing especially on the last element identified by Sandier. The use of the vast space of the Cartoucherie to evoke a *section* hall enclosing both actors and audience, the movement of actors around and amongst the audience, the use of lighting, all helped to create a very unusual actor–audience relationship, one in which the audience felt they had been a party to the events without (most of the time) a falsely induced sense of being part of them. The acting style partly accounted for this. As Brecht had recommended, the costumes were well broken in so as to convey the texture of everyday reality and be faithful to historical detail; like Stanislavsky's actors, the company rehearsed for months in costume. But the acting was directed more towards a demonstration of the individual's social reality than towards a very interiorised 'Stanislavskian' psychological realism. The costumes helped to define the class adherence of the characters; the flowing white shifts and white cotton bonnets worn by all the women helped to define them as a 'chorus'. Above all, the use of so much reported speech prevented the audience from becoming 'lost' in the action. The result was a fruitful to and fro for the spectators, now feeling that they were part of the *section*, now judging the events from a twentieth century standpoint. It was unlike any of Brecht's own productions, but it achieved just that interplay of human warmth and surprising strangeness that Brecht had worked for in his theatre practice.

In 1973 the Théâtre du Soleil found itself with a world-wide reputation but enormous debts. Despite the very large numbers of people who saw both *1789* and *1793*, their low ticket prices and insistence on a long rehearsal period before each new play meant that they ran up debts as soon as the old ones had been paid off. Their third collectively scripted show, *L'Age d'or*, took even longer to prepare and the whole company had to go on the unemployed register between the end of performances of *1793* in July 1973 and the opening of *L'Age d'or* in March 1975. With *L'Age d'or* they were determined to come up to date. Their desire had always been to dramatise contemporary reality and they were sensitive to the criticisms of those who said that they made things too easy for themselves by repeatedly going back to the late eighteenth century. All shared strong feelings about the sort of play they wanted to perform: 'We desire a theatre in direct contact with social reality, one which presents not just a statement but an incitement to changing the conditions in which we live' (Soleil 1975: 14). The difficulties they faced were those faced by any playwright: how to define and formulate the social reality in question and how to achieve the necessary transposition in order to be able to present that reality in the theatre. When dealing with historical subject-matter the necessary transposition was, they felt, partly inherent in the strangeness of a different period. But in dealing with today it was all too easy to fall into a sort of photographic copying, especially since our images of contemporary reality are so strongly conditioned by the camera.

In order to achieve this necessary transposition, they went back once again to work on clowns and then began to work with masks. They discovered that Meyerhold, in the immediate post-revolutionary period, had gone back to the Commedia dell'arte and attempted to use some of its techniques in the depiction of contemporary reality. The acrobatic acting style that Meyerhold termed bio-mechanics became a starting point for their work. Although they were not aware of this at the outset, Copeau had also seen the masks of the Commedia as a possible way forward, saying that if the theatre were once again to become both popular and artistically vital, it needed to discover a modern range of social types that would be the equivalent of the standard Commedia characters. Playing in masks had the advantage of forcing the Soleil actors to demonstrate everything with the whole body, while putting the accent on social relations rather than on psychology. This acting style built on the group's previous work towards making gesture as important as speech: 'We are trying to create a theatre of performance in which each gesture, each word, each intonation may have due importance, becoming a sign instantly recognisable by the spectator' (ibid. 13). Through the methods of collective improvisation they developed about forty characters, many of whom wore leather half-masks modelled on the style of the old Commedia masks by Erhardt Stiefel. Only about half of these characters appeared in the performances given to the public.

For the performance space, they required an open area in which a relationship of friendly intimacy between actors and spectators was possible but also one that would facilitate the festive spirit that had marked earlier Soleil productions. The solution was a space that borrowed its general features from the natural world: four large hollows made of piled earth covered in hessian matting on which the audience sat around, as if at some vast picnic on undulating grass or gently curving sand dunes. Overhead were reflecting panels of a coppery colour and a network of thousands of coloured fairground lights recalling both the circus-like décor of *Les Clowns* and the festive atmosphere of the *fête populaire* in *1789*. No additional scenic devices were used, the actors evoking every situation by means of gesture and words.

For the show's subject-matter, the company aimed to take a small news item, such as 'Immigrant worker falls to death from scaffolding' and then fill out the web of social and political reality within which such an event might have taken place. In their plays about the Revolutionary period, the actors had presented major historical events through the depiction of people who were situated on the bottom rung of the social hierarchy. The contemporary equivalent seemed to be the immigrant worker and so the main story-line of *L'Age d'or* involved the experiences of Abdallah, a Moroccan worker, from the moment of his arrival at Marseilles to his death from a fall on a building-site.

In the course of preparation, the company visited factories and mines, showing their improvisations to the workers and asking for their criticisms. This kind of empirical approach was particularly appropriate for this play, in which the company was determined to turn from the depiction of the past to the adumbration of the future. The golden age of the title is both the present age of capitalist conflict, in which money counts for everything, and also the future utopia of prosperity and friendliness, to which all aspire. The major stumbling block was one common to all political theatre: how to move beyond an analysis of present ills towards a prescription for future action?

In our conversation with Kodak staff we found ourselves asking them what they thought they could do to change their situation. They were just as puzzled about their future action as we were about how to portray it. It's exactly the same difficulty. The fact is that you only really know what to do about your situation when you find yourself doing it. The future cannot be invented theoretically (Mnouchkine, 1975: 10).

The whole play testified to this belief, combined with the feeling that only a performance avoiding crude propaganda could contribute anything new. Philippe Caubère, who played Abdallah, expressed his belief in the following terms:

The desire to portray the revolutionary struggle requires actors who are new both in their ideas and in their art. It is not sufficient just to hate the capitalists, the *flics* or the fascists in order to show them up on stage. If I put a *flic*'s képi on my head and parody him or make out he is a mental case, I have revealed nothing and its effect will be nil, both theatrically and politically. On the other hand, if I employ a form which allows me to say *who* this *flic* is, what interests make him tick, what power he possesses and how he uses it, ultimately *what* use he is and *to whom*, and if I can provoke laughter through this revelation, then I am creating a work of art, both at the theatrical and the political level (Soleil, 1975: 44).

L'Age d'or only achieved this stated aim in part. The characters such as Pantalon the greedy capitalist, Abdallah the optimistic immigrant worker, Mimi la minette, were portrayed with remarkable inventiveness making them much more than the mere cyphers they might have become. The complexities of the interdependence of exploiter and exploited in today's society was conveyed by weaving a number of incidental stories and episodes around the central theme of Abdallah's experience in France. Much fruitful contradiction was drawn from the dual meaning of the title. But in the performance, the inventiveness of the gags and *lazzi* took pride of place over the social analysis that was the play's avowed aim, and audiences were left with a feeling that the company had not succeeded in reproducing the same dense historical texture or sense of drive that had been achieved for the revolutionary period in *1793*.

L'Age d'or is the most elusive of the Soleil's shows for the theatre historian. No film version exists and although a *texte programme* was published by Stock in the same way as for *1789* and *1793*, it contains almost no text. Instead, it has interviews with the actors, accounts of the working methods, rehearsal diaries, sections on the masks, the characters, the playing space, and thirty photographs. Similar material was published in *Travail Théâtral* and other theatre publications. Reading these, one gets the impression that the working process has finally usurped the finished product altogether and this is confirmed by the play's subtitle *first version* (there has been no second version as yet). The company chose not to print the spoken text because of the way that this play, even more than any of their previous creations, depended on the sole presence of the actor on stage. The verbal element was important at the level of story-telling, but the power of the show was in the dangerously intimate relationship established between actor and audience. Like Peter Brook's actors on tour in Africa at this time, they performed on a simple matting carpet, in a space not separated off from the audience space and took up the challenge of bringing a whole world to life. Here was Copeau's dream of *le tréteau nu*, the bare boards, truly fulfilled, and to the extent that the play found its complete realisation in the ephemeral exchange between actor and audience, it died with the last performance.

In 1975 the annual subsidy of the group jumped from 500,000 francs to 1,000,000. In June 1976, with the same subsidy and a year of performing *L'Age d'or* to packed houses, the company had paid off all its debts, but no new play had been planned. The struggle to produce *L'Age d'or* by the collective method appeared to have exhausted the group's will to work in that way and although many of them remained within or close to activities at the Cartoucherie, productions over the next few years were more clearly reliant on particular individuals than upon collective creation. Jean-Claude Penchenat formed a break-away company, Le Théâtre du Campagnol, with which he wrote and directed a version of *David Copperfield*, others were involved in a production of Molière's *Dom Juan* and many of them were able to take part in a film about Molière scripted and directed by Ariane Mnouchkine. This film, entitled *Molière, ou la vie d'un honnête homme*, is very different from most films about great writers and should be seen as a continuation of the work of the Soleil. It is constructed around a series of key images, rather like the improvised scenes of the group's theatre performances.

These images are placed so as to surprise and delight the viewer, but are also dwelt on at length, so that he begins to see that the meaning of the film is contained within them. It is not that the film lacks a narrative thread, but rather that the story of Molière's private life is not the central element. As in the plays, the images are juxtaposed with a degree of self-consciousness through which is developed a commentary on the problems of viewing or constituting the very subject-matter itself. Just as *1789* contained a commentary on the different ways of reconstituting history, so *Molière, ou la vie d'un honnête homme* provides a commentary on the different ways of constructing the history of a theatre group. The well-known historical moments are included as rather self-conscious tableaux: for example the signing in 1645 of the contract establishing the Illustre Théâtre, with all the members of the company assembled in a very painterly group pose, reading over the contract and appending their signatures.

But the film also includes sequences when the public historical record is discarded in favour of an emotional or visionary image. A key sequence of the film depicts the carnival at Orleans and its suppression by the newly established local branch of Jesuits. The sequence is almost entirely wordless for about fifteen minutes. It shows the narrow streets of medieval Orleans being filled with an irresistible stream of masked and costumed carnival figures. The boys of the town's college, Molière among them, escape from their locked doors into this strangely appealing, yet also frightening world of misrule. But after a while mounted soldiers appear. They charge, and the procession turns into a massacre, with images of real blood soaking through false masks and costumes. In the confusion, the young Molière finds himself in a barn, where a group of travelling players is performing. He is spellbound and completely overwhelmed when, at the end of the performance, he wanders by mistake into the end of the barn where the actors and actresses are changing, washing, laughing together. Everything in the photography emphasises the sense of joy in Molière's discovery of a community not governed by hierarchies of authority, like the family and the church but by a mutual interdependence, willingly and generously accepted.

Afterwards, he walks outside with one of the actresses, who turns out to be Madeleine Béjart, and other members of the company. They are accompanied by a strange multi-coloured carnival ostrich whose presence is not explained; perhaps it is a survivor of the carnage. At one point they are pursued by a flaming waggon. They manage to squeeze up against a wall as it thunders past, almost singeing them with its heat and brilliance. The whole sequence is a dream-like metaphor for the discovery of theatre. It is presented as a utopian world of brilliant images, colourful masks and harmonious social relationships, devoid of possessiveness and power-seeking. As the story of Molière's life unfolds, this image is sometimes tarnished, but never forgotten. Theatre remains associated with festival, with those moments in life when normal constraints are temporarily lifted, when people come together with the spontaneous intention of common celebration, intent on asserting their collective force not on what they can get out of one another. In the conflict between the carnival procession and the authorities, we were being shown the struggle between the forces of life and of death. Molière's later attempts to celebrate the forces of life were thwarted at every turn by the authorities, and particularly the religious authorities, his only protection being the patronage, first of the king's brother and later of the king.

This life-long struggle was summed up in a final image on a flight of stairs leading to his apartment. He has collapsed on stage at the end of the performance of *Le Malade imaginaire*. The others rush him home in a carriage but the climb up the stairs seems to take an eternity. For several minutes the camera holds the group of Molière's friends in a desperate rush to carry him up the stairs but, as in a nightmare, the harder they run the less progress they make. This was achieved by a skilfully mimed movement of actors apparently climbing the stairs while in fact remaining in the same spot and the emotional impact of the sequence was reinforced by the playing of a theatrical bass aria from Purcell's *King Arthur*.

The film was first released in the cinema and later broadcast on both French and English television in five one-hour sections. It was not universally acclaimed. Many of the sequences were too unashamedly theatrical to appeal to film critics. Some people were disappointed not to find a familiar image of Molière and complained, with some justification, about the rather naïve psychology applied to Molière himself. But these criticisms missed the film's real strength, which is its meditation on the difficulties faced in creating and maintaining a festive theatre, and the evolution of the life and internal structure of a theatre company. It was also an answer by Mnouchkine to critics of *la création collective* by trying to show that the greatest French dramatist had also relied, to a great extent, on this method.

With *Mephisto* in 1979 the company pursued further this meditation on the life of a theatre company and its political role, while at the same time fulfilling an ambition to talk about the modern period. The play was adapted by Mnouchkine from the novel by Klaus Mann, at that time still unpublished in the west. Mann's novel is a *roman à clef*: its central character, Hendrik Höfgen, is modelled closely on the celebrated German actor Gustav Gründgens, and most of the other characters correspond to people whom Klaus Mann knew. It shows how an ambitious actor, with a strong awareness of the social function of theatre, develops from activity in communist cabaret in the early twenties to the point where he is superintendent of theatres under Hitler in the late thirties. In the novel the accent is on Gründgens' private drama as he sells his soul to Hitlerism, becoming the embodiment of the arguments he puts so well in his most famous professional role: Mephistopheles in Goethe's *Faust*. Mnouchkine's play is much more concerned with the life of a whole theatre company and the relations of work, creativity and friendship among its members. The fact that the real Gründgens had been able to survive the war with his reputation intact, and prevent the publication of Mann's novel, gave the subject a burning actuality.

Mann's anti-hero is a hollow man, narcissistically fascinated by his own technical expertise, carried by sheer histrionic talent from one role to another – a sequence of dazzling impressions. It is this aspect that was so well brought out in the recent film of the same title made by Szabo. Mnouchkine presents him as a rather weak person and lays emphasis on what he owed to his friends, especially those at the revolutionary cabaret 'The Stormbird'. In particular, for her, his relationship with his fellow actor Otto Ulrich (based on Hans Otto) is crucial: Höfgen relies on Otto but does not realise this until it is too late. Höfgen follows the incline on which he finds himself, leading to ever greater dependence on the Nazis; Otto, on the other hand, makes a genuine attempt to fight back and to counter Nazi propaganda. Where Szabo's film shows only one career, the play contrasts two: Höfgen's and Otto's. Mnouchkine's reason for this choice was that to show only the career of the man who sacrificed his friends and ideals to ambition, and fell into the Nazi trap, would be to imply that this was somehow inevitable, that Höfgen/Gründgens was shaped by history and had no choice. To contrast him with another actor who did not follow the same course is to demonstrate that other choices were possible. The attempt to trace the origins of choices, to show how one thing led to another is central to the play. In order to dramatise this process as vividly as possible, Mnouchkine constructed the play around oppositions and alternatives: to remain in Hamburg or stake all on getting to Berlin; to lampoon the Socialists or the Nazis; to hire or fire a self-confessed Nazi; to work in the state theatres or the oppositional theatres. As with earlier Soleil shows, the production sought not only to describe these alternatives, but to put its audience into the position of experiencing them for themselves.

This was achieved by the arrangement of the performance space. Two wings of the Cartoucherie were used. One was separated off by a wire mesh barrier and left completely bare. It acted as a permanent reminder throughout the performance of the bleak world of the concentration camps into which the victims of the great purges, Stalin's as well as Hitler's, disappeared in the thirties and forties. In the other, the audience was seated on wooden benches set out in straight lines facing a stage at one end. On the right was the wire mesh, on the left, a wall entirely covered with a huge fresco in the heroic style evoking the Germanic heroes and myths that were cultivated during the Nazi period. When the curtain went up, it revealed a theatre stage, but seen as if from the back wall, looking out at an imaginary audience. This was the Hamburg State Theatre and the company was taking its bow at the end of a performance. The play began with Höfgen holding up the applause in order to read out delightedly the news that Hitler's Munich putsch had just failed, and continued with the actors talking on stage after their performance.

The third scene taking place in the revolutionary cabaret 'The Stormbird', was acted on a stage placed at the opposite end of the hall immediately behind the audience. At this point the public discovered that the backrests of the seats were on pivots so that everyone could turn round and face the opposite way. As the play developed its oppositions and alternatives – popular culture versus official culture, the poor theatre versus the rich theatre, etc. – so the audience had to turn first one way then the other, following the dialectic of the play. The action of having to look now one way now the other, while conscious of the empty space threatening on one side, became a powerful metaphor for the two divergent political paths followed by characters in the play.

Three different groups of people are shown at two separate periods: Part I takes place in 1923–24 and Part II in 1930–33. The people are all connected with the theatre. The central group are the actors; flanking them are, on one side, the stage staff, on the other the literati. The stage staff are unpretentious, motivated by 'popular common sense' and an easy target for Hitler's propaganda. The literati are all sufficiently wealthy to feel (until it is too late) that they do not need to be involved. The Mann family entourage is depicted, under the alias of Bruckner, as a rather precious, inward-looking clan, for whom the Nazi phenomenon was so grotesquely vulgar that it could never be taken seriously. And yet the family has a kind of death-wish: their favourite pastime is reciting the last scene of Chekhov's *Cherry orchard*, so that when disaster strikes and they are obliged to leave their family home for exile, we feel that there is a kind of rightness in the event. It has been rehearsed and they have the language ready for it. In between these two groups, the members of the acting company adopt different attitudes according to a number of factors. Those who are not Jewish have to choose whether or not to oppose the drift of historical events: Otto Ulrich opposes, Hendrik Höfgen does not. Those with Jewish blood are obliged to seek some way out. Some emigrate, like Otto Ulrich's lover Carola, who goes, on his advice and against her better judgement, to Moscow. Her name was changed from Klaus Mann's original Dora in memory of Carola Neher, who disappeared in Stalin's purges. Others choose suicide, like the theatre director who is not a Jew and his wife who is. In a moving scene they are shown committing suicide together rather than be separated.

As well as its political subject-matter, the play is of considerable interest for its humour and its approach to characterisation. The humour is principally located in the scenes at the revolutionary cabaret and these were the most accomplished scenes in the Soleil's performance. The style of action drew on all the improvisation and clowning work of the previous ten years. The scenes were played with masks and false noses, large physical gestures and exaggerated voices, and they had their audiences in fits of laughter. But they are written in the form of rehearsals rather than finished performances and so the laughter is, every so often, interrupted by discussions in which all the difficulties in denouncing tyranny without making it seem either harmless or all-powerful emerge. Scene 6, for example, opened on a masterpiece of clowning showing Hitler in prison after the Munich putsch with the established powers discussing whether they can still use him. This is broken off for a brief discussion about whether fascism or social democracy is the main danger for the communist cause. The actors conclude that Hitler is no longer dangerous and move on to another sketch. But their conclusion is called into question because when they unroll the backcloth for the next sketch they find it has been daubed with the slogan 'Jews, Communists, Social Democrats . . . Patience . . . We'll destroy you.' The point about the dangers of disunity on the left had an obvious contemporary application as Giscard's first presidential term was drawing to an end and the communist and socialist parties in France were struggling to find a *modus vivendi* that would allow them to present some sort of united left-wing front.

The characterisation in the play also builds on the earlier work of the company, and its preoccupation with a redefinition of the actor, his social function and his art. In 1982, Mnouchkine described the actor as someone who 'metaphorises a feeling' and added that 'an actor is someone who possesses the art of metaphor . . . the art of transforming an interior state into exterior signs; not simply into words, but into acts' (1982: 25). It was with this in mind that she approached the characterisation in *Mephisto*, just as she had done in *Molière, ou la vie d'un honnête homme*. The result is a text in which the psychological development of each character is clearly visible through what is done as much as through what is said. Höfgen may call himself a 'red' and rejoice in the failure of Hitler's putsch, but his behaviour towards his friends in the theatre is authoritarian and cruel; he claims to be devoted to 'The Stormbird', but seldom appears there.

As a scripted play, *Mephisto* presents more opportunities for study after the event than *L'Age d'or*. Nevertheless, an important dimension of the performances cannot find a scripted equivalent, especially the cabaret sections covered by the bald stage direction '*lazzi*', and the conception and use of space. But the text provides a useful demonstration of the economy of the company's peculiar theatre idiom: everything is conveyed by demonstration rather than discussion, embodied in metaphor, not developed through explanatory dialogue. The text also shows the continuity of the company's preoccupations: research into comic performance style, but also into the connected area of politics and performance. The play poses two questions: what was the social responsibility of the actor in conditions such as those of Weimar Germany? And how might theatre companies have contributed towards an effective opposition to Nazism? The scenes in the state theatres at Hamburg and Berlin show that the social responsibility was a matter for a whole group and could not be isolated as simply an individual case of conscience; the scenes in 'The Stormbird' draw on the rich tradition of oppositional theatre that existed in Weimar Germany to develop the debate about effective political theatre and to show the limits of satire as a weapon.

Many other groups have attempted to work in a style similar to that of the Soleil. The best known is perhaps the Théâtre de L'Aquarium, which shares the Cartoucherie with the Soleil and the Tempête. Starting as a university troupe, its evolution in the course of the sixties closely paralleled that of the Soleil. Its first *création collective*, predating those of the Soleil, was *Les Guerres picrocholines*, in 1967, an adaptation of part of Rabelais' *Gargantua* making comments on contemporary history, with specific reference to Vietnam, Hiroshima and the irresponsibility of the modern military powers. In 1970 some members of the company decided to turn professional; their first show was *Les Evasions de M. Voisin*, performed in the Hérault region in the summer of 1970 and later in Paris at the Espace Pierre Cardin and at the Vieux-Colombier. The show was an improvisation on the theme of the contrast between the respectable bourgeois, Monsieur Voisin, and his alter ego, Zinzin, who embodied all Voisin's repressed desires. The script was written by Jacques Nichet, based on improvisations by the actors. Although Nichet is modest about his authorial role in the company, he has always had an important hand in shaping the material provided by the actors. In his view the Aquarium's distinctive contribution to *création collective* lies in the use of documentary material: 'we abandoned story, plot and psychology . . . our theatre was transformed by the use of documentary material; we no longer used the stage as a place to celebrate eternal cultural values, but as an instrument for elucidating social issues and as a form of group expression' (1981: 15). *Marchands de Ville* in 1972 marked the first successful use of this method. It was performed at the T.N.P., Salle Gémier, then at the Cité Universitaire and toured the Paris suburbs and provincial centres; its success was just in time to save the company from financial disaster and was sufficient to earn them the offer of one of the empty hangars at the Cartoucherie.

The theme of *Marchands de Ville* was corruption in housing policies based on wide-ranging research in which all the members of the company participated. As well as working from written documents, they conducted interviews with councillors, architects, developers and property magnates. Their main difficulty in finding the right theatrical transposition for this material was the familiar one of how to represent institutional power on stage. Their solution was to set two different performance styles in opposition to one another: the banks were presented by actors representing not individual bankers but the whole institution, whereas the tenants were given human depth. The 'banks' wore raised shoes and a pile of top-hats. Their enormous size was cleverly suggested by the miniature scale of the set, which consisted of Lilliputian buildings, which they brought on, carried away, or reordered as it suited them. In contrast to this grotesque style, the tenants of the buildings were presented as flesh-and-blood beings, using direct audience-address to involve the spectators in their problems at a human level. The play's structure followed that of a classic real-estate 'development', first finding a dilapidated district, then buying it up, then proceeding to eviction of the tenants, before tearing it down and rebuilding it. The show was widely praised for its theatrical inventiveness as well as for its exposure of shady property-dealings.

In 1973, *Gob, ou le journal d'un homme normal* took an incident reported by all of the press at the time, contrasting different versions of it and the different methods of reporting that led to these different versions. The incident was the murder, in 1972 in Bruay-en-Artois, of a 16-year-old girl, which was followed by the arrest of a local notary. The press whipped up a scandal over the supposed guilt of this pillar of respectable society. The play, constructed entirely from improvisation work, was centred on a character called Gob, a middlebrow reader of the press, attempting to work out the truth behind the reports. It stressed the semi-fictional quality of all reporting and showed how newspapers pander to their readers' prejudices (imagined or real). This play recalls the work of the Soleil in its use of *création collective* and its critical approach to the problem of how our images and understanding of the world are mediated.

Tu ne voleras point (1974) worked in the same vein, but built on a series of sketches on the theme of property and theft, rather than using documentary material. In 1975 the company temporarily abandoned *création collective* to perform *Ah Q*, adapted by Bernard Chartreux and Jean Jourdheuil from the Chinese novel, about poverty and revolution. But they returned to the collective method in 1976 with a play about factory occupations: *La Vieille Lune tient la jeune lune toute une nuit dans ses bras.* The performance was based on information they had acquired by visiting occupied factories, but rather than imitate striking workers, they attempted to present an account of what they had seen as *comédiens-enquêteurs* ('actor-investigators'). The play was appreciated by the particular, politically motivated audience that had been built up by the company, but Jacques Nichet later said that he felt the focus of the piece was too general. In their following shows, the Aquarium took cases that were more limited, sometimes very personal, although they continued to see themselves as actor-investigators.

For *La sœur de Shakespeare* (1978) they used an interview with a housewife recorded as part of a research programme in problems of female psychology. To this they added fragments from the testimonies of other women, of different ages and from different periods. Again they chose not to represent, in direct mimetic form, the life of a woman-in-the-home, but, rather, to present a collection of fragmented images of what it is to be a woman. The construction of the performance presented similarities with the work of the 'theatre of the everyday' (see following chapter), in which one finds characters presented in fragmentary form, often incapable of controlling their own language so that they become more 'spoken by it' than speaking. Nichet wrote that in *La Soeur de Shakespeare*, 'instead of presenting Madame A . . . on stage, we preferred to play with her words, to throw them about like a ball. We were no longer the bearers of her words; it was her words which bore us along . . . we followed the thread of her words, searched out what she had left unsaid, brought out her repetitions, emphases, lapses' (1981: 23). The play had a considerable success, especially in feminist circles, where it was praised for inventing a new structure that allowed the woman's voice to be heard. It was followed by a monologue entitled *Pépé*, constructed by Didier Bezace from recordings he had made in an old people's home. After this came a montage of texts by Flaubert, but the company's next major success was *Un Conseil de classe très ordinaire* (1981).

This performance had its origin in a tape-recording made clandestinely by Patrick Bonmard of an end-of-year 'conseil de classe' in a lycée. Bonmard persuaded Stock to publish the transcript and it acquired a certain notoriety as a document revealing just how decisions were made about pupils in a staff meeting. The problem for the Aquarium was how to develop this material into a performance. They were tempted to contextualise it, to add in other documentary material about the crisis in the education service, etc. But, fortified by the work on *La Sœur de Shakespeare* and *Pépé*, they decided to maintain the singularity of the tape-recording and to perform it without adding to it or changing a word. Given this approach, the element of mimetic performance was bound to be more important than in some of their previous shows, and yet they were determined to search for a 'transposition théâtrale', not simply to reproduce a realistic staff meeting. Jean-Louis Benoit, the director, explained the reason as follows:

The temptation to search for the psychology underlying the relationships in this little world was great; but we felt that any psychological development would simply become parasitic on the original document which, in the end, displayed nothing more than the institutional machine. I preferred the subjectivity of the characters to be limited to brief interruptions, quickly covered by the humming of the machine . . . Rather than a psychological coherence, or through-line for the character, we worked on scattered fragments superimposed on the text. (1981: 30)

The clearest embodiment of this principle was to be seen in the décor, which in the early stages had been planned as a realistic staff-room, but gradually took on elements borrowed from the dreams and fantasies of the characters. For example, part of the floor became a cabbage patch, which the Head would rake or weed from time to time, expressing his naïve belief in the role of education to bring up healthy young plants in orderly rows. The overall aim of the show was, in Benoit's words, 'to render strange what is familiar, so that one can laugh at it' (1981: 29). This was achieved by the movements, positioning and incidental activities of the various participants, which were used to express their differing relationships with institutional power, especially that embodied in the Head. For example, in the prologue, the parent-governor was ushered to a seat beside the Head, who thus appeared to make much of her, but was then ignored by him so that each teacher had to make his or her report speaking across the parent-governor as if she were not there at all. Above all, the show demonstrated the power of the institution to create its own little world with its self-perpetuating ceremonies and its own language: 'these teachers are caught in the trap of their language, which is not theirs but the language of the institution speaking through them' (Nichet, 1981: 26). Once again, it demonstrated the similarities between the work of the Aquarium and that of the 'theatre of the everyday', especially in its representation of people who become trapped in a language they cannot own. But it also demonstrated the company's continuing concern with documentary theatre, and with finding a theatrical transposition that can give free rein to the actor's creativity.

The work of the Aquarium makes an interesting point of comparison with that of the Soleil. Both companies gradually retreated from the thoroughgoing practice of *création collective* in the course of the 1970s; both sought for new ways to make theatrical discourse relevant to contemporary political process. The Aquarium did not develop so distinctive nor so theatrically brilliant a style as the Soleil, but it has been more successful in finding ways of forging a performance convention to deal with modern political and institutional realities. It also built up a faithful public of regular supporters who could be relied on to ensure its continuing success. Another group which experimented with collective methods of devising shows about contemporary institutions was the Théâtre Populaire de Lorraine, a group which started out with similar origins and objectives to those of the Soleil and the Aquarium. The most important difference between the T.P.L. and the two groups mentioned so far is that it was formed as a regional group to serve the interests of a particular community and continued to do so for more than two decades.

Jacques Kraemer, the director of the T.P.L., was particularly strongly influenced by Planchon. His first productions were of plays by Adamov (*Paolo Paoli*, 1963), Molière and Brecht. He adopted the Epic style, placing the classical plays in their social and historical context, attempting a delineation of character that relied on social relations as well as on psychological insight. In 1968 the group broke off performances of Corneille's *Le Menteur* to visit occupied works in the iron and steel industry. The discrepancy between the language of Corneille and that of the workers seemed too great to be bridged. The classic repertoire of decentralised theatre was abandoned in favour of plays about local concerns. These were not strictly speaking *créations collectives*, but were scripted by the director, Jacques Kraemer, after initial work of documentation and some preliminary improvisation had been carried out by the group.

The fundamental problem facing the workers of Lorraine at that time lay in the decline of the iron and steel industry of the Moselle basin. This accordingly became the subject of the group's first play, scripted in association with René Gaudy. They were very clear about the overriding need: to construct a stage language that would be both familiar and interesting to the iron and steel workers who, in the normal course of events, never attended a straight play. They had to feel that the language was part of their culture and their concerns. Starting from this premise, Kraemer and Gaudy had the idea of a satirical allegory punning on the name *Minette* which designates the low-grade iron ore of the area and can also mean a silly young girl. The sound is similar to 'Jeannette la bonne Lorraine' as Joan of Arc is called and the play was entitled *Splendeur et misère de Minette la bonne Lorraine*. Transformed from iron ore into a young girl, Minette became the heroine of a show about a gangland prostitution racket based on the cliché of the American gangster movie and transposing local economic problems onto a fictional plane as Brecht had transposed the history of the Nazi party onto the level of a story about vegetable trading.

The difficulties facing the iron and steel industries of the area at that time formed a classic case of how capitalist competition affects working people. The steel works in Lorraine exploit a type of iron ore which is poor in iron (30% on average). This makes it relatively uneconomic to mine. Rather than introduce costly enrichment procedures, it was more profitable for the trust, which owned all the area's steel works, to construct a new factory near Marseilles where it would import a better quality iron ore extracted at far less cost from French African countries. This was the dominant fact faced by steel workers at the time of 1968 and the task facing the T.P.L. was to dramatise it in a way that would permit a new approach to the bare economic facts. The play tells the story of the exploitation of Minette by a Mafia-like gang who live off immoral earnings and protection rackets. It moves rapidly with humour and excitement and can be enjoyed at a number of levels: it is a thriller, a send-up of American gangster movies and also an extended comment on the steel-working industry, since at every point in the story there are equivalences between the exploitation of the girls and the exploitation of natural resources. The success of the play, its fascination in performance as well as its satirical bite, is due to the fact that this double focus is maintained throughout and the plot works equally well on both levels. It is exciting at the level of a thriller in which the band of gangsters sets up a prostitution ring, but each development of the plot at this level also has a clear referent in the history of the mining industry.

The force of the political allegory stems from the position and role of Minette: she is always passive, quite unable to control her fate and indeed not very interested in doing so. When first discovered she is asleep. As a personification of the local ore, she naturally begins to take on in the spectator's mind the function of representing the area's human resources as well as its mineral riches, and the main political thrust of the play is its criticism of a situation where people's interests are fought over with no reference to the people themselves. A good example of how this works is Scene 1 of Part II, where Minette complains of being overworked. Her speeches are couched in terms which can be understood both as elements of the mining vocabulary and also the common vocabulary we use to describe ourselves:

Minette Avec M'sieur Jo, c'est toujours non. Il ne s'intéresse à moi que superficiellement. Il délaisse mes strates les plus profonds (67).

Both the following meanings are contained in this speech:

Minette Mr Jo always refuses. He's only interested in me superficially. He's only interested in creaming off the richest iron ore (a procedure that makes the rest of the seams unworkable). He's not interested in what I'm really like underneath. He refuses to mine at deeper levels.

This scene is developed with considerable verbal virtuosity. Minette complains that her I.Q. of 30 (i.e. also her iron content) is not being developed; her desire to have children can also be read as a request for additional machinery and is refused by Joseph on the grounds that he cannot afford her time off and her maternity benefits (i.e. he won't invest his profits). This exploitation of double meaning is not limited to economic commentary, but also works at the level of dream, imagination and myth. There are a number of dream sequences in which, for example, Minette sees herself as a heroine becoming famous and enriching the whole valley, or again experiences terror at the thought of being melted down.

A 'lexicon' of special terms was handed out to each spectator, but was not needed by most, because puns of this kind are familiar to those involved in the industry, so that the double level of meaning was effortlessly established from the outset. Everything that then occurred in the play, however unimportant, became charged with double significance. As well as providing great possibilities for comic dialogue, this helped to focus the audience's attention on more than just the economic facts and figures: by creating a startling framework of gangsters and prostitution within which to discuss the familiar problems of the industry, the play questioned the structures through which the audience normally perceived and understood their economic and political situation. This was reinforced by the prelude to each scene, in which a newsboy ran on stage shouting out the headlines of two different papers. One,

Spécial-Scandale, emphasised anything sensational or salacious (so that its announcements related more obviously to the prostitution plot-level). The other, *Vallée-Magazine*, was controlled by the steel bosses and exploited everything in the regular vocabulary of the right-wing press – appeals to tradition and patriotism and the presentation of management as responsible and fatherly. This technique provided an element of Brechtian alienation by introducing, in a different context, the double focus that is central to the action of the play. The effect of the play as a whole was thus to direct attention not just to the subject-matter but to our means of apprehending that subject-matter.

Minette had an enormous success and was seen by a very unusual audience for this or any other theatre: 11,000 spectators, 80% of them workers who had never before been to the theatre (Miller, 1977: 107). This is partly to be accounted for by what the group called 'L'Opération Minette'. This meant spending at least a week in each of the 15 different mining towns in which *Minette* was to be presented. During the first part of the week the group gave performances of two short flexible *montages* of poems, historical documents, songs and stories dealing directly with the mining industry. One of these was designed for schools and colleges, the other for factories and mines. These *montages* employed all the most direct techniques of agitprop, exploiting the miners' feelings, encouraging them to see themselves in heroic terms and persuading them to join in singing the miners' hymn (written in 1963 to celebrate the strike at Trieux).

Naturally enough, the industrial powers of the area took exception to seeing themselves represented as pimps and gangsters. As a result of their pressure, O.R.T.F. coverage of the play was prevented and the Metz municipality withdrew its subsidy. By 1970 the group was in severe financial straits and had been the object of a *mise en liquidation*. This threatened liquidation was in fact warded off with the help of loans from other theatre companies. But the next production of the T.P.L. took the subject of bankruptcy: *La Liquidation de Monsieur Joseph K* and again showed the power of the large financial trusts in monopoly capitalism. It traces the decline and bankruptcy of a small grocer (Joseph K) forced out of business by the competition of a supermarket chain called Gobkoloss. Like *Minette*, the play combines the documentary method with a style that is not simply factual, documentary or realistic. The progress of Joseph K from prosperous small grocer to bankrupt and tramp is accompanied by echoes of Kafka and Beckett, suggesting that the rather hallucinatory world view in which the individual is inexorably crushed suits very well the interests of the supermarkets and big financial trusts. A loudspeaker is used to suggest the deforming and alienating power of the media: a sexy female voice makes announcements praising the merits of the Gobkoloss goods and prices. As the play progresses, the content of the announcement shifts gradually away from mere commercial propaganda to government propaganda, and finally to J.K.'s internalised thought with a passage deliberately similar to the opening of Kafka's *The Trial*.

The group's next play was *Les Immigrés*, a witty satire on the cultural attitudes underlying racialism. The play is properly about ideology: it shows how ordinary French people live out their fears and fantasies relating to immigration. Rather than deal with the problem in realistic terms, which would have alienated much of his audience, Kraemer transposed it into a fantastic, comic-strip fable about 'anthropomorphes'. These are hybrid creatures, neither man nor beast (but possessing human form) who are discovered in a distant country and imported as cheap labour. They never appear on stage and the audience slowly realises that they are simply an amalgam constructed of all the fears and prejudices of the French concerning immigrant labour. The play consists of seventeen short sketches, some of which depict scenes similar to those of *L'Age d'or*, calling for a broad, physical acting style. But the variations of mood and rhythm later achieved by the Soleil are missing from *Les Immigrés* which, although successful in its own terms, remains at the level of social satire.

A similarly witty satire of the role of the press, *Noëlle de joie*, attacked the local newspaper *Le Républicain Lorrain* in 1975. In reprisal, the paper refused to print a single line about the T.P.L., even paid-up advertisements were rejected. Once again this led to conflict with the municipality, which blocked the Minister of Culture's plan to make the company an official Centre Dramatique National. But despite such hostile pressure, the group has continued, since *Minette*, to employ similar methods for similar purposes. These methods involve the use of research technique, followed by elaboration of the material in a parodistic style described by the group as 'comic expressionism' in which popular myths are lampooned and implications of common judgements are revealed.

Since *Les Immigrés*, the theatre has confronted a number of other subjects in similar style: the press in *Noëlle de joie*, women in society in *Jacotte*. But they have also broadened their scope: Kraemer has begun to write historical plays and other members of the company, Charles Tordjman and Anne-Marie Kraemer, have written plays of the *théâtre du quotidien* school. The most interesting among their recent plays is *Les Histoires de l'onkle Jakob* (1976). The play deals with the last few weeks in the life of a family living in the Lodz ghetto before the mass deportation to Auschwitz. Kraemer is himself of Polish-Jewish origins and drew on the experiences of his own family for the play. The danger that always threatens in works about the holocaust is of a descent into sentimentality. It can be seen in dramatic versions of Anne Frank's diaries or in Grumberg's *Dreyfus* (see chapter 10). Like Grumberg, Kraemer attempted to avoid this danger by an element of self-consciousness: as its title suggests, *Les Histoires de l'oncle Jakob* contains an extended reflection on whether and how it is possible to retell such appalling experiences. Kraemer is more successful than Grumberg because his text is more fragmented: his constant switches of tone and dramatic style serve to break any mood of helpless pathos and to focus the audience's attention on the problem of *making sense*: the audience trying to make sense of the stories and the characters trying to make sense of their own senseless situation.

This is a play about history and myth; about documentary knowledge and dramatic story-telling. Each of the characters in the play tells or enacts a story – we even see the rehearsal for a short agitprop sketch on the story of David and Goliath. It is also a play about trying to behave normally in abnormal circumstances; it suggests the unglamorous heroism of joking, writing poetry and even getting engaged when the future is apparently hopeless. The scene in which David and Rachel get engaged is particularly successful. Despite the absence of any food or drink, the family goes through the motion of a conventional celebration. The ceremony is as absurd as anything in Ionesco, but the scene is moving as well as humorous because the thrust of its meaning is not that *all* such ceremonies need be ridiculous (as, for example, in *Jacques ou la soumission*). This particular ceremony *could* carry the meaning with which the participants seek to invest it, if external circumstances were not there, making it wildly incongruous instead. In such scenes, Kraemer emphasises not only the horrors, but also the incongruities of the situation; not only the inevitable outcome in death and repression but also the kinds of resistance through which the will to survive finds expression. Against the Nazi attempt to liquidate the whole Jewish race, is set the attempts of the various characters to discover and affirm their identity. Against the temptation to slip back into an atemporal, fatalistic view of the events, is set the emphasis on cultural and historical awareness by members of the family.

The setting is carefully chosen: not the bare, sealed off attic of Anne Frank, but on the contrary a large, rather baroque room, half ruined and scarred by fire: the sort of place that might once have been used as a synagogue. There are books, seven-branch candlesticks, the remains of handsome panelling and one grand old wardrobe – the family's oldest and most valuable piece of furniture, the one thing they have managed to bring with them to this refuge; it will be broken up for firewood before the end of the play. There is also an enormous dusty mirror, partly broken, in which each character, at some stage of the action, searches for a meaningful image of him- or herself.

The work of the Théâtre Populaire de Lorraine is not so profound in either its political reflection or its research on performance styles as that of the Théâtre du Soleil. But it has been strikingly successful in forging its own theatre language – a language that has enabled it to communicate effectively with the people of Lorraine. It has achieved this through its permanent commitment to the region on the one hand and through its lively, questioning approach to given performance styles on the other. Few other groups have combined a consistent commitment to a community with consistent stylistic research of this standard. One of the few is André Benedetto's Nouvelle Compagnie d'Avignon. Benedetto's work since 1968 has been progressively more concerned with the rehabilitation of the Occitan language and culture. His plays employ symbol and allegory, ritual, verse forms and heightened language. They have sometimes been described as modern *chansons de geste* (Miller, 1977: 88). All include a role for Benedetto himself as master of ceremonies, and aim to provoke their audience to revolutionary action. They are directed particularly at those who, because of their poverty or because of linguistic oppression, feel themselves excluded by the established French-language civilization and culture. Benedetto is happier performing in the open air or in improvised spaces than in subsidised theatres. The weather in the south of France helps in this respect. His approach presents many similarities with that of Gatti (see chapter 7) and presents the same blurring of the distinction between professional and amateur performers. Gatti would have approved Benedetto's statement: 'Poetry and revolution are one and the same thing. Is this not because each can only truly be made by all?' (1969a: 120).

The groups so far discussed were among those present in 1971 at the 'rencontres du jeune théâtre' held at the Cartoucherie. As a result of these meetings, a federation was formed under the title Action pour le Jeune Théâtre. These young companies were complaining that there was no official status for them in the funding system; what they wanted was recognition by the Ministry of an official category of 'young theatre company' together with earmarked subsidies. Most of the groups who were affiliated had come together in one of the provincial centres, often in close proximity to an established decentralised theatre in France and they were fighting, not only for recognition and subsidy, but also for a more politicised and interventionist form of *le théâtre populaire*.

As well as groups working to raise political consciousness, there were others which interpreted 'popular' theatre in a different sense by attempting to revitalise those performance styles that had once possessed genuine mass appeal in the music halls and café concerts. The most successful of these groups is Le Grand Magic Circus, under the leadership of Jérome Savary. During the crisis that followed 1968, this group took the logical attitude that if the failure of the decentralisation movement lay in having played the game of the establishment, by making the working classes swallow bourgeois 'high culture', then 'high culture' must be fought with the weapons of 'low culture'. Their collectively scripted shows all had a strong satirical charge directed against the most admired artistic forms of the day. This usually involved a deliberate mobilisation of bad taste, nudity and other things calculated to shock middle class art-lovers. A prime example of such techniques was the scene in *De Moïse à Mao* (1973) devoted to Molière and the court of Louis XIV, which consisted in an elaborately pompous ceremony celebrating the king's egotism and building to a climax where Molière was obliged to wipe the king's arse. In the early seventies the appeal of these shows was limited to the iconoclastic pleasure of extreme irreverence. But as the group developed, their work acquired a comic inventiveness that by the end of the decade was quite outstanding. It appears that they had at first been afraid of demonstrating too much skill for fear of falling into the very culture trap they wished to avoid: so long as their shows were thoroughly bad by all normal canons, they could not possibly be *récupéré*. But their work gradually came to identify itself more with the mass popular theatre tradition of clowning, acrobatics, pantomime, etc. This tradition was offered as an alternative to the diet served out by the Maisons de la Culture and other official cultural establishments. It involved, among other things, an extraordinarily skilful use of song and dance and the deployment of trick stage effects.

Perhaps the most effective example of this expertise at work was in the first play from the repertoire ever attempted by this group: *Le Bourgeois gentilhomme* in 1981. In this production the play was prefaced by the arrival of a group of street theatre players in front of M. Jourdain's house. In the course of the action, they gradually invaded the domestic interior to the point at which the final 'mamamouchi' ceremony became the triumphant celebration of the defeat of high culture by low, of classic theatre by rough theatre. This was made an integral part of the play by interpreting M. Jourdain not as a fool to be despised, but as an ignorant man with a genuine thirst for knowledge. The succession of self-important teachers who try to exploit him came to represent the failure of high culture, and the triumph of the street musicians and actors the vigour of low culture. Its success depended on the excitement, comedy and sheer brilliance of the performers.

For some theatre groups, especially those working in the capital, a different solution to the problem of the repertoire was sought through adapting novels for the stage. Authors, who were finding it more and more difficult to get their plays staged, complained that this was another example of the extravagant power of the directors of subsidised theatres. To some extent this complaint was justified: many such adaptations were the result of particular directors' enthusiasms. But in other ways the decision not to act an existing play but to create a performance text out of something else was a liberating experience for every member of a theatre company. In his 'Dialogues', *The art of the theatre*, Edward Gordon Craig had predicted that the theatre of the future would be created from 'Action, scene and voice'. Through the working methods of *la création collective*, actors, designers, lighting designers, etc. became autonomous creative agents out of whose work the performance was created. In these circumstances the director sometimes had less power, since the separate theatre skills had acquired their freedom, and he became simply the initiator and co-ordinator (see Dort, 1980).

The complaints by authors were perhaps more justified when the director was also adaptor and therefore arrogated to himself the role of playwright. But in most cases, such directors were not acting out of misplaced pride. Their attitude was summed up by Georges Lavaudant, director of the Grenoble Centre Dramatique, who said: There was a gap in sensitivity between the theatre as it was then [1965] and what I really liked in the arts and in life. That's why I said to myself: 'We're going to do theatre but we won't do theatre-theatre, we won't stage classical plays: we'll try to write our own texts' (Miller, 1981: 431). This dissatisfaction with existing theatre in the second half of the sixties, which had led groups like the Soleil and the T.P.L. to create work of direct political relevance, had also pushed others like Lavaudant into new experiments. Some such experiments were strongly influenced by the visits to France of Bob Wilson, whose first French performance was *Le Regard du sourd* at the Nancy festival in 1971. This had an instant impact, helped by Aragon who proclaimed his enthusiasm in print: 'I have seen nothing so beautiful in the whole world' (cit. Godard, 1980: 52). Wilson's productions dispense with dialogue and plot, presenting instead a sequence of unexplained, dream-like images.

But a more frequent source of ideas was the cinema, the New Novel and the ideas related to structuralism and 'deconstruction' that were fashionable in critical circles and were published in the pages of *Tel Quel*. Since the novel appeared to be more advanced aesthetically than the theatre, it was natural for avant-garde directors to attempt adaptations of novels. Some of the most prolific and successful directors of the seventies, notably Antoine Vitez, helped to make the adaptation popular and in the latter part of the seventies, according to Judith Miller, one out of every five Parisian productions was an adaptation (1981: 431).

Most of these adaptations were not dramatised versions of novels in the old sense and did not consist of a text in dialogue form that could stand by itself – even to the limited extent that Brecht's *Schweyk*, Adamov's *Dead souls* or Mnouchkine's *Mephisto* do. The adaptations aimed to transfer the substance of the novel from a verbal code to a code of images and actions. In this way, for example, Geneviève Serreau's *Peines de coeur d'une chatte anglaise* (1977) was an adaptation of Balzac's *La Vie privée et publique des animaux* in which verbal language became almost irrelevant. The force of performance lay in the use of music and dance, mask and mime so that the play was able to visit London's Old Vic Theatre (in 1980) without the usual simultaneous translation headphones used for foreign-language productions.

Because the essence of such adaptations is in their displacement of the importance of the spoken or written word, they are, like *L'Age d'or*, ephemeral and cannot be given lengthy consideration in a study of this kind, despite their numerical and aesthetic importance. But it is worth briefly considering one or two representative examples because the aesthetic considerations involved are similar to some of those encountered in studying the new writing of the seventies (see following chapter).

A first example is Vitez's adaptation of Aragon's novel *Les Cloches de Bâle* under the title of *Catherine*, elaborated and performed with his company, the Théâtre des Quartiers d'Ivry, in 1976, and subsequently televised by the O.R.T.F. Vitez believes in a productive tension between the material and its staging: 'The theatre is *someone* who takes his material wherever he finds it – even things not made for the stage – and puts them on stage. Or, rather, stages them' (Miller, 1981: 432). 'Theatre can be made from anything . . . novels, poems, press cuttings, the Gospel' (Temkine, 1977: 197). *Catherine* consisted of eleven actors sitting down and having dinner around a table, going slowly through each of the courses in French style, from the soup at the beginning to coffee and liqueurs at the end. At the beginning Vitez seized a copy of Aragon's novel and began to read aloud from it. The reading passed from one actor to another, with occasional movements when the readers took on some of the characteristics of Aragon's people. But it remained essentially a *reading* of a novel, not a dramatisation in the usual sense. Vitez claimed that to stage a novel means not simply to put it into dialogue but to stage its narrative texture as well. He took a similar approach to Pierre Guyotat's book *Tombeau pour cinq cent mille soldats* in 1981 at the Théâtre National de Chaillot. Guyotat's dense prose attempts to embody all the sordid horror and fascination of the Algerian War in the very texture of its words. Vitez presented chunks of Guyotat's prose intact, accompanied by images of torture, killing, rape, blood, excrement and sperm, not telling a story but presenting the raw experience of a twentieth century war. Through such adaptations, Vitez achieves something similar to the effect of a play by Vinaver (see next chapter): he creates for his audience an experience of overlapping realities or time scales (e.g. both that of the actors' meal and that of the story of Catherine) drawing from the clashes between them a reflection on how we constitute and experience our own realities and our own stories.

An even more thoroughgoing reflection of this nature was provoked by the version of *David Copperfield* produced in 1977 by the Théâtre du Soleil and Théâtre du Campagnol (Jean-Claude Penchenat's splinter group). Their version was elaborated through character improvisations, like much of the Soleil's earlier work, but its real originality lay in finding a scenic equivalent for the novel's particular reflection on the processes of memory and on how our relationship to our own childhood alters over the years. In the course of rehearsal improvisations, the actors worked, not only on David Copperfield's memories, but also on their own, so that the performances became for all of them a rediscovery of childhood. The child David was at the centre of the performance, rather like the figure of the dreamer in an Expressionist play. The structure of the play was like the flow of memories and free associations, with unlikely juxtapositions and involuntary memories sometimes covering the scenes that David was struggling to recall.

The many aspects of memory inform the conception of the playing area as well as influencing the lighting, costumes, movement, and music. Through the physical elements of the performance, the domain of memory becomes palpable. The playing area, cavernous and dusty, resembles a grandparent's attic or a marvellous pawn shop, with old clothes, bric-à-brac, bits and pieces of material and furniture suspended from the flies or propped against the walls. Divided into two halves by the lighting, the front portion is the domain of present memory while the dimmed back half houses all the memories, past or about to sally forth. Splendid Victorian chandeliers bathe the players in a haze of yellow light, while the greyed greens and violets of the opulent costumes complete the illusion of a long-ago engraving. The movement reinforces the spectators' discernment of memories passing before their eyes. Characters fade in and out from one level of consciousness to another. Their exaggerated gestures give them the mythic dimension of a childhood still present in the mind (Miller, 1981: 447).

The achievements of *création collective* and group theatre in the seventies were very considerable, and although there are now fewer companies working in this way, those discussed here are all alive and kicking. Their work has been of great importance for the development of the French theatre in two main respects. First, it has helped to impel the theatre into the post-structuralist age. The theatre no longer lags behind the other arts in the matter of critical self-consciousness or experimentation with new forms. Plays no longer present uncomplicated subjects whose stability is never questioned and who have only to speak in order to be. The sense of crisis in the accepted concept of man's solid subjective reality has broken out of the 'absurdist' ghetto to be explored in all manner of realistic or concrete situations. Much of the credit for this must go to groups like those I have discussed (as well as others I have not had space for, such as L'Aquarium); the work of the playwrights studied in the next chapter was, to some extent, made possible by their experiments.

Secondly, the participation by numerous actors and technicians in work of this kind has had a profoundly liberating effect upon the professional structures of the French theatre. If the inter-war period saw the liberation and establishment of the director, the post-war period has seen a similar creative liberation for actors, designers and technicians. Although many theatres still operate with a rather old-fashioned, authoritarian hierarchy, the model of groups like the Soleil, with equality of salaries and responsibilities, demonstrates that alternative methods can work. It may have been difficult for new playwrights to get their work performed during the early seventies, but when the inevitable reaction came and theatre companies began once again to search for plays, it was often with a profounder understanding of theatre language and of how the different creative skills involved in constructing a performance can work together.

10

Playwrights of the seventies

The decade of the 1970s was a difficult one for playwrights in France. In the excitement of the *création collective* experiments, during the early years of the decade, the traditional role of the playwright almost seemed to have disappeared: instead of starting with a text, theatre companies started from an idea, theme or situation; where playwrights were still employed, it was as literary advisers or adaptors, serving the interests of actors and directors. Among the factors contributing to this situation were: the emphasis on group responsibility; developments in literary theory; the questioning of established artistic methods; and the all-pervading *'gauchisme'*. *Gauchisme* was the pejorative name given to that brand of extreme intellectual left-wing attitude that proclaims the revolution now. Among actors, it led to the insistence that, as the 'proletariat' of the theatre, they had to be free to speak with their own voice. To speak a text written by someone else, especially if that someone was a professional writer (i.e. 'bourgeois individualist'), was to accept an oppressive and authoritarian practice: all theatre texts had to be the result of a collective voice. It was the squabbles arising from just such a superficial approach that had made Gatti's *Treize Soleils de la rue Saint Blaise* so unsatisfactory (p. 161).

In places where such crude over-simplifications were avoided, the writer did not necessarily fare any better, because of the predominance of 'directors' theatre'. The brilliant success of Planchon's methods had produced many imitators. The tendency towards a theatre of images had been further reinforced by the impact of Grotowski, the Living Theatre, Bread and Puppet, Bob Wilson and other similar foreign companies, whose work drew its power from images as much as from texts. Foreign influences of this kind continued to play an important role throughout the seventies, especially after the discovery of Tadeusz Kantor. It was these models that fired the imaginations of many of the new young directors and companies.

The power of the director was further reinforced by a change in the government's method of paying subsidies. Annual subsidies for a given theatre had always been paid to a named director rather than to an author or company, but extra money was available for the staging of new plays under the 'Aide à la Première Pièce' (originally established by Jeanne Laurent in 1947). After 1967 this was replaced by a 'Commission d'Aide à la Création Dramatique' (see Allen, 1981: 247). Under the new system, the director no longer had to find an unperformed playwright, but could claim the subsidy for a *création collective* or an adaptation of the kind discussed in the previous chapter.

The new playwrights of the forties and fifties had seen their work performed in the privately-owned Parisian 'art' theatres. During the sixties, the state-owned theatres had, to a large extent, taken over as the main presenters of new plays. But as the recession of the seventies began to make itself felt, the surviving Parisian theatres were no longer able to take risks and, as we shall see, the state theatres also ran into financial difficulties. The result was a sudden reduction in the number of outlets for new writing.

In this situation it became fashionable to declare that the era of the playwright was past. After all, had not writers of real quality, such as Gatti, chosen to abandon playwriting in search of new, collaborative forms of expression? This climate of ideas found its counterpart in structuralist and post-structuralist literary theory, which was proclaiming the 'death of the author'. By this was meant that works of literature should no longer be viewed as if they were letters, written by one person to convey information to another. Rather, they should be seen as slabs of discourse, whose meanings are constructed as much by the different readers as by the author who first set them down. Moreover, the old-fashioned notion of meaning was itself called into question and the suggestion made that there is in fact no such thing as a stable meaning that can be located in a literary text (see for example Eagleton, 1983: 127–45). The impact of these theoretical developments contributed to the fashion for the production of adaptations rather than of play texts (see pp. 221–3). As the intentions and the authority of the author lost much of their traditional importance, so it became more frequent for directors to put together 'collages' of texts drawn from many different literary periods and genres. The tradition of literary introspection was particularly favoured: texts that call into question the whole basis upon which we sum up and judge a human character. These preoccupations were to come to the fore in the work of certain playwrights, too, especially those playwrights known as *le théâtre du quotidien*. But, as we shall see, their writing was also fuelled by social considerations.

The crisis that faced playwrights in the early seventies also had straightforward economic causes: put simply, many of the larger decentralised theatres had become too expensive to run. By the middle seventies the large building programme begun by Malraux, and which had carried on under its own momentum, had resulted in the existence of fifteen Maisons de la Culture, four national theatres, eighteen Centres Dramatiques and a further two dozen or more theatre companies of some size, all competing for subsidies. During the seventies around 0·5% of the national budget was devoted to the arts (as against 0·3% in Britain), but as the increase in labour costs and the general rise in inflation made the theatre more expensive, it became apparent that most of the government subsidies were being spent on administrative and running costs. Simply to keep a large theatre or Maison open was absorbing so much of the money that the creative work, for which the whole structure was supposed to exist, was being starved of funds. Often the only solution seemed to be to abandon creative work altogether and simply open the theatre to touring productions. This practice became known as 'garaging'.

The situation was aggravated by the suspicious attitude of successive Ministers of Culture towards the theatre. The ruling class had been profoundly shocked by the events of 1968. They were determined to do what they could to prevent state subsidy going to those whose professed aim was revolutionary socialism. On his appointment as Minister of Culture in 1973, Maurice Druon declared that he would not tolerate people who came to him with a begging bowl in one hand and a Molotov cocktail in the other. This inflammatory remark produced outraged response from theatre workers all over France, culminating in a massive demonstration by the Action pour le Jeune Théâtre. They claimed, with some justification, that it suited the Ministry very well to have a state-subsidised theatre so top-heavy with administrative costs that it could mount few new productions. Matters appeared to have reached an impasse during the last years of Giscard d'Estaing's presidency. Even the Association Technique pour l'Action Culturelle, which had performed a vital role in publishing regular news of activities throughout the decentralised theatres, was forced out of business. It became common to declare that 'decentralisation was dead'.

Like most slogans, of course, this gave only a very one-sided view of the true picture. Despite a hostile financial climate, the period of the seventies was marked by a constant increase in the number of new young theatre groups springing up in the provinces. Moreover, many of the major theatres continued to perform original work, notably the T.N.P.-Villeurbanne, the Comédie de Caen and the Théâtre National de Strasbourg. The work of the Strasbourg theatre was particularly influential and provides a good example of the profound change that was taking place in the practice of French playwrights.

In 1975 Jean-Pierre Vincent was appointed director of the Strasbourg theatre. He had made his name with productions of Brecht, Büchner, Vyshnevsky, as well as modern French plays by Rezvani and Grumberg, and a very successful revival of *La Cagnotte* by Labiche. He was an admirer of Peter Stein and had worked in Germany. From his appointment in 1975 until his move to direct the Comédie Française in 1983, Vincent established a pattern of working practice modelled on that of the German civic theatres. He drew the Strasbourg acting school into close collaboration with the professional theatre company and appointed two 'dramaturges' – Bernard Chartreux and Michel Deutsch. Their function was not just to act as literary advisers, but to write new material for performance by both the company and the students, mostly adaptations of non-dramatic work, such as Zola's *Germinal*, which formed the basis of the first production by Vincent at Strasbourg. The position of Chartreux and Deutsch typifies that of many playwrights in France today: they work from within a professional theatre company. This means that although they may write their own plays, they will also spend much of their time working on projects commissioned by the director, who thus reinforces his predominant role in the production of new theatre work.

In order to protect the interests of the independent author, an organisation called Théâtre Ouvert was established in 1970 by broadcaster and publisher Lucien Attoun. At first this consisted only of play-reading sessions at the

Avignon festival, broadcasts on France-Culture and a special series of publications for Stock. But its activities have increased to include work at other times of the year and in other places. It now owns its own premises, at the Jardin d'Hiver in Paris, where it arranges for small-budget productions of new plays, usually directed by the author himself. The list of authors helped by Théâtre Ouvert during the seventies runs to nearly 200. It includes Gatti, Grumberg, Deutsch, Wenzel, Kalisky and Vinaver. It has shown that despite a changed intellectual climate and a reduction in the number of outlets for new work in the French theatre, plays of quality are still being written (see Jeffery 1984a).

The main casualty of the changes and cutbacks in the seventies was the particularly Parisian tradition of the lyrico-whimsical play, examples of which had featured in every Paris theatre season since the war. Its authors had resisted the polarisation into Brechtian or absurdist camps, combining sardonic social comment with humorous situations, often more or less 'absurd'. This tradition included writers such as Schéhadé, Dubillard, Billetdoux, Félicien Marceau, as well as Audiberti and Vauthier, who had made the link between the avant-garde and the boulevard in Paris during the fifties before their rediscovery by Maréchal in the sixties. New authors of secondary importance, writing in a similar style, emerged in the course of the sixties, notably Romain Weingarten and René de Obaldia.

Weingarten's *L'Eté* was a big success in the Paris season of 1966/7. It depicts two talking cats and two children, through whose eyes the relationship of two lovers (never seen on stage) is observed. It sparkles with *bons mots* and insights into adolescent psychology. It also offers two very amusing acting parts for the cats (played by Nicholas Bataille and Weingarten himself). But it marked no significant new departure. Much the same can be said of Obaldia's plays, the first of which, *Génousie*, had been part of Vilar's 1960 season of new plays at the Récamier. His *Le Satyre de la Villette* was produced in 1963 by André Barsacq, who had produced so many of Anouilh's early plays. In 1965 *Du vent dans les branches de sassafras* provided the great comic actor Michel Simon with one of his last triumphs; the play is a spoof western, in which Simon took the part of an accident-prone cowboy. Obaldia's plays always present slightly unexpected characters in strange situations, but their verbal antics are neither so 'absurd' as those of Ionesco, nor so precocious as those of Arrabal, nor so cynical as those of Vian.

Jean-Claude Grumberg

This variety of whimsical writing, which had flourished in the fifties and sixties has almost entirely died out since the beginning of the seventies. The playwrights who now make the link between the boulevard and the avant-garde are those who have managed to combine the lessons of the New Theatre with the discoveries of the *théâtre populaire* movement and of Epic theatre. The outstanding example is Jean-Claude Grumberg. Grumberg was born in 1939 in Paris of immigrant Jewish parents. Soon afterwards, his father was deported during the purges of the Occupation. He never returned and so his mother went out to work as a seamstress in the clothing trade to support her children. Becoming first an apprentice tailor, then an actor, Jean-Claude only began to write for the stage in the middle sixties. His first plays, heavily influenced by the New Theatre, dealt with the themes of racism and intolerance through violent images of incomprehensible conflicts taking place in everyday circumstances. They aim to create a sense of the grotesque by introducing into conventional situations a language so violent and cruel that the spectator experiences the shock of seeing, in the open, the normally hidden or unconscious desires and drives of the characters.

This was also the style of writing employed in the play that gave Grumberg his first commercial success, *Amorphe d'Ottenburg*, published by Stock in 1970, and produced the following year by J.-P. Roussillon at the Odéon theatre on a set resembling an enormous spider's web. The play is a parable of Nazism, with the dumb Amorphe as Hitler, his parents as the establishment powers who encouraged him, Uncle Merle as the Pope and an evil hunchback who represents the finance and business houses which benefited from the Nazi régime and came out of it even stronger than before. Most of the time, the play works as a parody of gothic melodrama, and its force is to demystify the process through which high-sounding ideological motives are made to cover base instincts. Amorphe has an irresistible compulsion to stab in the back anyone who is old and helpless. This liquidation of the infirm is an enormous boon to the Ottenburg economy and so his crimes are covered up by his father, the Lord of Ottenburg. When Amorphe kills the 'troubadour' (in fact a neighbouring prince in disguise) it seems as though he has gone too far, but his father succeeds in winning back sympathy for him by a forceful speech about the parasitism of all artists and musicians.

There is a strong influence of Jarry in the cruelty, systematic distortion of truth, and general base egotism of most of the characters in the play. This influence is also visible in the language, especially in the use of archaic French for scurrilous purposes and in the names of the Lord of Ottenburg's opponents, Stanislas, Matolas and Pamolas, recalling the good King Wenceslas of *Ubu Roi* and his noble son Bougrelas. There is a grotesque quality to the language throughout, well exemplified by the play's running gag which is in the murderous but mute Amorphe's struggles to articulate his own name. He finally succeeds as he mounts the throne over the dead bodies of father and uncle and his stammering of his name is taken up by those around him as a battle cry: 'A mort . . .' (Death to . . .; 167). Those opposed to Amorphe appear just as corrupt as he is, interested only in how they can keep their own peasantry down with less blatant methods than those used by Amorphe. After a prolonged war, they conquer Ottenburg and kill Amorphe, but the hunchback saves his skin by presenting the victors with his perfectly kept account books. The audience's horror is shifted from its focus on Amorphe himself to the evil financial genius and suddenly, at the final curtain, we see a whole line of hunchbacks, each holding account books.

As a black farce the play is successful; as a political allegory it is less so. This is because the generalised nature of the vaguely medieval setting prevents the author from treating the problems of the relationship between power and finance in any but the most schematic way. Rather than discovering anything new about Nazism, the spectator's pleasure is limited to the amusement of exerting his wits in the recognition of the models to which each character refers. The parallel with the history of the Third Reich only becomes clear as the play progresses, so that recognition dawns slowly. Grumberg attempted to give the play a more general significance by making each character speak and act in the name of 'Gott' but, once again, since the terms of the analysis are so vague, nothing significant is revealed about the causes or effects of religious persecution. The play is both entertaining and brilliantly theatrical but there is a certain incongruity between this and its subject-matter.

Grumberg's subsequent plays show him turning more towards real events and situations and drawing more on his own personal experience. They also show an increased, self-consciously critical attitude towards the problems of form. This is most clearly evident in *Dreyfus*, in which the problem of how to write and present a play about anti-semitism is the central concern of a group of Polish Jews who are themselves the victims of anti-semitism. *Dreyfus* was first produced by Jacques Rosner at the Théâtre du Lambrequin, Tourcoing, the new name given to the Centre Dramatique du Nord when Rosner became its director in 1971.

Its content is more specifically political and its setting is precisely identified in a Yiddish-speaking suburb of a Polish town, where an amateur theatre group is working on a play (by one of their members) about Dreyfus (see fig. 19). The time is around 1930 and the play dramatises the murderous incongruity of people struggling to understand the anti-semitism of a previous generation while failing to see the growth of the new, more brutal anti-semitism in their own time.

The play turns on two questions: how is it possible to understand anti-semitism? and how is it possible to represent it in such a way that the audience will learn something that they can use? The first question is not really answered. The central character, Maurice, the one who has written a play about Dreyfus, concludes that it can only be understood in the context of a large Marxist theory of history, but this intuition only emerges at the very end of the play in a letter sent by Maurice to his friends. Most of the characters in the play remain completely baffled by the hostility they face, clinging all the more strongly to their Jewish identity. They cannot understand Maurice's fascination with the fact that Dreyfus did not even consider himself as a Jew, but was first and foremost an officer, thinking of himself simply as a French soldier. This was why the accusation of treason hit him so hard: it created a difference of species that had not existed before.

It is in the discussions about Dreyfus' view of himself that the answer to the second question is developed: Maurice insists that their play must show that there is essentially no difference between Jew and Gentile, that indeed the supposed differences do not emerge until someone needs to find a victim to protect himself from blame. Maurice has to struggle for his understanding of these issues against the traditionalism and inflexibility of his colleagues. Arnold, for example, sees the whole subject in melodramatic terms and would like to perform the whole play as a piece of traditional Yiddish theatre with song and dance routines. Motel, the tailor, believes that the only important ingredient of the play will be the costumes. Michel, the actor playing Dreyfus, finds it quite impossible to understand his role until one night a rehearsal is broken up by a couple of violent anti-semitic drunks. Michel terrifies them by charging, in his officer's uniform and with drawn sword. By not adopting his usual apologetic, self-effacing posture, he has stepped outside himself, realized that he need not be imprisoned by ideas of racial groups. Maurice's play is never finally performed. He leaves for Warsaw, where he joins the communist party, explaining his discovery of the concept of direct action to his former friends by letter.

Grumberg's play is well constructed. It draws richly on the Yiddish tradition for some very funny and some very moving dialogue. It employs the device of the play within the play most effectively, unashamedly exploiting the stock devices such as the scene in which the young lovers enact a declaration of love that turns into the real thing. The general atmosphere of the small, protective Jewish community is depicted with warmth and affection. Above all,

19 *Dreyfus* (Grumberg): design sketch by Jacques Voizot for the production by Jacques Rosner, Théâtre du Lambrequin, Tourcoing, 1974.

Grumberg conveys a kind of amazement that such a group of people can persist in an almost blind idealism in the face of a brutally hostile world. But as in the case of *Amorphe d'Ottenburg*, the play is too self-contained to really illuminate the historical themes upon which it touches – they become submerged beneath the brilliantly observed surface detail of the Jewish community, and the large questions raised by the play remain unanswered.

What links *Dreyfus* with *En r'venant d'l'Expo* (1975) is an element of self-consciousness about the formal devices employed. In *Dreyfus* we saw a theatre group struggling to put on a play. Here we are asked to consider the function of the *cafés concerts* in the period leading up to the First World War. Once again, the play is extremely well constructed, the opening scenes, at the Universal Exhibition of 1900, being a particularly successful piece of dramatic exposition. The idea of showing how *la belle époque* led up to the First World War had already been used by Adamov in *Paolo Paoli*. While Adamov exploited the hypocrisies of the bourgeois *commerçants*, Grumberg attempts to juxtapose the sincere idealism of the syndicalist movement with the frivolity of the *cafés concerts*.

This enables him to use the popular songs of the period to some effect, although the play rather disappointingly shows only the superficial or escapist aspects of popular songs, failing to show how they could also be subversive. Rather like Maurice in *Dreyfus*, the syndicalists of this play are great idealists, believing up until the last moment that war is impossible since the workers' International will simply call a universal strike to prevent it. As a piece of documentary drama about the period, it is fascinating; as a piece of political theatre it seldom goes beyond stating the obvious.

The attractions of the play are in its surface texture rather than in its overall coherence. The setting of the play's opening scenes in the Universal Exhibition is particularly successful, since an exhibition provides the ideal public meeting point where the social and political clichés of the period are rehearsed, but where more intimate family and sentimental relationships can also be developed. Everything that occurs amongst the imposing exhibits is superficial and meretricious, from the curé's homily on the value of colonial wars because of the glorious deaths they provide, to the invocation of Joan of Arc by the Anglophobe. The various bugbears of the period are introduced: the Jews, the revolutionaries, indiscipline of any kind; and the exposition of plot is achieved with great vitality, economy and humour of dialogue and character.

The remainder of the play alternates between the *café concert* and the workers' hall. The *café concert* revels in jingoistic songs designed to stir up militaristic fervour, while in the workers' hall the union meets to discuss the politics of peace. The link between the two worlds is Louis, son of a waiter who begins to make a hit as a singer at the café, but realises the destructive effects of his songs and so searches for an alternative. The difficulty is that the second half of the play tends to degenerate into a series of debates with little dramatic force – a tendency already evident in *Dreyfus*. There is a debate about whether popular songs should do more than 'faire oublier'; there is a debate about pacifist politics. But in the end what is shown to matter is not these reasoned discussions, but the sheer emotional force of a militaristic song or the call to arms in 1914. In the end the pacifist workers have to admit their impotence in the face of the emotive power of nationalism, however false and short-sighted it may be.

The overall effect of the play is thus rather fatalistic. In the syndicalist scenes the writing expresses Grumberg's evident sympathy for their cause but the main emphasis of the action is on the disunity within the movement. Similarly, the author shows evident dislike of the chauvinistic traditions of the *cafés-concerts*, but stresses their attractions by including a number of examples of such songs. The message, that superficial passions and resentments are more powerful than reason, was emphasised most effectively by Jean-Claude Penchenat in his production of the play for the Théâtre du Campagnol (1979). The play was staged in a large arena which allowed the audience to feel they were part of the crowds at the exhibition or the clients at the *café-concert*. A last scene was added, in which the on-stage band played heroic military music while all the characters joined in a military parade. As they marched around the arena, their expressions and gestures became gradually more violent and hysterical until we were faced with a powerful, literal image of the lunacy and bestiality of war.

Grumberg's following play *L'Atelier* opened at the Odéon in 1979. It transferred to a boulevard theatre where it enjoyed a long run. It is a largely autobiographical story of Jewish survivors of the Nazi Occupation, and the pain of surviving when so many have died. It depicts the life of a small clothing workshop between 1945 and 1952. The action is entirely confined to the workshop so that everything the audience learns is filtered through the work process. This is treated entirely naturalistically. In the Odéon production (Grumberg both acting and helping to direct), the actresses playing the six seamstresses did not pretend to sew: they really did it and the audience saw whole suits take shape before their eyes as the evening progressed. To live through such a period was, the play suggests, a matter of survival. It was essential for the women to produce suits sufficiently fast and cheaply to stay ahead of the competition so that there would be a through-flow of cash enabling all who worked there to eat. The moments of crisis or movement on stage occurred when a consignment had been returned or deliveries were not going smoothly. At such points Léon, the owner, shouted and screamed at the women, who accepted it because they knew it was their survival as well as his that was at stake. This work was the most vital and most physically demanding thing in their lives and so had to be presented as such.

But the play does not develop a denunciation of the alienating effect on the women of having to sell their labour. Its mood remains broadly nostalgic, emphasising the simple contradiction that although the workshop was experienced as a treadmill, it also gave respite from the anguished loneliness of those who had survived the holocaust. Simone, the character based on Grumberg's mother, has to spend every waking hour that she is not in the workshop searching for news of her deported husband and caring for her children. The occasional moments of emotional depth occur when she is working late, alone in the workshop, and hears from Léon, or from the presser, about other men's experiences of deportation. The ending of the play comes with the collapse of Simone, exhausted from the years of privation and hard labour. The news that she has been taken to hospital is brought to the workshop by her son, aged about eleven. Grumberg, at this point, gives way completely to the sentimental tone as the women all kiss him and he announces that soon he will be old enough to do a man's work so that his mother need no longer go out to support him and his brother.

After flirting with the methods of the Absurd and the Epic, Grumberg here returns to the most traditional form of naturalism: he relies on reproducing, by means of set, costumes and actors' behaviour, an imitation of a real workshop so perfect that his audience will believe in its reality. So long as they are convinced by the imitation, they will experience the play's events through the eyes of the fictional characters, identifying with their sufferings and delights. Because the method has been well established for more than a century, an audience expects a story of high emotional voltage before it will allow itself to be convinced. The holocaust supplies the necessary power: suffering of such magnitude compels the submergence of one's own identity in awe-struck sympathy with the sufferings of the characters on stage. The final descent into sentimentality confirms our sense that although unquestionably a master of his craft, Grumberg has, for the time being, abandoned experiment with dramatic form for the well-tried formulae of the past.

Eduardo Manet

Like Grumberg, Eduardo Manet possessed a thorough grounding in theatre practice when he wrote his first play *Les Nonnes* in 1967. He had left his native Cuba to train with Jean-Louis Barrault and Jacques Lecoq during the 1950s. In 1960 he joined with many other Cuban exiles returning to help create a socialist society under Fidel Castro. He was put in charge of the Cuban National Theatre Ensemble, but spent much of his time making films, and assisting like-minded film directors from Europe. Among those who came to make films with Manet were Chris Marker (*Cuba; si*) and Armand Gatti (*El otro Christobal*). But after eight years in Cuba he began to feel less sympathetic towards the Castro revolution and he returned to France, where Roger Blin's production of *Les Nonnes* (1969) was received with enthusiasm by the critics and enjoyed a considerable commercial success. During the 1970s he continued to write and sometimes to direct his plays; eight were produced, mostly in small studio theatres, culminating in the massive production at the Nouveau Théâtre de Nice in 1979 of *Un balcon sur les Andes*.

Manet's plays all demonstrate a keen sense of the telling theatrical image or situation. The dramatic devices he employs frequently have a self-conscious quality reminiscent of Pirandello. This quality is particularly clear in Manet's one-act play *Le Jour où Mary Shelley rencontra Charlotte Brontë*, an amusing sketch concerning the relationship of the writer with his/her characters. The play shows Jane Eyre and Frankenstein's monster both demanding that their respective authors free them from the constraints imposed by their situations and allow them to dictate their own stories. Though witty enough, this play has nothing very original about it, whereas *Les Nonnes* certainly took Paris critics and audiences by surprise. The setting of the play is given as 'Haïti dans les jours où eut lieu la révolte des esclaves'. It shows three nuns, a Mother Superior and two sisters, trapped in a cellar; they have lured a rich Señora to join them by promising escape from the rebels but in fact they murder her for her jewels. As their situation grows more desperate, they attempt to tunnel their way out of the cellar amid fierce quarrelling, which culminates in a fight to the death between the Mother Superior and Sister Inés. The play ends as the mob is about to break down the cellar door. The dramatic interest of what might have been simply an historical 'fait divers' stems from the fact that the three nuns are men: they talk like men, behave like men, drink, smoke, fight like men. But at the same time some of their expectations and thought patterns are those of nuns conditioned by convent life. These two different levels of reality remain entirely separate, they are never resolved. The audience is denied any explanation, in realistic terms, of why the nuns are men: they are not men dressed up as nuns, nor are they nuns experiencing a sex change. They remain *both* nuns *and* men. The result is an unusual mixture of farce and horror which can properly be termed *grotesque*. Audiences found it very comical to watch whisky-swilling, cigar-smoking nuns. They also found it horrific to watch members of a religious order, whose lives are supposedly devoted to the service of others, motivated simply by murderous self-interest.

The name of Artaud was much invoked by critics who first wrote about this play but in reality it borrows little from Artaud. Instead, it uses a particularly striking theatrical device to make a fairly straightforward Marxist point: that social conditions govern ideas and behaviour. The nuns' frantic attempts to save their skins are merely, Manet suggests, an extreme expression of their normal self-interested behaviour. Normally, this is masked by the repressive apparatus of Catholic ideology, but the social revolution reveals the nuns in an entirely new light and the best way to portray this dramatically was not just to show them behaving *like* cut-throats and thieves, but to present them literally embodied as cut-throats and thieves. This literal embodiment was something Manet had learned from the New Theatre and the black humour of his plays has obvious similarities with the early plays of Adamov or Ionesco. The setting is vague and timeless: apart from the sentence in the stage directions already quoted, there is nothing to anchor the action in nineteenth-century Haïti. As the play unfolds and all possibility of escape from the cellar dwindles, the struggle of the nuns takes on nightmarish proportions. Yet Manet has attempted to harness this technique to a demystification of ideological structures and here the force of his play is dulled by the very vagueness of its target. As Ionesco discovered with *Rhinocéros*, the playwright who seeks to give a political slant to an intensely personal vision is in danger of either being generally misunderstood or of enunciating statements so general as to be almost valueless.

Manet attempted a much more precise demystification of Catholic ideology with his next major play, *Holocaustum ou le borgne*, produced at the Athénée by Michel Fagadau in 1973. This is set at the time when the Roman Empire was being Christianised and makes a contrast between the epicurean enjoyment here and now of earthly pleasures and what he presents as the mendacious 'combine' of Christianity: the belief that all will be given after death to those who renounce the pleasures of life. The character named 'le borgne', who persuades a group of prisoners to face the lions in the arena by means of the slogan 'foi . . . joie . . . don de soi', is revealed at the end of the play to be a complete charlatan. The play's argument is simplistic but it offers considerable opportunities for performance as the alternatives of indulgence and self-denial are made physically real on stage. Manet's gift for the exciting theatrical image was evident in his subsequent plays and particularly in the 'Groupe d'expérience libres' founded by him in 1977. The culmination of his work during the 1970s was *Un balcon sur les Andes*, a large-cast play including songs and dances, produced by Jean-Louis Thamin at the Nouveau Théâtre de Nice in 1979. Manet described this, as he might have described *Les Nonnes*, as 'une fausse pièce historique' since, like the earlier play, it begins in an historically situated moment and then moves into fiction.

The play follows the fortunes of some French actors, arrested in 1848 for performing an anti-monarchist street show, incarcerated in the château d'If for a while, who escape to South America and attempt to make their living there as travelling players. Manet is able to make good use of the device of theatre within the theatre, as the actors put on their shows for different audiences: civilians, soldiers, peasants, rulers. Their journeys from one country to another and their various changes of fortune are dealt with rapidly and economically with plenty of opportunity for music, movement, colour and crowd scenes. The popular image of the strolling player is exploited by Manet, but in the first part of the play he is content to tell the story of the author's travels without emphasising any particular message. The second part of the play, however, shows the actors being drawn into the political struggles of the area. They are hired by a grotesque tyrant to perform a version of his life for propaganda purposes. When, in ubuesque fashion, the tyrant is assassinated by his general-in-chief, one of the actors, Tarrasin, accepts the post of 'Ministère des Réjouissances Publiques' in the new government, while the others leave in disgust. They soon fall into the hands of guerillas and, after initial hesitations, are converted to their cause. They first agree to perform for them and later take up arms beside them. Meanwhile Tarrasin has been employed by the general for his diplomatic talents and has patched up a system of alliances which succeeds in wiping out the guerilla forces. His friends are captured and witness Tarrasin's triumph: the arrival of a United States ambassador who presents the victorious general with the M.G.M. lion as a sign of his government's esteem.

In this second part of the play Manet attempts to show how theatre cannot escape being used, for one side or the other, in the political struggle. There is nothing very complex about the depiction of this struggle in the play: it involves a simple contrast between right-wing dictatorship and left-wing freedom fighters. The actor who sides with the dictatorship ends up being used by it for purposes of propaganda and diplomacy. He claims to be accepting the post of minister in the cause of stability and for the greater good of art, but in fact soon finds that he is used by the forces he imagined he could use. The actors who side with the guerillas end up militating in their struggle – it is not enough, Manet suggests, simply to entertain and to celebrate; there comes a point when one is drawn into active commitment. The play presents interesting parallels with Mnouchkine's *Mephisto* (see pp. 210–13). Like *Mephisto*, it achieves some of its best effects through skilful use of theatre within the theatre. Like *Mephisto* it also attempts a meditation on the relationship between theatrical power and political power. But Manet's play seems rather simplistic by comparison with Mnouchkine's, because neither the characters nor the situation have precise historical referents. Part of *Mephisto*'s fascination lies in its historical value. The characters are all drawn from life and their history is open to research, to questioning, to discussion. Manet's characters do not have this advantage, nor do they hold much intrinsic interest: they are summed up by their roles in the political opposition of left and right. Their view of the role of art in society never develops beyond the naïvely utilitarian and so the element of real debate about the function of art that is part of *Mephisto* is absent from *Un balcon sur les Andes*. Manet's sure sense of theatre enables him to create lively plays which have been successful in performance. He is possessed of a rich imagination in which Catholicism and revolutionary politics constantly confront one another. But despite the novelty of his first play he has failed to develop an original vision of the world through his plays.

Georges Michel

Another playwright whose early work brought the methods of the Absurd to bear on the real world was Georges Michel. His plays were mainly written in the 1960s but, in their themes and structure, they point towards the preoccupations of the playwrights of the following decade. Michel is a watchmaker who lives in Paris and who shares Grumberg's Jewish proletarian origins. He was adopted in the early sixties by Sartre, who published his first play, *Les Jouets*, in *Les Temps Modernes* in 1963 and also provided a preface for his play *La Promenade du dimanche* in 1967. Michel's plays employ the dramaturgical methods of literalisation that were so successfully used by the New Theatre playwrights, presenting grotesque concrete images of the fears and fantasies of social conformism. *La Promenade du dimanche* depicts a typical French bourgeois family on its Sunday afternoon stroll. The dialogue is composed almost entirely of clichés; the common clichés of family life which are used to train children to accept authority and which were employed to similar effect in Ionesco's *Jacques ou la soumission*. But in Ionesco's plays both language and the world may be transformed: the deep subjective needs of Jacques and Roberte can be expressed through the ecstatic evocation of the flaming horse (Ionesco, 1954: 122).

No such transformation occurs in Michel's plays. The only unexpected occurrences are incursions of sudden violence, as first the grandfather, then the grandmother, and finally the little boy are shot or knifed. But these acts of violence produce no change in the survivors, for whom the cliché has become an impenetrable defence. When the grandfather is killed the mother simply comments:

It's an unlucky day . . . it started badly . . . I could feel it. First of all the fuses went this morning, it was an omen . . . then the waste pipe was blocked in the bathroom. I've always said: it goes in threes . . . well, at least we shan't have any more today (1968a: 12).

She is wrong, as her own death is shortly to show. Every so often on their walk the family passes a scene of torture or brutality, but a cliché response is always to hand: 'he's only doing his job' or 'it's not our business to interfere'. The consequences of blind acceptance of authority enshrined in such statements take literal shape before their eyes without ever altering their behaviour: as their son lies dead, the mother shouts,

Your father's right; come on, that's enough now, get up, get up, you hear me? All right, you'll have no pudding . . . no pudding, you hear? (ibid.: 75).

The characters in most of Michel's plays behave, in similar fashion, like programmed automata. The only exceptions are children, who are presented as creatures with a certain naïve independence, still able to question the solidified clichés that have become the adults' stock responses to whatever experiences they encounter. *Arbalètes et vieilles rapières* (1969) contains one such child, who begins by questioning the need for war, but ends up indoctrinated with chauvinistic and militaristic propaganda, to the point where he is transformed into a bundle of senseless aggressive drives, ready to kill anything that crosses his path.

The violence in this play is not physical but verbal. The coagulated clichés of aggression and chauvinism are what drive the people to war, and the two opposing armies find that they, too, coagulate in the final scene, where, after hurling insults at one another, they freeze 'in an arrogant warrior's pose such as may be seen in our war memorials' (98), while the sound of bombs exploding fills the theatre. The merit of Michel's plays is that they do not remain at the level of cliché, but attempt to show how the reliance on pre-digested ideas and expressions places one entirely at the mercy of the dominant ideology and, ultimately, blinds one to the reality of violence. In *Arbalètes et vieilles rapières* the boy's family is incapable of seeing that the indoctrination they put him through is literally one of *alienation*: he ends up *aliéné*, i.e. mad. In *L'Agression*, produced by Wilson at the T.N.P. in 1967, a group of passers-by is equally incapable of understanding the revolt of a group of adolescents as they try to fight back against the subtly aggressive forces of the consumer society.

Un Petit Nid d'amour (1970) shows how the fears generated in people by the consumer society may be played on in order to create a hysteria of acquisition which also culminates in violence. It is a very simple story of a young couple falling in love and setting up house together. Michel cleverly exploits all the clichés of the *Love Story* variety to show how their ideological basis relies on the determination to feather one's own nest at the expense of others. The salesman, who is always near at hand, is able to persuade them to keep changing their house for one with thicker walls, first just to keep out the noise, later to defend themselves against enemies, real or imagined. In the end they acquire a nuclear bunker; the last scene of the play shows them shooting down someone who was asking for help and retiring into their bunker with the words:

Him Did you see how he insisted on coming in?
Her Our little love-nest is not a dormitory, after all! *They kiss* (79–80).

In the aftermath of 1968 Michel wrote *La Ruée vers l'ordre* (a pun on the French translation of *the goldrush: la ruée vers l'or*). In this, for the first time, he attempted to treat public figures in the same manner as the couples and families of his early plays. It shows the President of France calming his panic-stricken cabinet, making a televised appeal to the nation, and winning an election campaign, after which the population is force-fed on the benefits of the consumer society. The play is a series of rather predictable left-wing images, although one or two of the scenes have considerable power, especially the preparation for the President's broadcast, in which we see just how the correct, reassuring image is constructed by the media men. There are also some good passages on the abuse of language in modern consumer societies, saturated by advertising, that compare with *L'Aboyeuse et l'automate* by Cousin and *Off limits* by Adamov. But the paradox of Michel's writing is that it has the greatest force when it is least applicable to a specific historical case. It is a style that aims to reveal the violence concealed behind familiar structures and, as such, must work with typical cases. As soon as it is applied to a precise set of circumstances, such as France in 1968, the results are bound to seem over-simplified. Its appeal lies not in historical investigation but in the intensely literal enactment of situations we all recognise to be real. Similar methods were to be employed by the writers of the *théâtre du quotidien* that flourished in the seventies.

Le théâtre du quotidien – Kalisky, Deutsch, Wenzel

This was the name given by critics to a school of playwrights influenced by the new authors and film makers of Germany and Austria. In the course of the seventies many translations from German were performed in France, especially at the Comédie de Caen, where Michel Dubois and Claude Yersin produced Handke (1972), Kroetz (1973) and Fassbinder (1975). In the work of these authors, audiences were confronted with fragmentary scenes showing ordinary, often inarticulate people in very ordinary situations, which were nevertheless presented in a syle of heightened realism. Behind the ordinariness of the situations, the hidden violence of contemporary social structures emerged with great force.

The French writers we shall now examine employ similar dramatic methods: not linear plots, but a discontinuous structure of fragmented reality; not well-rounded characters in control of their language, but a demonstration of how language can control and articulate character. Together with Georges Michel, Kalisky, Deutsch and Wenzel all illustrate Vinaver's contention that modern man is 'both crushed by a system but at the same time in perfect communion with it' (see below, p. 253). Kalisky's cycling champion in *Skandalon* (1970) is a man who allows his life to be constructed entirely by the *interests* of others: the financial interests of his backers and trainers; the sexual interests of his friends and wives; the interest the journalists take in building up an idol and then destroying him again. He consents in the whole process, becoming pure object; as a subject he has no existence. When his second wife sees his status as champion on the decline, and tries to persuade him to give up racing, she is talking to an absence. He only exists as the champion; there is no longer any private individual 'behind' this public figure who could take an alternative path. He can only use the arguments of his backers that justify the brief glory of the racing cyclist: he articulates his own oppression.

The plays of Michel Deutsch exhibit characters who are similarly constructed from alien forms of discourse. Deutsch's work exemplifies the logical end-point of existentialist attitudes towards character which had been explored by Sartre in the fifties and Gatti in the sixties. In Deutsch's plays the idea of the character as a fixed entity has entirely vanished. Like Sartre, he sees human beings not as creations but as shapeless emergent existences. Sartre, however, used the dramatic situation to show the process through which these existences acquire an essence: he showed characters who, in choosing a course of action or a value, choose themselves. In this philosophy, a character can only be summed up after death, since every new moment of life presents new choices, and this is why Sartre needed the fiction of hell for *Huis clos*.

Deutsch reduces the scope of his enquiry, pinpointing not a whole life but particular moments. His characters are a collage of the many different types of behaviour of the different people they have encountered in their lives. They have copied a phrase here, an action there, and frequently these different elements contradict one another quite blatantly. As well as being shaped by other people, Deutsch's characters are constructed and deconstructed by the various public institutions that dominate their lives. Because his characters owe their reality to these other people and institutions outside themselves, the dividing lines that separate one character from another can never be established with absolute clarity. *Partage* (1981), showed two of the Manson girls, after their murder of Sharon Tate, trying to make sense of their actions. In his programme note, Deutsch wrote 'They tear one another apart, devour one another, tremble, become motionless, close their eyes . . . One becomes the other who becomes the one who is the other. The boundaries are uncertain, hazy. There is no exact dividing line between them.' The play is a rite of attempted possession and expiation in which each girl tries to articulate her own character in an acceptable manner, projecting onto her companion those things she cannot face up to. Much more simply, one of Deutsch's earliest plays, *Dimanche*, published in 1974 and produced at Strasbourg in 1976, shows a girl whose personal reality is lost in her desire to become a perfect majorette.

The alien, mechanical image of a long-legged American high-kicker imposes itself upon her to the point where she can live only for her training, submerges her subjective reality in the pursuit of this image, and dies of exhaustion.

A similar change in the subjective realities of two women is shown in *Convoi* (1980), set in the south-west of France during the German Occupation. Anne, a sixty-year-old peasant woman, takes in an eighteen-year-old Jewish refugee. She christens her Marie, treats her like a daughter, behaving as if the girl were a young cousin or niece who had lost her memory. For a while 'Marie' almost becomes Anne's daughter. But she cannot rid herself of the memory of the concentration camps or the columns of refugees being strafed by planes. Neither is she allowed to live in isolated exile, independent of Anne's family and neighbours. When the Germans invade the 'free zone' she is denounced, and the militia come to arrest both women. Jean-Pierre Vincent, who directed the play at Strasbourg in 1980, commented that the theme of the play was 'exile, physical exile or interior exile, a certain reaction to misfortune' (Deutsch, 1980: 109). He also suggested that all of Deutsch's characters could be summed up by a phrase from *Ruines*: 'you are pierced with slices of text' (*vous êtes traversés par des pans de texte*) (ibid.). They are martyred by their language, invaded and defined by it without wanting to be.

The outbursts of Marie in which she evokes her suffering have great lyrical force, but, outside of these passages, Marie seems inarticulate. Many of Deutsch's characters display this linguistic schizophrenia. The character named Jules in *La Bonne Vie* (produced by Vincent at Strasbourg in 1976) is a factory worker whose conversation consists of the most banal clichés interspersed with extraordinary, dream-like statements, e.g. 'In the Bois de Boulogne, coming back from work the other night, I caught sight of a pterosaurus. It was gliding on the rising air currents in search of carrion' (1975: 51). Jules' mind is filled with undigested chunks of unrelated text, or language. In order to improve himself he has been reading about evolutionary theory. He is also a devoted follower of 'Boggy' – Humphrey Bogart. At the end of the play the Bogart language overwhelms him entirely and articulates his destruction, as he talks through what might be one of Bogart's last scenes in the role of the tough guy driven into a corner finally having no alternative but to shoot both himself and his girl. The characters have little or no control over these slices of language which appear and then disappear, like icebergs, occasionally colliding with one another.

Most of Deutsch's characters are drawn from the bottom rungs of the social scale, peasants or urban workers. He has explained that at first he believed that their speech must be recorded and copied. 'That did not last long. I realized that the only thing that one could record was *silence* and the rhythm of that silence; the speech of these people escaped me' (Sarrazac, 1976: 97). But, unlike Kroetz, he did not reproduce the silence of the inarticulate in his plays. This would have been to fall into the 'ever-present threat' of 'reactionary naturalism' (ibid.). Instead, he introduced other discourses struggling for supremacy: the slogans of advertising, the small-talk of the secretarial office, the glamourised dialogue of Hollywood westerns. The emotional force of his plays arises from his use of dramatic irony: the audience observes characters struggling for independent life who are so deeply alienated that they seize on just that language or behaviour that is the very instrument of their destruction.

Violence is a constant factor in Deutsch's work, and while he is alert to the danger of naturalism, he does not always avoid the opposite danger of melodrama. Sometimes he even seems to welcome it, as in *L'Entraînement du champion avant la course*, a bloody tale of a man who murders his mistress (a butcher), and is poisoned by his wife. But the violence is only an extreme aspect of both the language and the behaviour imposed on his characters by external forces. In order to achieve a contemporary realism, Deutsch feels that it is essential to see that 'power relationships do not simply express themselves through state apparatus but they pierce us through completely, *pierce through our bodies*' (Sarrazac, 1976: 95). Some of his plays present scenes of almost unbearable violence, like the penultimate scene of *La Bonne Vie*, when Marie finds herself miscarrying in the toilets of a café. But the violence is not presented aggressively. It is violence suffered, helplessly.

What prevents these plays most of the time from seeming melodramatic, inflated or superficial is the fragmentation of the action. In traditional melodrama the causes and effects are too easily explained: the stereotype wicked landlord oppresses the poor widow because he is a greedy monster with no pity. But in Deutsch's plays the stories are so disjointed that the audience is never allowed to supply simple explanations of this kind. Instead, they are confronted with the irreducible reality of suffering and alienation and encouraged to look for explanations that lie outside the fictive world of the play. This is achieved partly by questioning the familiar expressions of everyday experience. Sarrazac (1981: 72) points out the centrality of the table in many of Deutsch's plays as an expression of the woman's everyday experience of reality. On it she has to provide, share out, labour, sometimes even offer herself to be shared out as in the case of *L'Entraînement*, in which the table is a butcher's chopping block. Deutsch explodes the whole concept of the bourgeois interior as a location for meaningful action. The interiors in his plays are evacuators of meaning: they contain nothing but destructive forces and the harder a character tries to deny this, like the butcher in *L'Entraînement*, the more destructive is the final result.

Deutsch has said that his aim is to present moments of revolt since even in the most oppressive situations 'there are always actions with a liberating content' (Sarrazac, 1976: 97). He gives, as an example, the moment in *L'Entraînement* when Maurice's wife and his mistress meet and discover that by coming together they can find a comfort and strength that is not possible while they remain separated in the roles of wife or mistress. But this is a very brief, utopian moment in the depiction of an otherwise violent and sordid reality. Where Deutsch is most successful in provoking a *prise de conscience* is in his whole treatment of women. For although their character outlines may be blurred by shifting contradictions, their physical reality is presented with great feeling and truth. Released from the traditional imagery of saintly, maternal love, or devilish, sexy seduction, their immediate problems are all to do with the realities of physical existence.

Jean-Paul Wenzel was responsible for founding a company entitled 'Le Théâtre du Quotidien', which performed *L'Entraînement* in 1975 under his direction. He has also written a number of plays, the best known being *Loin d'Hagondange*. This shows an ordinary working class couple at the end of their lives. After an unremarkable working life in Hagondange, they have retired to a little love-nest in the country, where they quietly die of boredom. Like the couple in Georges Michel's *Un Petit Nid d'amour*, they have accepted the model of married bliss that fits the needs of consumer society: they have cut themselves off from community life and concentrated instead on acquisitions. All their energies have been directed towards the purchase of the ideal retirement house. Now that they are there, they have no mental or spiritual resources with which to fill it or give it meaning. Without the familiar clichés of the husband's workaday routine to fall back on, the couple have nothing to say to one another. The husband continues to go to work in his garden shed each day, as he had previously gone off to the steel-works, the wife continues to clean up a house that never gets dirty. Their words express the alienation that has been forced upon them in the course of a working life: nothing of passion or personal value is left. Their language simply reproduces the slogans and clichés with which they have been force-fed.

Loin d'Hagondange was a sudden success for Wenzel, particularly after its production by Patrice Chéreau (T.N.P. 1977), who set the couple's retirement house in a Surrealist desert landscape. Chéreau's production exploited to the full the quality that much of the *théâtre du quotidien* shares with Pinter: its use of silence. The emptiness of these two old people's lives, their unspoken desires and repressed longings were conveyed as much by the intervals between their words as by the words themselves. Wenzel's subsequent plays have tended to develop the theme of latent violence, rejecting the passivity of the old couple in *Loin d'Hagondange*: 'I felt that the sentimentality of *Loin d'Hagondange* reassured and comforted too many people, that it veiled the violence of daily life that is contained in the play' (1982: 12). In his next play, *Marianne attend le mariage* (1975), he showed this violence erupting openly in a working class family, where one of the daughters is made to feel so guilty about a minor shop-lifting incident that she commits suicide and provokes the disintegration of the family group.

The authors of *le théâtre du quotidien* are always in danger of belittling their working class characters, of emphasising their alienation and victimisation to the point of patronising or even scorning them. This is why Deutsch insists that he wishes to avoid 'reactionary naturalism', i.e. the mere stating of lamentable facts. In his best plays he escapes from this danger by an approach that is more questioning than stating: he probes at the very concept of character, calling into question the received ideas of fixed personality and conscious value choices. His most successful plays are those like *Convoi*, in which the interplay of public violence and private suffering is evoked by means of a precise historical situation. The result is not 'reactionary naturalism' but a surprising revelation of a situation that had at first seemed familiar. By contrast, the stereotyped characters of Georges Michel's plays seem excessively arid by the end of a performance, lacking the detail and complexity of lived experience.

The work of the authors I have been discussing is an attempt to come to terms with the fragmented reality of a daily life which can no longer be made sense of, where both the personal motivations of individuals and the behaviour of public bodies seem beyond control. Their authors see them as political plays, provoking a *prise de conscience* in their audiences, but eschewing the neat demonstration formulae of plays which try to show how to have a revolution. Where they succeed, it is by their use of contradiction and discontinuity. In this way they demonstrate rather than discuss the broken lives that they choose to dramatise. Because of this, they all rely heavily on the immediacy of performance. Where the drama is chiefly one of language, the different forms of discourse must be enacted, permitting the language to establish its own rhythms and to impose its own life (or death) on the characters. Frequently these dramatists leave considerable scope to the director and actors to fill the spaces in the text with appropriate actions that will challenge its claims to dominance. Attempts to define a new relationship between text and action in this fragmented world have led to impressive experiments in staging such as Chéreau's production of *Loin d'Hagondange* (see Burgess: 1977) or a montage of fragmented scenes from many different plays including extracts from Molière, Beckett, Büchner, Brecht, Handke, Kroetz, Deutsch and Wenzel at the Comédie de Caen entitled *Le Désamour* (1980). For this production a multiple set was constructed that used all the spaces in the theatre, representing a street and a three-storey block of flats with the front wall removed. The audience itself was fragmented, not sitting in a single block, but separated into male and female and placed on different sides of the structure so as to observe the different scenes from different points of view. To many critics, this production appeared to represent the culmination of a decade of experimentation in new writing and staging methods, because it had found a concrete form of expression for the drama of multiple viewpoint towards which writers of the *théâtre du quotidien* school had been reaching (see *Loisir* (Caen) 35, 1980).

In the work of authors such as Kalisky, Wenzel and Deutsch, we can see a fusion of the discoveries of both New and Epic theatre. From Epic theatre they have acquired a skill in presenting lived experience in such a way as to reveal its socially determining factors. From the New Theatre, they have borrowed what Kalisky calls 'an interpenetration of space, of locality, of time, of consciousness, giving rise to new realities, ephemeral, unfixed' (1978: 223). Kalisky's later plays demonstrate this 'interpenetration' at work. In *Dave au bord de la mer* (1978), we see the experiences of Saul, David and Jonathan from the Old Testament superimposed on the relationships of a group of modern Israelis facing the threat of terrorist attack. Or, rather, the surface of the twentieth century characters' reality is constantly disturbed by the eruption of the mythical archetypes. The result is a fascinating attempt to show how the violent lives of modern men and women are experienced through the reliving of subconscious mythical models. Kalisky presents a multiple view of his characters' reality, refusing to provide his audience with a single, authoritative interpretation.

Michel Vinaver

The outstanding playwright of the seventies, also employing a drama of multiple viewpoint, is Michel Vinaver. In fact Vinaver's early plays were written in the course of the fifties, but he experienced a long fallow period during the sixties, becoming identified with the *théâtre du quotidien* in the middle seventies. Vinaver's first play, *Aujourd'hui ou les Coréens*, had enjoyed some success two decades previously: it had been produced by Planchon at the Théâtre de la Comédie in 1956, by Jean-Marie Serreau at the Alliance Française in 1957, by Charles Joris with the company that was to become the Théâtre Populaire Romand in 1959 and by Gabriel Monnet at the Comédie de Saint Etienne in 1960. After *Aujourd'hui ou les Coréens* Vinaver wrote *Les Huissiers* in 1957, translated Dekker's play *The Shoemaker's Holiday* for Jean Vilar in 1958 and completed *Iphigénie Hotel* in 1959. But none of these had the same success as his first play. In the 1960s his working life began to make greater demands on his time and he wrote no further plays until *Par-dessus bord* nearly a decade later.

The action of *Aujourd'hui ou les Coréens* alternates between half a dozen French soldiers in the Korean war who have lost contact with their company and a group of Korean villagers. One of the soldiers stumbles on the village, where he is accepted and becomes integrated into the village life. In the course of this process the fixed ideologies and labels that have hitherto structured his experience of life fall away and simply lose their use. In a perceptive review, Barthes noted that '*Aujourd'hui*, as its title indicates, offers the present as a material that is *immediately* structurable and contradicts the traditional dogma of Revolution as an essentially eschatological time span' (1978: 59). Vinaver's original insistence on the immediate experience of the here and now as his basic dramatic material was to be the basis of his mature plays in the seventies. Both *Les Coréens* and *Iphigénie Hotel* are youthful plays in which he can be seen trying out a new form that would allow him to escape from the false alternative: *either* political theatre *or* absurdist theatre. The result is two plays concerning violent events but recounted, as it were, from a distance. In *Les Coréens* the villagers are awaiting the arrival of the liberation army, but the French forces fall back more quickly than expected, the army presses ahead and does not, after all, come to the village. In *Iphigénie Hotel*, the fall of the Fourth Republic is experienced by a group of tourists cut off in a hotel in Mycene, listening to unreliable radio reports. Instead of presenting historical events at first hand, these plays present history as experienced by the mass of people, having only partial information, feeling cut off from the centre of interest, yet discovering themselves in the seemingly unimportant details of everyday life.

In between *Iphigénie Hotel* and *Par-dessus bord* there was a period when his energies were fully absorbed by the multi-national corporation for which he worked. Moreover, he was unable to see how to bridge the gap between the cut-throat realities of a big international business concern and the fictions of theatre. He finally overcame this difficulty by writing *Par-dessus bord*, a work

247

of enormous dimensions that would take at least eight hours to stage in its entirety, but in which melodrama is rigorously excluded by a style that is faithful to Vinaver's special feel for the everyday. Later, he explained that the centre of his creative life had always been located in the experience of 'astonishment at being permitted the simplest of things, such as opening a door, running, stopping, etc. . . all my (literary) activity has been an attempt to penetrate this territory of the everyday, which was never *given* to me but which had to be discovered, forced open. In other words, for the writer that I am, nothing exists before writing; to write is to try to give consistency to the world and to myself within it' (Vinaver, 1979: 73).

With this style of writing, the challenge was of course to avoid boredom, since 'the everyday is what is both repetitive and flat. An alchemy must operate so that the most uninteresting magma is transmuted into an object of enjoyment and understanding' (Vinaver, 1982: 132). The success of productions, both of *Les Coréens* in the late fifties and of his more recent plays, shows that in performance his texts do achieve this alchemical operation, and the fascination of Vinaver's theatre is to discover how this is done. The most striking feature of his plays is that they are not committed in the usual sense of the word, they do not take sides or present the pros and cons of an idea or situation. At first sight they are in fact more like stream of consciousness novels than plays. The text of *Iphigénie Hotel* seemed so undramatic that no director would take it on until Vitez produced it in 1977. As a director, Vitez likes to work by contradictions. Rather than construct a unified character, he encourages his actors to look for discontinuities, to show abrupt, even inexplicable changes of mood. He also encourages them to play against the text so that a tension emerges from, say, a suave piece of writing and a jerky delivery, or vice versa. He was attracted by the rather undramatic nature of Vinaver's work and appreciated his attempt to write 'not so much *for* the theatre . . . but rather against the theatre' (Vinaver, 1982: 294–5). Vinaver, in turn, appreciated Vitez's 'rare virtue of considering a text for what it is, as a *non-soluble element*' (ibid. 286). He considers that the best texts do not necessarily transfer easily to the stage but that 'what is productive are the tensions caused by the meeting of text and performance' (ibid. 151). The dialogue in his plays since *Par-dessus bord* is entirely devoid of punctuation except for the use of question marks. Sometimes the name of the speaker is not even specified. There is very little in the way of stage directions. The result is a verbal texture of great complexity and ambiguity. On the page it appears to be an unstructured copy of conversations that might be overheard in a great many everyday situations. But in performance the effect is more like that of exposing a cross-section of a human brain. On the bared surface are revealed mental or spiritual movements that range from the most superficial to the most profound, from those easily accounted for to those that are seemingly incomprehensible. Each page of text offers the possibility of many different interpretations because different kinds of statement jostle with one another quite unseparated by the verbal fabric, and leaving a permanent uncertainty about what the characters may be *doing* as they speak a given line.

248

One way of understanding Vinaver's writing is to compare it to painting. He is fond of such comparisons and has even written that he wishes he had been born with a talent for painting or composing rather than writing, carrying the ability to work simply with form, tone and rhythm (1979: 74). He claims that his work deals not so much with people, ideas, conditions, as with the relations between these things, just as Braque claimed that the important thing in his pictures was less the objects depicted than the space between them. This comparison is both accurate and helpful, for the discontinuities and contradictions of Vinaver's style are the marks of the first thoroughly successful drama of multiple viewpoint. Just like Picasso, Braque, Joyce, Eliot and the whole Modernist school of painters, poets and novelists, Vinaver's fragmented viewpoint is both statement and formal device. It states the impossibility of ever reaching the unified, coherent world view and asserts that only *meanings* not *meaning* can be found. It is not surprising that this drama of multiple viewpoint should have arrived in the theatre so slowly and so tentatively. The experience of theatre is immediate and cannot easily be interrupted or held at a distance like paintings, poems or novels. Vinaver wanted to find a way of combining the immediate experience with self-conscious reflection on the problems of fragmented vision. He could see that in some way the usual linear form of dramatic story-telling had to be changed, something new put in its place. That something, he describes as the very material of human intercourse, the texture of language itself (see 1982: 310).

In this way Vinaver is able to write plays that reflect both on society and on the means available to the theatre for depicting that society: his plays are both socially satirical and theatrically satirical. *Par-dessus bord*, written at the end of the sixties, employs elements of all the theatre styles fashionable at that time: total theatre, archaic myth, nudity, happenings, music theatre, dance theatre, etc. etc. It has a Rabelaisian quality; the subject is a toilet-paper manufacturing business and its attempts to change with the times: both from hard and crinkly to 'soft strength' and from the methods of an old-fashioned family firm to aggressive American marketing techniques. The story is commented on from within at different levels. The most obvious comments come from Passemar, who is both on the management staff of the firm and an autobiographical figure for Vinaver. His comments and interruptions have the same self-conscious ironic quality as those of Gide in *Les Faux-Monnayeurs*. Passemar gives us a running commentary on both theatrical and management techniques. Another commentator figure who intrudes is an old-school professor lecturing on Norse myths. Linked to his lectures is a group of dancers who want to use the myths for a mime and movement performance. The incomprehensible battles of the Norse gods provide an ironic counterpoint to the equally incomprehensible manoeuvres of the business world. There is also a group of jazz musicians who arrange 'happenings' in order to increase their popularity with a certain middle class public. This provides scope for the author to introduce discussion of the ultimate temptation in the happening: to create an event through other people's blood and suffering. The happenings of a tired avant-garde are contrasted with similar *Aktionen* inflicted by the Nazis on Jewish groups in Poland.

As well as this kind of comment, the social and economic function of a business like the toilet-paper firm is presented from a number of different viewpoints: that of the travelling salesman; of the secretaries; the various heads of department; the different members of the owning family; a banker; a Dominican father and the marketing consultants who come in to advise on plans for expansion; as well as the American president of the competing firm, who finally concedes defeat but buys them up as a profitable subsidiary. The play presents a kind of war of different languages: office jargon; franglais marketing jargon; old-fashioned academic language; new media slang; jazzmen's roughtalk; salesmen's smoothtalk; high-finance talk, etc. It is through the juxtaposition of these different languages that Vinaver scores his best ironic effects. For example, the story of the killing of Baldr, the visionary hero whose good judgements could never be put into practice, is enacted by the dancers immediately before the crushing analysis of the firm's management methods by Donohue and Frankfurter, the American marketing consultants. The two different ways of talking about the painful relinquishing of the old values reverberate against one another.

Many of the play's high points are achieved through Vinaver's sensitivity to the humorous possibilities inherent in displaying the place of linguistic manipulation in people's relations with one another and with their social conditions. Two scenes, one near the beginning and one near the end, depict the firm's annual office party. They are written like choral passages in Greek tragedy with no attribution of lines to speakers. The effect they create is of a group voice expressing a guarded loyalty towards the firm, a sense of outrage at the behaviour of fellow employees who have overstepped the unwritten rules of management, a grudging admiration for business success and a generalised feeling of being taken for a ride. These responses to the firm are interwoven with concerns of a more personal nature, so that the overall effect of the passage is to suggest how corporate life invades private life and vice versa. The choric device is used again for an outrageously comic 'brainstorm' session, in which the firm's executives get together to practise free association so as to produce a new name for their product. The final choice, 'Mousse et Bruyère' is only one of a list of some 200 similarly fatuous ideas, including such suggestions as 'Gair Sourire', 'Doux Baiser', 'Chaud Baiser' or 'Toison d'Or', 'Mon Plaisir', 'Sable d'Or', 'Vigne Vierge'. More insidious, as John Burgess has pointed out, are the passages in which the marketing consultants are able to manipulate the glib commercial jargon and newspeak of international commerce to mask the sterility of the economic competition and the inhumanity of the procedures it dictates (1974b).

Out of this rich kaleidoscope, Vinaver thought, the material for several different productions could be extracted. In 1956 and 1957 he had felt that neither of the two productions by Planchon and Serreau conveyed the full *Coréens*, but that taken together they did. He allowed Planchon to rewrite his own version of *Par-dessus bord* in the hopes that other productions would follow. In fact Vinaver was disappointed. The situation had changed, Planchon was no longer an interesting young outsider but the acknowledged leader, and no other producer was ready to invite invidious comparisons. What had impressed Planchon about the play was its documentary accuracy (the development of the toilet-paper industry in the seventies was, in fact, almost exactly as predicted in the play). He admired Vinaver's unique insight into the business world, and his vivid sense of contemporary dialogue. But he could see no solution to staging it as written, since it calls for many of the different actions to overlap or take place simultaneously. He therefore looked for a solution that would achieve the effect of fragmenting the story and ironically undermining it, but by scenic rather than verbal means. He used a technique that he had perfected over a long period, introducing features of the American musical comedy form to undermine the American economic conquest of French business. He considered that seeing American advertising consultants moving like Gene Kelly while discussing submerged drives and sales psychology had just the right derisive effect. Many of the subsidiary actions were cut and the whole play treated in a highly theatrical manner (see fig. 20).

Planchon claimed that it was permissible to treat Vinaver's text in this way *because* it was so brilliantly exact about what life is like in business. He contrasted it with *Paolo Paoli* which, he said, had required a realistic

20   *Par-dessus bord* (Vinaver): Planchon's production employing burlesque musical comedy techniques. T.N.P.-Villeurbanne, 1973.

production because Adamov did not really know business life from the inside, but 'the truth of Vinaver's play is so strong, at the textual level, that everything can be transposed' (1975b: 36). At the time, Vinaver accepted Planchon's manipulation of his text, but, in later comments, he regretted the fact that in Planchon's production the linear story-line had once again become predominant and he felt that a production reproducing more faithfully the texture of the original might have been possible. He was no doubt encouraged by the faithful production in 1980 by Jacques Lassalle of *A la renverse*, a second play about the fortunes of a French firm, this time a manufacturer of sun-tan cream. The play presented many of the same features as *Par-dessus bord*, including the use of choral passages, though it was a more manageable length for stage performance. In between these two major works, Vinaver had written four shorter plays: *La Demande d'emploi* (produced in Paris and Lausanne in 1973 and in Caen in 1975); *Dissident, il va sans dire* and *Nina, c'est autre chose* (T.E.P. 1978); and *Les Travaux et les jours* (Annecy 1980).

Les Travaux et les jours is a masterpiece. Its title is borrowed from Hesiod (with overtones of Proust's *Les Plaisirs et les jours*) and demonstrates Vinaver's tendency, like T. S. Eliot whom he admires, to fill his work with obscure references to the ancient world. By studying this play we can discover the quintessential Vinaver more easily than from *Par-dessus bord* because this play is so much more pared down. It has a cast of only five and is set in the after-sales office of a firm making coffee grinders. There are three secretaries who take phone calls from the customers and explain how and where to send the machines for repair. In addition, there is the office manager and one blue-collar worker with a workbench at which he repairs urgent or special cases.

The three women talk amongst themselves when they are not on the phone – and sometimes even in the middle of a call – revealing not only the development of the firm but the progress of their private lives as well. Theirs is a world in which people are supposed to give meaning to their lives through their work. It is also the world of immense technical improvements in communications equipment. Through this work that is supposed to satisfy, and this equipment that is supposed to improve communications, the five characters live out their frustrated and fragmented lives. The only language that any of them can speak with perfect fluency is the language of the firm's promotional publications. But the more thoroughly they have mastered it, the more of themselves they have invested in it, the more it lets them down in the end.

To a greater or lesser extent each character finds a way of preserving his or her personal integrity. It is easiest for the men because in the unwritten law of the office world they always dominate: Guillermo by virtue of his proletarian past, Jaudouard by virtue of his power as boss. Each of the three women finds herself in competition for the favours of one or both of these men. In addition they cannot help noticing that many of the people who ring up do so less because of their broken coffee grinders than because they need to talk to someone. Beside these demands on them, they struggle to establish some space for their own emotional needs but end up simply articulating their own oppression: the comforting phrases that they offer to one another when troubles come are the echo of those they offer to the customers. Vinaver's analysis of modern man is that he is 'both crushed by a system but at the same time in perfect communion with it' (1982: 286). This paradox had been exploited by Adamov, particularly in *Le Ping-Pong*, but without quite the same vividness of lived everyday reality: *Le Ping-Pong* was still to some extent a dream play. Vinaver's play follows rigorously the pattern of real life: the company is bought up, economies are discussed, the work force goes on strike. The girls cope heroically with increasing calls, explaining to anxious customers that repairs will continue – as soon as the situation is normal. But as soon as this is so, it transpires that the after-sales service will be a victim of the economies. There will be no one to talk to callers; instead a computer will be installed to send the customer one of a range of 64 standard replies drawn up in advance. In the end only the youngest of the three is kept on because she has made eyes at the appropriate director in the lift.

The story element has been reduced to a minimum and is fairly ordinary. The play's brilliance ˎ is in Vinaver's dialogues which are ambiguous and fragmentary, mixing up different streams of consciousness and sequences of ideas. Questions and answers do not correspond, they are interrupted by other lines of discussion, but through these shifting perspectives five different worlds are built up, each with a point of intersection in the office, but reaching beyond it, too, into the subconscious and emotional worlds of the characters. The method avoids all the usual traps of melodrama, sentimentality or didacticism by this subtle interweaving of themes and languages.

It is instructive to compare this play with Grumberg's *L'Atelier* (see above p. 235). Both plays present a group of women in their place of work dominated by structures of male authority. In *L'Atelier*, Grumberg skilfully arranges every event in a sequence that appears to be self-explanatory and gives the impression of reality. Vinaver, on the other hand, asks his audience to abandon this privileged perspective and to experience something of the confusions and ambiguities of the characters themselves. He makes it difficult for his audience to lose themselves in sympathy with the characters, because they are constantly having to re-assess the truth of those characters' situations. In Grumberg's play we are not invited to doubt or to question the veracity of the narrative. In Vinaver's we receive as many different versions of the events as there are characters on stage. All have a different understanding of what is happening to them and the play does not gradually reveal the falsehood of one view set against the truth of another: it obliges us to construct the reality of the situation as we go along from the patchwork of views, emotions and actions that appear before us. The play asks its audience, not to admire a particular behaviour pattern, but to work out what freedom of action is available to a given character in a given situation. Each slightly different image of the modern world that is presented carries an ethical and political value. The spectator must constantly accept or reject these values. In Vinaver's play the humour arises from the discrepancies and disjunctions between things that appear to the characters on stage to fit together but can be seen not to do so by the audience. They leave the theatre having had their emotions touched by an understanding of how we all love the system that destroys us – how easily we project human values onto an inhumane enterprise that serves only efficiency and profitability. In both plays the problems of a whole society are evoked through a microcosm. But Grumberg's microcosm is self-contained, specific to a particular class group. Vinaver's is at once more limited and more open. We do not receive the same sense of a homogeneous group. But we do see how everything hangs together – how a decision taken in an American boardroom may influence the emotional development of a French secretarial worker.

When Vinaver talks about his own writing, he emphasises the importance, in dramatic dialogue, of being able to set in relation one to another elements having, at the outset, nothing in common, so that 'a line by a character who is not in any way part of the dramatic situation of the character who spoke the line before will nevertheless influence the situation in question' (Vinaver, 1982: 288). What is offered to the spectator is a collage of fragments which generate meanings by collisions and reverberations. The meanings produced in this way tend to be ironic. Vinaver defines irony as: 'brutal discrepancy between what is expected and what happens' and maintains that its effect is like an electric shock in which a circuit is established and through which the current passes – 'a current of meaning' (Vinaver, 1979: 75). These principles are particularly well illustrated in *A la renverse*, where the sun-tan cream firm is ruined because of a popular television programme in which the princess of Bourbon-Beaugency, dying of skin cancer, talks week by week of the progress of her illness and her former devotion to acquiring a sun-tan. For the 1980 production by Jacques Lassalle at the Chaillot theatre, a special television film was made, which was inserted into the stage performance using playback monitors. For the audience the experience was of two distinct discourses – the sentimentalised bravery of the dying princess and the desperate attempts to stimulate the market by the firm's executives – which completely failed to intersect but threw up richly comic ironies.

Because of their unusual form, the experience of watching these plays can at first be strange but it is not mystifying: 'after a few minutes' acclimatisation', wrote the critic Michel Cournot, 'the spectator-listener has the feeling that he holds within his grasp the multiple series of causes and effects contributing to a given event, whereas classic linear dialogue reduces these series to a single thread. From this grasp there arises, in the audience, a profound emotion, stemming no doubt from the fact that life itself seems to be captured in the fullness of its flux and all its mystery' (*Le Monde* 14 March 1980). Although all Vinaver's plays present moments of profound emotion, a mood of ironic humour is perhaps even more characteristic of them. In his view the role of the dramatist is to provoke cracks in the established order, to uncover the world in an unexpected light, and the method for doing this is ironic humour. He rejects the Romantic notion of the artist as a man with a mission, because if he presents a new vision he always ends up suppressed or censored by the established order. He claims instead the role of the fool, whose function is to say what nobody dares think and to confuse people's views (Vinaver, 1982: 316). His achievement is, as Sarrazac points out (1981), to have abandoned a theatre of *stories* for a theatre of *possibilities* which goes beyond the failure of the linear plot-line as explored, say, in *En attendant Godot*. In the fragmented structures of their plays in the sixties, writers such as Adamov and Gatti had already pointed towards this theatre of possibilities. Like Kalisky (see above p. 240), Gatti had invoked the need for different, parallel realities to be shown simultaneously on stage (Gatti, 1964: 15). Vinaver's plays represent a further refinement of similar ideas: he suggests that if it is impossible to make sense of our lives as linear sequences, then we must go back to each separate situation, and try out their possible combinations. In this way a new form of Epic theatre is created, opposed to the Aristotelian like Brecht's, and depending on the Modernist aesthetic of the tableau viewed kaleidoscopically from multiple viewpoints. Like Gatti and the other writers of the sixties, Vinaver and the writers of the *théâtre du quotidien* have been reaching for a *new way of seeing*; in so doing, they have helped to create a new dramatic form.

11

The eighties

After the relative stagnation of the 1970s, the decade of the 1980s was a period of renewed expansion for theatre in France. As the decade began, there was widespread dissatisfaction with the centre-right government of Giscard d'Estaing. He was seen as having attempted, but failed, to play the part of a latter-day de Gaulle. From the cultural point of view he certainly had none of de Gaulle's appeal: where de Gaulle had vigorously pursued an expansionist cultural policy, Giscard offered only austerity. The Socialist party decided to give a prominent place to the revitalisation of cultural institutions in their campaign for the elections in the spring of 1981. Mitterrand saw clearly that in Jack Lang he had a cultural spokesman with mass appeal. He accordingly authorised him to pledge an increase in spending on cultural affairs to 1 per cent of the national budget. Mitterrand was duly elected president and his Socialist party achieved a majority in parliament, which they retained throughout the decade, apart from a two-year interruption between 1986 and 1988. The pledge was honoured: by the end of the decade the 1 per cent level had been achieved and the budget of the theatre section alone had gone above one billion francs (one hundred million pounds).

The new government came to power with an ambitious programme for political reforms, the key to which was regionalisation. They were responding to a widespread feeling that the processes of government were excessively centralised and that, if the country were to be run more efficiently, power needed to be devolved to the regions. In the theatre, this move was welcomed by those struggling to maintain the dream of decentralised theatre that had been such a driving force in the 1950s and 1960s. Morale had dropped to a low point among theatres in the late 1970s, but all this changed with the rapid increase in funding and the altered political atmosphere. The building programme of earlier decades had come to fruition and running costs were once again provided for the buildings to function as they should, with the result that by the end of the 1980s every sizeable town in France had its own municipal theatre, often with a company resident for at least part of the season. Alongside these officially sanctioned institutions, and challenging their right to set the agenda for the community's cultural life, there was a proliferation of independent companies, many of which also received subsidies. By the end of the decade there were over 500 independent professional companies in receipt of public funds. This was in addition to the forty national dramatic centres, or establishments of similar status, and the five national theatres: the Comédie

Française, the Théâtre National de l'Odéon (also home for part of the year to the Théâtre de l'Europe under Giorgio Strehler) the Théâtre National de Chaillot, the Théâtre National de la Colline (formerly Théâtre de l'Est Parisien) and the Théâtre National de Strasbourg.

The most striking fact about French theatre in the 1980s is that despite this increase in level of funding and activity, no new school of playwriting emerged to compare with the New Theatre of the 1950s, the popular and political work of the 1960s or the *création collective* of the early 1970s. The reasons for this are difficult to identify, but certain features of the theatrical life of the period help to point towards an explanation. In the first place, the period saw yet further consolidation of the power of the director. Because subsidies were still paid to directors, the increased subsidy simply served to confirm and increase their power. After the directors, the group of theatre workers that benefited most from the increased spending was the designers. The coherence of the director's concept and the visual brilliance brought to it by the designer became the hallmarks of French theatre in the 1980s. The use of the words *décor* and *décorateur* for designer and set design were abandoned in favour of the terms *scénographe* and *scénographie*, and this change of vocabulary signalled a shift of emphasis in the production process, as the visual element acquired greater importance in the construction of meaning.

In the perception of the theatre-going public the major stars of the decade were the directors. It was they rather than the playwrights or actors who were seen as the key to any new developments; where theatre journalists had once concerned themselves mostly with writers and performers, they now spent most of their time discussing the ambitions and achievements of directors. Chéreau's regime at the Théâtre des Amandiers (Nanterre) from 1982 to the end of the decade was a major source of interest. This was partly because of the spectacular quality of his production work, aided by his designer Richard Peduzzi. But it was also because of the brilliance of his repertoire: as well as outstanding productions of the classics (e.g. his *Hamlet*, 1988, and Marivaux's *La Fausse Suivante*, 1985) he directed a powerful revival of *Les Paravents* (1983), did the first French performance of Heiner Müller's *Quartett* (1985) and presented the four major plays of Bernard-Marie Koltès, perhaps the most exciting new young playwright of the decade. He also invited Peter Stein to bring his Schaubühne production of *The three sisters* and Luc Bondy to direct *The winter's tale*, thus strengthening the link with the successful director's theatre of Germany.

Another talking-point was Jean-Pierre Vincent's move from Strasbourg to head the Comédie Française in 1983. This was seen as a vindication of the decentralisation movement and a recognition of the leading role that had been played by the Strasbourg centre (where his place was taken by Jacques Lassalle). Vincent announced a policy of increasing the amount of new work done at France's oldest theatre, and of introducing more flexible working methods into the company. However, the traditional structures of the 'Maison de Molière' proved too much for even his reforming zeal and he did not seek a renewal of his mandate three years later. The biggest star director of all was perhaps

Antoine Vitez, who succeeded in the Herculean task of breathing new life into the Théâtre National de Chaillot. He took charge in 1980 with the slogan 'un théâtre élitaire pour tous', and a policy of presenting the broadest possible range of work in experimental productions. He accepted no limits, including work never meant for the stage such as Guyotat's *Tombeau pour 500,000 soldats* or Tahar Ben Jelloun's journalistic *Entretiens avec M. Saïd Hammadi, ouvrier algérien* as well as plays from the classic repertoire from Racine to Claudel. With major means at his disposal, he displayed a penchant for taking on those works presenting the largest and most difficult challenge: *Hamlet, Faust*, and the first uncut version of *Le Soulier de satin* ever to be performed. The Théâtre National de Chaillot acquired a reputation for work that was exciting and experimental without being marginal; by the end of the decade it once again held a recognised place in the avant-garde of French theatre. In 1988 Vitez was invited to become director of the Comédie Française. He was able to establish his authority because of his success as a teacher at the Conservatoire (1968–81), but only had time to begin on a programme of reforms before his sudden death in April 1990.

Jérome Savary's move into the established theatre was demonstrated by his gradual progress in a northerly direction, starting from Béziers, where he was appointed director of a new Maison de la Culture in 1982, to the Théâtre du Huitième, Lyon, in 1985, finally taking over from Vitez at Chaillot in 1988. Planchon remained faithful to Villeurbanne, where Lavaudant replaced Chéreau as co-director, but after the grand Racine–Molière production (see pp. 135–8) his main energies became diverted into film: he planned and wrote scripts for a series of films based on the work of Molière but, when production was about to begin, a change of management at the film company led to the project being cancelled. Instead, he was able to make a film version of Molière's *George Dandin*, which came out in 1987 entitled simply *Dandin*.

It is difficult to discern any guiding pattern in these various moves around the chess-board of French subsidised theatre, but one thing was clear: the watertight distinctions between Paris and the provinces that had held good throughout the 1950s and 1960s no longer operated in the 1980s. The system of 'co-productions', in which several theatres contributed the funds to mount a production which then toured round several venues, had finally put paid to the idea of specifically regional theatre work. Moreover, the enhanced awareness of the visual aspects of theatre production, while giving rise to some very brilliant productions, also tended to engender a situation in which each director–designer team had to reach for ever more lavish productions in order to justify their yearly increase in subsidy, and so theatrical brilliance became an end in itself. The sense of taking theatre to culturally deprived audiences that had been the driving force behind the decentralisation movement seemed to have evaporated without any very positive aim coming in to replace it. It would be wrong, however, to underestimate the achievements of French directors in the 1980s. Despite the loss of an overall sense of direction, the period was distinguished by some extremely brilliant work; director–designer teams such as Chéreau and Peduzzi, Vitez and Kokkos, Mnouchkine and Guy-Claude

François deservedly acquired international reputations for the quality of their productions.

The development of director's theatre in France continued to be strongly influenced by international visits and exchanges. Tadeusz Kantor followed his visits to France with *The dead class* in 1976 by bringing *Wielopole Wielopole* in 1984 and *Let the artists die* in 1985. Several of Bob Wilson's productions were also seen in French theatres. But the major intercultural event of the decade was Peter Brook's production of the *Mahabharata*, translated and adapted in collaboration with Jean-Claude Carrière. This was performed in its entirety for the first time at the Avignon festival in 1985 after being developed at Brook's Paris base, the Bouffes du Nord. It had an enormous success and was followed by a world tour that occupied Brook's company for the rest of the decade, culminating in the filming of the production in 1988/9 (for a discussion of Brook's work in this period, see Bradby and Williams, 1988).

The continuing predominance of the director did not preclude a certain improvement in the conditions for playwrights. In the course of the 1970s the diminishing opportunities for playwrights had taken two principal forms, each of which tended to reinforce the other. First there had been the trend towards *création collective*. Although a few companies invited authors to participate in the creative process, most dispensed with the services of the professional writer altogether, developing and scripting their own material. Second, there was the demise of theatre publishing. In the early 1970s at least four publishing houses had respectable collections of plays: Gallimard published plays in its 'manteau d'arlequin' series, the brain-child of Jacques Lemarchand. When Lemarchand died Gallimard decided not to continue his work. The collection was not abandoned, but new titles became extremely rare. The same slow strangulation was applied to the 'L'Arche' collection published by Robert Voisin. Voisin had been one of the driving forces behind *Théâtre Populaire* in the 1950s. His failure to publish new playwrights in the 1970s was prompted by a long-running argument with the Société des Auteurs concerning rights for the performance of published plays. Another major collection at the start of the decade had been 'Théâtre Ouvert' edited by Lucien Attoun and published by Stock. The text of *1789* appeared in this collection and achieved the status of a bestseller. But few of the other titles in this collection sold in sufficient quantities to cover their costs and Stock closed down the series. A fourth notable casualty of the mid-1970s was the small firm of J. P. Oswald, based in Honfleur. Oswald specialised in plays, but he knew that these were hard to sell, so he demanded payments from authors by way of subsidy. Because it was so hard to get plays into print, many authors who would not normally have indulged in vanity publishing agreed to Oswald's terms. When this firm went bankrupt, it left a bad taste in many mouths.

By the beginning of the 1980s, the situation had reached the point where interventionist measures were required. The new director of theatre in Jack Lang's Ministry of Culture was Robert Abirached, a professor of theatre studies who had also written plays and had been published in the Stock collection. Among the new measures he introduced was a special subsidy for theatres putting on plays by young playwrights. Subsidies were also made available through the Centre National des Lettres to publishers of plays and two important new series were started: 'Théâtrales', published by Eidilig and 'Papiers' published by Actes Sud. The latter series was the creation of Christian Dupeyron who proved, as Nick Hern did in Britain, that given the right marketing techniques and sufficient level of commitment from the publisher, play publishing can be a commercially successful enterprise. The result was that by the end of the 1980s playwrights once again had a reasonable expectation of seeing their work in print.

Most vigorous and most consistent of all the encouragements to young playwrights has been that provided by the organisation Théâtre Ouvert, run by Lucien and Micheline Attoun. From its modest beginnings as a once-yearly event at the Avignon festival, Théâtre Ouvert has developed into a larger-scale organisation by acquiring its own premises in Paris at the old winter garden near the place de Clichy. This is used as a base from which to launch a series of initiatives, including the dissemination of new play scripts and the testing out of new work in performance. Among the opportunities provided for young authors is the possibility of trying out an as yet unfinished new play with a group of actors and a director. The author is given the studio space for three weeks, during which time he or she can work in whatever way seems best with the aim of bringing the play to its conclusion. One of the most useful services provided by Théâtre Ouvert is the typing and duplicating of new work so that it can be circulated among theatres and professionals who might be able to perform it. This has led naturally to a full-scale publishing venture and there are now a number of titles commercially available under Théâtre Ouvert's own imprint. In 1987 the organisation experienced a budgetary crisis and was threatened with closure. A major campaign to mobilise arts organisations and professional opinion succeeded in persuading the Ministry of Culture of its usefulness, and, with the return to power of the Socialists in 1988, it was given a new status as a Centre de Création National and a budget of half a million pounds.

At the time when increased subsidy was made available to new writing, the Centre National des Lettres was fortunate to have Michel Vinaver as the chairman of its theatre committee. Vinaver's personal experience of marketing techniques on the one hand, and of the difficulties facing creative writers on the other, made him uniquely suited to the job of deciding how best to use subsidy. In order to clarify the particular problems involved, he undertook a report and a survey on the state of play writing and publishing in France. This was published in 1987 as *Des mille maux dont souffre l'édition théâtrale et des trente-sept remèdes pour l'en soulager* (Actes Sud: 1987). The major conclusion of the report was that there had been a change in the status of the writer of plays. In the 1950s a writer would turn to the theatre as naturally as to the novel; indeed, the major writers of the period – Camus, Sartre, etc. – were carrying on the traditions of pre-war literary life, in which authors as various as Gide, Giraudoux, Mauriac, Montherlant, Cocteau had not seen the need to choose between prose and drama. The rise of the all-powerful director and the post-1968 revolution had had the effect of clarifying the specific qualities of the art of theatre. This process had already been set in motion by the work of the New Theatre playwrights, whose work had laid such a strong emphasis on the importance of performance. As a result, the playwright had come to be seen as a specialist, and dramatic dialogue as something that could be written only by those who had chosen it as their particular vocation. He concluded that plays had ceased to be considered as part of the mainstream of the nation's cultural life and had been marginalised in a sort of specialist ghetto.

This tendency was reinforced by the new practice, copied from the German theatre, of employing a *dramaturge* in many large theatres. A number of playwrights benefited greatly from developing a close relationship with a working theatre, notably Michel Deutsch and Bernard Chartreux at Strasbourg and Daniel Besnehard at Caen. The work of the *dramaturge* involves adapting foreign plays or non-dramatic writing for performance as well as being given the chance to write his or her own plays. While providing an excellent training for the young playwright, this work obviously leads a writer to become even more specialised in the dramatic field. The fashion for staging adaptations rather than new plays ensured that there was plenty of work for the *dramaturges*, but work which served the interests of the theatre establishment rather than developing their careers as original playwrights. Nevertheless, there was a steady growth in the number of new plays being performed in the 1980s and the fact that many were also published in one of the new collections made for a very different atmosphere from the 1970s.

A special supplement on playwrights published by *Le Monde* in February 1988 contained references to dozens of new writers. A few of these could be grouped together by theme or preoccupation; for example the writers concerned to raise public consciousness of women's issues: Denise Bonal, Louise Doutreligne, Denise Chalem, Yasmina Reza, Jeanine Worms. But most were developing their own distinctive voices that could not be seen as part of any school. Enzo Cormann wrote plays that were bitterly anti-capitalist, with some similarities to the 'quotidien' school and to Botho Strauss. Jean-Pierre Sarrazac's work was eclectic and post-modernist, juxtaposing elements borrowed from Surrealism, from historical or philosophical writings. Michel Deutsch continued to experiment with the theatre of discourse analysed in chapter 10. Daniel Besnehard wrote plays in a more naturalistic style, returning obsessively to the history of Normandy during the German Occupation. Studies of working-class life were written by Daniel Lamahieu and Gildas Bourdet, whose *Station Service* was a great success in 1985. Richard Demarcy produced satirical comedies which blended the nonsense tradition of Lewis Carroll with comments on contemporary French customs. Jean-Christophe Bailly wrote works of mythological dimensions, Valère Novarino spun webs of densely structured poetic images, and many other remarkable new voices emerged, such as the extraordinary dramatic monologues of Raymond Cousse. The dramatic monologue became a very popular form, perhaps under the influence of German-language playwrights such as Achternbusch and Müller, combined with that of the late Beckett. For the new writer, it has the advantage of enabling him or her to stress the singularity of the individual voice, with the added advantage that monologues are cheap and easy to mount. The first work of Bernard-Marie Koltès to be staged was a monologue: *La Nuit juste avant les forêts*. This was performed at the Avignon festival in 1977 and Koltès went on to become the most successful young dramatist of the 1980s with four new plays all directed by Patrice Chéreau. (See below, pp. 270–9).

As greater emphasis was once more placed on the role of the writer in the theatre, the contribution of playwrights considered as 'modern classics' was re-evaluated; Beckett, Genet, Claudel and Duras were all the subject of new production work and fresh critical evaluation in the course of the decade. Beckett's work had earlier been considered the special preserve of the Parisian intellectual elite; in the years leading up to his death in 1989, his universal appeal became more evident and there was hardly a theatre that did not put on at least one of his plays. Added inspiration came from seeing his own productions of his work, for example at the Orsay theatre in 1978, when he directed *Pas moi*, *Pas*, and *Histoires* two years after their English-language premières at the Royal Court theatre. Genet's presence was evident in two much-publicised productions of his work: *Les Paravents* directed by Chéreau at Nanterre in 1983 and *Le Balcon* directed by George Lavaudant at the Comédie Française in 1985. Chéreau's production was faithful to the scenic ideas originally evolved by Genet and Blin, even casting Maria Casarès in the same role (the Mother) that she had played in Blin's original production. The final death scenes were performed exactly as specified by the author, with the characters bursting through paper screens. Genet's self-reflective world of performance and image was enhanced by the setting: Richard Peduzzi converted the whole theatre, stage and auditorium into a space that suggested a run-down cinema in the Arab quarter of a large French city; the racial antagonisms out of which the play grows were thus central to the play's performance, and much of the action was played out between stage and auditorium. This production won high critical acclaim, unlike Lavaudant's *Le Balcon* at the Comédie Française. But in this case it was not so much the quality of the performance that was seen as important, rather the simple fact of Genet's entry into the repertoire of Comédie Française, which marked his transition from 'poète maudit' into officially sanctioned modern classic.

Claudel's plays, too, showed that they were strong enough to survive in unexpected environments. Where his work had been considered the exclusive preserve of Jean-Louis Barrault, it was now taken up by directors with a very different approach. The first to challenge Barrault's rather baroque, mystical style was Antoine Vitez who directed an austere *Partage de midi* at the Comédie Française in 1976. He followed this with *L'Echange* at Chaillot in 1986, a production underpinned by Marxist theories of value and exchange. A similarly austere, materialist approach was taken by Gildas Bourdet in his 1984 production of *Le Pain dur* and by Bernard Sobel, director of the Théâtre de Gennevillers, who was invited to direct *La Ville* at Nanterre in 1986. In 1987 Vitez boldly confronted *Le Soulier de satin*, a play that had not been attempted since Barrault's production (analysed in chapter 2) and had never previously

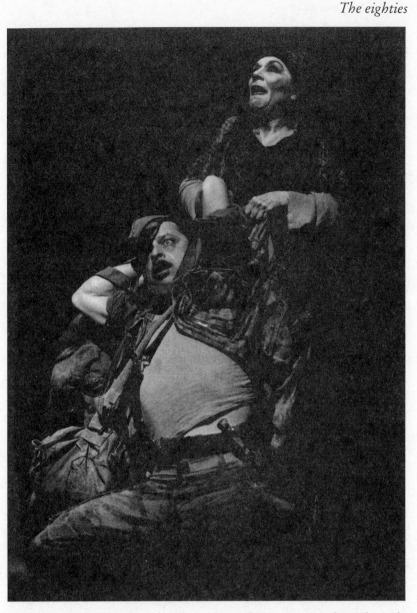

21 *Les Paravents* (Genet): Bernard Ballet as Pierre and Maria Casarès as the Mother in the production by Patrice Chéreau, Théâtre des Amandiers, Nanterre, 1983.

been performed uncut. Vitez capitalised on the theatrical qualities of the text, emphasising its vitality and mixture of styles. The cumulative effect of these and other productions was to confirm Claudel's status as the major French playwright of the early twentieth century.

The decade also provided Marguerite Duras with an opportunity to renew her interest in the theatre. In 1983 she wrote a new version of *Savannah Bay*, which she directed herself in a production at the Rond-Point theatre. This was followed, two years later, at the same theatre, by a revival of her early play *La Musica*, also directed by the author. The renewed interest in Duras's work can be ascribed to two causes. The first is the new interest in non-dramatic texts as foundations for theatre performance. Marguerite Duras had never seen herself as a dramatic writer; all her work, whether it is published as narrative or film or drama, shares the same characteristic stream-of-consciousness style. In different versions of the same stories or situations, the same lines are attributed to different characters, showing that it is the act of utterance itself rather than the nature of the character who speaks that is important to the author. In fact the problem of finding a voice, of shaping the various fragments of discourse that babble ceaselessly in our heads is a continuing preoccupation of Duras, together with the nagging of memories that are unstable, seeming to change each time they are rehearsed. This quality of her writing, making it closer in many ways to monologue than to dramatic dialogue, coincided with much new writing that was being performed in the 1980s. It was a common feature of much that was grouped together under the heading *théâtre du quotidien* (see chapter 10): dialogues consisting of webs of discourse, in which characters were unstable, and the boundaries between memory, dream and real event could not be established once and for all. As critics took stock of such developments, they realised that these had been the characteristics of Duras's work since the 1950s. The first major success of this technique for Duras had been in the film *Hiroshima mon amour*, directed by Alain Resnais in 1959, for which she wrote the script.

The second reason had to do with developments in psychoanalytic and feminist theory. The writings of Julia Kristeva, which had become widely known in the 1970s, depend on establishing a crucial role for the maternal body in the shaping of Western consciousness. It is the mother who initiates the child into what Kristeva calls the symbolic order (i.e. the area in which rules and laws are established). Nevertheless, the language and the structures of patriarchy intervene, and so prevent free access between child and mother. The maternal body thus becomes an object of forbidden desire and Kristeva sees Western society as based on the alternating permission and occlusion of the mother. Considered afresh from these theoretical perspectives, Duras's fiction was seen to be challenging the myths and structures of patriarchal society and seeking to create a space for female desire. The role of the maternal body is clearest in *L'Eden cinéma*, first performed by the Renaud–Barrault company under the direction of Claude Regy in 1977, that of female desire in *Véra Baxter* and *Savannah Bay*.

L'Eden cinéma has a narrative structure with very little dramatic tension or conflict. The semi-autobiographical story is that of a mother, but told from the point of view of her children. The emotional centre of the story is the mother's obsessive determination to right the wrong that has been done to her: she has spent all her savings on a plot of ground in South-East Asia that has been sold to her as good planting ground, but, as she discovers too late, is regularly flooded by sea water. She struggles to build dams to keep out the sea and when her plans fail remains only more determined to continue. Her children are both implicated in her schemes but also separate – she comes close to selling her daughter when tempted by a sum sufficiently large to allow her to start rebuilding the dams. The story constantly questions and upsets the normal boundaries one would expect to find in matters of ownership, parenthood, marriage, identity. The mother's only source of income is playing the piano in a cinema to accompany silent films. She had no voice of her own but her story is voiced by her children.

Like Michel Deutsch, but with greater conviction and greater control than him, Duras presents women who are only half in control of their text. The words they utter are composed of fragments of memory, of a confirmation of their own reality. That reality is always elusive, but however hard it is to pin down, articulation of reality becomes a necessary condition for survival. In *Savannah Bay*, as La Jeune Femme talks to Madeleine, the lives of three generations of women are evoked on stage through speech impulses that take on a life of their own. The published text of 1983 contains two versions of the same play, the first as written by Duras before rehearsals started and the second as performed in her production at the Rond-Point by Madeleine Renaud and Bulle Ogier. The second text is starker and relies more on the development of a clear relationship between grandmother and granddaughter, where the first text had left their respective identities and hence their relationships less clearly defined. Nevertheless, within this relationship they take on different identities and exchange roles in a deliberately self-referential allusion to their condition as performers in a theatre.

The strength of Duras's plays lies in their economy. There are no details brought in for atmosphere or for local colour: every word counts and every thought expressed contributes to the central concern. The pleasure of listening to these texts is similar to that derived from a text by Beckett, akin to the pleasure of poetry. Her plays allow for very little dramatic conflict of the traditional kind: since the boundaries between the characters is so fluid, there is little scope for antagonism. But almost all of them generate a tension between character and place. The setting for key actions is constantly evoked, for example the rock, the sea and the salt marshes where Madeleine's daughter is first seduced and then commits suicide in *Savannah Bay*, or the grand villa on the Atlantic Coast in *Véra Baxter* (performed at the Théâtre de Poche in 1983).

The tension set up between the characters and their spaces may be the result of hostility and struggle, as in the account of the mother's attempt to hold back the Pacific Ocean in *L'Eden cinéma*, but more often it is the product of a relationship through which the character strives to define herself. An example is the use to which Duras puts the large villa in which Véra Baxter attempts to come to terms with her situation. The grand but abandoned mansion, with its succession of empty rooms, becomes the object of her desire, a desire displaced from her husband, who is inaccessible to her. As she struggles to articulate her feelings, and through this to come to terms with being abandoned, the villa takes on the quality of a mausoleum in which she is tempted to end her life. By the end, helped by the gentle but insistent presence of an unknown man, she is persuaded to leave the house behind and with it her thoughts of suicide.

Duras's work at the Rond-Point was reinforced by that of Simone Benmussa who had worked for many years as secretary to Jean-Louis Barrault and Madeleine Renaud and who gradually developed her own style as writer and director. In 1984 she staged an adaptation of *Enfance* by Nathalie Sarrante, another author who, like Duras, had a strong influence on the development of theatre without being principally a playwright. Another case of an established feminist writer turning to the stage was that of Hélène Cixous, already well known for her literary and philosophical work, who wrote two epic plays for the Théâtre du Soleil. The year 1980 marked a clear watershed for Ariane Mnouchkine and the Théâtre du Soleil. The work of the company up until that point had been collaboratively scripted and revolutionary in its politics. In the 1980s Mnouchkine devoted her work and the work of the company exclusively to the production of plays by Shakespeare – *Richard II* (1981); *Twelfth night* (1982); *Henry IV Part I* (1984) – and Hélène Cixous: *L'Histoire terrible mais inachevée de Norodom Sihanouk roi du Cambodge* (1985) and *L'Indiade ou L'Inde de leurs rêves* (1987). The Shakespeare plays were chosen as a way of returning to first principles. In the late 1960s work on *A Midsummer night's dream* had given her company the impulse to begin working on clowns and on the performance techniques of the popular theatre traditions. At the beginning of the 1980s, wanting to perform a play about the political situation in South-East Asia, but finding that improvisational methods were not producing work that satisfied her, she decided to embark on a cycle of Shakespeare plays 'in the spirit of an apprentice entering the master's workshop, hoping to learn how to depict the world on a stage' (programme for *Richard II*). The three Shakespeare plays that reached the stage of public performance gave evidence both of the continuity of the company's pre-1980s preoccupations and of new developments.

The working methods were similar to those that had been employed earlier; the company contained a large number of new young actors and for them the work on the Shakespeare plays was their apprenticeship to Mnouchkine's methods. The aim was to discover, through improvisations and exercises, a gestural performance style that could give physical expression to basic emotional states. There was a continuity between this and the work on *commedia*-inspired performance in *L'Age d'or*. The expressive flamboyance of the actors was enhanced by the musical improvisations of Jean-Jacques Lemêtre, who accompanied the text continuously on a wide range of instruments drawn from all over the world. For *Richard II* inspiration for costume, music and movement was drawn principally from classical Japanese theatre; for *Twelfth night* there was a marked Indian influence. In both productions, as in *Henry IV*, where stylistic borrowings were even more eclectic, there appeared a desire to reach beyond the limits of particular European traditions to a universal language of performance, mixing elements from all the major traditions, Eastern as much as Western. In this respect it was evident that the company was preparing itself for a new work that would be capable of matching up to the awareness, provided to us today by electronic media, of living in a single world community, where events in Hong Kong or Vietnam may have as much relevance for us as events in the next town. (For a discussion of the Shakespeare productions, see Bradby and Williams, 1988.)

This preparation reached fruition in the two new plays by Hélène Cixous, one about Cambodia and the other about India. In both cases the productions were heavily marked by the utopian idealism that had always been a feature of Mnouchkine's work. But this idealism was no longer expressed in revolutionary terms. Because the company had worked for five years on Shakespeare, and because Cixous's two plays are closely modelled on the Shakespearian Historical Epic, the utopian images that emerged were of a feudal society. Just as the most moving moments of *Richard II* had come at the end of the play with Richard's naked body draped across Bolingbroke, the image of a *pietà*, so in the play about Sihanouk all the sympathies of the audience were enlisted on behalf of this deposed king of Cambodia, whose relationship with his people was presented as an ideal image of paternalist harmony, disrupted only by the machinations of evil empires, whether American or Chinese. This uncritical portrayal of the divine right of kings, updated to apply to twentieth-century Cambodia, was extraordinarily simplistic, especially coming from the pen of a writer who had shown considerable sophistication in analysing the myths of paternalism in modern Western society.

In *L'Indiade*, the history of Indian independence was not quite so crudely handled, and more space was given to popular protest movements, but the play again followed the model of the history play that concentrates on the personalities and motives of the political leaders, a model that had been so effectively called into question by *1789* and *1793*. After the play, Mnouchkine and Cixous collaborated on a film, *La Nuit miraculeuse*, commissioned for the bicentenary celebrations of the French Revolution but not completed until 1990. This attempted to employ some of the same techniques that had gone into the construction of *1789*, but had none of the zest or the hard political content of that show. It depicts a small boy, observing a waxwork exhibition of the first Assemblée Nationale, for whom the scene comes to life. Beneath his wondering gaze, the députés re-enact the debate over the declaration of the Rights of Man. He is joined by his ne'er-do-well parents, two cleaning women, the librarian of the Assemblée Nationale, and the craftsmen who had made the waxworks. There is also a villain in the form of the owner of a department store who tries to prevent the vote by placing a bomb. But his dastardly plot is foiled and the vote is taken amidst applause from representatives of the nations of the world and such historical luminaries as Victor Hugo, Emile Zola, Mrs Pankhurst and Gandhi. Gandhi provides the link with *L'Indiade*: the work of Mnouchkine and Cixous in the second half of the 1980s appears to have degenerated into a simplistic programme for setting up a pantheon of secular saints, whose mawkish over-simplications are all the more astonishing in view of the vigorous critique of received historical images that had been mounted by the work of the Théâtre du Soleil in the 1970s.

At the end of the 1970s, Michel Vinaver had emerged as a major force in contemporary play writing – both as a leader of the 'quotidien' school and an author whose work went beyond the limitations of that school. In 1986 his collected plays were published in two volumes. This apparently straightforward event was remarkable for two reasons: it was the *only* publication of the complete works of a living dramatist to appear in the ten-year period, and it was issued not by a big Parisian publisher but by Actes Sud in Arles, with some help from a Lausanne-based firm, L'Aire. More important still, Vinaver wrote four new full-length plays: *L'Ordinaire* in 1981, *Les Voisins* and *Portrait d'une femme* in 1984 and *L'Emission de télévision* in 1988.

In these plays he continued with the methods and preoccupations of the previous decade, though he also added some significant developments. His basic approach retains all the experimental qualities of his earlier work: the texts are devoid of punctuation and their dramatic technique stresses multiple viewpoint. It is a technique similar to that of Pirandello, for which the Italian dramatist coined the term *umorismo*. By this, Pirandello meant an awareness of how a person might look ridiculous when viewed from a particular standpoint, but tragic from another. Like Pirandello, Vinaver's plays do not mock or satirise; instead, they induce in their audience a mood which is constantly oscillating between laughter and sympathy. The need to arouse such opposite responses from an audience always creates difficulties for an actor. Just as actors find Pirandello's plays among the most difficult to perform, so they frequently fail with Vinaver's characters, making them either uniformly tragic or uniformly comic. An exception to this rule was the fine production of *L'Emission de télévision* directed by Jacques Lassalle at the Odéon with members of the Comédie Française in 1990. Alain Pralon was particularly successful in the role of Pierre Delile, a middle-aged man who had been out of work for a long period and who was offered a job as customer adviser in a D.I.Y. supermarket. His performance was sufficiently complex and warm to make us sympathise with his plight, but just enough physical clowning to arouse mirth. Seeing this performance reminded one of the observation by Jacques Rivière (editor of Vinaver's collected plays) to the effect that Vinaver the playwright is a close cousin of Tati the film-maker: 'If the characters in Tati's films began to talk they would do so like those of Vinaver.'

This is an apt comparison, for like Tati's scenarios, Vinaver's plays never depart from everyday reality, yet they manage to present images that startle, and situations that provoke laughter, by means of chance incongruities or collisions of disparate elements. Moreover, as Rivière points out, Vinaver, like Tati, displays a brilliantly acute observation of those peculiar habits, preoccupations, and quirks that go to make up what we call 'the national character' so that a film by Tati or a play by Vinaver exudes a quality of 'frenchness' that almost seems to proceed from an ethnographical concern. Vinaver's plays are particularly rich in the everyday speech patterns of French life and part of their humour is similar to the humour of English playwrights like James Saunders or Alan Bennett – amusement that stems from the recognition of a particular speech idiom accurately caught by the dramatist.

268

Thematically, the plays of the 1980s continue with similar concerns to those of the 1970s: the impact of modern marketing methods on business life; friendship and rivalry in the workplace; the tendency of human relationships to be moulded by the institutional structures through which much social life is experienced; the close ties between self-respect and the value that the employment market sets on one's skills; the trauma of job loss, etc. A new and powerful theme also emerges: the theme of justice or, as Vinaver himself put it, justice on trial. *Portrait d'une femme* and *L'Emission de télévision* both raise questions about the legal process and leave their audiences or readers with considerable doubts about the impartiality of the law. *Portrait d'une femme* is based entirely on the reports of a real murder case published by *Le Monde* at the time of the trial (1951). This makes it the only play text Vinaver has written that is not set in the present or very close to it. The play brings together a range of different situations in the life of Sophie Auzanneau, on trial for the murder of her boyfriend and lover. We see her with parents, friends, teachers, earlier lovers. But she is constantly at odds with other people's expectations of her. Each of the people or groups has a different idea of what she should be, an image that each tries to impose on her. Gradually it becomes apparent that every one of these relationships is, each in its own way, a power relationship: Sophie is never allowed to take a dominant role. Her predicament is to a large extent the consequence of having to conform to role models proposed by men. In court, she resembles Meursault, the hero of Camus's novel *L'Etranger*, in that she appears to remain untouched by the proceedings. Once again she does not adopt the attitudes projected onto her – she is neither contrite nor defiant. Her one defence against the encroachment of the men who surround her is to refuse to enter into their linguistic field. Her own emotional needs only emerge in scenes of flashback to her youth.

Where *Portrait* is centred on Sophie Auzanneau and her trial, *L'Emission de télévision* also brings into play the character of the Juge d'Instruction. The opening scene is set in his office and the action is to some extent constructed through his eyes as he interviews the various witnesses in the investigation into a murder case. The audience itself becomes witness to the process whereby the statements of these people coagulate into the shape of official depositions. The judge has these typed out and signed with the ritual words 'reconnaissez-vous là vos paroles?' (Do you recognise these as your words?) – manifestly they do not, but they can do nothing about it. The author makes particularly good use of the relationship between the judge and his secretary. She specialises in lurid dreams which, she believes, give her prophetic knowledge of the true criminal. The judge's contemptuous dismissal of these is mirrored in the audience's scepticism *vis-à-vis* his own theories as to what occurred.

The larger theme of the play could be described as the process of how one makes sense of one's life when one has to 'rehearse' it. When a television producer wants to make a programme about one's situation, how does one present or represent it, and what sort of shaping or deforming processes enter into this representation? The play demonstrates in witty detail how, as soon as the television gets hold of reality, there is a fundamental de-realisation or alienation that takes place, whatever the intentions of the programme-makers. The investigations of the Juge d'Instruction are thus contextualised and commented on by two parallel investigations – the investigation by the television researchers trying to find a good subject for a programme about middle-aged people thrown out of work, and the investigations of a local journalist who is determined to play the private detective in order to make her name.

The play thus has a 'whodunnit' interest, but the answer to the question of who committed the murder is never finally revealed. Instead, the interest is displaced onto a demonstration of how the personal aims and ambitions of each character affect their favoured reconstruction of the events. Nevertheless, the suspense element is important to the play's theatrical appeal and it is worth noting that this is a feature of all of Vinaver's later plays. Without sacrificing multiplicity of voice and of viewpoint, and without returning to a simple time sequence in the construction of his plays, he has given greater prominence to the interest of the story-line. In *L'Ordinaire*, which depicts the crash of a company plane in the Andes, there is the suspense as to which of the characters will survive and whether rescue teams will reach them in time; in *Les Voisins*, the suspense turns on a series of thefts, more or less unexplained, which constantly threaten to disrupt the harmonious relations of two neighbouring families; in *Portrait* there is suspense as to the outcome of the trial and in *L'Emission* suspense on several grounds: which character will be chosen for the programme; will the judge succeed in outfacing the television producer; will the murderer be found; will Delile retain his new-found job; will he accept a role in the television programme after the death of his old rival, etc.? In this way, without abandoning the structural openness that characterised his most experimental work of the 1970s, Vinaver has succeeded in reintegrating the element of what Brecht called the *fable*.

Bernard-Marie Koltès was undoubtedly the most important new young playwright of the 1980s. His four full-length plays were all staged by Patrice Chéreau and designed by Richard Peduzzi: *Combat de nègre et de chiens*, 1983; *Quai ouest*, 1986; *Dans la solitude des champs de coton*, 1987, and *Le Retour au désert*, 1988. This immensely promising career was cut short when he died in 1989, aged 41. He had trained as a director at the Strasbourg school under Hubert Gignoux in the 1970s, had travelled widely in Africa, and translated the work of Athol Fugard into French. His first performed piece was a monologue, *La Nuit juste avant les forêts*, spoken by an Arab immigrant, destitute, lost and frightened in some French city; the language is intense, powerful, carefully worked without departing from the idioms of ordinary speech. This form of monologue was to be integrated into all of Koltès's full-length plays. All of these are constructed on the pattern of a 'deal' that is done, and it is in the bargaining, the give and take that build up to the 'deal' that dramatic tension of his work is located. The precise meaning he attached to the word 'deal' is set out in the epigraph to *Dans la solitude des champs de coton*:

A *deal* is a commercial transaction, turning on values that are banned or subject to strict controls, and which is concluded in a neutral space, indeterminate and not intended for this purpose, between suppliers and consumers, by means of tacit agreement, conventional signs or conversations with double meanings – with the aim of circumventing the risks of betrayal or swindle implied by this kind of operation – at any hour of the day or night, with no reference to the regulation opening hours for officially registered trading establishments, but usually at times of closure on the part of the latter. (1986: 7)

Beneath the mock-bureaucratise of this paragraph the reader may detect the precise analysis of a fundamental quality that is present in all successful dramatic dialogue: a tension arising from an encounter between two people, each of whom wants something from the other, each of whom is trying to *do* something to the other through the words that he or she speaks. Moreover, an additional source of tension in dramatic dialogue is identified by Koltès: the tension established between the dialogue and the situation or environment in which it takes place – often a tension arising from the fact that the 'deal' under discussion is not entirely innocent. This analysis could be applied, *mutatis mutandis*, to a great many plays from the classical tradition: the action of *Tartuffe*, to take an obvious example, is very largely taken up with a series of 'deals' conducted for motives that are not entirely innocent and in a space not at all designed for that purpose. Every one of Koltès's plays follows this pattern. The other constant presence in his theatre is the racial mix: West African and French in *Combat de nègre et de chiens*; American – both black, white, and Quechua Indian, in *Quai ouest*; North African and French in *Dans la solitude des champs de coton* and *Le Retour au désert*. This, naturally, is also a factor that creates dramatic tension. An examination of how these different kinds of tension are put to work by Koltès will provide an appropriate method for analysing his plays and throw light on both the formal and the thematic peculiarities of his work.

In *Combat de nègre et de chiens* the deal concerns a body. One party has it, the other party wants it. The setting is neither a cemetery nor a morgue – it is a space usually associated more with construction and regeneration rather than with death: a building-site where a new road bridge is going up. The building-site is located somewhere in West Africa and the project is riven with the contradictions that are typical of so many 'development projects' (funded by Western capital and employing European expertise) that have played a preponderant role in the economics of the former African colonies. The play has only four characters: two white engineers, a black labourer and a woman who has just arrived on a plane from Paris. Work on the site has come to a halt, partly because the funds appear to have dried up, and partly because one of the labourers has been killed. As the play opens Alboury, the labourer, comes to ask for the body of his dead brother. Horn, the older and more responsible of the two Europeans, tries to do a deal: he offers Alboury whisky, tries to get him to accept compensation. But Alboury is adamant that he (and his whole village) insist on having the body returned. Horn, meanwhile, is trying to cope with pressures from two different directions: from Léone, the Parisian woman whom he encountered on a recent visit back home and intends to marry, and from Cal, the other engineer employed on the project, who is a loner. Léone is in culture-shock; Cal is racist, self-pitying and violent (the only affection he shows is for his missing dog). As the play unfolds, it becomes clear that Cal was responsible for the death and subsequent disposal of Alboury's brother. While Alboury is always there as a dominating presence, much of the play's action is taken up in the confrontation between Horn and Cal. In the end Cal is shot, seemingly by one of the invisible African guards, whose presence is audible throughout the play, just off-stage; Léone departs for Paris; and Horn is left with the bodies of Cal and Cal's dog.

The dialogue of the play is highly charged, fluent, and filled to bursting with the myths of fear and guilt that have haunted the white European imagination from Conrad onwards. Much of the action concerns a duel of wills played out between Horn and Cal. Horn, the boss, is an idealist, and an organisation man; the only thing that really impresses him is the company he works for, with its tentacular, world-wide structure and its ability to function above the constraints of governments, politics, law and morality. He sees himself as a loyal member and servant of this 'extended family'. With this attitude goes a paternalist belief in 'co-operation', that is, the masterminding by Westerners of large engineering schemes for the good of the Third World. Cal, on the other hand, owes allegiance to nothing. His reasons for accepting foreign postings are greed and racism: they pay well and enable him to parade his prejudices against 'inferior races'. Each of these two characters employs his own rhetoric of domination: Cal's is cruder than Horn's: Cal brags about his toughness, his skill with weapons and women. But when faced with danger, he panics or whines. Horn, on the other hand, keeps his nerve and avoids confrontational behaviour. He disapproves of Cal and of everything he stands for.

And yet Horn, too, is limited by his total inability to enter into Alboury's way of seeing the world (something that, surprisingly, is not beyond Léone). At the end of scene four, Horn has a long speech in which he expounds his theories concerning the city. Every one of Koltès's plays contains a meditation on the desolate state of the city in the late twentieth century. Contrasting violently with the concrete jungle which he has helped to create and in which he is standing, Horn has a comically utopian plan for world harmony that would involve bringing the whole population of the globe together in a single megacity, to be located in France:

France seems ideal to me. It's a temperate country, with good rainfall and no extreme in climate, vegetation, animal life, health risks; ideal, France is ideal. It [the city] could of course be built in the southern part, the sunniest part. As for me, I like the winter; good rough winters; you don't know what a good rough winter is like. So it would be best to build this city lengthwise, from the Vosges to the Pyrenees, running down beside the Alps; people who like winter could live in the region that had once been Strasbourg and those who couldn't stand the snow, asthmatics and people who are afraid of the cold, could go to the areas where Marseille or Bayonne had been razed. The last of humanity's conflicts would be a theoretical debate between the attractions of winter in Alsace as against spring on the Cote d'Azur. (1983: 37)

In this scheme of things the role of the rest of the world would be to provide food and recreation for the inhabitants of the great city in France.

The action of the play takes place in the course of a single night. By the end of it, in the struggle that has taken place between the 'dogs' and the black, no one has achieved what they wanted from the others; all are losers. But the 'dogs' – the Europeans – have all paid the price for being in complete contradiction with their situation. Faced with the patient strength of Alboury, each is compelled to recognise his or her impotence. This is all the more striking since the speeches of the 'dogs' are all to do with civilisation, superiority, control, whereas their behaviour demonstrates the opposite qualities. Gradually the false rhetoric of the 'European civilising mission' is stripped bare and revealed for what it is: desire for power, and above all for *ownership*. The world is seen only as a place for supplying the needs of white west Europeans. As for the real needs of the people of the world, these are never considered: Horn's Franco-centric utopian speech quoted above is delivered, with no sense of irony on his part, to Alboury, who has come with one simple, concrete request: the body.

In its use of dramatic technique, the play very clearly lays claim to the classical heritage. It observes the unities of time, place and action; it is structured on a succession of impassioned encounters between two characters in which their respective positions are stated with considerable use of the long 'tirade' and some recourse to monologue as well. The language has all the power and precision that we associate with French classical theatre: it is in no sense a copy of the language in which people on a West African construction site would really address one another. And yet Koltès does not use abstruse or unusual words: he remains strictly within the limits of the vocabulary that *might* be used in such circumstances and by such people. The consequence is

22 *Combat de nègre et de chiens* (Koltès): Philippe Léotard as Cal in the production by Patrice Chéreau, Théâtre des Amandiers, Nanterre, 1983.

23 *Combat de nègre et de chiens* (Koltès): Philippe Léotard as Cal and Michel Piccoli as Horn in the production by Patrice Chéreau, Théâtre des Amandiers, Nanterre, 1983.

that, as the characters speak, the audience sees their rhetoric undermined and understands clearly the discrepancy between their real intentions and the alibis they repeatedly try to construct. By this particular combination of dramatic technique, subject-matter and use of dramatic language, Koltès's play achieves an allegorical resonance within a situation that remains strictly contemporary and sharply focussed on the issue of race. In this he resembles the author with whom he has frequently been compared (and whom he greatly admired): Jean Genet.

The production of *Combat* by Chéreau took realism to its extreme point: Peduzzi's design faithfully reproduced an enormous concrete bridge whose pillars strode across the stage, and the action took place in a dusty space beneath. Where the text mentions a truck, a real vehicle was driven onto the stage and the monumental production style was in danger of swamping the play's central encounter between characters and languages. Chéreau adopted similar tactics for Koltès's second play, *Quai ouest* (1986), set in an anonymous American dockland hangar. The same design and production team filled the stage with sections of freight containers and massive stretches of warehouse wall which moved as if possessed of a life of their own, shifting to and fro behind the actors. It was only the charismatic power of the actors Chéreau was able to attract that prevented the plays from being completely overwhelmed: Michel Piccoli played Horn and Philippe Léotard Cal; in *Quai ouest* Maria Casarès took the female lead.

Quai ouest has a larger cast and the 'deals' that each character tries to negotiate are more complex. The setting was inspired by a riverside warehouse that Koltès had found on a visit to New York. The action begins with Maurice Koch, a rich 60-year-old trying to bargain with some down-and-outs to assist him in a suicide attempt. As more characters are brought in and the action develops, we find that each one is linked to the others by a network of bargains and compromises of a financial or emotional nature. The setting is again a source of dramatic tension: it is a place that has been created by the economic forces that have made Koch rich. Yet it is hostile to him, as Monique, his companion, points out: once it was full of people who lived and traded there; now it has become a wasteland, inhabited only by drop-outs. As Koch pursues his ultimately successful quest for annihilation, the tensions set up by the developing action reveal the underlying social and racial stratification of these characters, and through his depiction of these Koltès makes his comments on the state of society under late capitalism.

In his notes on how to produce the play, Koltès wrote: 'the worst thing would be for a performance to become sentimental rather than comic ... These are scenes of trade, exchange, barter and must be played as such' (1985: 108). His desire for the comedy of the play to be emphasised perhaps reveals an uneasiness about the nature of his own work. For Koltès's main fault is a tendency to over-write, to fall into inflated, repetitive speeches with a rather portentous tone, and almost nothing that could be described as comic. By comparison with *Combat*, *Quai ouest* seems over-long and unnecessarily complicated, even self-indulgent at times.

This is a mistake he did not repeat in his last two plays: *Dans la solitude des champs de coton* (1987) is stripped down to bare essentials, and *Le Retour au désert* (1988), while much more complex, also emulates the concentrated power of *Combat* and contains some scenes of powerful black comedy. *Dans la solitude des champs de coton* contains only two characters, named simply Le Dealer and Le Client, and it comes straight to the point, presenting human intercourse entirely through a single bargaining encounter, in which one person tries to supply what he thinks the other person wants and the second person seeks to maintain his freedom of movement, refusing to be pinned down as to what it is he wants or the price he is willing to pay. Once again, the setting is the urban wasteland that is inevitably created when the city is seen as something purely instrumental and not as a habitat designed with the aim of fulfilling human needs. The dealer, whose role was played in Chéreau's 1987 production by Isaach de Bankolé, employs the language of earthly realities, spiced with proverbs in the African style. The language of the client is more evasive and more abstract. He normally lives 'above' the ground and is uneasy at being stopped:

I was going from that lighted window, behind me, up there, to that other lighted window, over there in front of me, following a straight line which goes through you since you have deliberately positioned yourself there. Now there is no other way, for a person wishing to pass from one high place to another high place, to avoid coming down in order once again to go up, with all the absurdity of two movements which cancel one another out, and the risk, between the two, of squashing rubbish at every step, rubbish that has been thrown out of the windows; the higher up you live, the cleaner the space, but the harder the fall. (1986: 13)

The dialogue between them develops into a trial of strength. They circle round one another, taking care to give nothing away, each searching for the weakness that will give him a purchase on the other. Every conceivable need is evoked, whether emotional, spiritual or material, that might provide a basis for bringing the two men together. In the end they find no ground for negotiation on which they can agree, other than the reality of their struggle – this reaches its logical conclusion when what began as a purely verbal challenge develops into a duel to the death. The last words spoken are: 'Alors, quelle arme?' (Well, choose your weapon; 1986: 61).

Le Retour au désert is in some ways more accessible than Koltès's earlier plays. In the first place, it tells an absorbing story – the story is of a struggle for power played out between a brother and sister, both in late middle age, with children on the verge of adulthood. For most of their married lives Mathilde and Adrien have lived apart, she in Algeria and he in the provincial town, somewhere in the East of France, where they were both born and brought up. Now, in the early 1960s, the Algerian conflict has provoked the return of the sister with her two children, Fatima and Edouard. Their arrival disturbs everything in the settled pattern of this upper bourgeois household: the relationships within the household, where Adrien's son Mathieu is kept in a state of dependency and where his second wife Marthe is drunk most of the time, as well as the relationships outside in the town, where Adrien's clubby contacts with the local powers will be upset. Mathilde provokes this revolution partly out of sheer cussedness, partly because she wants to regain her part of the inheritance, and partly because she is genuinely upset at the death of Adrien's first wife, Marie, who had been her friend, and the way her sister Marthe has taken her place. In the course of the play the dead Marie returns, to haunt the family, though she is visible only to Fatima.

The action all takes place in the large town house that is itself almost a character in the drama, since the play is centrally concerned with rights, property, inheritance and ownership. Mathilde and Adrien can only relate to one another through activities of barter and exchange, and their children become commodities in this process just as much as the house and factory that they have inherited from their father. But although their disputes centre on such very ordinary subjects, Koltès's dialogue has the power, as in his earlier works, of bringing into play the whole range of cultural and ideological values that secrete this particular mode of interaction between siblings. The multi-layered quality of Koltès's work is epitomised in his title *Le Retour au désert*. The title sets up the questioning, challenging tone that is characteristic of the whole play: what exactly is the desert of the title? Is it Algeria, or is it France? Since the opening scene shows one of the central characters, Mathilde, returning to France after years of living in Algeria, the immediate supposition is that conventional ways of thinking are being reversed and we are being invited to think of the provincial French town as *le désert*. But at the end of the play both she and her brother Adrien are on the point of leaving once again. We are not sure of their exact destination; it may be North Africa, or Andorra, Monaco, Geneva – one of those places where the rich are efficiently cushioned from the unpleasant realities of life: 'where you are surrounded by people who are sterile, old and satisfied and where no one gets on anyone else's nerves' (1988: 81). So in retrospect the title also takes on a different meaning, a social desert, recalling perhaps Alceste's departure at the end of *Le Misanthrope*.

The atmosphere of the play owes something to the worlds of stifling bourgeois propriety evoked by Mauriac, but the language of the dialogue has the power and intensity as well as the poetic resonance of Genet. The clashes between different members of the family are entirely credible at a personal and social level, but the author employs a deliberately artificial dramatic structure so as to create a sense of distance and to enable us to observe them coolly and critically. The structure once again borrows the characteristics of classical dramaturgy, but occasionally allows the action to tip over into black farce. There is a classical concern for symmetry in the exchange of speeches between the main characters. The first encounter between Mathilde and Adrien, for example, is in the style of two warriors matching up to one another, each measuring the other's spirit, probing for the other's strengths and weaknesses. The battle between these two later reaches extraordinary levels of linguistic violence; when this in turn erupts into action they remind us of characters from farce rather than from classical tragedy, as they attempt to come to blows and each has to be held back by a servant. As Colette Godard commented in *Le Monde* (8 Oct. 1988), 'we move from the Atrides to Dallas and Dynasty, by way of the Absurd'. In Chéreau's production the roles were taken by Jacqueline Maillan and Michel Piccoli, who succeeded in conveying the whole range, from profound hatred or jealousy, to futile temper-tantrums that reveal the sterility of an approach to the world concerning itself only with property and ownership (a sterility finally recognised and welcomed by Mathilde at the end).

Koltès decided to write the play as a vehicle for Jacqueline Maillan, who normally performs in Boulevard comedy, and this may explain the lighter touch that he achieved. Even the use of the neo-classical structure is ironically subverted, since, although unity of place and action are preserved, the time sequence is more epic than classical and is broken up into units named after the devotions that punctuate the Muslim day; *sobh* (the dawn prayer); *zohr* (the midday prayer); *'acr* (the afternoon prayer); *maghrib* (the evening prayer); and *'icha* (the night-time prayer). The last scene of all is given the title of the feast that marks the end of Ramadan, so that the play's action can be seen, in retrospect, as a long period of trial and discipline. By imposing this Islamic structure on the play, Koltès brings home the interpenetration of the two cultures that is one of his main themes.

Like Genet, Koltès systematically exploited a juxtaposition of African and French ways of thought in order to question the inherited assumptions of his own culture. *Combat de nègre et de chiens*, for example, sets the attitudes of the three representatives of the 'developed' world in contrast with those of a representative of the 'underdeveloped' world in order to cast doubt on these terms and to question their interrelationship. *Quai ouest* does something similar in bringing together American and European value systems. In *Le Retour au désert* the convenient myth of the 1950s, according to which North Africa was just another part of France, is questioned and challenged by placing French customs under the scrutiny of North African characters. The play opens with a passage in Arabic, as Aziz, the manservant of the house, expresses himself freely about his master. Mathilde, on her entrance, reveals that she too can speak Arabic; in fact her responses are those of a colonial who assumes ownership of both cultures, maintaining a pretence that both have equal value. She has named her daughter Fatima, which scandalises her conventional brother. But her real attitude towards Arabs will be revealed in a magnificent *coup de théâtre* at the end of the play when Fatima, who has already shocked her mother by revealing she is pregnant, gives birth to twins that are black. Mathilde's son, Edouard, also brings a taste for adventure to his staid surroundings; he soon discovers the local brothel, the cafe Saifi, and amazes his cousin (Adrien's over-protected son) by taking him there. Aziz accompanies them and the scenes in the cafe serve to cast a critical light on the town's vaunted defence of justice and morality, especially when the cafe Saifi is blown up by a racist French gang led by the Ortonesque police chief.

Le Retour au désert resembles all Koltès's earlier work in its central action: the intense struggle for power by two adversaries, whose language is carefully crafted by the author so as to evoke wider perspectives and to call into question the inherited European value system. But in addition to this it succeeds, where his earlier plays had failed, in introducing a note of comedy, however black. The tendency of the action to tip over into grotesque farce only increases the savagery of his attack on the provincial business class of the post-war years in France. At the time of his death, Koltès was working on a play about Roberto Succo, a man who was convicted of killing his parents for no apparent reason, underwent psychiatric treatment, and was released, but, after living quietly for some years, committed further murders before taking his own life. The subject suggests that he was trying to tackle head-on the violence that he perceived underlying all personal relationships in our time.

As a playwright, Koltès presents interesting similarities with Vinaver. His use of heightened language and intense theatricality are, of course, very different from Vinaver's rather cool dramatic writing. But beneath the differences in the surface texture of their work, both dramatists are searching for the fundamental qualities that make for dramatic specificity. Both have found original ways of representing the individual's complex relationship to the wider social realities of late twentieth-century life. Both write for performance but have *also* been able to establish the claim of the playwright to be considered as an author, whose works must be published as well as performed. At the end of the decade, these two authors stand out for the quality of their work. They represent a profession that is once again thriving, that has recovered from the near-extinction it suffered in the 1970s, and has begun to re-establish its right to a place at the centre of cultural life in France.

Although the playwrights have successfully re-established their claim to a central place in the business of making theatre, the outstanding names in the French theatre at the start of the 1990s are still those of directors. Audiences still flock to see Chéreau's *Hamlet* (which has been running, intermittently, for three seasons), or Savary's *Le Bourgeois Gentilhomme* (a revival of his 1980 production to celebrate his arrival at the former T.N.P.). But such repetitions and revivals suggest a sense of fatigue in directors' theatre: perhaps the death of Vitez, in April 1990, will come to be seen as marking the end of its heyday. In its early, heroic phase, it had been underpinned by a strong sense of mission: the urge to take theatre to new audiences outside Paris and to discover, in the popular traditions, effective forms of political theatre. In the seventies and the eighties, the spectacular successes of directors such as Planchon, Chéreau, Mnouchkine frequently appeared self-indulgent, and the sense of mission appeared to have been lost. Nevertheless, there has been no reduction in the number of new young companies being formed and of new works being produced.

In all its diversity, the French theatre of the fifty-year period from 1940 to 1990 has one or two clear unifying characteristics. From Sartre to Vitez, almost every departure by a major practitioner or writer has echoed Artaud's call to do away with the theatre of psychological case-studies. This has been accompanied by a debate about the specificity of theatre, in which there has been agreement that the main strength of the best theatre is not the depiction and analysis of character; this is better done in the cinema or the novel, art forms that can probe and distort a single personal viewpoint. What the theatre does best is to provide a multi-layered view of human beings in their complex relations to other human beings within a whole social order, with its cultural, metaphysical and ideological conditions. This kind of theatre does not reject psychology, but shows how it is constructed through the interplay of conditions and actions, relationships and choices.

The long-term influence of Brecht and the rediscovery of the tradition going back through the German Romantics to the Elizabethan theatre has had a powerful impact, both on productions of the classics and on new writing. The division into absurdist and political camps during the fifties and sixties was a symptom of the enormous wrench that was needed before Aristotelian models of organic unity could be abandoned and the virtues of an art of discontinuity could be appreciated. But the disagreements and contradictions sometimes proved fruitful, producing new work in which 'the social analysis never crushes the individual psychology of the characters, while at the same time the characters do not mask the general view of the society that is being described' (Planchon above, p. 125).

The unique richness of the period lies in a new, critical attitude towards the conventions of theatre and the art of playwriting. The early plays of Beckett, Ionesco and Adamov, together with those of Genet, constitute such a controlled display of self-conscious experimentation, such a radical challenge to the old theatre forms, that critics and creators alike were dazzled: it seemed impossible to go beyond these achievements. For some people, the only way forward was to go to the opposite extreme, to claim that the individual avant-garde author was a lackey of the establishment powers, and that only the creations of collective groups were worth staging.

More importantly, authors and practitioners alike began to question this need to see the theatre in terms of stark alternatives: regional *or* Parisian, political *or* absurdist, Brechtian *or* Artaudian. The plays of Adamov, Planchon, Césaire, Gatti, Vinaver and Koltès have probed those areas in the experience of both individuals and collectives at which fears, fantasies and dreams intersect with the material realities of social conditions. Adamov's plea was for a theatre linking 'the individual, not only with his own dreams and imaginings (*fantômes*), but also to other men, and hence to their dreams, and set in a time that is not imaginary' (1964: 240), and this has found an echo in the most interesting work of recent years. The approach of the authors and directors we have studied has often been tentative, as they have struggled to come to terms with the realities of late twentieth century life and to avoid the temptation to despair. In so doing, the best have managed to combine the critical, experimental attitudes of the New Theatre with the rediscovered Elizabethan-Romantic-Brechtian tradition, thus creating complex dramas of multiple viewpoint. In these plays and productions, we have discovered an exploration of the relationships between ideology and dramatic form that has proved capable of calling forth fresh creative responses from theatre practitioners, and of confronting audiences once again with the most fundamental questions.

Bibliography

SECTION I: AUTHORS AND PRACTITIONERS

Adamov, Arthur

1950   *La Parodie, L'Invasion*, Paris: Charlot.
1953   *Théâtre I (La Parodie, L'Invasion, La Grande et la Petite Manoeuvre, Le Professeur Taranne, Tous contre tous)*, Paris: Gallimard.
1955   *Théâtre II (Le Sens de la marche, Les Retrouvailles, Le Ping-Pong)*, Paris: Gallimard.
1958   *Théâtre de Société (Intimité, Je ne suis pas français, La Complainte du ridicule)*, Paris: Editeurs français réunis.
1964   *Ici et maintenant*, Paris: Gallimard.
1966   *Théâtre III (Paolo Paoli, La Politique des restes, Sainte Europe)*, Paris: Gallimard.
1968a   *Théâtre IV (Le Printemps 71, M. le Modéré)*, Paris: Gallimard.
1968b   *L'Homme et l'enfant*, Paris: Gallimard.
1969a   *Off limits*, Paris: Gallimard.
1969b   *Je . . . Ils . . .*, Paris: Gallimard.
1970   *Si l'été revenait*, Paris: Gallimard.
     See Abirached, Bradby, Dort, Gaudy, Mélèze.

Anouilh, Jean

1942a   *Pièces noires (L'Hermine, La Sauvage, Le Voyageur sans bagage, Eurydice)*, Paris: Calmann-Lévy.
1942b   *Pièces roses (Le Bal des voleurs, Le Rendez-vous de Senlis, Léocadia)*, Paris: Calmann-Lévy.
1946   *Nouvelles Pièces noires (Jézabel, Antigone, Roméo et Jeanette, Médée)*, Paris: La Table Ronde.
1951   *Pièces brillantes (L'Invitation au château, Colombe, La Répétition, Cécile)*, Paris: La Table Ronde.
1956   *Pièces grinçantes (Ardèle, La Valse des toréadors, Ornifle, Pauvre Bitos)*, Paris: La Table Ronde.
1960   *Pièces costumées (L'Alouette, Becket, La Foire d'empoigne)*, Paris: La Table Ronde.
1970   *Nouvelles Pièces grinçantes (L'Hurluberlu, La Grotte, Le Boulanger, la boulangère et le petit mitron, Les Poissons rouges)*, Paris: La Table Ronde.
1974   *Pièces baroques (Cher Antoine, Ne réveillez pas Madame, Le Directeur de l'Opéra)*, Paris: La Table Ronde.
1977   *Pièces secrètes (Tu étais si gentille quand tu étais petite, L'Arrestation, Le Scénario)*, Paris: La Table Ronde.
1980   *La Belle Vie*, Paris: La Table Ronde.
1984   *Pièces farçeuses (Chers Zoiseaux; La Culotte, Episode de la vie d'un auteur; Le Nombril)*, Paris: La Table Ronde.
     See Gignoux, Howarth, Malachy, Vandromme.

Bibliography

Arrabal, Fernando

1967 *Théâtre V (Théâtre panique, L'Architecte et l'Empereur d'Assyrie)*, Paris: Bourgois.

1968a *Théâtre I (Oraison, Les Deux Bourreaux, Fando et Lis, Le Cimetière des voitures)*, Paris: Bourgois.

1968b *Théâtre II (Guernica, Le Labyrinthe, Le Tricycle, Pique-nique en campagne, La Bicyclette du condamné)*, Paris: Bourgois.

1969a *Théâtre III (Le Grand Cérémonial, Cérémonie pour un noir assassiné)*, Paris: Bourgois.

1969b *Théâtre IV (Le Lai de Barabbas, Concert dans un oeuf)*, Paris: Bourgois.

1969c *Théâtre VI (Le Jardin des délices, Bestialité érotique, Une tortue nommée Dostoievski)*, Paris: Bourgois.

1969d *Théâtre VII (Théâtre de guérilla: Et ils passèrent des menottes aux fleurs, L'Aurore rouge et noir)*, Paris: Bourgois.

1969e *Entretiens avec Alain Schifres*, Paris: Belfond.

1970 *Théâtre VIII (Ars Amandi, Dieu tenté par les mathématiques)*, Paris: Bourgois.

1972a *Théâtre IX (Le Ciel et la merde, La Grande revue du XXe siècle)*, Paris: Bourgois.

1972b *Théâtre X (Bella Ciao, La Guerre de mille ans)*, Paris: Bourgois.

1974 *Sur le fil ou la ballade du train fantôme*, Paris: Présence Africaine.

1976 *Théâtre XI (La Tour de Babel, La Marche royale, Une orange sur le mont de vénus, La Gloire en images)*, Paris: Bourgois.

1978a *Théâtre XII (Théâtre bouffe: Vole-moi un petit milliard, Le Pastaga des loufs ou ouverture orang-outan, Punk et punk et colégram)*, Paris: Bourgois.

1978b *Entretiens avec Arrabal*, Grenoble: Presses Universitaires.

1981 *Théâtre XIII (Mon Doux Royaume saccagé, Le Roi de Sodome, Le Ciel et la merde II)*, Paris: Bourgois.

1982 *Théâtre XIV (L'Extravagante réussite de Jésus Christ; Karl Marx et William Shakespeare, Lève-toi et rêve)*, Paris: Bourgois.

1984 *Théâtre XV (Les Délices de la chair; La Ville dont le prince était une princesse)*, Paris: Bourgois.
 See Aslan, Bérenguer.

Artaud, Antonin

1956– *Oeuvres complètes*, Paris: Gallimard.

1964 *Le Théâtre et son double*, Paris: Gallimard (idées 114).
 See Esslin, Innes, Virmaux.

Audiberti, Jacques

1948 *Théâtre I (Quoat-quoat, L'Ampélour, Les Femmes du boeuf, Le Mal court)*, Paris: Gallimard.

1952 *Théâtre II (La Fête noire, Pucelle, Les Naturels du Bordelais)*, Paris: Gallimard.

1955 *Le Cavalier seul*, Paris: Gallimard.

1956 *Théâtre III (La Logeuse, Le Ouallou, Opéra parlé, Altanima)*, Paris: Gallimard.

1959 *L'Effet Glapion*, Paris: Gallimard.

1961 *Théâtre IV (Coeur à cuir, Le Soldat Dioclès, La Fourmi dans le corps, Les Patients, L'Armoire classique, Un bel enfant)*, Paris: Gallimard.

1962 *Théâtre V (Pomme, Pomme, Pomme, Bâton et ruban, Boutique fermée, La Brigitta)*, Paris: Gallimard.

1965 *Entretiens avec Georges Charbonnier*, Paris: Gallimard.

Barrault, Jean-Louis

1949   *Réflexions sur le théâtre*, Paris: Vautrin.
1959   *Nouvelles Réflexions sur le théâtre*, Paris: Flammarion.
1961   *Le Phénomène théâtral*, Oxford: University Press.
1972   *Souvenirs pour demain*, Paris: Seuil.
1973   'Three early essays', *Theatre Quarterly* 10: 2–5.
1975   *Comme je le pense*, Paris: Gallimard.
1978   'Dialogue sur le théâtre avec Eugène Ionesco', *The French Review* 51(4): 514–28.
1983   *Paris notre siècle*, Paris: Messine (with Madeleine Renaud).
       See Chancerel, Frank.

Beckett, Samuel

1951a   *Molloy*, Paris: Minuit.
1951b   *Malone meurt*, Paris: Minuit.
1952   *En attendant Godot*, Paris: Minuit.
1953   *L'Innommable*, Paris: Minuit.
1954   *Waiting for Godot*, New York: Grove Press.
1956   *Waiting for Godot*, London: Faber (expurgated).
1957a   *Fin de Partie, Acte sans paroles I*, Paris: Minuit.
1957b   *All that fall*, London: Faber.
1957c   *Tous ceux qui tombent*, Paris: Minuit.
1958   *Endgame, Act without words 1*, London: Faber.
1959a   *Krapp's last tape, Embers*, London: Faber.
1959b   *La Dernière Bande, Cendres*, Paris: Minuit.
1959c   *Molloy, Malone dies, The unnamable*, London: Calder.
1961a   *Poems in English*, London: Calder.
1961b   *Happy days*, New York: Grove Press.
1962   *Happy days*, London: Faber.
1963a   *Cascando*, Paris: Minuit.
1963b   *Oh les beaux jours*, Paris: Minuit.
1964   *Play, Words and music, Cascando*, London: Faber.
1965   *Waiting for Godot*, London: Faber (revised).
1966   *Comédie, Va et vient, Cascando, Paroles et musique, Dis Joe, Acte sans paroles II*, Paris: Minuit.
1967a   *Eh Joe, Act without words II, Film*, London: Faber.
1967b   *Come and go*, London: Calder and Boyers.
1971   *Breath and other short plays*, London: Faber.
1973   *Not I*, London: Faber.
1977   *Ends and odds*, London: Faber.
1978   *Pas*, Paris: Minuit.
1982   *Catastrophe et autres dramaticules*, Paris: Minuit.
        See Asmus, Cohn, Fletcher, Louzon, Reid, Robbe-Grillet, Simon.

Benedetto, André

1968   *Napalm*, Honfleur: Oswald.
1969a   *Zone rouge, Feux interdits*, Honfleur: Oswald.
1969b   *Le Petit Train de Monsieur Kamodé*, Honfleur: Oswald.
1970a   *Emballage*, Honfleur: Oswald.
1970b   *Rosa Lux*, Honfleur: Oswald.

Bibliography

1971a *Auguste et Peter, Lola Pelican*, Honfleur: Oswald.
1971b *Commune de Paris*, Honfleur: Oswald.
1972   *Le Chine entre à L'O.N.U.*, Honfleur: Oswald.
1973   *La Madone des ordures*, Honfleur: Oswald.
1975a *Aie! Les lunes de Fos*, Honfleur: Oswald.
1975b *Alexandra K*, Honfleur: Oswald.
1975c *Esclarmunda*, Honfleur: Oswald.
1975d *Geronimo*, Honfleur: Oswald.
1975e *Pourquoi et comment on a fait un assassin de Gaston D.*, Honfleur: Oswald.
1976   *Théâtre I (Les Drapiers Jacobins, Le Siège de Montauban, Mandrin)*, Honfleur: Oswald.

Benoit, Jean-Louis

1981   'Un Conseil de classe très ordinaire: quelques notes de travail sur la mise en scène', *Théâtre Public*, 38: 24–30.

Billetdoux, François

1961–4 *Théâtre* (2 vols.), Paris: La Table Ronde.

Blin, Roger

1963   'An interview with Bettina Knapp', *The Drama Review* 7(3): 111–24.
1967   'Two interviews with Bettina Knapp and Paul Gray', *The Drama Review* 11(4): 109–12.
1981   'An interview with J. L. Savona', *Modern Drama* 24(2): 127–34.
1986   *Souvenirs et propos*, Paris: Gallimard.
       See Aslan, Knapp.

Brecht, Bertolt

1955–62 *Théâtre* (10 vols.), Paris: L'Arche.
1963   *Ecrits sur le théâtre*, Paris: L'Arche.
       See Benjamin, Dort, Willett.

Camus, Albert

1962   *Théâtre, récits, nouvelles* (Pléiade edition), Paris: Gallimard.
1970   *Selected essays and notebooks* (ed. and trans. P. Thody), Harmondsworth: Penguin.
       See Freeman, Thody.

Césaire, Aimé

1955   *Discours sur le colonialisme*, Paris: Présence Africaine.
1956   *Et les chiens se taisaient* (arrangement théâtral), Paris: Présence Africaine.
1963   *La Tragédie du roi Christophe*, Paris: Présence Africaine.
1966   *Une saison au Congo*, Paris: Seuil.
1969   *Une tempête*, Paris: Seuil.
       See Harris, Laville, Mbom, Pestre de Almeida.

Cixous, Hélène

1985   *L'Histoire terrible mas inachevée de Norodom Sihanouk roi du Cambodge*, Paris: Théâtre du Soleil.

1987   *L'Indiade ou L'Inde de leurs rêves*, Paris: Théâtre du Soleil.

Claudel, Paul

1965   *Théâtre II* (Pléiade edition), Paris: Gallimard. (Contains both original and stage versions of *Le Soulier de satin*.)

1966   *Mes Idées sur le théâtre*, Paris: Gallimard.

Cocteau, Jean

1948a   *Théâtre I (Antigone, Les Mariés de la Tour Eiffel, Les Chevaliers de la Table Ronde, Les Parents terribles)*, Paris: Gallimard.

1948b   *Théâtre II (Les Monstres sacrés, La Machine à écrire, Renaud et Armide, L'Aigle à deux têtes)*, Paris: Gallimard.

1952   *Bacchus*, Paris: Gallimard.

1976   *Orphée, the play and the film* (ed. E. Freeman), Oxford: Blackwell.

Copeau, Jacques

1941   *Le Théâtre populaire*, Paris: Presses Universitaires (Bibliothèque du Peuple no. 1).

1974   *Registres I: Appels*, Paris: Gallimard.

1976   *Registres II: Molière*, Paris: Gallimard.

1979   *Registres III: Les Registres du Vieux-Colombier* 1, Paris: Gallimard.
    See Anders, Borgal.

Cousin, Gabriel

1958   *L'Ordinaire Amour*, Paris: Gallimard.

1963   *Théâtre I (L'Aboyeuse et l'automate, L'Opéra Noir)*, Paris: Gallimard.

1964   *Théâtre II (Le Voyage de derrière la montagne, Le Drame du Fukuryu-Maru)*, Paris: Gallimard.

1969   *Le Cycle du crabe*, Paris: Gallimard.
    See Chambers, Jeffery, *Théâtre Populaire* 45, 1962.

Craig, Edward Gordon

1911   *On the art of the theatre*, London: Heinemann.

Dasté, Jean

1977   *Voyage d'un comédien*, Paris: Stock.
    See Mignon.

Deutsch, Michel

1974   *Ruines, Dimanche*, Paris: Stock.

1975   *La Bonne Vie, L'Entraînement du champion avant la course*, Paris: Stock.

Bibliography

1979   *Le Chanteur, L'Amour du théâtre*, Paris: Bourgois.
1980   *Convoi*, Paris: Stock.
1982   *Tel un enfant a l'écart, Partage, MGC 148*, Paris: Bourgois.
1984   *Thermidor*, Paris: Bourgois.
1986   *El Sisisi*, Paris: Bourgois.
1987   *Théâtre (Dimanche, La Bonne Vie, Convoi, Tamerlan)*, Paris: Union Générale
       d'Editions.
       See Sarrazac.

Dubillard, Roland

1962   *Naïves hirondelles, Si Camille me voyait*, Paris: Gallimard.
1966   *La Maison d'os*, Paris: Gallimard.

Dullin, Charles

1946   *Souvenirs et notes de travail d'un acteur*, Paris: Lieutier.
1969   *Ce sont les dieux qu'il nous faut*, Paris: Gallimard.
       See Arnaud.

Duras, Marguerite

1965–8   *Théâtre* (2 vols.), Paris: Gallimard.
1977   *L'Eden Cinéma*, Paris: Mercure de France.
1980   *Véra Baxter ou les plages de l'Atlantique*, Paris: Albatros.
1983   *Savannah Bay* (new revised edition), Paris: Minuit.

Gatti, Armand

1958   *Théâtre I (Le Poisson noir)*, Paris: Seuil.
1959   *Le Crapaud-bufle*, Paris: L'Arche (répertoire du T.N.P.).
1960   *Le Quetzal, Europe 374*, June 1960, 58–87.
1960   *Théâtre II (L'Enfant-Rat, Le Voyage du Grand'Tchou)*, Paris: Seuil.
1962   *Théâtre III (La Deuxième Existence du camp de Tatenberg, Chroniques d'une
       planète provisoire, La Vie imaginaire de l'éboueur Auguste Geai)*, Paris: Seuil.
1964   *Chant public devant deux chaises électriques*, Paris: Seuil.
1967a   *V comme Vietnam*, Paris: Seuil.
1967b   'Un théâtre pour la cité', *La Nef* 24(29): 71–3.
1968a   *La Passion du Général Franco*, Paris: Seuil.
1968b   *La Naissance*, Paris: Seuil.
1968c   *Les Treize Soleils de la rue Saint-Blaise*, Paris: Seuil.
1969   *Un Homme seul*, Paris: Seuil.
1971a   *La Cigogne*, Paris: Seuil.
1971b   'Interview avec Denis Bablet', *Travail Théâtral* 3:3–21.
1973   *Rosa collective*, Paris: Seuil.
1973   'La Colonne Durutti', *Cahiers Théâtre Louvain* 14–17:5–126.
1975   *La Passion du Général Franco par les émigrés eux-mêmes*, Paris: Seuil.
1977   'Armand Gatti dans le Brabant Wallon', *Cahiers Théâtre Louvain* 26–29:
       1–121.
1982   'Time, place and the theatrical event', *Modern Drama* 25(1): 69–81.
1987   *Opéra avec titre long*, Perpignan: L'Ether Vague.
       See Campos, Champagne, Coe, Gozlan and Pays, Knapp, Knowles, Kravetz,
       Long, Tancelin.

Gatti, Stephane

1987 *Gatti: Journal illustré d'une écriture*, Paris: La Parole Errante.

Gémier, Firmin

1925 *Le Théâtre*, Paris: Grasset.
      See Blanchart.

Genet, Jean

1947a *Les Bonnes* in *L'Arbalète* 12.
1947b *Haute Surveillance* in *La Nef* 28.
1951   *Oeuvres complètes II (Notre-dame des fleurs, Le Condamné à mort, Miracle de la rose, Un chant d'amour)*, Paris: Gallimard.
1954   *Les Bonnes* (including 'Préface à Pauvert'), Paris: Pauvert.
1956   *Le Balcon*, Décines: L'Arbalète.
1958   *Les Nègres*, Décines: L'Arbalète.
1960   *Les Nègres* (including 33 production photographs), Décines: L'Arbalète.
1961   *Les Paravents*, Décines: L'Arbalète.
1964   'Interview', *Playboy* 11(4): 454–53.
1966   *Lettres à Roger Blin* (including 26 production photographs of *Les Paravents*), Paris: Gallimard.
1968   *Oeuvres Complètes IV* (Includes *Le Balcon, Les Bonnes*, 'Comment jouer *Le Balcon*', 'Comment jouer *Les Bonnes*', *Lettres à Roger Blin*), Paris: Gallimard.
1977   'Jean Genet talks to Hubert Fichte', *The New Review* 37: 9–21.
1981   'Jean Genet par lui-même', *Magazine Littéraire* 174: 16–49.
       See Blin, Coe, Dort, Goldmann, *Obliques*, Thody, Vais, Walker.

Ghelderode, Michel de

1950–57 *Théâtre* (5 vols.), Paris: Gallimard.

Giraudoux, Jean

1982 *Théâtre Complet* (Pléiade edition), Paris: Gallimard.

Grand Magic Circus

1970 'Zartan, a scenario', *The Drama Review* 15(1): 88–91.
1972 *Zartan ou le frère mal aimé de Tarzan* and *Les Derniers Jours de solitude de Robinson Crusoe* in *L'Avant-Scène Théâtre* 496.
1974 *De Moise à Mao* in *L'Avant-Scène Théâtre* 539.
      See Savary.

Grumberg, Jean-Claude

1970   *Amorphe d'Ottenburg*, Paris: Stock.
1974   *Dreyfus*, Paris: Stock.
1975   *En r'venant d'l'Expo*, Paris: Stock.
1979a *Michu, Demain une fenêtre sur rue, Rixe, Chez Pierrot*, Paris: Stock.
1979b *L'Atelier*, Paris: Stock.

Bibliography

Haim, Victor

1971   *La Peau d'un fruit sur un arbre pourri*, Paris: Stock.
1979   *La Baignoire, La Servante*, Paris: Stock.

Halet, Pierre

1963   *La Provocation*, Bourges: Comédie de Bourges.
1965   *Le Cheval-caillou*, Bourges: Comédie de Bourges.
1967   *La Butte de Satory*, Paris: Seuil.
1968   *Little boy*, Paris: Seuil.
1970   *La Double Migration de Job Cardoso*, Paris: Seuil.

Ionesco, Eugène

1954   *Théâtre I (La Cantatrice chauve, La Leçon, Jacques ou la soumission, Les Chaises, Victimes du devoir, Amédée ou comment s'en débarrasser)*, Paris: Gallimard.
1958   *Théâtre II (L'Impromptu de l'Alma, Tueur sans gages, Le Nouveau Locataire, L'Avenir est dans les oeufs, Le Maître, La Jeune Fille à marier)*, Paris: Gallimard.
1962a *Notes et contre-notes*, Paris: Gallimard.
1962b *La Photo du colonel*, Paris: Gallimard.
1963   *Théâtre III (Rhinocéros, Le Piéton de l'air, Délire à deux, Le Tableau, Scène à quatre, Les Salutations, La Colère)*, Paris: Gallimard.
1964   *Notes and counternotes*, London: Calder.
1966a *Entretiens avec Claude Bonnefoy*, Paris: Belfond.
1966b *Théâtre IV (Le Roi se meurt, La Soif et la faim, La Lacune, Le Salon de l'automobile, L'Oeuf dur, Pour préparer un oeuf dur, Le Jeune Homme à marier, Apprendre à marcher)*, Paris: Gallimard.
1967   *Journal en miettes*, Paris: Mercure de France.
1968   *Présent passé, passé présent*, Paris: Mercure de France.
1973a *Théâtre V (Jeux de massacre, Macbett, La Vase, Exercices de conversation et de diction françaises pour étudiants américains)*, Paris: Gallimard.
1973b *Le Solitaire*, Paris: Mercure de France.
1975   *L'Homme aux valises, Ce formidable bordel*, Paris: Gallimard.
1977   *Antidotes*, Paris: Gallimard.
1978   'Dialogue sur le théâtre avec Jean-Louis Barrault', *The French Review* 51(4): 514–28.
1979   *Un homme en question*, Paris: Gallimard.
1981   *Théâtre VII, (Voyages chez les morts)*, Paris: Gallimard.
       See Coe, Hubert, Knowlson, Serreau.

Jarry, Alfred

1962   *Tout Ubu*, Paris: Livre de Poche.
       See Béhar, Schumacher, Vais.

Jourdheuil, Jean

1976   *L'Artiste, la politique, la production*, Paris: Union Générale d'Editions.
1979   *Le Théâtre, l'artiste, l'état*, Paris: Hachette.

Jouvet, Louis

1938   *Réflexions du comédien*, Paris: La Nouvelle Critique.
1952   *Témoignages sur le théâtre*, Paris: Flammarion.
1954   *Le Comédien désincarné*, Paris: Flammarion.

Kalisky, René

1969   *Trotsky etc. . .*, Paris: Gallimard.
1970   *Skandalon*, Paris: Gallimard.
1972   *Jim le téméraire*, Paris: Gallimard.
1973   *Le Pique-nique de Claretta*, Paris: Gallimard.
1978   *La Passion selon Pier Paolo Pasolini, Dave au bord de la mer*, Paris: Stock.
1983   *Falsch*, Paris: Théâtre National de Chaillot.

Koltès, Bernard-Marie

1980   *Combat de nègre et de chiens* and *La Nuit juste avant les forêts*, Paris: Stock.
1985   *Quai Ouest*, Paris: Minuit.
1986   *Dans la solitude des Champs de Coton*, Paris: Minuit.
1988   *Le Retour au désert*, Paris: Minuit.
1989   *Struggle of the Dogs and the Black* (trans. Matthew Ward), in *New French Plays*, ed. Bradby and Schumacher, London: Methuen.

Kraemer, Jacques

1970   *Splendeur et misère de Minette la bonne Lorraine*, Paris: Seuil (in collaboration with René Gaudy).
1973a   *Les Immigrés*, Honfleur: Oswald.
1973b   *Le Retour du Graully*, Honfleur: Oswald.
1974   *La Liquidation de Monsieur Joseph K., Jacotte ou les plaisirs de la vie quotidienne*, Honfleur: Oswald.
1975   *Noëlle de joie, Les Ciseaux d'Anastasie*, Honfleur: Oswald.
1977   *Les Histoires de l'oncle Jakob* in *L'Avant-Scène théâtre* 601: 3–24. *See* Miller.

Manet, Edouardo

1969   *Les Nonnes*, Paris: Gallimard.
1972   *Holocaustum ou le borgne*, Paris: Gallimard.
1973   *L'Autre Dom Juan*, Paris: Gallimard.
1975   *Madras, la nuit où*, Paris: Gallimard.
1979   *Un Balcon sur les Andes*, Paris: Stock.

Maréchal, Marcel

1974   *La Mise en théâtre*, Paris: Union Générale d'Editions.

Meyerhold, Vsevolod

1963   *Le Théâtre théâtral*, Paris: Gallimard.
        See Braun.

Bibliography

Michel, Georges

1963   *Les Jouets*, Paris: Gallimard.
1967   *La Promenade du dimanche*, Paris: Gallimard.
1968a *The Sunday walk* (trans. Jean Benedetti), London: Methuen.
1968b *L'Agression*, Paris: Gallimard.
1969   *Arbalètes et vieilles rapières*, Paris: Gallimard.
1970   *Un Petit Nid d'amour*, Paris: Gallimard.
1971   *La Ruée vers l'ordre* in *Travail Théâtral* 2: 84–118.
1975   *Lit cage*, Paris: Galilée.
1980   'Ecrire le quotidien de demain', *Atac informations* 113: 16–17.
       See Prendergast.

Mnouchkine, Ariane

1968   'Une prise de conscience', *Le Théâtre* 1: 119–26.
1971a 'Entretien avec Ariane Mnouchkine', *Travail Théâtral* 2: 3–14.
1971b 'L'Aventure du Théâtre du Soleil', *Preuves* 7: 119–27 (with Jean-Claude
       Penchenat).
1972   'An interview with Irving Wardle and a public discussion with Michael Kustow,
       Jonathan Miller, Kenneth Tynan, Arnold Wesker', *Performance* 2: 129–41.
1975   '*L'Age d'or*: the long journey from 1793–1975', *Theatre Quarterly* 5(18): 5–13.
1982   'Le Besoin d'une forme', *Théâtre Public* 46–7: 8–11.
       See Soleil.

Montherlant, Henry de

1958   *Théâtre* (Pléiade edition), Paris: Gallimard.

Nichet, Jacques

1981   'La Mise en pièces du document', *Théâtre Public*, 38: 14–26.

Obaldia, René de

1966–8 *Théâtre* (4 vols.), Paris: Grasset.

Pinget, Robert

1959   *Lettre morte*, Paris: Minuit.
1960   *La Manivelle*, Paris: Minuit.
1961   *Ici ou ailleurs*, *Architruc*, *L'Hypothèse*, Paris: Minuit.

Piscator, Erwin

1962   *Le Théâtre politique*, Paris: L'Arche.
1980   *The political theatre* (translated with chapter introductions and notes by Hugh
       Rorrison), London: Methuen.
       See Innes, Willett.

Planchon, Roger

1955   'Propos sur Bertolt Brecht', *Théâtre Populaire* 11: 65–7.
1959   'Notes pour *Dandin*', *Théâtre Populaire* 34: 47–50.

1962   'Orthodoxies', *Théâtre Populaire* 46: 117–34.
1969a   'La Mise en scène du *Tartuffe*', *Art et Education* (Lyon) 21: 16–18.
1969b   'Conversation avec Planchon: Le Living et Grotowski', *Art et Education* (Lyon) 21: 42–8.
1969c   'Journée débat avec Roger Planchon', *Art et Education* (Lyon) 22–3: 15–95.
1970   [Untitled text on Adamov], *Les Lettres Françaises* 25 March: 5.
1972   'Creating a theatre of real life', *Theatre Quarterly* 2(5): 46–55.
1973   *Le Cochon noir, La Remise*, Paris: Gallimard.
1974a   'Un théâtre qui mobilise', *Preuves* 18: 47–51.
1974b   '*Blues whites and reds*: the humours of a history play', *Theatre Quarterly* 4(15): 27–31.
1975a   *Gilles de Rais, L'Infâme*, Paris: Gallimard.
1975b   'Marx, les fruits et la spéculation. A propos de *Par-dessus bord*', *La Nouvelle Critique* 85: 34–7.
1977a   'Le Sens de la marche d'Arthur Adamov par lui-même', *La Nouvelle Critique* 100: 34–8.
1977b   'Taking on the T.N.P.', *Theatre Quarterly* 7(25): 29–33.
1977c   'D'Artaud à Racine', *Etudes* August: 217–34.
1981   'I'm a museum guard', *Performing Arts Journal* 16: 97–109.
        See Bataillon, Burgess, Copfermann, Daoust, Kowzan, Kustow, *Théâtre Populaire*.

Rezvani

1970a   *Le Rémora*, Paris: Stock.
1970b   *Théâtre (Body, L'Immobile, Le Cerveau)*, Paris: Bourgois.
1971   *Capitaine Schelle, Capitaine Eçço*, Paris: Stock.
1972   *Le Camp du drap d'or*, Paris: Stock.
1974   *La Colonie*, Paris: Stock.
1975   *Le Palais d'hiver*, Paris: Bourgois.

Salacrou, Armand

1943   *Théâtre III (Une femme libre, L'Inconnue d'Arras, Un homme comme les autres)*, Paris: Gallimard.
1945   *Théâtre IV (La Terre est ronde, Histoire de rire, La Marguerite)*, Paris: Gallimard.
1947   *Théâtre V (Les Fiancés du Havre, Le Soldat et la sorcière, Les Nuits de la colère)*, Paris: Gallimard.
1954   *Théâtre VI (L'Archipel Lenoir, Poof, Dieu le savait*, 'La Vie et la mort de Charles Dullin', 'Mes Certitudes et incertitudes'), Paris: Gallimard.
1957   *Théâtre VII (Pourquoi pas moi?, Sens interdit, Les Invités du bon Dieu, Le Miroir)*, Paris: Gallimard.
1966   *Théâtre VIII (Une femme trop honnête, Boulevard Durand, Comme les chardons)*, Paris: Gallimard.

Sarraute, Nathalie

1978   *Théâtre*, Paris: Gallimard.

Sarrazin, Maurice

1970   *Comédien dans une troupe*, Toulouse: Grenier.

Bibliography

Sartre, Jean-Paul

1943   *L'Etre et le néant*, Paris: Gallimard.
1947a *Théâtre I (Les Mouches, Huis clos, Morts sans sépulture, La Putain respectueuse)*, Paris: Gallimard.
1947b *Situations I*, Paris: Gallimard.
1948   *Les Mains sales*, Paris: Gallimard.
1951   *Le Diable et le bon Dieu*, Paris: Gallimard.
1952   *Saint Genet comédien et martyr*, Paris: Gallimard.
1954   *Kean*, Paris: Gallimard.
1956   *Nekrassov*, Paris: Gallimard.
1960a *Les Séquestrés d'Altona*, Paris: Gallimard.
1960b *Critique de la raison dialectique*, Paris: Gallimard.
1965   *Les Troyennes*, Paris: Gallimard.
1969   'Dullin et *Les Mouches*', *Le Nouvel Observateur* 8 December.
1973   *Un Théâtre de situations*, Paris: Gallimard (idées).
1974   *Between Existentialism and Marxism*, London: New Left Books.
        See Contat and Rybalka, Jeanson, McCall, Palmer, Thody.

Savary, Jérome

1972   'Une grande fête pour adultes tristes', *Preuves* 11(3): 137–45.
1974   *Album du Grand Magic Circus*, Paris: Belfond.

Schéhadé, Georges

1951   *Monsieur Bob'le*, Paris: Gallimard.
1954   *La Soirée des proverbes*, Paris: Gallimard.
1957   *Histoire de Vasco*, Paris: Gallimard.
1960   *Les Violettes*, Paris: Gallimard.
1961   *Le Voyage*, Paris: Gallimard.
1965   *L'Emigré de Brisbane*, Paris: Gallimard.

Serreau, Jean-Marie

1974   'Jean-Marie Serreau aux Amandiers', *Atac informations* 55: 31–2.
        See Auclaire-Tamaroff, Laville, Masson.

Soleil

1967   *La Cuisine* in *L'Avant-Scène Théâtre* 385.
1971a *1789*, Paris: Stock.
1971b 'Où est la différence?' *Travail Théâtral* 2: 15–20.
1972a *1793*, Paris: Stock.
1972b 'La Justice telle qu'on la rend' *Esprit* 40 (417): 524–55.
1973   *1789* and *1793* in *L'Avant-Scène Théâtre* 526–7.
1975   *L'Age d'or*, Paris: Stock.
1979   *Mephisto*, Paris: Solin.
        See Bablet, *Esprit*, Mnouchkine, Mounier, Temkine, *Travail Théâtral*.

Tardieu, Jean

1955   *Théâtre de chambre*, Paris: Gallimard.
1960   *Poèmes à jouer*, Paris: Gallimard.

1975 Une soirée en Provence, Paris: Gallimard.
1978 Le Professeur Froeppel, Paris: Gallimard.

Vauthier, Jean

1955 Le Personnage combattant, Paris: Gallimard.
1958 Les Prodiges, Paris: Gallimard.
1960 Le Rêveur, Paris: Gallimard.
1966 Capitaine Bada and Badadesques, Paris: Gallimard.
1967 Médéa, Paris: Gallimard.
1970 Le Sang, Paris: Gallimard.

Vian, Boris

1965–71 Théâtre (2 vols.), Paris: Union Générale d'Editions.

Vilar, Jean

1955 De la tradition théâtrale, Paris: L'Arche.
1971 Chronique Romanesque, Paris: Grasset.
1972 Mot pour mot, Paris: Stock.
1975 Le Théâtre, service public, Paris: Gallimard.
1981 Mémento, Paris: Gallimard
      See Leclerc, Serrière, Wehle.

Vinaver, Michel

1956 Les Coréens, Paris: Gallimard.
1958 Les Huissiers in Théâtre Populaire 29.
1960 Iphigénie Hotel in Théâtre Populaire 39; version scénique: Gallimard, 1963.
1972 Par-dessus bord, Paris: L'Arche.
1973 La Demande d'emploi, Paris: L'Arche.
1975 'Marx, les fruits et la spéculation. A propos de Par-dessus bord', La Nouvelle Critique, 85: 34–7.
1978 Théâtre de chambre (Dissident, il va sans dire and Nina, c'est autre chose), Paris: L'Arche.
1979 Les Travaux et les jours, Paris: L'Arche.
1980 A la renverse, Lausanne: Editions de l'Aire.
1982 Ecrits sur le théâtre, ed. Michelle Henry, Lausanne: Editions de l'Aire.
1983 L'Ordinaire, Lausanne: Editions de l'Aire.
1986 Théâtre Complet (2 vols.), Arles: Actes Sud.
1987 Des mille maux dont souffre l'édition théâtrale et des trente-sept remèdes pour l'en soulager, Arles: Actes Sud.
1989a Portrait of a woman (Portrait d'une femme, trans. Donald Watson), in New French Plays, ed. Bradby and Schumacher, London: Methuen.
1989b Les Voisins, précédé de: entretien avec Jean-Loup Rivière, St Imier, Switzerland: Canevas.
1990a L'Emission de télévision, Arles: Actes Sud.
1990b Le Dernier Sursaut, Arles: Actes Sud.
      See Ubersfeld.

Vitez, Antoine

1981 De Chaillot à Chaillot (with Emile Copfermann) Paris: Hachette.
      See Benhamou.

Bibliography

Weingarten, Romain

1967   L'Eté, Akara, Les Nourrices, Paris: Bourgois.

Wenzel, Jean-Paul.

1975a   Loin d'Hagondange, Paris: Stock.
1975b   Marianne attend le mariage, Paris: Stock.
1981   Doublages, Paris: Albin Michel.
1982   'D'une écriture à l'autre', Partenaires 4: 12–13.
1983   Vater Land, Paris: Théâtre Ouvert.

Yacine, Kateb

1959   Le Cercle des représailles (Le Cadavre encerclé, La Poudre d'intelligence, Les
        Ancêtres redoublent de férocité, Le Vautour), Paris: Seuil.
1970   L'Homme aux sandales de caoutchouc, Paris: Seuil.

SECTION 2: CRITICS AND THEATRE HISTORIANS

Abirached, Robert

1978   La Crise du personnage dans le théâtre moderne, Paris: Grasset.

Abirached, Robert, Ruhe, Emstpeter and Schwaderer, Richard

1983   Lectures d'Adamov, Tübingen: Gunter Narr; and Paris: Jean-Michel Place.

Allen, John

1981   Theatre in Europe, Eastbourne: John Offord.

Anders, France

1959   Jacques Copeau et le Cartel des quatre, Paris: Nizet.

Architecture d'Aujourd'hui

1970   Oct.–Nov. no. spéc.: 'Les Lieux du spectacle'.

Aristotle

1920   On the art of poetry, trans. Bywater, Oxford: Clarendon Press.

Aronson, Arnold

1981   'Theatres of the future', Theatre Journal 33(4): 489–503.

Arnaud, Lucien

1959   Charles Dullin, Paris: L'Arche.

Aslan, Odette

1970 *'Le Cimetière des voitures'* in *Les Voies de la création théâtrale I*, Paris:
C.N.R.S.: 309–40.
1972 *'Les Paravents* de Jean Genet' in *Les Voies de la création théâtrale III*, Paris:
C.N.R.S.: 11–107.
1973 *Jean Genet*, Paris: Seghers.
1974 *L'Acteur au vingtième siècle*, Paris: Seghers.
1975 *'Les Bonnes* de Jean Genet mise en scène de Victor Garcia' in *Les Voies de la création théâtrale IV*, Paris: C.N.R.S.: 103–315 (in collaboration with others).
1988 *Roger Blin*, Cambridge: University Press.

Asmus, Walter D.

1975 'Beckett directs *Godot'*, *Theatre Quarterly* 5 (19): 19–26.

Auclaire-Tamaroff, Elizabeth and Barthélémy

1986 *Jean-Marie Serreau: découvreur de théâtres*, Paris: L'Arbre Verdoyant.

Bablet, Denis

1970 etc. (editor) *Les Voies de la création théâtrale*, Paris: C.N.R.S.
1975 *Les Révolutions scéniques du XXe siècle*, Paris Société International d'Art XXe siècle.

Bablet, Denis and Jacquot, Jean (editors)

1969 *Le Lieu théâtral dans la société moderne*, Paris: C.N.R.S.

Bablet, Denis and Marie-Louise

1979 *Le Théâtre du Soleil* ('Diapolivre'), Paris: C.N.R.S.

Baecque, André de

1964 *Le Théâtre d'aujourd'hui*, Paris: Seghers.
1967 *Les Maisons de la culture*, Paris: Seghers.

Bair, Deirdre

1980 *Samuel Beckett*, London: Pan.

Banu, Georges

1984 *Le Théâtre, sorties de secours*, Paris: Aubier.

Barthes, Roland

1953 *Le Degré zéro de l'écriture*, Paris: Seuil.
1957 *Mythologies*, Paris: Seuil.
1959 'Le Soulier de satin', *Théâtre Populaire* 33: 121–3.
1960 'Le Balcon', *Théâtre Populaire* 38: 96–8.
1964a *Essais critiques*, Paris: Seuil.

Bibliography

1964b *Eléments de sémiologie*, Paris: Seuil.
1971 'Réponses', *Tel Quel* 47: 89–107.
1977 *Image – music – text*, London: Fontana.
1978 'Note sur *Aujourd'hui*', *Travail Théâtral* 30: 58–60.

Bataillon, Michel

1982 *Expoplanchon* (catalogue of exhibition), Vénissieux: Centre Culturel.
1983 'Arthur Adamov et Roger Planchon' in Abirached *et al.*, *Lectures d'Adamov*.

Behar, Henri

1980 *Jarry dramaturge*, Paris: Nizet.

Benhamou, Anne-Françoise, *et al.*

1981 *Antoine Vitez: toutes les mises en scène*, Paris: Godefroy.

Benjamin, Walter

1969 *Essais sur Bertolt Brecht*, Paris: Maspéro.
1973 *Understanding Brecht*, London: New Left Books.

Berenguer, Angel

1977 *L'Exil et la Cérémonie dans le premier théâtre d'Arrabal*, Paris: Union Générale d'Editions.

Bishop, Thomas

1960 *Pirandello and the French theatre*, New York: University Press.

Blanchart, Paul

1954 *Firmin Gémier*, Paris: L'Arche.

Borgal, Clément

1960 *Jacques Copeau*, Paris: L'Arche.
1963 *Metteurs en scène*, Paris: Lanore.

Bradby, David

1975 *Adamov*, London: Grant and Cutler (Research Bibliographies and Checklists).
1983 'Finita la Commedia – l'emploi du jeu dans le théâtre Adamovien des années soixante' in Abirached *et al.*, *Lectures d'Adamov*.

Bradby, David and McCormick, John

1978 *People's theatre*, London: Croom Helm.

Bradby, David and Williams, David

1988 *Directors' theatre*, London: Macmillan.

Braun, Edward

1969   *Meyerhold on theatre*, London: Methuen.
1979   *The theatre of Meyerhold*, London: Methuen.
1982   *The director and the stage*, London: Methuen.

Brenner, Jacques

1978   *Histoire de la littérature française de 1940 à nos jours*, Paris: Fayard.

Burgess, John

1974a   'Roger Planchon's *The black pig* at Villeurbanne', *Theatre Quarterly* 4(14):
        56–86.
1974b   'Paris', *Plays and Players* November 1974, 37–8.
1976   'Roger Planchon's *Gilles de Rais* at Villeurbanne', *Theatre Quarterly* 6(22):
        3–24.
1977   '*Loin d'Hagondange*', *Plays and Players* 24(9): 34.

Busson, Alain

1986   *Le Théâtre en France: contexte socio-économique et choix esthétiques*, Paris: La
       Documentation française.

Cacérès, Beningno

1967   *L'Espoir au coeur*, Paris: Seuil.

Campos, Christophe

1976   'What Gatti did next: the wild ducks of Saint–Nazaire', *Theatre Quarterly*
       8(31): 7–16.

Campos, Christophe and Sadler, Michael

1981   'The complex theatre of Antoine Vitez', *Theatre Quarterly* 10(40): 79–96.

Cavell, Stanley

1969   *Must we mean what we say?*, New York: Scribner.

Chambers, Ross

1965a   'A Lebensraum for love: the work of Gabriel Cousin' *Meanjin* (Melbourne) 4:
        473–81.
1965b   'Antonin Artaud and the contemporary French theatre' in *Aspects of Drama
        and Theatre*, Sydney: University Press: 113–42.

Champagne, Lenora

1981   'Armand Gatti: toward spectacle without spectators', *Theater* 13(1): 26–42.

Bibliography

Chancerel, Léon

1953   *Jean-Louis Barrault*, Paris: Presses Littéraires de France.

Coe, Richard

1968   *The vision of Jean Genet*, London: Peter Owen.
1970   *The theatre of Jean Genet: a casebook*, New York: Grove Press.
1971   *Ionesco: a study of his plays*, London: Methuen (revised).
1983   'The theatre of the last chance: catastrophe-theory in the plays of Armand Gatti', *Australian Journal of French Studies* 20(1): 71–92.

Cohn, Ruby

1980   *Just play: Beckett's theatre*, Princeton: University Press.
1987   *From Desire to Godot: pocket theatres of postwar Paris*, Berkeley and Los Angeles: University of California Press.

Contat, Michel and Rybalka, Michel

1970   *Les Ecrits de Sartre*, Paris: Gallimard.

Copfermann, Emile

1977   *Théâtres de Roger Planchon*, Paris: Union Générale d'Editions (revised edition).
1989   'La Décentralisation' in Jomaron, *Le Théâtre en France*.

Corvin, Michel

1963   *Le Théâtre nouveau en France*, Paris: Presses Universitaires de France.
1989   'Une Ecriture plurielle' in Jomaron, *Le Théâtre en France*.

Da Costa, Bernard

1978   *Histoire du Café-Théâtre*, Paris: Buchet-Chastel.

Daoust, Yvette

1981   *Roger Planchon*, Cambridge: University Press.

Davison, Peter

1965   'Contemporary drama and popular dramatic forms' in *Aspects of Drama and Theatre*, Sydney: University Press: 143–97.
1983   *Contemporary drama and the popular dramatic tradition in England*, London: Macmillan.

Delcampe, Armand

1973   'La Colonne Durruti-Gatti', *Travail Théâtral* 10: 129–38.

298

Section 2: critics and theatre historians

Demarcy, Richard

1973   Eléments d'une sociologie du spectacle, Paris: Union Générale d'Editions.

Dhomme, Sylvain

1959   La Mise en scène contemporaine d'André Antoine à Bertolt Brecht, Paris: Nathan.

Domenach, Jean-Marie

1967   Le Retour du tragique, Paris: Seuil.

Dort, Bernard

1960   Lecture de Brecht, Paris: Seuil.
1967   Théâtre public, Paris: Seuil.
1971   Théâtre réel, Paris: Seuil.
1974   'Entre la magie et l'histoire', Travail Théâtral 17: 49–51.
1979   Le Théâtre en jeu, Paris: Seuil.
1980   'Entre la nostalgie et l'utopie: esquisse pour une histoire du théâtre français au XXe siècle', Cahiers Théâtre Louvain 43: 7–35.
1988   La Représentation émancipée, Arles: Actes Sud.
1989   'L'Age de la représentation' in Jomaron, La Théâtre en France.

Duvignaud, Jean

1965   Sociologie du théâtre, Paris: Presses Universitaires de France.
1966   L'Acteur, esquisse d'une sociologie du comédien, Paris: Gallimard.
1970   Spectacle et société, Paris: Denoel.
1973   Fêtes et civilisations, Paris: Weber.
1974   Le Théâtre contemporain, Paris: Larousse (with Jean Lagoutte).

Eagleton, Terry

1976   Marxism and literary criticism, London: Methuen.
1983   Literary theory, Oxford: Blackwell.

Esprit

1965   Esprit 33 (338), 'Notre théâtre: Théâtre moderne et public populaire'.
1975   Esprit 43 (447), 'Théâtre et création collective'.

Esslin, Martin

1976   Artaud, London: Fontana.
1980   The Theatre of the Absurd, Harmondsworth: Penguin (revised edition).

Bibliography

Fanon, Frantz

1952   *Peau noire, masques blancs*, Paris: Seuil.
1961   *Les Damnés de la terre*, Paris: Maspéro.

Fletcher, John (editor)

1972   *Forces in modern French drama*, London: University Press.

Fletcher, John and Spurling, John

1972   *Beckett. A study of his plays*, London: Methuen.

Frank, André

1971   *Jean-Louis Barrault*, Paris: Seghers.

Freeman, Edward

1971   *The theatre of Albert Camus*, London: Methuen.

Gaudibert, Pierre

1972   *Action culturelle. Intégration et/ou subversion*, Paris: Casterman

Gaudy, René

1967   'Planchon répète', *La Nouvelle Critique* 1: 54–7.
1971   *Arthur Adamov*, Paris: Stock.

Gignoux, Hubert

1946   *Jean Anouilh*, Paris: Temps Présent.

Godard, Colette

1971   *Lavelli*, Paris: Bourgois (with Dominique Nores).
1977   'Patrice Chéreau: poets invent the future', *The Drama Review* 21(T–74): 25–44.
1980   *Le Théâtre depuis 1968*, Paris: Lattès.

Goldmann, Lucien

1970   'Le Théâtre de Genet. Essai d'étude sociologique' in *Structures mentales et création culturelle*, Paris: Maspéro.

Gontard, Denis

1973   *La Décentralisation théâtrale en France*, Paris: SEDES.
1974   *Le Journal de bord des Copiaus*, Paris: Seghers.

Gouhier, Henri

1943   *L'Essence du théâtre*, Paris: Plon.

Gozlan, Gérard and Pays, Jean-Louis

1970   *Gatti aujourd'hui*, Paris: Seuil.

Gripari, Pierre

1979   *Café-Théâtre*, Lausanne: L'Age d'Homme.

Guicharnaud, Jacques and June

1967   *Modern French theatre from Giraudoux to Genet*, New Haven and London: Yale University Press (revised edition).

Gunthert, André

1983   *Le Voyage du Théâtre National de Strasbourg*, Paris: Solin.

Harris, Rodney

1973   *L'Humanisme dans le théâtre d'Aimé Césaire*, Ottawa: Naaman.

Henderson, John

1971   *The first avant-garde*, London: Harrap.

Hill, Victoria

1978   *Bertolt Brecht and post-war French drama*, Stuttgart: Hans-Dieter Heinz.

Howarth, William

1972   'Anouilh' in *Forces in modern French drama*, ed. Fletcher, London: University Press.

Hubert, Marie-Claude

1987   *Language et corps fantasmé dans le théâtre des années 50: Beckett, Ionesco, Adamov*, Paris: Corti.
1988   *Le Théâtre*, Paris: Colin.
1990   *Eugène Ionesco*, Paris: Seuil.

Hufner, Agnes

1968   *Brecht in Frankreich 1930–63*, Stuttgart: Metzlersche.

Innes, Christopher

1972   *Erwin Piscator's political theatre*, Cambridge: University Press.
1979   *Modern German drama*, Cambridge: University Press.
1981   *Holy theatre*, Cambridge: University Press.

Inskip, Donald

1958   *Jean Giraudoux: the making of a dramatist*, Oxford: University Press.

Bibliography

Jacquart, Emmanuel

1974   *Le Théâtre de dérision*, Paris: Gallimard.

Jeanson, Francis

1955   *Sartre par lui-même*, Paris: Seuil.
1973   *L'Action culturelle dans la cité*, Paris: Seuil.

Jeffery, David

1976   'Evolution in the theatre of Gabriel Cousin', *Theatre Research International* 1(3): 205–15.
1977   'Les Compagnons de la Saint-Jean: an experiment in popular theatre', *Modern Languages*, 58(3): 123–9.
1980   *Social drama in France in the new subsidised theatres 1945–68 with special reference to the work of Gabriel Cousin.* Ph.D. Thesis for Bedford College, London University.
1984a   'Théâtre Ouvert', *Theatre Research International* 9(1).
1984b   'Gabriel Cousin: sa conception du théâtre populaire', *Zagadnienia Rodzajow Literackich.*

Jomaron, Jacqueline

1981   *La Mise en scène contemporaine II*, Bruxelles: Renaissance du Livre.
1989   *Le Théâtre en France* (2 vols.), Paris: Colin.

Knapp, Bettina

1975   *Off-stage voices*, New York: Whitston.

Knowles, Dorothy

1967   *French Drama of the inter-war years 1918–39*, London: Harrap.
1971   'Michel Parent and theatrical experiments in simultaneity', *Theatre Research* 11(1): 23–41.
1972   'Principles of staging' in *Forces in modern French drama*, (ed.) Fletcher, London: University Press.
1975a   'Le Théâtre, lieu d'une prise de conscience du monde contemporain', *Zagadnienia Rodzajow Literackich* 18(1): 25–30.
1975b   'Ritual theatre: Fernando Arrabal and the Latin Americans', *The Modern Language Review* 70(3): 526–38.
1976   'Le Théâtre, miroir du monde contemporain', *Synthesis* (Bucharest) 3: 179–91.
1989   *Armand Gatti in the theatre*, London: Athlone.

Knowlson, James

1972   'Ionesco' in *Forces in modern French drama*, (ed.) Fletcher. London: University Press.

Kowzan, Tadeusz

1978   '*Le Tartuffe* de Molière mise en scène de Roger Planchon' in *Les Voies de la création théâtrale VI*, Paris: C.N.R.S. 279–340.

302

Kravetz, Marc

1987   *L'Aventure de la parole errante*, Toulouse: L'Ether vague.

Kustow, Michael

1972   'Life and work of an illuminated man', *Theatre Quarterly* 2(5): 42–5.

Lang, Jack

1968   *L'Etat et le théâtre*, Paris: Librairie Générale de droit et de jurisprudence.
1978   *Eclats* (with Jean-Denis Bredin), Paris: Simoen.

Larthomas, Pierre

1972   *Le Langage dramatique, sa nature, ses procédés*, Paris: Colin.

Laurent, Jeanne

1955   *La République et les beaux-arts*, Paris: Julliard.

Laville, Pierre

1970   'Aimé Césaire et Jean-Marie Serreau, un acte politique et poétique', *Les Voies de la Création Théâtral* II, Paris: C.N.R.S.

Leclerc, Guy

1971   *Le T.N.P. de Jean Vilar*, Paris: Union Générale d'Editions.

Long, Joseph

1979   'Armand Gatti: theatre without walls', *Threshold* 30: 6–20.

Louzon, Myriam

1977   '*Fin de partie* de Samuel Beckett. Effacement du monde et dynamisme formel', *Les Voies de la création théâtrale* V, Paris: C.N.R.S.: 377–445.

McCall, Dorothy

1969   *The Theatre of Jean-Paul Sartre*, New York and London: Columbia University Press.

Madral, Philippe

1969   *Le Théâtre hors les murs*, Paris: Seuil.

Malachy, Thérèse

1978   *Jean Anouilh. Les problèmes de l'existence dans un théâtre de marionettes*, Paris: Nizet.

Marsh, Patrick

1981   'Le Théâtre à Paris sous l'occupation allemande', *Revue de la Société d'histoire du théâtre* 33(3): 197–369.

Bibliography

Masson, Joel

1966 'Les Aventures et inventions de Jean-Marie Serreau', *Loisir* (Caen) 24: 12–13.

Mbom, Clément

1979 *Le Théâtre d'Aimé Césaire*, Paris: Nathan.

Mélèze, Pierre

1973 *Adamov*, Paris: Seghers.

Merle, P.

1985 *Le Café-Théâtre*, Paris: Presses Universitaires de France.

Mignon, Paul-Louis

1953 *Jean Dasté*, Paris: Presses Littéraires de France.

Miller, Judith

1977 *Theatre and revolution in France since 1968*, Lexington: French Forum.
1981 'From novel to theatre: contemporary adaptations of narrative to the French stage', *Theatre Journal* 33(4): 431–52.

Mounier, Catherine

1977 'Deux créations collectives du Théâtre du Soleil: *1793, L'Age d'or*,' *Les Voies de la création théâtrale V*, Paris, C.N.R.S.: 121–278.

Moussinac, Léon

1966 *Le Théâtre des origines à nos jours*, Paris: Flammarion.

Obliques

1972 *Genet* (special issue): 2.
1976 *Artaud* (special issue): 10–11.

O'Connor, Garry

1971 'Press reactions (to *Rabelais*) December '68', *Theatre Quarterly* 1(3): 97–8.
1975 *French theatre today*, London: Pitman.

Palmer, Jeremy

1970 '*Les Séquestrés d'Altona*: Sartre's black tragedy', *French Studies*, 24(2): 150–62.

Partisans

1967 *Partisans* 36, 'Théâtres et politique'.
1969 *Partisans* 47, 'Théâtres et politique bis'.

Pavis, Patrice

1976   *Problèmes de sémiologie théâtrale*, Quebec: Presses Universitaires.
1979   'Notes towards a semiotic analysis', *The Drama Review*, 84: 93–104.
1980   *Dictionnaire du théâtre*, Paris: Editions Sociales.
1981   'The Interplay between avant-garde theatre and semiology', *Performing Arts Journal*, 15: 75–86.

Pestre de Almeida, Lilian

1982   'Le Comique et le tragique dans le théâtre d'Aimé Césaire', *Présence Africaine* 121–2: 180–92.

Pierron, Agnès

1977   *Maréchal*, Lausanne: L'Age d'Homme.

Polieri, Jacques

1971   *Scénographie-sémiographie*, Paris: Denoel.

Prendergast, Christopher (editor)

1971   *La Promenade du dimanche* by Georges Michel, London: Methuen.

Puaux, Paul

1983   *Avignon en festivals*, Paris: Hachette.

Reid, Alec

1968   *All I could manage more than I could. An approach to the plays of Samuel Beckett*, Dublin: Dolmen press.

Robbe-Grillet, Alain

1963   *Pour un nouveau roman*, Paris: Minuit.

Roubine, Jean-Jacques

1980   *Théâtre et mise en scène 1880–1980*, Paris: Presses Universitaires de France.
1985   *L'Art du comédien*, Paris: Presses Universitaires de France.

Sandier, Gilles

1970   *Théâtre et combat*, Paris: Stock.
1982   *Le Théâtre en crise*, Grenoble: La Pensée Sauvage.

Sarrazac, Jean-Pierre

1975   'L'Ecriture au présent', *Travail Théâtral*, 18–19: 55–85.
1976   'L'Ecriture au présent', *Travail Théâtral*, 24–25: 88–102.
1981   *L'Avenir du drame*, Lausanne: L'Aire.

Bibliography

Schumacher, Claude

1988   *Jarry and Apollinaire*, London: Macmillan.
1989   *Artaud on theatre*, London: Methuen.

Serreau, Geneviève

1966   *Histoire du 'nouveau théâtre'*, Paris: Gallimard.

Serrière, Marie-Thérèse

1959   *Le T.N.P. et nous*, Paris: Corti.

Simon, Alfred

1976   *Les Signes et les songes*, Paris: Seuil.
1979   *Le Théâtre à bout de souffle*, Paris: Seuil.
1983   *Beckett*, Paris: Belfond.

Surer, Paul

1969   *Cinquante ans de théâtre (1919–1969)*, Paris: SEDES.

Surgers, A.

1982   *La Comédie française*, Paris: Hachette.

Tancelin, Philippe (editor)

1989   *Théâtre sur paroles*, Toulouse: L'Ether vague.

Temkine, Raymonde

1967   *L'Entreprise théâtre*, Paris: Cujas.
1968   *Grotowski*, Lausanne: La Cité.
1970   'La Commune au théâtre', *Europe* 499–500: 210–26.
1977   *Mettre en scène au présent I*, Lausanne: La Cité.
1979   *Mettre en scène au présent II*, Lausanne: La Cité.

Théâtre Populaire

1970   *Itinéraire de Roger Planchon*, Paris: L'Arche.

Theatre Quarterly

1976   *Theatre Quarterly* 6(23), 'People's theatre in France since 1870'.

Thody, Philip

1960   *Jean-Paul Sartre. A literary and political study*, London: Hamish Hamilton.
1961   *Albert Camus 1913–60*, London: Hamish Hamilton.
1968   *Jean Genet. A study of his novels and plays*, London: Hamish Hamilton.
1971   *Sartre. A biographical introduction*, London: Studio Vista
1977   *Roland Barthes. A conservative estimate*, London: Macmillan.

306

Travail Théâtral

1976   *Différent: le Théâtre du Soleil*, Lausanne: La Cité.

Ubersfeld, Anne

1978a   *Lire le théâtre*, Paris: Editions Sociales.
1978b   *L'Objet théâtral*, Paris: Centre National pour la Documentation Pédagogique.
1979   *L'Espace théâtral* (with Georges Banu), Paris: Centre National pour la Documentation Pédagogique.
1981   *L'Ecole du spectateur*, Paris: Editions Sociales.
1990   *Vinaver dramaturge*, Paris: Librairie Théâtrale.

Vais, Michel

1978   *L'Ecrivain scénique*, Quebec: Presses Universitaires.

Vandromme, Paul

1965   *Jean Anouilh: un auteur et ses personnages*, Paris: La Table Ronde.

Veinstein, André

1955   *La Mise en scène théâtrale et sa condition esthétique*, Paris: Flammarion.
1968   *Le Théâtre expérimental: tendances et propositions*, Bruxelles: La Renaissance du Livre.

Vernois, Paul (editor)

1974   *L'Onirisme et l'insolite dans le théâtre français moderne*, Paris: Klincksiek.

Vessilier, Michèle

1973   *La Crise du théâtre privé*, Paris: Presses Universitaires de France.

Virmaux, Alain

1970   *Antonin Artaud et le théâtre*, Paris: Seghers.
1977   *Antonin Artaud et le théâtre*, Paris: Union Générale d'Editions.
1979   *Artaud: un bilan critique*, Paris: Belfond.
1980   *Artaud vivant*, Paris: Nouvelles Editions Oswald.

Walker, David (editor)

1982   *Le Balcon* by Jean Genet, London: Methuen.

Wallis, Roger

1971   'Jean-Louis Barrault's *Rabelais*', *Theatre Quarterly* 1(3): 83–97.

Webb, Richard

1976   *Experimental theatre in France 1945–75*, Ph.D. Thesis, University of Hull.

Bibliography

Wehle, Philippa

1981   *Le Théâtre populaire selon Jean Vilar*, Avignon: Barthélemy.

Weightman, John

1973   *The concept of the avant-garde*, London: Alcove.

Willett, John

1959   *The theatre of Bertolt Brecht*, London: Methuen.
1967   *The theatre of Bertolt Brecht*, London: Methuen (revised ed.).
1973   *Brecht on theatre* (ed. and trans.), London: Methuen.
1978   *The theatre of Erwin Piscator*, London: Methuen.

Williams, Raymond

1968   *Drama from Ibsen to Brecht*, London: Chatto and Windus.
1972   *Drama in performance*, Harmondsworth: Penguin.
1976   *Keywords*, Glasgow: Fontana.
1981   *Culture*, Glasgow: Fontana.

Historical table of productions referred to in this book

Date	Author	Title	Director	Theatre (in Paris except where specified)
1940	Anouilh	Le Bal des voleurs (revival)	André Barsacq	Atelier
	Cocteau	Les Monstres sacrés	André Brulé	Michel
	Corneille	Le Cid	Jacques Copeau	Comédie Française
1941	Obey	800 Mètres	Jean-Louis Barrault	Stade Roland-Garros
	Cocteau	La Machine à écrire	Jean Cocteau	Hébertot
1942	Giraudoux	L'Apollon de Marsac	Louis Jouvet	Rio de Janeiro
	Montherlant	La Reine morte	Pierre Dux	Comédie Française
	Vermorel	Jeanne avec nous	George Douking	Comédie des Champs-Elysées
1943	Cocteau	Renaud et Armide	Jean Cocteau	Comédie Française
	Copeau	Le Miracle du pain doré	Jacques Copeau	Hospice de Beaune
	Claudel	Le Soulier de satin	Jean-Louis Barrault	Comédie Française
	Giraudoux	Sodome et Gomorrhe	George Douking	Hébertot
	Sartre	Les Mouches	Charles Dullin	Cité (Sarah-Bernhardt)
	Strindberg	The dance of death	Jean Vilar	Private room
	Strindberg	Storm	Jean Vilar	Poche
1944	Anouilh	Antigone	André Barsacq	Atelier
	Camus	Le Malentendu	Marcel Herrand	Mathurins
	Sartre	Huis clos	Raymond Rouleau	Vieux-Colombier
1945	Camus	Caligula	Paul Oettly	Hébertot
	Eliot	Murder in the cathedral	Jean Vilar	Vieux-Colombier
	Giraudoux	La Folle de Chaillot	Louis Jouvet	Athénée
	Obey	Noé (revival)	Jean Dasté	Grenoble
	Salacrou	Le Soldat et la sorcière	Charles Dullin	Sarah-Bernhardt
	Strindberg	The dance of death (revival)	Jean Vilar	Noctambules
1946	Audiberti	Quoat-Quoat	André Reybaz	Gaîté-Montparnasse
	Plautus	The Carthaginian	Maurice Sarrazin	Grenier de Toulouse
	Salacrou	Les Nuits de la colère	Jean-Louis Barrault	Marigny
	Shakespeare	Hamlet	Jean-Louis Barrault	Marigny

Date	Author	Title	Director	Theatre (in Paris except where specified)
1947	Anouilh	L'Invitation au château	André Barsacq	Atelier
	Audiberti	Le Mal court	Georges Vitaly	Poche
	Brecht	The exception and the rule	Jean-Marie Serreau	Noctambules
	Daudet	L'Arlésienne	André Clavé	Centre Dramatique de l'Est (Strasbourg)
	Genet	Les Bonnes }	Louis Jouvet	Athénée
	Giraudoux	L'Apollon de Bellac }		
1948	Gide (ad. Kafka)	Le Procès	Jean-Louis Barrault	Marigny
	Pichette	Les Epiphanies	Georges Vitaly	Noctambules
	Shakespeare	Richard II	Jean Vilar	Avignon festival
	Buchner	Danton's death	Jean Vilar	Avignon festival
	Camus	L'Etat de siège	Jean-Louis Barrault	Marigny
	Claudel	Partage de midi	Jean-Louis Barrault	Marigny
	Montherlant	Le Maître de Santiago	Paul Oettly	Hébertot
	Sartre	Les Mains sales	Pierre Valde	Antoine
1949	Camus	Les Justes	Paul Oettly	Hébertot
	Corneille	Le Cid	Jean Vilar	Avignon festival
	Genet	Haute Surveillance	Jean Genet and Jean Marchat	Mathurins
1950	Ghelderode	Fastes d'enfer	André Reybaz	Atelier
	Adamov	La Grande et la Petite Manoewvre	Jean-Marie Serreau	Noctambules
	Adamov	L'Invasion	Jean Vilar	Studio des Champs-Elysées
	Ionesco	La Cantatrice chauve	Nicolas Bataille	Noctambules
	Salacrou	Poof	Yves Robert	Edouard VII
	Synge	The playboy of the western world	Hubert Gignoux	Comédie de l'Ouest (Rennes)
1951	Brecht	Mother Courage	Jean Vilar	T.N.P. Chaillot
	Claudel	L'Echange	Jean-Louis Barrault	Marigny
	Ionesco	La Leçon	Marcel Cuvelier	Poche
	Schéhadé	Monsieur Bob'le	Georges Vitaly	Huchette
	Sartre	Le Diable et le bon Dieu	Louis Jouvet	Antoine

1952	Adamov	*La Parodie*	Roger Blin	Lancry
	Gide (ad. Kafka)	*Le Château*	Jean-Louis Barrault	Marigny
	Ionesco	*Les Chaises*	Sylvain Dhomme	Lancry
	Pichette	*Nucléa*	Gérard Philipe	T.N.P. Chaillot
	Ponson du Terrail	*Rocambole*	Roger Planchon	Comédie (Lyon)
	Vauthier	*Capitaine Bada*	André Reybaz	Poche
	Vauthier	*La Nouvelle Mandragore*	Gérard Philipe	T.N.P. Chaillot
1953	Adamov	*Le Professeur Taranne* } *Le Sens de la marche* }	Roger Planchon	Comédie (Lyon)
	Adamov	*Tous contre tous*	Jean-Marie Serreau	Oeuvre
	Anouilh	*L'Alouette*	Jean Anouilh and Roland Piétri	Montparnasse
	Beckett	*En attendant Godot*	Roger Blin	Babylone
	Claudel	*Christophe Colomb*	Jean-Louis Barrault	Marigny
	Ionesco	*Victimes du devoir*	Jacques Mauclair	Quartier Latin
	Molière	*Dom Juan*	Jean Vilar	T.N.P. Chaillot
	Sartre (ad. Dumas)	*Kean*	Pierre Brasseur	Sarah-Bernhardt
1954	Brecht	*The Good Woman of Setzuan*	Roger Planchon	Comédie (Lyon)
	Brecht	*A man's a man*	Jean-Marie Serreau	on tour
	Brecht	*Mutter Courage* (in German)	Bertolt Brecht	Berliner Ensemble at Sarah-Bernhardt
	Ionesco	*Amédée ou comment s'en debarrasser*	Jean-Marie Serreau	Babylone
	Montherlant	*Port-Royal*	Jean Meyer	Comédie Française
	Schéhadé	*La Soirée des proverbes*	Jean-Louis Barrault	Petit Marigny
1955	Adamov	*Le Ping-Pong*	Jacques Mauclair	Noctambules
	Aeschylus	*Oresteia*	Jean-Louis Barrault	Bordeaux festival and Marigny
	Brecht	*The exception and the rule*	André Steiger	Comédie du Centre Ouest (Bellac)
	Brecht	*Der kaukasischer Kreidekreis* (in German)	Bertolt Brecht	Berliner Ensemble at Sarah-Bernhardt
	Ionesco	*Jacques ou la soumission*	Robert Postec	Huchette

Date	Author	Title	Director	Theatre (in Paris except where specified)
1956	Brecht	*The Caucasian chalk circle*	Jean Dasté and John Blatchley	Comédie de Saint Etienne
	Brecht	*Fear and misery of the Third Reich*	Roger Planchon	Comédie (Lyon)
	Brecht	*Mother Carrar's rifles*	Cyril Robichez	Théâtre Populaire des Flandres (Lille)
	Ionesco	*L'Impromptu de L'Alma*	Maurice Jacquemont	Studio des Champs-Elysées
	Vauthier	*Le Personnage combattant*	Jean-Louis Barrault	Petit Marigny
	Vinaver	*Aujourd'hui ou les Coréens*	Roger Planchon	Comédie (Lyon)
1957	Adamov	*Paolo Paoli*	Roger Planchon	Comédie (Lyon)
	Beckett	*Fin de partie*	Roger Blin	Royal Court (London) and Studio des Champs-Elysées
	Genet	*The balcony*	Peter Zadek	Arts (London)
	Ionesco	*Le Nouveau Locataire*	Robert Postec	Aujourd'hui
	Shakespeare	*Henry IV*	Roger Planchon	Cité (Villeurbanne)
1958	Molière	*George Dandin*	Roger Planchon	Cité (Villeurbanne)
	Planchon (ad. Dumas)	*Les Trois Mousquetaires*	Roger Planchon	Cité (Villeurbanne)
1959	Anouilh	*Becket*	Jean Anouilh and Roland Piétri	Montparnasse
	Arrabal	*Pique-nique en campagne*	Jean-Marie Serreau	Lutèce
	Brecht	*Mother Courage*	Jacques Mauclair	Grenier de Toulouse
	Claudel	*Tête d'or*	Jean-Louis Barrault	Odéon
	Gatti	*Le Crapaud-Buffle*	Jean Négroni	T. N. P. Récamier
	Genet	*Les Nègres*	Roger Blin	Lutèce
	Ionesco	*Tueur sans gages*	José Quaglio	Récamier
	Marivaux	*La Seconde Surprise de l'amour*	Roger Planchon	Cité (Villeurbanne)
	Sartre	*Les Séquestrés d'Altona*	François Darbon	Renaissance
	Vian	*Les Bâtisseurs d'empire*	Jean Négroni	T. N. P. Récamier
1960	Adamov (ad. Gogol)	*Les Ames mortes*	Roger Planchon	Cité (Villeurbanne)
	Beckett	*La Dernière Bande*	Roger Blin	T.N.P. Récamier
	Brecht	*The resistible rise of Arturo Ui*	Jean Vilar	T.N.P. Chaillot

	Author	Play	Director	Theatre
1961	Genet	Le Balcon	Peter Brook	Gymnase
	Ionesco	Rhinocéros	Jean-Louis Barrault	Odéon
	Obaldia	Génousie	Roger Mollien	T.N.P. Récamier
	Aristophanes	Peace	Jean Vilar	T.N.P. Chaillot
	Beckett	En attendant Godot (revival)	Roger Blin	Odéon
	Brecht	Schweyk in the Second World War	Roger Planchon	Cité (Villeurbanne)
	Cousin	L'Aboyeuse et l'automate	Jacques Lecoq	Quotidien (Marseilles)
	Genet	Les Paravents (in German)	Hans Lietzau	Schlosspark (Berlin)
	Salacrou	Boulevard Durand	André Reybaz	Centre Dramatique du Nord (Le Havre)
1962	Schéhadé	Le Voyage	Jean-Louis Barrault	Odéon
	Cousin	Le Drame du Fukuryu-Maru	Jean Dasté	Comédie de Saint Etienne
	Gatti	La Deuxième Existence du camp de Tatenberg	Gisèle Tavet	Celestins (Lyon)
	Gatti	La Vie imaginaire de l'éboueur Auguste Geai	Jacques Rosner	Cité (Villeurbanne)
1963	Ionesco	Le Roi se meurt	Jacques Mauclair	Alliance Française
	Molière	Le Tartuffe	Roger Planchon	Cité (Villeurbanne)
	Parent	Gilda appelle Mae West	Jean-Marie Serreau	Dijon festival
	Planchon	La Remise	Roger Planchon	Cité (Villeurbanne)
	Adamov	Paolo Paoli (revival)	Jacques Kraemer	Théâtre Populaire de Lorraine
	Adamov	Scavengers (translation of La Politique des restes)	O. Bernhardt	Unity (London)
1964	Adamov	Le Printemps 71	Claude Martin	Gérard Philipe (Saint Denis)
	Audiberti	Le Cavalier seul	Marcel Maréchal	Cothurne (Lyon)
	Beckett	Oh! les beaux jours	Roger Blin	Odéon
	Ionesco	Le Piéton de l'air	Jean-Louis Barrault	Odéon
	Obaldia	Le Satyre de la Villette	André Barsacq	Atelier
	Adamov (ad. Gorki)	Les Petits Bourgeois	Ariane Mnouchkine	Montreuil
	Beckett	Comédie	Jean-Marie Serreau	Pavillon de Marsan
	Césaire	La Tragédie du roi Christophe	Jean-Marie Serreau	Salzburg festival
	Gatti	Le Poisson noir	Armand Gatti	Daniel Sorano (Vincennes)

Date	Author	Title	Director	Theatre (in Paris except where specified)
1965	Shakespeare	Troilus and Cressida	Roger Planchon	Cité (Villeurbanne)
	Yacine	Le Cadavre encerclé	Jean-Marie Serreau	Récamier
	Duras	Des Journées entières dans les arbres	Jean-Louis Barrault	Odéon
	Léotard (ad. Gautier)	Capitaine Fracasse	Ariane Mnouchkine	Montreuil
	Obaldia	Du Vent dans les branches de sassafras	René Dupuy	Grammont
1966	Sartre (ad. Euripides)	Les Troyennes	Michel Cacoyannis	T. N. P. Chaillot
	Vauthier	Badadesques	Marcel Maréchal	Lutèce
	Arrabal	Le Cimetière des voitures	Victor Garcia	Dijon festival
	Cousin	Le Voyage de derrière la montagne	Françoise Lepeuve	Arras festival
	Gatti	Chant public devant deux chaises électriques	Armand Gatti	T. N. P. Chaillot
	Genet	Les Paravents	Roger Blin	Odéon
	Grotowski (ad. Calderon)	The constant prince	Jerzy Grotowski	Odéon (Théâtre des Nations)
	Ionesco	La Soif et la faim	Jean-Marie Serreau	Comédie Française
	Michel	La Promenade du dimanche	Maurice Jacquemont and Georges Michel	Studio des Champs-Elysées
1967	Racine	Bérénice	Roger Planchon	Cité (Villeurbanne)
	Shakespeare	Richard III	Roger Planchon	Cité (Villeurbanne)
	Vauthier	Capitaine Bada (revival)	Marcel Maréchal	Cothurne (Lyon)
	Weingarten	L'Eté	Jean-François Adam	Poche
	Aquarium (ad. Rabelais)	Les Guerres picrocholines	Jacques Nichet	Vieux-Colombier
	Arden	Armstrong's last goodnight	Jacques Rosner	Cité (Villeurbanne)
	Arrabal	L'Architecte et l'empereur d'Assyrie	Jorge Lavelli	Montparnasse
	Béjart (ad. Flaubert)	La Tentation de Saint-Antoine	Maurice Béjart	Odéon
	Césaire	Une saison au Congo	Jean-Marie Serreau	Venice and Théâtre de l'Est Parisien
	Cousin	L'Opéra noir	Gabriel Garran	Commune (Aubervilliers)
	Gatti	V comme Vietnam	Armand Gatti	Grenier de Toulouse

Year	Author	Title	Director	Theatre
	Michel	*L'Agression*	Georges Wilson	T. N. P. Chaillot
	Montherlant	*La Ville dont le prince est un enfant*	Jean Meyer	Michel
	Planchon	*Bleus blancs rouges ou les libertins*	Roger Planchon	Cité (Villeurbanne)
	Vauthier (ad. Seneca)	*Médéa*	Jean-Louis Barrault	Odéon
	Wesker	*The kitchen*	Ariane Mnouchkine	Cirque Médrano
	Yacine	*Les Ancêtres redoublent de férocité*	Jean-Marie Serreau	T. N. P. Chaillot
1968	Audiberti	*La Poupée*	Marcel Maréchal	Huitième (Lyon)
	Barrault (ad. Rabelais)	*Rabelais*	Jean-Louis Barrault	Elysée-Montmartre
	Gatti	*La Cigogne*	Jean Hurstel	Strasbourg University theatre
	Gatti	*Les Treize Soleils de la rue Saint-Blaise*	Guy Rétoré	Théâtre de l'Est Parisien
	Living Theatre	*Paradise Now*	Julian Beck and Judith Malina	Avignon festival
	Sartre	*Le Diable et le bon Dieu* (revival)	Georges Wilson	T. N. P. Chaillot
	Shakespeare	*A midsummer night's dream*	Ariane Mnouchkine	Cirque Médrano
	Wyspianski	*Akropolis*	Jerzy Grotowski	Theatre Laboratory at Epée de bois
1969	Adamov	*Off limits*	Gabriel Garran	Commune (Aubervilliers)
	Adamov	*Off limits*	Klaus-Michael Grüber	Piccolo (Milan)
	Césaire	*Une tempête*	Jean-Marie Serreau	Hammamet (Tunisia) and Cité Universitaire (Paris)
	Kraemer and Gaudy	*Splendeur et misère de Minette la bonne Lorraine*	Jacques Kraemer	Théâtre Populaire de Lorraine
	Manet	*Les Nonnes*	Roger Blin	Poche-Montparnasse
	Planchon	*L'Infâme*	Roger Planchon	Cité (Villeurbanne)
	Planchon	*La Mise en pièces*	Roger Planchon	Cité (Villeurbanne)
	Soleil	*Les Clowns*	Ariane Mnouchkine	Commune (Aubervilliers)
1970	Aquarium	*Les Evasions de M. Voisin*	Jacques Nichet	Tour
	Jarry	*Jarry sur la butte*	Jean-Louis Barrault	Elysée-Montmartre
	Shakespeare	*Richard II*	Patrice Chéreau	Nouveau Gymnase (Marseilles)
	Soleil	*1789*	Ariane Mnouchkine	Piccolo (Milan)
	Vauthier	*Le Sang*	Marcel Maréchal	Huitième (Lyon)

Date	Author	Title	Director	Theatre (in Paris except where specified)
1971	Grumberg	*Amorphe d'Ottenburg*	Jean-Pierre Rousillon	Odéon
	Kraemer	*La Liquidation de Monsieur Joseph K*	Jacques Kraemer	Théâtre Populaire de Lorraine
	Michel	*Un Petit Nid d'amour*	Raymond Pacquet	Compagnie dramatique d'Aquitaine (Bordeaux)
	Michel	*La Ruée vers l'ordre*	Marcel Robert	Mobile (Geneva)
	Wilson	*Deafman glance (Le Regard du sourd)*	Bob Wilson	Nancy festival
1972	Adamov	*Si l'été revenait*	Michel Berto	Cartoucherie
	Aquarium	*Marchands de ville*	Jacques Nichet	Cartoucherie
	Claudel	*Sous le vent des îles Baléares*	Jean-Louis Barrault	Orsay
	Marlowe	*Massacre in Paris*	Patrice Chéreau	T. N. P. Villeurbanne
	Kraemer	*Les Immigrés*	Jacques Kraemer	Théâtre Populaire de Lorraine
	Soleil	*1793*	Ariane Mnouchkine	Cartoucherie
1973	Aquarium	*Gob*	Jacques Nichet	Cartoucherie
	Dorst	*Toller*	Patrice Chéreau	T.N.P. Villeurbanne
	Grand Magic Circus	*De Moïse à Mao*	Jérome Savary	Théâtre National de Strasbourg
	Kroetz	*Upper Austria* and *Request concert*	Claude Yersin	Comédie de Caen
	Manet	*Holocaustum ou le borgne*	Michel Fagadau	Athénée
	Molière	*Le Tartuffe* (2nd version)	Roger Planchon	T.N.P. Villeurbanne
	Planchon	*Le Cochon noir*	Roger Planchon	T.N.P. Villeurbanne at Caen
	Vinaver	*La Demande d'emploi*	Jean-Pierre Dougnac	Théâtre 347
	Vinaver	*Par-dessus bord*	Roger Planchon	T.N.P. Villeurbanne
1974	Aquarium	*Tu ne voleras pas*	Jacques Nichet	Cartoucherie
	Gatti	*La Colonne Durruti*	Armand Gatti	Schaelbeek (Belgium)
	Grumberg	*Dreyfus*	Jacques Rosner	Lambrequin (Toucoing)
1975	Adamov	*A.A. théâtres d'Adamov*	Roger Planchon	T.N.P. Villeurbanne
	Chartreux and Deutsch	*Germinal*	Jean-Pierre Vincent	Théâtre National de Strasbourg
	Chartreux and Jourdheuil	*Ab Q*	Jacques Nichet	Aquarium (Cartoucherie)
	Cousin	*Le Cycle du crabe*	Gabriel Cousin	Théâtre Populaire Occitan (Auch)
	Deutsch	*L'Entraînement du champion avant la course*	Jean-Paul Wenzel	Théâtre du Quotidien (Corbeil)

Year				
1976	Fassbinder	*Bremen freedom*	Michel Dubois	Comédie de Caen
	Grumberg	*En r'venant d'l'Expo*	Jean-Pierre Vincent	Odéon
	Kalisky	*Skandalon*	Daniel Benoin	Daniel Sorano (Vincennes)
	Soleil	*L'Age d'or*	Ariane Mnouchkine	Cartoucherie
	Vinaver	*La Demande d'emploi* (revival)	Claude Yersin	Comédie de Caen
	Aquarium	*La Vieille Lune*	Jacques Nichet	Cartoucherie
	Deutsch	*La Bonne Vie*	Jean-Pierre Vincent	Théâtre National de Strasbourg
	Deutsch	*Dimanche*	Dominique Muller	Théâtre National de Strasbourg
	Kraemer	*Les Histoires de l'oncle Jakob*	Jacques Kraemer	Théâtre Populaire de Lorraine
	Marivaux	*La Dispute*	Patrice Chéreau	T. N. P. Villeurbanne
	Planchon	*Gilles de Rais*	Roger Planchon	T. N. P. Villeurbanne
	Vitez (ad. Aragon)	*Catherine*	Antoine Vitez	Quartiers d'Ivry
	Wagner	*Ring cycle*	Patrice Chéreau (with Pierre Boulez)	Festspielhaus (Bayreuth)
1977	Wenzel	*Loin d'Hagondange*	Jean-Paul Wenzel	Comédie de Caen
	Gatti	*Le Cheval qui se suicide par le feu*	Armand Gatti	Avignon festival
	Serreau (ad. Balzac)	*Les Peines de coeur d'une chatte anglaise*	Alfredo Rodriguez Arias	Shiraz festival and Gérard Philipe (Saint-Denis)
	Soleil and Campagnol (ad. Dickens)	*David Copperfield*	Jean-Claude Penchenat	Cartoucherie
1978	Vinaver	*Iphigénie Hôtel*	Antoine Vitez	Quartiers d'Ivry
	Wenzel	*Loin d'Hagondange* (revival)	Patrice Chéreau	T. N. P. Villeurbanne
	Aquarium	*La Soeur de Shakespeare*	Jacques Nichet	Cartoucherie
	Beckett	*Pas moi; Pas; Histoires*	Samuel Beckett	Orsay
	Grand Magic Circus	*Les 1001 nuits*	Jerome Savary	Orsay
	Molière	*L'Ecole des femmes; Le Tartuffe; Dom Juan; Le Misanthrope*	Antoine Vitez	Ivry
	Vinaver	*Dissident, il va sans dire; Nina, c'est autre chose*	Jacques Lassalle	Théâtre de l'Est Parisien
1979	Aquarium	*Pépé*	Jean-Louis Benoit	Cartoucherie
	Grumberg	*L'Atelier*	Jean-Claude Grumberg	Odéon
	Grumberg	*En r'venant d'l'Expo*	Jean-Claude Penchenat	Campagnol
	Kafka	*Théâtre Complet*	Engel-Pautrat-Riety	Théâtre National de Strasbourg

Date	Author	Title	Director	Theatre (in Paris except where specified)
	Kalisky	Dave au bord de la mer	Antoine Vitez	Odéon
	Mnouchkine	Mephisto (ad. Klaus Mann)	Ariane Mnouchkine	Cartoucherie
	Müller	Hamlet Machine	Jean Jourhdeuil	Gérard Philip (Saint Denis)
	Pinter	No man's land	Roger Planchon	TNP Villeurbanne
1980	Chartreux	Violences a Vichy }	Jean-Pierre Vincent	Théâtre National de Strasbourg
	Deutsch	Convoi }		
	Molière	Dom Juan }	Roger Planchon	TNP Villeurbanne
	Racine	Athalie }		
	Various	Le Desamour	Michel Dubois	Comédie de Caen
	Vinaver	A la renverse	Jacques Lassalle	Chaillot
	Vinaver	Les Travaux et les jours	Alain Françon	Théâtre Eclaté (Annecy)
1981	Aquarium	Un conseil de classe très ordinaire	Jean-Louis Benoit	Cartoucherie
	Campagnol	Le Bal	Jean-Claude Penchenat	Antony
	Chekhov	The cherry orchard	Peter Brook	Bouffes du Nord
	Deutsch	Partage	Michel Deutsch	Théâtre Ouvert
	Ibsen	Peer Gynt	Patrice Chéreau	TNP Villeurbanne
	Molière	Le Bourgeois gentilhomme	Jérome Savary	Grand Magic Circus (at the Théâtre de L'Est Parisien)
	T.N.S.	Palais de Justice	Jean-Pierre Vincent	Théâtre National de Strasbourg
	Shakespeare	Richard II	Ariane Mnouchkine	Cartoucherie
	Various	L'Amour de l'amour	Jean-Louis Barrault	Rond-Point
1982	Demarcy	L'Etranger dans la maison	Richard Demarcy	Tempête (Cartoucherie)
	Dumas	Les trois mousquetaires	Marcel Maréchal	Criée (Marseille)
	Shakespeare	Twelfth Night	Ariane Mnouchkine	Cartoucherie
	Duras	Savannah Bay	Marguerite Duras	Rond-Point
1983	Duras	Véra Baxter	Jean-Claude Amyl	Théâtre de Poche
	Genet	Les Paravents	Patrice Chéreau	Amandiers (Nanterre)
	Ionesco	Voyages chez les morts	Roger Planchon	TNP Villeurbanne
	Kafka	Le Gardien du tombeau	Jean-Marie Patte	Théâtre de la Bastille
	Koltès	Combat de nègre et de chiens	Patrice Chéreau	Amandiers (Nanterre)
	Molière	Le Tartuffe	Jacques Lassalle	Théâtre National de Strasbourg
	Molière	L'Avare	Roger Planchon	TNP Villeurbanne

Year	Author	Title	Director	Venue
	Vinaver	L'Ordinaire	Alain Françon and Michel Vinaver	Chaillot
1984	Wenzel and Bloch	Vater Land	Jean-Paul Wenzel	Tempête (Cartoucherie)
	Claudel	Le Pain dur	Gildas Bourdet	Porte St. Martin
	Cormann	Noises	Alain Françon	Théâtre Eclaté (Annecy)
	Kantor	Wielopole Wielopole	Tadeusz Kantor	Théâtre de Paris
	Lemahieu	Usinage	Claude Yersin	Comédie de Caen
	Sarraute	Enfance	Simone Benmussa	Rond-Point
	Shakespeare	Henry IV Part 1	Ariane Mnouchkine	Cartoucherie
1985	Bourdet	Station service	Gildas Bourdet	Salamandre (Lille)
	Brook and Carrière	Le Mahabharata	Peter Brook	Bouffes du Nord and Avignon Festival
1986	Cixous	Norodom Sihanouk	Ariane Mnouchkine	Cartoucherie
	Duras	La Musica	Marguerite Duras	Rond-Point
	Genet	Le Balcon	Georges Lavaudant	Comédie Française
	Kantor	Qu'ils crèvent les artistes	Tadeusz Kantor	Avignon Festival
	Muller	Quartett	Patrice Chéreau	Amandiers (Nanterre)
	Campagnol	Vautrin (ad. Balzac)	Jean-Claude Penchenat	Chatenay-Malabry
	Claudel	L'Echange	Antoine Vitez	Chaillot
	Claudel	La Ville	Bernard Sobel	Amandiers (Nanterre)
	Koltès	Quai Ouest	Patrice Chéreau	Amandiers (Nanterre)
	Manet	Mendoza en Argentine	Thérésa Thiérot	Centre culturel des Prémontrés
	Molière	George Dandin	Roger Planchon	TNP Villeurbanne
	Vinaver	Les Voisins	Alain Françon	Théâtre Ouvert
1987	Cixous	L'Indiade	Ariane Mnouchkine	Cartoucherie
	Claudel	Le Soulier de satin	Antoine Vitez	Avignon Festival
	Koltès	Dans la solitude des champs de coton	Patrice Chéreau	Amandiers (Nanterre)
1988	Müller	Paysage sous surveillance	Jean Jourdheuil	Bobigny
	Besnehardt	Arromanches	Claude Yersin	Nouveau Théâtre d'Anger
	Koltès	Le Retour au désert	Patrice Chéreau	Rond-Point
	Shakespeare	Hamlet	Patrice Chéreau	Amandiers (Nanterre)

Index

Index

Index

Index

328